Millennial Dreams in Oil Economies

This book shifts the analysis of economic development in Oman from the traditional focus on oil to the perspective of labour. Focusing on the experiences of workers, jobseekers, and the governance of labour markets, Crystal A. Ennis offers a fresh perspective on regional development and rentier neoliberalism in the Gulf. Uniquely, the book treats Gulf labour markets as part of the story of global labour. Highlighting Oman's position within global capitalism, Ennis makes a compelling case for de-exceptionalising the Gulf, arguing that the region's labour markets are global and subject to similar pressures as other global economies. Moving beyond oil also allows Ennis to focus on the social conditions of Oman, where over 64 per cent of the population are under the age of thirty. Ennis offers a rich analysis of historical lineages of labour governance and class formation and how, following protests after 2011 as youth unemployment soared in the region, authoritarian states react to public pressure and social unrest around perceived economic decline.

CRYSTAL A. ENNIS is University Lecturer of Political Economy at Leiden University, the Netherlands. She is co-editor of *The South Asia to Gulf Migration Governance Complex* (2022) and has published in *New Political Economy*, *Third World Quarterly*, *Global Social Policy*, *International Journal*, *Cambridge Review of International Affairs*, among others. She is currently serving as an associate editor of the *International Studies Review* and president of the *Association for Gulf and Arabian Peninsula Studies*.

The Global Middle East

The Global Middle East series seeks to broaden and deconstruct the geographical boundaries of the "Middle East" as a concept to include North Africa, Central and South Asia, and diaspora communities in Western Europe and North America. The series features fresh scholarship that employs theoretically rigorous and innovative methodological frameworks resonating across relevant disciplines in the humanities and the social sciences. In particular, the general editors welcome approaches that focus on mobility, the erosion of nation-state structures, travelling ideas and theories, transcendental techno-politics, the decentralization of grand narratives, and the dislocation of ideologies inspired by popular movements. The series will also consider translations of works by authors in these regions whose ideas are salient to global scholarly trends but have yet to be introduced to the Anglophone academy.

Other Books in the Series

Millennial Dreams in Oil Economies

Job Seeking and the Global Political Economy of Labour in Oman

CRYSTAL A. ENNIS
University of Leiden

CAMBRIDGE
UNIVERSITY PRESS

CAMBRIDGE
UNIVERSITY PRESS

Shaftesbury Road, Cambridge CB2 8EA, United Kingdom

One Liberty Plaza, 20th Floor, New York, NY 10006, USA

477 Williamstown Road, Port Melbourne, VIC 3207, Australia

314–321, 3rd Floor, Plot 3, Splendor Forum, Jasola District Centre,
New Delhi – 110025, India

103 Penang Road, #05-06/07, Visioncrest Commercial, Singapore 238467

Cambridge University Press is part of Cambridge University Press & Assessment,
a department of the University of Cambridge.

We share the University's mission to contribute to society through the pursuit of
education, learning and research at the highest international levels of excellence.

www.cambridge.org
Information on this title: www.cambridge.org/9781009499477

DOI: 10.1017/9781009499422

First published 2024

A catalogue record for this publication is available from the British Library.

Library of Congress Cataloging-in-Publication Data
Names: Ennis, Crystal A., author.
Title: Millennial dreams in oil economies : job seeking and the global political
    economy of labour in Oman / Crystal A. Ennis.
Description: Cambridge, United Kingdom ; New York, NY : Cambridge University Press,
    2024. | Series: The global Middle East 29 | Includes bibliographical references.
Identifiers: LCCN 2024010962 (print) | LCCN 2024010963 (ebook) |
    ISBN 9781009499477 (hardback) | ISBN 9781009499446 (paperback) |
    ISBN 9781009499422 (ebook)
Subjects: LCSH: Labor supply–Oman. | Generation Y–Oman. | Oman–Economic
    conditions. | Petroleum industry and trade–Oman–History.
Classification: LCC HD5812.44 .E56 2024 (print) | LCC HD5812.44 (ebook) |
    DDC 331.1095353–dc23/eng/20240517
LC record available at https://lccn.loc.gov/2024010962
LC ebook record available at https://lccn.loc.gov/2024010963

ISBN 978-1-009-49947-7 Hardback

Contents

Figures

Maps

x

Tables

Preface

I walked into the first class of the semester. It was early 2007. I had already spent over a year teaching at Shinas College of Technology, watching it grow from a fledgling new addition to Oman's Ministry of Manpower's chain of technical colleges across the country. The college started with offering engineering and information technology diplomas along with an English foundation year when it opened in the fall of 2005. By 2007, I had been tasked with shepherding the new business studies program as the acting head of department. But this was not a business class. This was a research methods and communication class for engineering students. The room was full of young female students, most of whom were from the various corners of the Al-Batinah governorate in north Oman. Eager faces looked up from their chairs. It was the first Shinas cohort of engineering students in their last year of the diploma programme. There were two men seated awkwardly between them. Yes, in rural Oman, with students from the growing port city of Sohar, small towns along the coast, and further inland villages across Al-Batinah and Al-Buraimi governorates, the percentage of female engineering students was far higher than I had ever encountered in North American engineering programmes, which even today remain overwhelmingly male. I was inspired. I loved that even in the far corners of the Arabian Peninsula women were defying tired Western stereotypes of their oppression and role in the economy and society.

Their employment opportunities were not as promising. Jobs for engineers at the time were often concentrated in the oil industry, and many required field stays in the desert or offshore. Few women in rural communities, it was thought, would be willing, or have families willing to permit them, to be the only female living in work accommodations and spending nights away from the home. Companies reproduced these excuses without asking female graduates themselves. Moreover, the companies in the growing Sohar Industrial Estates rarely hired young Omanis of any gender, preferring trained expatriates from the

Indian subcontinent. I tried several times, unsuccessfully, to arrange internships and work placements for our students there. Companies simply did not want to commit to training local labour even when it was offered through educational schemes. Supervisors were uninterested in local knowledge transfer. The impression among Omanis who did work there, and those who wished to, was that mid-level and senior management, often from South Asia, wanted to hire their own compatriots rather than young Omanis. Omani employees were perceived as threats to expatriate job security. Knowledge transfer and local hiring were usually only discussed in the context of corporate social responsibility – a necessary expense of doing business.

Upon graduation, women were even less likely to find work here. One evening on my way to a later-than-usual meeting in the industrial area, I was stopped from driving through the control gate instead of being waved through. The sun was setting and darkness was beginning to extend across the stretches of concrete blocks and fences ahead. The security guard, looking bored, informed me '*al-nisā' mamnū' bi-al-layl*' (women are forbidden at night). I explained I had a meeting and was allowed to pass. It is true, however, that the state has rules (only intermittently implemented), supposedly in the interest of protecting women, that limits their employment during evening or nighttime hours with the exception of some industries like health care. Better job prospects could be found in Muscat, but this would usually mean taking up accommodation during the working week in the capital region. But very often, young women remained frustrated and unemployed for long periods or became busy with building homes and families. Educated young men and women felt alienated from the job market, frustrated by a lack of prospects, and uncomfortable with the few opportunities that were presented.

These anecdotes offer a simple introduction to the many labour market contradictions I was confronted with during the years I first worked in Oman between 2005 and 2008. It also hints at the broader empirical puzzle that shapes my work on the country. Why do economic development plans from the state appear to respond so clearly to labour market problems yet fail so dramatically to address them evenly across sectors? Why are labour market reforms so unevenly adopted and so rapidly changed, while the conditions that restrict young jobseekers' productive engagement in the economy and alienate them from the private sector persist and continue intensifying? And finally, how can we understand the experiences and range of responses from Omani millennials?

This book addresses these puzzles. It is dedicated to my former students and to the youth of Oman.

Acknowledgements

I am deeply grateful to many individuals and communities who contributed their time, energy, friendship, advice, and solidarity at various stages of the research and writing journey. The greatest debt is to my students, friends, colleagues, and many interlocutors, interviewees, and research participants over the years. Without the time and generosity of people and communities across Oman, this book would not have been possible. I hope my deep respect for you comes through in my writing. I do my utmost to do justice to your ideas, experiences, and perspectives.

I am overwhelmed with gratitude to Raya Al-Maskari, the inspiring artist of the painting featured as the cover illustration on the book, for allowing me to use her beautiful work. It is truly an honour. Her painting is entitled *bāḥthūn ʿan āmal*, meaning 'hope seekers', which is a play on words in Arabic to *bāḥthūn ʿan ʿamal* – job seekers. The painting, to me, encapsulates both an awareness and a yearning for hope among a generation of citizens – a hope that is wrapped up in the dream of working.

I thank the Oman Studies Centre, and its director Joachim Düster, for awarding me the Omani Studies Fellowship that allowed me to spend the Fall of 2021 at the Leibniz Zentrum Moderner Orient (ZMO) in Berlin, German. I benefitted tremendously not only from the time to write but also for the vibrant intellectual community at ZMO. Special thanks to Ulrike Freitag, Kai Kresse, and Katrin Bromber for many thoughtful exchanges, as well as to Olly Akkerman, Zahir Bhalloo, and Taha, and to Kadara Swaleh, Jacob Nerenberg, Silke Nagel, and many others who made Berlin or ZMO feel like home.

There are many other people and institutions to thank, and I apologise in advance if I have unintentionally left anyone out. I am grateful to Bank Al-Markazi, the Chamber of Commerce, the Ministry of National Economy (and its various name changes), and the National Centre for Statistics and Information in Oman for giving me access to their respective archives. I have also benefitted from archives at the International Institute for Social History in Amsterdam and the British National Archives in Kew, United Kingdom.

In Oman, I thank Yahya Al-Jabri and the SEZAD team for facilitating my research visit to Duqm, Col Yousef Al-Nabhani and Ahmed Al-Darai at the National Survey Authority for permitting me to include the NSA map of Oman at the start of the book, and Omar Al-Mahrizi, CEO of Sohar Port and Freezone, for the map of the port area. I am grateful to Said Al-Saqri for his friendship through the years and willingness to exchange ideas, offer advice, perspectives, and support. I thank Aisha for her abundantly generous friendship that has stood the test of time. Kawthar AlHarthi's friendship, teaching, and intellectual debate has been both sustaining and heartwarming. Many thanks also to exchanges and conversations with Khalid Al-Azri, Riyadh Al-Balushi, Khalid Al-Haribi, Ann Al-Kindi, Nawra Al-Lawati, Hatem Al-Shanfari, Abbas al-Zadjali, M. Reda Bhacker and Bernadette Millard, Sandhya Rao Mehta, and many others who must remain anonymous. I am grateful for so many friendships I have made along the way, from Sohar to Nizwa, to Muscat, to my hiking group from near and far. All arguments and opinions in the book remain my own and do not represent the views of the generous people who supported me with their knowledge and friendship.

Several colleagues have read and commented on drafts and exchanged ideas along the way. I am especially indebted to Omar Al-Shehabi and Talal Al-Rashoud who took the time to offer detailed feedback on complete drafts. I presented an early introduction to this book at the European Workshop on International Studies, of the European International Studies Association (EISA), in Krakow, Poland in 2019. The fantastic workshop organised by Hannes Baumann and Roberto Roccu, 'IPE and the Middle East: Beyond Mutual Neglect', offered me the opportunity to exchange ideas and benefit from feedback from a wonderful group of scholars. Adam Hanieh, Michael Herb, Adam Fishwick, and Toufic Haddad commented on different drafts of chapters at various stages of readiness. I presented chapters at several International Studies Association and Middle Eastern Studies Association annual conventions. My reflection for the roundtable 'Citizenship and Belonging in the Arabian Peninsula' convened by Gwenn Okruhlik in *International Journal of Middle East Studies* 52, no. 4 (2020) grew out of Chapter 5 of this book. Gwenn and the other roundtable participants offered me insightful reactions to my arguments. I first developed the analysis of intersecting logics at work in entrepreneurship promotion (in Chapter 6) in my *New Political Economy* article 'The Gendered Complexities of Promoting Entrepreneurship in the Gulf' (24, no. 3 [2019]). Reactions to this piece have allowed me to strengthen and clarify the approach. Establishing a good foundation in Arabic was also key, and I am grateful to the many Arabic teachers I have had over the years, including Kawthar AlHarthi, Kanan Al-Ali, Khadige Abboud, among others.

A wealth of thanks are due to many other friends, colleagues, and comrades who, in one way or another, have helped with this project, including Sahar Al-Khulaidi, Aziz Al-Riyami, Wafa Al-Sayed, Fahad Al-Sumait, Anique Bakker, Fahad Bishara, Lindsay Black, Nicolas Blarel, Malia Bouattia, Martijn Boven, Christa Braccio, Patricia Chraiteh, Sai Englert, Beatrix Futak-Campbell, Radhika Gupta, Emily Hemlow, Christian Henderson, Yih-Jye Hwang, Michelle Johnson, Stella Morgana, Eftychia Mylona, Mari Nakamura, Tsolin Nalbantian, Amber Neumann, Gwenn Okruhlik, Nicola Pavanini, Namrata Raju, Cyrus Schayegh, Saori Shibata, Remy Sirls, Cristiana Strava, Sanjukta Sunderason, Limin Teh, Abdel Razaq Takriti, Keye Tersemette, Maghiel van Crevel, Gerdien Verheuvel, Tracey Wagner-Rizvi, Jue Wang, Nira Wickramasinghe, Rafeef Ziadah, and Rawan Ziadah. A special thanks to my writing group filled with inspiring creatives, especially to Megin Jimenez, Janelle Ward, and Katie Sweeney.

Thanks to the three anonymous reviewers, whose comments and engagement with the text helped me strengthen the final outcome. At Cambridge University Press, I am grateful to Arshin Adib-Moghaddam for believing in the project and to the numerous editors I have worked with along the way including Daniel Brown, Maria Marsh, Natasha Burton, and Biju Singh. Thanks to Trent Hancock for careful copy editing, and Francis Young for expertly compiling the index.

Writing took place in many locations but mostly in Leiden, Muscat, and Berlin. The love and companionship of my husband Ra'id, and our many adventures together, sustained me through the long writing process. I am immensely grateful to his family as well, Um Ra'id, Najla, and Wa'il. An incredible amount of gratitude also belongs with my beautiful blended family, my mother and father and stepmother and stepfather, and siblings, Tawnya, Vince, and Shaylyn, and Sarah, Lisa, and David.

A Note on Transliteration

I mostly follow the *International Journal of Middle Eastern Studies* (*IJMES*) guide for Arabic transliteration except in cases where the name or word has a commonly used spelling within Oman, where local pronunciations differ, or where it is widely used in English otherwise. For example, I spell the city of Ṣuḥār as Sohar. Rial is used instead of *riyāl* for the unit of Omani currency based on its official spelling on banknotes. For personal names that are not pseudonyms, I have used the transliteration that appears favoured by them according to business cards, personal websites, or personal communication, etc.

Abbreviations

BOT	Build, Operate, and Transfer (BOT) agreements
CEO	chief executive officer
CSR	corporate social responsibility
GCC	Gulf Cooperation Council
GDP	gross domestic product
GFOW	General Federation of Oman Workers – sometimes General Federation of Oman Trade Unions (GFOTU)
GPE	Global Political Economy
FDI	foreign direct investment
FTA	free trade agreement
FYP	five-year plan
ICV	in-country value
IFIs	international financial institutions
ILO	International Labour Organization
IMF	International Monetary Fund
IOM	International Organization for Migration
IOR	India Office Records
IPC	Iraq Petroleum Company
IPE	International Political Economy
IR	International Relations
ISCO	International Standard Classification of Occupations
LCC	local community contractors
MAN	Movement of Arab Nationalists
MENA	Middle East North Africa
MNC	multinational company
MoM	Ministry of Manpower (renamed Ministry of Labour in 2020)
NCSI	National Centre for Statistics and Information

NOC	no-objection certificate
NSA	National Survey Authority
OMR	Omani Rial
OU	Oman Union
PDO	Petroleum Development Oman (PD(O) until May 1980)
PFLOAG	Popular Front for the Liberation of Oman and the Arabian Gulf
PPP	public–private partnership
PRO	public relations officer
SDGs	sustainable development goals
SEZ	Special Economic Zone
SEZAD	Special Economic Zone Authority of Duqm
SME	small- and medium-sized enterprise
SOE	state-owned enterprise
USD	US dollars
VAT	value-added tax
WTO	World Trade Organisation

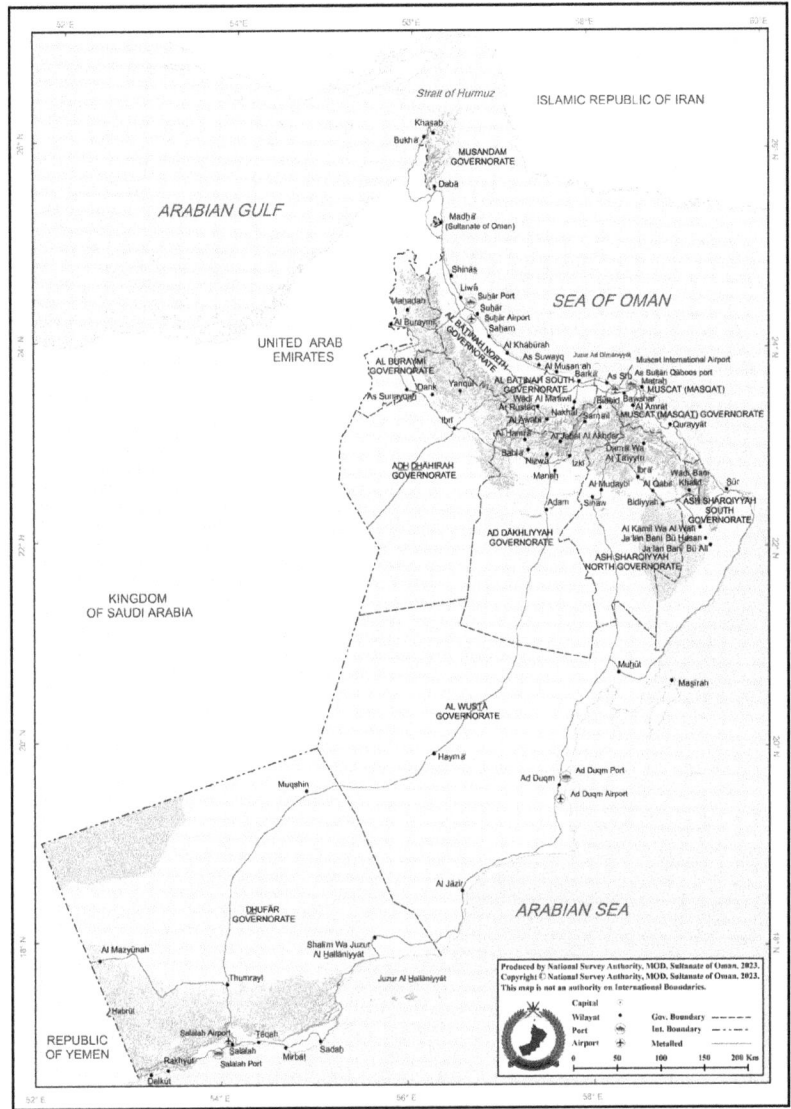

Map 0.1 Map of Oman (Governorates and Wilayats).
National Survey Authority, MOD, Sultanate of Oman (2023)

1 | *Bringing Citizen Labour into IPE Scholarship on the Gulf*

Oman's population is a youthful one. Like their peers globally, jobs are at the forefront of many young people's minds. Life choices consume the imagination with visions of what can be. What do you want to do with your life when you finish school, when you finish college or university? What kind of job do you want? These are the questions asked of young people the world over. With over 64 per cent of Oman's population under the age of thirty, dreams of the future might just be a national pastime.[1] Yet, increasingly, young people's dreams are being fractured by the reality that jobs are neither as plentiful nor as secure as they once were, that even the possession of a university or college degree or diploma does not necessarily improve one's chances on the labour market.

This book is interested in young adults in the labour market in Oman. While it centres on Oman, and Omanis, this is very much a story relevant for Gulf economies and for oil-dependent and foreign labour–dependent countries elsewhere. A dominant feature of Gulf economies since the early twentieth century has been the presence of, and economic dependence on, hydrocarbon export. This unsurprisingly structures much political economy analysis of the region, with questions probing the causal relationship between oil and various economic and political outcomes. Yet in most of these inquiries, Gulf citizens fall to the background. What happens when we shift the entry point from oil to human beings, or in this case, from one factor of production to another – labour? Fresh insights can be derived by asking new questions and reorienting our research. Such analytical shifts do not mean hydrocarbons hold less importance but signal that we lose valuable comparative insights by focusing on one analytical puzzle and emphasising exceptional narratives rather than comparative and transnational ones.

---

[1] NCSI, 'Statistical Year Book 2021' (Muscat: National Centre for Statistics and Information, August 2021), 66, www.ncsi.gov.om/Elibrary/.

This book represents a new direction in international political economy (IPE) research on the Gulf. In it, I shift from the rentier state entry point in scholarship on oil-exporting countries and begin with labour. That is, this book shows how to take labour seriously in Gulf development governance discourses and does this by dislodging labour from the margins of IPE analysis. Centring Omani voices, experiences, and economic governance histories, I explain the ways through which Oman's young citizens navigate and interpret the labour market in parallel with the conditions and trajectories that have shaped the contemporary labour market milieu. My central argument is twofold. Oman's labour market is global; and Omani labour must be understood *globally* and *relationally* – within and beyond segmentation. Explaining the position, experiences, and contradictions of Gulf labour, especially of youth, requires grounding an understanding of locally segmented labour markets within the wider global political economy. It also requires understanding labour and class relations amongst citizens and foreigners. The ways millennials perceive economic life and the governance of their participation in it are shaped by the constitution and reconfiguration of the global labour market, the ways governance unfolds at multiple scales, and the promises and discourses concerning national development. Gulf labour markets are both a direction for global labour and a space of formation for the global labour market and for class. In the chapters that follow, I unpack this argument through seven sub-arguments:

- Gulf labour markets are global and subject to capitalist pressures present in labour markets globally. Simultaneously, Gulf labour markets and economies present economic nationalist sentiments and pressures.

- The presence and formation of a global Gulf labour market mediates and shapes the ways in which Gulf labour of any citizenship performs labour and participates in economic activities. This global character is therefore a key component of class formation and social relations.

- Labour's contemporary governance, regulatory, and resistance milieus have lineages that extend from the colonial and oil industry labour practices and discourses through the era of neoliberal reform to the present.

- Gulf economies are both rentier and neoliberal. Rather than challenging neoliberalism, rentierism has gone to bed with it. The labour market and related economic reform areas illustrate this dysfunctional relationship well.

- Young Omanis, despite their legal belonging vis-à-vis political citizenship, face multiple exclusions in their economic citizenship.
- Millennial citizen expectations take shape in the interaction of perceived outcomes from economic globalisation, neoliberalism, and government responsibilities for governing hydrocarbon windfalls.
- Evidence from Oman suggests that Gulf states react to public pressure during periods (or expected periods) of social unrest especially around issues of national unemployment. Three policy reform areas highlight these reactions: (1) labour nationalisation, (2) labour migration control, and (3) entrepreneurship promotion.

Centring the Omani story, often relegated to the margins of Gulf and Middle East Studies scholarship, and centring labour illustrates other dimensions of the development trajectory and the transnational, shared connections and transformations of local and regional economic life and its governance. Uniquely, this book treats Gulf labour markets as part of the story of global labour, viewing connections between transformations across multiple levels of global labour governance. It takes citizen youth seriously and enters its analysis with the largest generation in the region at the core. By looking at young citizens in the labour market, we are able to understand Gulf economies in ways previously unexplored. The Sultanate of Oman takes centre stage as the empirical focus and driving data. Through this case and this book, I demonstrate how using labour as a departure point provides novel interpretations of economic transformations, economic history, and economic policy in the Gulf. This exhibits the potential and value of including the region in debates on the comparative and global political economy of development.

1.1 Setting the Stage

Youth economic dreams emerge in the context of a country and region that has experienced dramatic economic growth and social change over the past fifty years. Parents and grandparents of today's millennials witnessed a visible expansion of economic opportunities and radical improvements in human development indicators. Literacy rates in Oman leapt from 36.2 per cent in 1980 to 96 per cent in 2017, with youth literacy at nearly 99 per cent today. Life expectancy increased from 50 years of age in 1970 to 77.9 in 2019.[2] Oil-led growth supported quality infrastructure, health care, and educational development. It also underpinned the establishment of a large public sector that became a major employer of citizens across the country. From serving in burgeoning national bureaucracies, an expanding security apparatus, and various functions in the local *baladīyyāt* (municipalities), public sector employment expanded alongside the employment and economic opportunities in the oil industry. Millennial dreams have been influenced by such expectation structures.

The uprisings of 2011 abruptly attuned the Omani and Gulf political space to potential political outcomes of unrequited millennial dreams and expectations. The size and scale of the protests and level of civil unrest between February and May represented one of the largest and most widespread social movements in Oman since the end of the Dhofar war in 1976. Among the economic demands were loud calls for jobs, for social protection for the unemployed, for increasing the minimum wage, and for more higher educational opportunities. Government officials were surprised and alarmed by the intensity of the demands. Protests emerged across most of the major population centres including Muscat, Salalah, and Sur, but they were most severe in Sohar. The promised employment opportunities from economic windfalls after years of reform and economic investment in diversification initiatives and industrialisation in places like Sohar were not trickling down. Educated and unskilled young people alike felt ignored and isolated from systems and institutions perceived as corrupt, lacking transparency, and exclusionary to young citizens.

Today, millennial dreams continue to emerge in a context of high youth unemployment in the country and wider Arab world and in a context of uncertain economic futures under post–oil wealth conditions. Omani youth unemployment is felt everywhere: 90 per cent of Omani families have jobseekers in them according to the latest census.[3] If 2011 made policymakers more acutely aware of youth labour market demands, the long 2010s should have driven the message home. Trending social media hashtags between 2017 and 2021 in

---

[2] 'World Development Indicators' (World Bank Databank, 2019), https://databank.worldbank.org/reports.aspx?source=world-development-indicators#.

[3] 'al-Taʿdād al-iliktrūniyy l-lsukān wa-l-masākin wa-l-munshaʾāt 2020' (Muscat: NCSI, January 2021), 59, www.ncsi.gov.om/Elibrary/.

Oman included *'Umānīyūn bilā waẓā'if* (Omanis without jobs), *bāḥthūn 'an 'amal yastaghīthūn* (Jobseekers are calling out), and *mwūlāy at-tawẓīf maṭlabunā* (My lord, jobs are our demand). The census shows that it takes over half of Omani jobseekers three or more years to find a job. This rises to 67 per cent for those looking for their first job.[4] Estimates of youth unemployment in the country are inconsistent and controversial. Calculating from the official census data shows an unemployment rate of 8.02 per cent, with unemployment among those aged fifteen to thirty-four reaching 17.10 per cent.[5] A World Bank report claims youth unemployment may even be as high as 49 per cent, and recent ILO data estimates the percentage of youth not in employment, education, or training is 22.6 per cent.[6] What is clear from these estimates and from conversations with young people, their families, and employers around the country is that these issues are real and feel palpable among youth. Indeed, 74 per cent of the country's registered jobseekers are under the age of thirty.[7] Dreams risk turning into disillusionment and disenfranchisement.

In addition to being young, Oman's population is also diverse. This diversity stems not only from its own population but especially from the vast number of foreigners flocking to the country for economic opportunities. Only a little over half of Oman's population are citizens, a feature that the government is keen to emphasise. That is, it wishes to highlight that there are more citizens than foreigners in the country in contrast with the much larger demographic 'imbalances' in some of Oman's smaller Gulf neighbours like the United Arab Emirates (UAE) and Qatar. Local dailies regularly mention this feature, and the welcome page of the National Centre for Statistics and Information keeps readers abreast of the current numbers with a live population clock.[8] Yet the country looks less demographically 'balanced' with a view of

---

[4] 'al-Ta'dād al-iliktrūniyy l-lsukān wa-l-masākin wa-l-munsha'āt 2020', 65.

[5] This is calculated on the basis of the registered number of jobseekers ÷ labour force x 100. 'Ta'dād 2020'.

[6] World Bank, 'Oman's Economic Outlook – April 2018' (Washington, DC: World Bank, 16 April 2018), www.worldbank.org/en/country/gcc/publication/economic-outlook-april-2018-oman; 'Statistics on Youth' (International Labour Organization, 2022), https://ilostat.ilo.org/topics/youth/.

[7] "al-Shabāb: silsilat al-iḥṣā'āt al-mujtam'iyya (Muscat: National Centre for Statistics and Information, 2018), 16.

[8] National Centre for Statistics and Information (NCSI), 2021, www.ncsi.gov.om/Pages/NCSI.aspx.

the private sector labour market, where Omanis only hold 12.5 per cent of jobs.[9]

Herein lies an enduring policy paradox at the heart of economic governance in Oman. Local and international capital interests demand access to global, competitively priced labour flows while, at the same time, unemployment among educated graduates rises. Saudi Arabia and Bahrain face similar tensions. Even in wealthier members of the GCC, demands for youth employment have emerged, often alongside more xenophobic concerns about cultural erosion or economic leakage from remittance flows. Here, the pressure is not as much about jobless rates as the creation of meaningful jobs in the context of bloated, redundant public sectors and unfulfilled dreams of potential and contribution.[10] Such demands underline how the expectations of what the state should provide, and the conditions it should create, are powerful drivers of social sentiment and pressure points. This paradox also lays bare the tension between neoliberalising pressures, rentier economic characteristics, and nationalist regulatory pressures. That is, when does the state regulate in favour of protecting citizen labour, and when does it do so to accommodate private sector interests? This tension is a thread running through this book, present from the historic context wherein today's labour structures emerged, as we see in Chapter 3, through to the present.

1.2 Understanding Labour in a Rentier World

Gulf labour markets are intensely global. It is one of the first things outside observers notice about Gulf cities when they visit. The sheer diversity and visibility of multiple ethnicities from across the Indian Ocean and the Middle East make these economic spaces instantly interesting. Yet IPE scholarship on the region is dominated by the analysis of another major feature of Gulf economies – the importance of oil and gas in the modern development story.[11] Rentier state

---

[9] Ministry of Manpower, 'Open Data', 2019, www.manpower.gov.om/OpenData/home/home.

[10] Abeer Allam, 'Kuwaitisation: Youth Demands Action to Meet Expectations', *Financial Times*, 23 April 2013, www.ft.com/content/9fda70fc-a81d-11e2-b031-00144feabdc0.

[11] The term 'rentier' defines states with a heavy reliance on resource revenue as a percentage of government income and export earnings. By this definition, Oman

literature has provided rich theorising on the region over several decades, advancing our understandings of how oil rent impacts politics, economics, and society in resource-dependent economies.[12] Newer generations of scholarship on the resource curse from both quantitative and qualitative traditions, which Sean Yom calls 'revisionist', have developed sophisticated and increasingly nuanced theorising on rentierism that IPE scholarship draws on.[13] Outside of this contribution,

---

is a rentier state. Among rentiers, Gulf states are often considered archetypal, and much of the theorising on the causal impact of rent on politics emerges from these cases rather than other oil-wealthy countries. The generation of hypotheses around these links has led to well-debated contradictions and shortcomings in the literature, as shown by Benjamin Smith and David Waldner, *Rethinking the Resource Curse* (Cambridge: Cambridge University Press, 2021), among others.

[12] Hazem Beblawi and Giacomo Luciani, *The Rentier State* (New York: Routledge, 1987); Kiren Aziz Chaudhry, 'Economic Liberalization and the Lineages of the Rentier State', *Comparative Politics* 27, no. 1 (1994): 1–25, https://doi.org/10.2307/422215; Donald L. Losman, 'The Rentier State and National Oil Companies: An Economic And Political Perspective', *The Middle East Journal* 64 (Summer 2010): 427–45, https://doi.org/10.3751/64.3.15; Matthew Gray, 'A Theory of "Late Rentierism" in the Arab States of the Gulf', Center for International and Regional Studies Georgetown University School of Foreign Service in Qatar, Occasional Paper, no. 7 (2011); Mehran Kamrava, ed., *Political Economy of the Persian Gulf*, 1st ed. (Oxford: Oxford University Press, 2012); Marc Lynch and Michael Herb, eds., *The Politics of Rentier States in the Gulf* (Washington, DC: POMEPS, 2019), https://pomeps.org/pomeps-studies-33-the-politics-of-rentier-states-in-the-gulf; Michael L. Ross, 'Does Oil Hinder Democracy?', *World Politics* 53, no. 3 (2001): 325–61, https://doi.org/10.1353/wp.2001.0011; Michael L. Ross, 'Oil, Islam, and Women', *American Political Science Review* 102, no. 1 (February 2008): 107–23, https://doi.org/10.1017/S0003055408080040.

[13] David Waldner and Benjamin Smith, 'Rentier States and State Transformations', in *The Oxford Handbook of Transformations of the State*, ed. Stephan Leibfried et al. (Oxford: Oxford University Press, 2015), https://doi.org/10.1093/oxfordhb/9780199691586.013.38; Jessie Moritz, 'Reformers and the Rentier State: Re-Evaluating the Co-Optation Mechanism in Rentier State Theory', *Journal of Arabian Studies* 8, no. 1 (2018): 46–64, https://doi.org/10.1080/21534764.2018.1546933; Jessie Moritz, 'Re-Conceptualizing Civil Society in Rentier States', *British Journal of Middle Eastern Studies* 47, no. 1 (2020): 136–51, https://doi.org/10.1080/13530194.2020.1714268; Michael Herb, 'No Representation without Taxation? Rents, Development, and Democracy', *Comparative Politics* 37, no. 3 (1 April 2005): 297–316, https://doi.org/10.2307/20072891; Lynch and Herb, *The Politics of Rentier States in the Gulf*; Sean L. Yom, 'Oil, Coalitions, and Regime Durability: The Origins and Persistence of Popular Rentierism in Kuwait', *Studies in Comparative International Development* 46, no. 2 (1 June 2011): 217–41, https://doi.org/10.1007/s12116-011-9087-y; Martin Beck and Thomas Richter, eds., *Oil and the*

however, IPE has largely ignored the region.[14] This book does not disregard rentier state research but instead shows how IPE scholarship can also be enriched by situating other units at the centre of analysis, in this case, labour.

Certainly, Gulf labour markets are impacted by the huge role of hydrocarbons in the modern development of the region. Since the oil discoveries in the early twentieth century and especially following the first oil boom beginning in 1973, the heightened importance of oil and its dominance in the regional economic landscape necessarily influenced the type, availability, and structure of work. The influx of oil income not only funded institutional growth and the development of huge public sectors but also increased the demand for labour across many sectors of the economy. The birth and growth of extractive industries in the region created the foundation for two addictions that have become deep structural features of Gulf economies – an addiction to oil revenue and to foreign labour. It is both using these resources productively and shaking these addictions prodigiously that consume the economic planning policy space.[15]

Political Economy in the Middle East: Post-2014 Adjustment Policies of the Arab Gulf and Beyond (Manchester: Manchester University Press, 2021).

[14] Hannes Baumann and Roberto Roccu, 'International Political Economy and the State in the Middle East', *Globalizations* (2023): 1–13, https://doi.org/10.1080/14747731.2023.2223951; Hannes Baumann, 'Avatars of Eurocentrism in International Political Economy Textbooks: The Case of the Middle East and North Africa', *Politics*, 28 October 2021, https://doi.org/10.1177/02633957211054739; Erin A. Snider, 'International Political Economy and the New Middle East', *PS: Political Science & Politics* 50, no. 3 (July 2017): 664–67, https://doi.org/10.1017/S104909651700035X.

[15] Michael Herb and Steffen Hertog have made large contributions both to understanding Gulf labour markets under conditions of resource abundance and to situating political or economic outcomes in the region in comparative frameworks. Comparative politics work that includes the Gulf is rare, making their contribution all the more valuable. Their treatments and the value of their findings thus underscore the necessity of further developing such analysis. Michael Herb, *The Wages of Oil: Parliaments and Economic Development in Kuwait and the UAE* (Ithaca, NY: Cornell University Press, 2014); Steffen Hertog, 'State and Private Sector in the GCC after the Arab Uprisings', *Journal of Arabian Studies* 3, no. 2 (2013): 174–95, https://doi.org/10.1080/21534764.2013.863678; Steffen Hertog, 'Defying the Resource Curse: Explaining Successful State-Owned Enterprises in Rentier States', *World Politics* 62, no. 2 (2010): 261–301, https://doi.org/10.1017/S0043887110000055; Steffen Hertog, *Princes, Brokers, and Bureaucrats: Oil and the State in Saudi Arabia* (Ithaca, NY: Cornell University Press, 2010).

In fact, when you speak to policymakers, business owners, or managers in Oman over the last decade, the almost universal comment is that creating employment is the major national concern. Oman is among the countries Herb describes as 'middling' rentiers, which he contrasts with the wealthier, 'extreme rentiers' Kuwait, Qatar, and the UAE.[16] Extreme rentiers are those that are extremely hydrocarbon wealthy with small populations; and middling rentiers – Bahrain, Oman, and Saudi Arabia – are those with relatively lower resource income but larger indigenous populations to employ. Oil rents, as Herb argues, facilitated 'badly distorted' labour markets in the extreme rentiers.[17] While his work focuses on extreme rentier cases, this book attends to a middling one. Herb's focus on the labour market to study the relationship between political outcomes and rentierism, one of the rarer political economy works to do so, is important but still begins with oil. Here, I instead centre the margins, labour and Oman, to trace other trajectories alongside and beyond, as well as before and after, oil.

Domestic and regional structures of oil economies do not materialise in a vacuum and thus are not the whole story influencing the shape of labour markets in the region. Movements of capital and labour from and across the region are features intimately tied to global economic transformations, vital for understanding Gulf political economy. Scholars like Hanieh, Khalili, Mitchell, and Vitalis have made essential contributions to what transformations in oil and capital have meant for the region and the global political economy.[18] In particular, Hanieh's starting point of capitalism and Khalili's on logistics and transportation infrastructure demonstrate clearly the crucial advances we can make in examining the region in transnational and global patterns by varying our departure points and primary analytical foci. With a view of the global economy, Hanieh has documented how the Gulf is 'fully capitalist and subject to the same dynamics as other

---

[16] Herb, *The Wages of Oil*, 14.   [17] Herb, *The Wages of Oil*, 184.

[18] Adam Hanieh, *Capitalism and Class in the Gulf Arab States* (New York: Palgrave Macmillan, 2011); Adam Hanieh, *Money, Markets, and Monarchies: The Gulf Cooperation Council and the Political Economy of the Contemporary Middle East* (Cambridge: Cambridge University Press, 2018); Laleh Khalili, *Sinews of War and Trade: Shipping and Capitalism in the Arabian Peninsula* (London: Verso Books, 2020); Timothy Mitchell, *Carbon Democracy: Political Power in the Age of Oil* (London; New York: Verso Books, 2011); Robert Vitalis, *America's Kingdom: Mythmaking on the Saudi Oil Frontier* (Stanford: Stanford University Press, 2007).

neighbouring states'.[19] Such dynamics portended dramatic shifts in global production networks based on capital's search for cheaper more flexible labour. This story of global labour, and the re-erosion of labour's power relative to capital, has underpinned and perpetuated systems of hierarchy, unequal power, and structural exclusions in Gulf political economies.

In conversation with this literature, I view Gulf labour markets as global. They exist within the 'global economy that is part of the actual essence of the Gulf itself'.[20] Drawing on an expanding scholarship on the international political economy of labour allows me to develop and substantiate my conceptualisation of *global* Gulf labour markets in contrast with their usual description as particular national spaces.[21] The shape and the past, present, and future of labour in the Gulf is tied up in the development of what Henk Overbeek calls 'a global labour market'.[22] That is, the trajectory and continuity of the Gulf's reliance on low-cost, available, and flexible labour from across Asia is entangled within Asia's transformation into 'a continent of labour'.[23] As Daeoup Chang has persuasively shown, the development and rise of Asia has lifted people out of absolute poverty by creating jobs but simultaneously pushed the labouring classes into various forms of wage labour and capitalist social relations where the vast majority of Asia's labour force suffers under low paying, insecure, and informal

---

[19] Adam Hanieh, *Lineages of Revolt: Issues of Contemporary Capitalism in the Middle East* (Chicago: Haymarket Books, 2013), 124.

[20] Hanieh, *Capitalism and Class in the Gulf Arab States*, 16.

[21] Jeffrey Harrod, 'Towards an International Political Economy of Labour', in *Global Unions? Theory and Strategies of Organized Labour in the Global Political Economy*, ed. Jeffrey Harrod and Robert O'Brien (London; New York: Routledge, 2002), 49–63; Stephen Castles, 'Migration, Crisis, and the Global Labour Market', *Globalizations* 8, no. 3 (1 June 2011): 311–24, https://doi.org/10.1080/14747731.2011.576847; Jon Las Heras, 'International Political Economy of Labour and Gramsci's Methodology of the Subaltern', *The British Journal of Politics and International Relations* 21, no. 2 (2019): 462–80, https://doi.org/10.1177/1369148118815403; Jon Las Heras, 'International Political Economy of Labour and Collective Bargaining in the Automotive Industry', *Competition & Change* 22, no. 3 (2018): 313–31, https://doi.org/10.1177/1024529418764350.

[22] Henk Overbeek, 'Neoliberalism and the Regulation of Global Labor Mobility', *The Annals of the American Academy of Political and Social Science* 581, no. 1 (1 May 2002): 78, https://doi.org/10.1177/000271620258100108.

[23] Daeoup Chang, 'From Global Factory to Continent of Labour: Labour and Development in Asia', *Asian Labour Review* 1, no. 1 (1 January 2015): 5–48.

jobs.[24] Many turn to internal and external migration, where West Asia is a major destination.[25] Indeed, the Gulf space is an embodiment of how globalisation and neoliberalism 'integrates an increasing proportion of the world population directly into capitalist labour markets and locks national and regional markets into a global labour market'.[26] This is visible in workplaces and labour policy-making spaces in the Gulf.

The course of Oman's capitalist, labouring, and job-seeking classes are bound up within this global labour market. Through a domestic lens, the record of Oman's economic and labour market reforms has been decidedly uneven and frequently contradictory. More and more young Omanis are graduating from higher education institutions, and like their peers globally, they expect this to pay off in the labour market. Yet many increasingly find not only a hostile employment environment but also contracting state benefits. What explains the weak labour market outcomes and expectation gap for millennials in Oman? Gulf labour markets are situated in a limbo space, confronting their position in a global labour market and the struggles of citizen labour and migrant labour for better lives and livelihoods. They face intense neoliberal pressures for economic growth, visible through pressures from international institutions to liberalise and deregulate labour markets, from businesses for cheap labour, and from regional competition to be the most attractive markets for FDI and business operations. Simultaneously, they face pressures from below that push for regulation that privileges citizens in the economy and reserves jobs and benefits for them. One can in fact observe a form of Polanyi's double movement'[27] around Omani labour, where the first movement involves individuals decrying political control and pushing for greater market

[24] Dae-oup Chang, 'Informalising Labour in Asia's Global Factory', *Journal of Contemporary Asia* 39, no. 2 (May 2009): 161–79, https://doi.org/10.1080/00472330902723766; Chang, 'From Global Factory to Continent of Labour'.

[25] Andrea Wright, *Between Dreams and Ghosts: Indian Migration and Middle Eastern Oil* (Stanford: Stanford University Press, 2021); Crystal A. Ennis and Nicolas Blarel, eds., *The South Asia to Gulf Migration Governance Complex* (Bristol: Bristol University Press, 2022); Mehran Kamrava and Zahra Babar, eds., *Migrant Labor in the Persian Gulf* (New York: Columbia University Press, 2012).

[26] Overbeek, 'Neoliberalism and the Regulation of Global Labor Mobility', 78.

[27] Karl Polanyi, *The Great Transformation: The Political and Economic Origins of Our Time* (Beacon Press, 1944).

dominance, while the second involves citizens seeking to reassert control over the market or, at least, find their place within it. This book details this story.

Conventionally, 'organized labour has been concerned that the liberalisation of national economies shifts the balance further in favour of capital over labour'.[28] The means and mechanisms of this concern evolves differently in the Gulf labour space where the possibilities and potential for collective action are more difficult, fragmented by the structures of the labour market.[29] Here, labour is segmented across multiple ethnic, class, skill-level, and gender lines, as explained in Chapter 2. The interests of different labour market constituents divide their organisation and demands, and any resultant empowerment usually involves the disempowerment of another. This fragmentation does not remove contestation but means scholars need new tools and approaches to view and interpret it.

The high degree of stratification in Gulf labour markets is in many ways an exceptional feature of the regional political economy. Yet this social ordering is not only endogenously created but also reflects structural features of the global labour market. Indeed,

the interplay between market forces demanding freedom of movement and political forces demanding control can be seen as highly effective in creating a global labour market stratified not only according to 'human capital' (possession of education, training, and work skills), but also according to gender, race, ethnicity, origins, and legal status. The new global labour market is thus an expression of a global class hierarchy, in which people with high human capital from rich countries have almost unlimited rights of mobility, while others are differentiated, controlled, and included or excluded in a variety of ways.[30]

---

[28] Robert O'Brien, 'The Varied Paths to Minimum Labour Standards', in *Global Unions? Theory and Strategies of Organized Labour in the Global Political Economy*, ed. Jeffrey Harrod and Robert O'Brien (London; New York: Routledge, 2002), 222.

[29] This different pattern is also due to the contemporary, neoliberal conditions across Asian labour markets which resulted in 'struggles of labour' no longer following the 'usual model of working class mobilisation' (Chang, 'From Global Factory to Continent of Labour', 38). Across Asia, many trade unions have been unable to move beyond being 'subordinate development partners of state and capital' (38), a trend I also discuss in the Omani union experience in Chapter 4.

[30] Castles, 'Migration, Crisis, and the Global Labour Market', 312.

The segmentations in Gulf labour markets correspond to these broader divisions, inclusions, and exclusions. Regulatory measures that constrain or liberate labour inevitably impact certain classes more powerfully than others. The stratification within Gulf political economies also fragments any empowerment that can be derived from regulatory change. That is, measures that protect national labour often erodes the empowerment of foreign labour and vice versa. Such division and differentiation mean any collective action is more commonly found within a singular segment rather than across a wider, unified labour. This is elaborated in greater detail in Chapters 3–5.

When a population is so young, particular socio-political and economic concerns inform policy and civil society discourses, such as the promise of economic growth or the threat of social unrest. A young population can be an economic blessing or a curse, we are told, and one would expect global political economy (GPE) scholarship might also find reason to examine issues of youth or demography in the region. Yet, peculiarly, these matters are rarely given attention.[31] Young Gulf citizens open up the so-called black box of policy-making and politics in Gulf states in ways that other approaches and entry points have been unable to accomplish. Rentier theorising on the Gulf has been so adamant that citizens are apolitical, disinterested in political change, and unengaged in policy matters (unless they are technocrats involved in its construction), that scholarship has failed to understand the political economy transformations as they matter to some of the region's major constituents.[32]

Much of this exclusion stems from a failure to engage with insights from other fields or view the Gulf as part of a wider global economy when oil is not the central unit of analysis. I identify three layers of this neglect. First, studies of Gulf economies almost entirely ignore Gulf citizens, outside passing remarks on their concentration in

---

[31] Few monographs provide explicit examinations of the Gulf in IPE, Hanieh, *Capitalism and Class in the Gulf Arab States*; Kristian Coates Ulrichsen, *The Gulf States in International Political Economy* (New York: Palgrave Macmillan, 2016); and fewer still take seriously the citizen/non-citizen relationship in the labour market. Abdulhadi Khalaf, Omar AlShehabi, and Adam Hanieh, eds., *Transit States: Labour, Migration & Citizenship in the Gulf* (London: Pluto Press, 2015); Herb, *The Wages of Oil*.

[32] A notable exception here is Vitalis' historical examination of Saudi labour in *America's Kingdom*.

public sector employment and weak representation in the private sector.[33] Political economy work that does consider Gulf labour is primarily descriptive of the segmentation between expatriates and citizens.[34] Deeper, idiographic work in anthropology rarely engages with IPE and tends to focus on singular migrant communities.[35] Second, labour is marginalised in IPE research in general.[36] Third, studies of labour and class relations in oil economies are sparse and accompanied by claims of their weak salience to analysis.[37] Moreover, much political economy literature on the Gulf treats the region as exceptional across global cases but generalisable at the regional level. This not only ignores the substantial diversity across and within Gulf states but also isolates them from meaningful cross-regional comparison.[38]

---

[33] Herb, *The Wages of Oil*, bucks this trend. .

[34] E.g., Gabriella Gonzalez et al., *Facing Human Capital Challenges of the 21st Century: Education and Labor Market Initiatives in Lebanon, Oman, Qatar, and the United Arab Emirates* (Santa Monica: Rand Corporation, 2008); Nasra Shah, 'Recent Labor Immigration Policies in the Oil-Rich Gulf: How Effective Are They Likely To Be?', *International Publications* 52, Working Paper no. 3 (1 January 2008), http://digitalcommons.ilr.cornell.edu/intl/52; Onn Winckler, *Arab Political Demography: Population Growth, Labor Migration and Natalist Policies*, rev. and expanded 2nd ed. (Sussex Academic Press, 2009); Steffen Hertog, 'A Comparative Assessment of Labor Market Nationalization Policies in the GCC', in *National Employment, Migration and Education in the GCC*, ed. Steffen Hertog (Berlin: Gerlach Press, 2012).

[35] Some of the most compelling and helpful work on the Gulf is, in fact, coming out of anthropology. Neha Vora, *Impossible Citizens: Dubai's Indian Diaspora* (Durham; London: Duke University Press, 2013); Andrew M. Gardner, *City of Strangers: Gulf Migration and the Indian Community in Bahrain* (Ithaca: Cornell University Press, 2010); Moreover, a recent turn has seen more frequent engagement with the dimensions of global capitalism. See, for example, Wright, *Between Dreams and Ghosts*; Ahmed Kanna, Amélie Le Renard, and Neha Vora, *Beyond Exception: New Interpretations of the Arabian Peninsula* (Ithaca: Cornell University Press, 2020).

[36] Phoebe Moore, 'Where Is the Study of Work in Critical IPE?', *International Politics* 49, no. 2 (1 March 2012): 215–37, https://doi.org/10.1057/ip.2011.40; Robert O'Brien, 'Labour and IPE: Rediscovering Human Agency', in *Global Political Economy: Contemporary Theories*, ed. Ronen Palan (New York: Routledge, 2000), 89–99, https://doi.org/10.4324/9780203978740.

[37] Kaveh Ehsani, 'Disappearing the Workers: How Labor in the Oil Complex Has Been Made Invisible', in *Working for Oil: Comparative Social Histories of Labor in the Global Oil Industry*, ed. Touraj Atabaki, Elisabetta Bini, and Kaveh Ehsani (Cham: Springer, 2018), 11–34; Mitchell, *Carbon Democracy*.

[38] Important exceptions include both Herb and Hertog's work and use of a comparative politics approach, as discussed (p8, footnote 15). Herb, *The Wages of Oil*; Hertog, 'Defying the Resource Curse'.

Shifting the focus in rentier state literature from oil to labour aids in resituating the Gulf within comparative and global political economy analysis. This shift, alongside integrating methods from economic anthropology with IPE, allows us to take the voices of youth as agents in economic development more seriously. This contributes to understanding Gulf development challenges within the story of global capitalist expansion, the rise of neoliberalism and its tensions with economic nationalism, and strains in globalised labour markets. Building from here, the project connects Gulf development trajectories to scholarship on authoritarian neoliberalism[39] and asks what explains the persistence of regulatory interventions in the face of pressures toward deregulation and flexibilisation of the labour market. Who wins and who loses from these tensions and the tendency toward one or the other? It examines what the global nature of Gulf labour markets means for its participants and what this means for domestic political economy within Oman.

At the crux of this research agenda are two real-world, global problems – youth unemployment and socio-political tensions around migration. Youth unemployment has been signalled by international financial institutions and consultancies as both a policy problem and opportunity to promote market-friendly reforms and business-friendly economies. The Arab world is no exception. Youth unemployment is rising in several resource-abundant Gulf countries alongside growing numbers of migrant workers. Tensions develop from the marginalisation of Omani youth in the private sector and the exclusion of non-nationals from political belonging. Yet scholarship views young Gulf citizens as reluctant to engage in the private sector because of a 'rentier mentality' associated with the 'resource

---

[39] Ian Bruff, 'The Rise of Authoritarian Neoliberalism', *Rethinking Marxism* 26, no. 1 (2 January 2014): 113–29, https://doi.org/10.1080/08935696.2013 .843250; Ian Bruff and Cemal Burak Tansel, 'Authoritarian Neoliberalism: Trajectories of Knowledge Production and Praxis', *Globalizations* 16, no. 3 (2019): 233–44, https://doi.org/10.1080/14747731.2018.1502497; Cemal Burak Tansel, ed., *States of Discipline: Authoritarian Neoliberalism and the Contested Reproduction of Capitalist Order* (Lanham: Rowman and Littlefield, 2017), www.rowmaninternational.com/buy-books/product-details/.

curse',[40] or, more crassly, a so-called Arab disease.[41] Such essentialisation limits the comparative appeal of work on the region. Crucially, many of the aspirations, expectations, and worries young people express are reflective of (disenfranchised / non-elite) youth globally – especially in welfare states with certain expectations of public goods delivery. This is not to say various impacts of oil dependence have not made their mark. The economic structures that derive from oil and foreign labour dependence are visible. However, by focusing on authoritarianism and elite preferences, such scholarship has failed to include a 'bottom-up' analysis of economic change in the region – and to probe youth views on oil, rentierism, or uncover their employment preferences, expectations, and aspirations.[42] It is incumbent on IPE scholars to not only engage with statist and institutionalist perspectives but also directly interrogate issues of youth, gender, segmentation, inequality, and opportunity in labour markets. It is time to treat the region as more than an oil spot not only to expand analysis of the region and its integration in the global economy but also to generate grounded solutions to tangible problems.

---

[40] Hazem Beblawi, 'The Rentier State in the Arab World', in *The Rentier State*, ed. Hazem Beblawi and Giacomo Luciani (New York: Routledge, 1987), 49–62; Martin Hvidt, 'Economic and Institutional Reforms in the Arab Gulf Countries', *The Middle East Journal* 65, no. 1 (2011): 85–102.

[41] Atif A. Kubursi, 'Prospects for Arab Economic Integration After Oslo', in *The Middle East Dilemma: The Politics and Economics of Arab Integration*, ed. Michael C. Hudson (New York: Columbia University Press, 1999), 310.

[42] There are notable exceptions to the absence of youth and citizens from academic analysis on the region, including insightful work on young Saudis and Emiratis. On Oman, Al-Farsi discusses Omani youth and democracy. The literature is scarce and does not centre on labour. Pascal Menoret, *Joyriding in Riyadh: Oil, Urbanism, and Road Revolt* (Cambridge: Cambridge University Press, 2014); Amélie Le Renard, *A Society of Young Women: Opportunities of Place, Power, and Reform in Saudi Arabia* (Stanford: Stanford University Press, 2014); Mark C. Thompson, *Being Young, Male and Saudi: Identity and Politics in a Globalized Kingdom* (Cambridge: Cambridge University Press, 2019); Calvert W. Jones, 'Seeing Like an Autocrat: Liberal Social Engineering in an Illiberal State', *Perspectives on Politics* 13, no. 1 (March 2015): 24–41, https://doi.org/10.1017/S1537592714003119; Ahmed Kanna, 'Flexible Citizenship in Dubai: Neoliberal Subjectivity in the Emerging "City-Corporation"', *Cultural Anthropology* 25, no. 1 (February 2010): 100–29; Sulaiman H. Al-Farsi, *Democracy and Youth in the Middle East: Islam, Tribalism and the Rentier State in Oman* (London; New York: I. B.Tauris, 2013).

1.3 Gulf Millennials?

At the heart of the book sit the voices and perspectives of young Omanis – in particular the millennial generation.[43] Following Sukarieh and Tannock, I understand youth and millennials as a social category influenced by the structures of capitalism, where it is essential to give 'renewed attention to global political economy' and to the 'social construction of youth in a global context'.[44] Doing so grounds our understanding of 'the shifting terrain on which youth is understood, invoked and experienced' by Omani millennials and how 'youth' is engaged in economic and labour market governance by local and international policymakers.[45] I use the term 'millennials' loosely, roughly corresponding with international usage that speaks of the demographic born between 1980 and 2000.[46] I use millennials to refer to young people both preparing to enter the work force and in the early stages of their labour market participation. That is, those over eighteen years of age and usually under the age of thirty-five participated in interviews, focus groups, and surveys. These research tools focused on perspectives, expectations, and engagements in the labour market, looking at a range of stages including students of technical colleges and universities, school leavers, unemployed youth, new entrants to workplaces, and those nearing the end of the early career to mid-career period.

The term millennials is more commonly used in reference to this generation in the West. The Gulf social and historical space does not attach the same meaning to recent generational labels such as Baby Boomer or Generation X, which refer to particular socio-political and historical contexts. Indeed, the millennial generation in the Middle

---

[43] My field research centres on Omani millennials, but the broader book includes and centres on young Omanis over time, historically (see Chapter 3), and subsequent generations, paying particular attention to the intersections of youth with class, gender, and race. It is therefore especially worth noting, as Sukarieh and Tannock say in their important work on youth in the global economy, the concept of youth is 'notoriously fuzzy' and its boundaries difficult to determine. Mayssoun Sukarieh and Stuart Tannock, *Youth Rising? The Politics of Youth in the Global Economy* (New York: Routledge, 2014), 3.

[44] Sukarieh and Tannock, 5–8.   [45] Sukarieh and Tannock, 5.

[46] Increasingly, Generation Z has been interjected into this long time span, depending on definition. Some accounts mark the generational break between millennials (Gen Y) and Gen Z around 1995. Gen Z is also known as the Zoomer generation, or digital natives.

East is at the same time a baby boom generation. It is regularly referred to as a youth bulge[47] and makes up the largest demographic group in Oman. As Figure 1.1 illustrates, over 73 per cent of Omanis are under the age of thirty-five.

Overall, I think generational terms and definitions offer sketchy typologies of limited analytical value. Yet broad-brush generalisations of millennials in the West, and all the critique of their inappropriateness, reflects in some ways a dialogue of the deaf between generations. I find similar stereotyping dialogues in Oman and the Gulf between generations but also between expatriates and citizens. Such sweeping generalisations, whether about young people in America or young people elsewhere, tells us something about expectations and perceptions and how these, however imperfect, influence policy discourse and the policy-making space. Thus, the term millennial in this text may be apt in more ways than one.

In early Western writing on millennials, the generation differentiates itself from previous ones largely by the economic and technological repercussions of the Internet.[48] Some writers add to the technological divide and suggest a greater civic-mindedness and strengthened sense of community at both local and global levels in comparison to previous generations.[49] These broad characteristics could also be applied to other socio-political spaces transformed by increased connectivity and technological change. The Gulf region has one of the highest mobile usage and social media penetration rates in the world. Young people there tend to be early adopters of technology.[50]

More specifically, comparisons can be drawn between depictions of millennials by older generations. In Western economies, millennials are criticised for an alleged sense of entitlement, high expectations of the

---

[47] World Bank, 'Unlocking the Employment Potential in the Middle East and North Africa: Toward a New Social Contract' (Washington, DC: The World Bank, 2004); 'Rethinking Arab Employment: A Systemic Approach for Resource-Endowed Economies' (Geneva: World Economic Forum, October 2014), http://wef.ch/1uAr60x.

[48] See, for example: William August Draves and Julie Coates, *Nine Shift: Work, Life and Education in the 21st Century* (River Falls: LERN Books, 2004).

[49] Neil Howe and William Strauss, *Millennials Rising: The Next Great Generation* (New York: Random House LLC, 2000).

[50] Jane Kinninmont, 'To What Extent Is Twitter Changing Gulf Societies?' (London: Chatham House, February 2013), www.chathamhouse.org/sites/default/files/public/Research/Middle%20East/0213kinninmont.pdf.

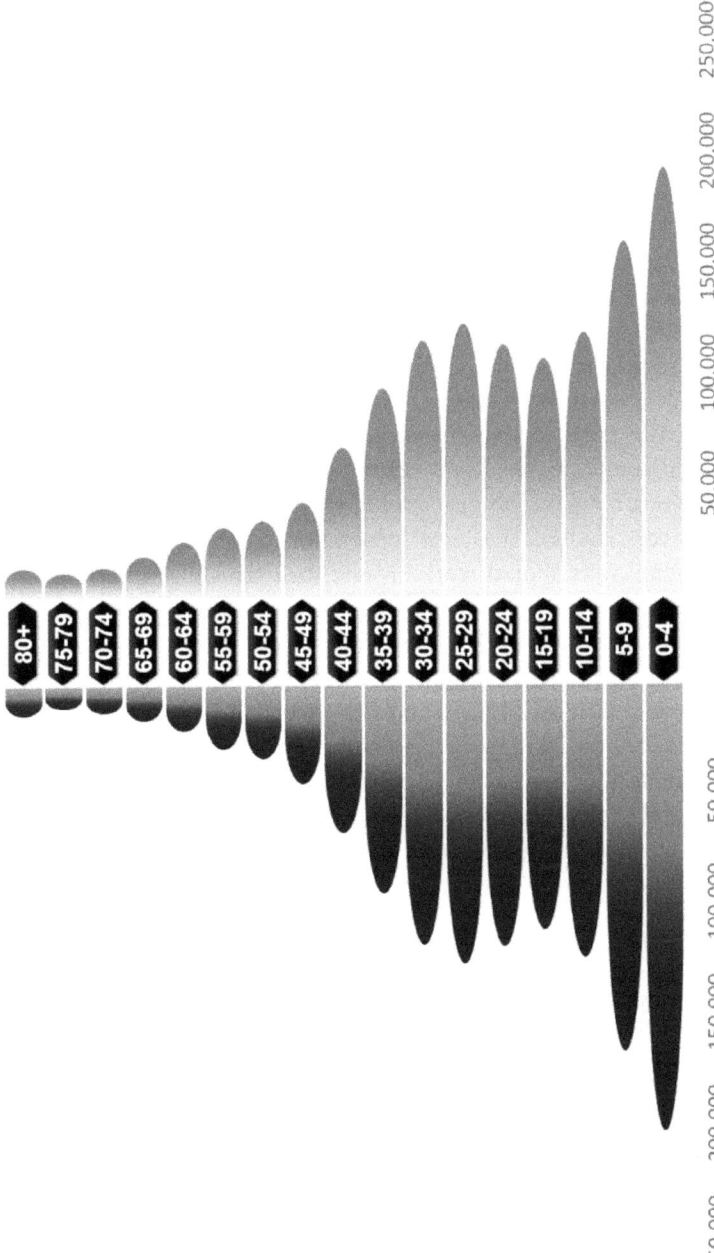

Figure 1.1 Omani population pyramid.
Calculated from NSCI, Statistical Year Book 2019

19

job market, and an apparent need for praise and affirmation.[51] One of the common accusations is that 'childhoods of constant praise, self-esteem boosting, and unrealistic expectations did not prepare [millennials] for an increasingly competitive workplace and the economic squeeze'.[52] In the workforce, Western millennials are criticised for 'demanding too much too soon' and wanting to be 'CEO tomorrow'.[53] Along with expecting higher pay, flexible work schedules, rapid promotions, and more vacation and personal time, there is a prevailing perception that millennials 'desire to shape their jobs to fit their lives rather than adapt their lives to the workplace'.[54]

Many of these hyper-capitalist criticisms mirror those toward Gulf millennials. In personal interviews, individuals from earlier generations often shared similar sentiments. Business managers regularly claimed that millennials frequently changed jobs 'in pursuit of higher salaries', wanted to 'get a profit fast' without working particularly long or hard.[55] Omani young people, I was regularly told, had unrealistically high expectations for pay, job title, and flexible working hours. Even Omani employers claimed the 'new' generation were presumptuous and thought employers should work around their schedule, adjusting for personal commitments and family obligations.[56] Many interviewees suggested that higher levels of education came with a sense of entitlement to better jobs despite lacking practical experience. Everyone spoke of how technology had changed the mode of communication, connectedness, and social openness.[57] I do not think it useful to stress the similarities too much. There are significant differences and diverse historical paths that led to the types of expectations as well as the perceptions of older generations toward millennials. However,

---

[51] Ron Aslop, 'The "Trophy Kids" Go to Work', *Wall Street Journal*, 21 October 2008, http://online.wsj.com/article/SB122455219391652725.html; Jean M Twenge, *Generation Me: Why Today's Young Americans Are More Confident, Assertive, Entitled – and More Miserable Than Ever Before* (New York: Free Press, 2006).

[52] Twenge, *Generation Me*, 7.   [53] Aslop, 'The "Trophy Kids" Go to Work'.

[54] Aslop, 'The "Trophy Kids" Go to Work'.

[55] Interviews with business managers and policymakers, Muscat, 25 October 2011, 8 January 2012.

[56] Interviews with business managers and policymakers, Muscat, Summer 2014, 2017–2018, January 2019.

[57] Interviews with business managers and policymakers, Muscat, Summer 2014, 2017–2018, January 2019.

some of the implied meaning behind the term also paints a picture that is illustrative beyond a simple age category.

Further, understanding youth and millennials, and centring on the issue of employment that consumes them, requires understanding the confluence of interests (political, economic, and ideological) surrounding the issue area, the global context in which job seeking and youth unemployment exists, and the labour market struggles of all ages and generations in conversation.[58] In Oman, even the term *baṭāla* (unemployment) itself is politically sensitive and seen as taboo in official and policy spaces. *Bāḥthūn 'an 'amal* (jobseekers) is used instead to refer to the unemployed.[59] Since they constitute the bulk of the unemployed and a major source of pressure on the state, *al-shabāb* – youth – are the target of national discourse and policy-making around the labour market. Even the National Centre for Statistics and Information started producing regular reports on youth and the labour market over the last ten years.[60] The experiences of millennial jobseekers, and multigenerational labour struggles, need to be understood within a multi-scalar, structural, and historically specific analysis of the material and discursive conditions of their lives in local, national, regional, and global contexts.

1.4 A Note on Method

Oman is a valuable case not only because it is under-researched but also because it is considered a laboratory of reform within the Gulf.[61] Its more limited hydrocarbon earnings suggest Oman must prepare for a post-oil future more urgently than many Gulf counterparts. Reforms attempted in Oman are sometimes considered test cases for rolling out new policies on socially complicated portfolios like labour. Focusing on one of the middling rentiers, and starting with labour instead of oil, gives IPE scholarship a new angle of approach for examining not only

---

[58] Sukarieh and Tannock, *Youth Rising?*, 55–78.
[59] NCSI, 'Khaṣā'iṣ al-Bāḥth 'an 'amal' (Muscat: National Centre for Statistics and Information, 2015), www.ncsi.gov.om/Elibrary/.
[60] 'al-Shabāb wa al-'Amal' (Muscat: National Centre for Statistics and Information, 2017); 'aAl-Shabāb wa sūq al 'amal' (Muscat: National Centre for Statistics and Information, 2020), www.ncsi.gov.om/Elibrary/.
[61] Marc Valeri, 'Oligarchy vs. Oligarchy: Business and Politics of Reform in Bahrain and Oman', in *Business Politics in the Middle East*, ed. Steffen Hertog, Giacomo Luciani, and Marc Valeri (London: Hurst, 2013), 18.

how labour is governed but how young nationals engage with the bifurcated and globalised labour markets of the region.

I make two distinct methodological choices in this work – centring the margins by focusing on labour and embedding the study in global development trends and transformations.[62] The first allows me to centre Omani experiences and voices, while the second allows me to escape the methodological nationalism that characterises much of the rentier state and political economy scholarship on the Gulf.[63]

Omanis of varying social classes have described to me the history and present of Oman as a 'labour country'. Taking inspiration from my interlocutors and the experience of working with Omani youth, I find understanding the global political economy of the country requires understanding the human beings that contribute to it. That is, one can learn a great deal about the present and past of the economy by 'follow[ing] the workers'.[64] Today, this also includes understanding the unemployed. What I hope my work does – and what I'm calling for intellectually – is to ground our scholarship in the human experience even when we are discussing economic governance; that is, do not just look from the top down but also engage the bottom up. Processes of governing, and discourses on, labour are not radically new but rather part of longer historical processes of governing and framing labour by colonial, nationalist, and neoliberal forces and processes. Taking a longer view shows this continuity and change. Analysis from the top down shows the evolution of policy choices. Analysis from the bottom up allows us to read the landscape through the eyes of actors and visualise it as a 'contradictory space of social struggle and asymmetrical power relations, engaging through contingent analyses of inherently messy socioeconomic relations and cluttered institutional

---

[62] I thank Tsolin Nalbantian for suggesting the turn of phrase 'centring the margins'.

[63] Methodological nationalism refers to a tendency in the literature to focus on individual national case studies and treat them 'as self-contained, enclosed sets of social relations, separate from the wider region and world market'. Adam Hanieh, 'Overcoming Methodological Nationalism: Spatial Perspectives on Migration to the Gulf Arab States', in *Transit States: Labour, Migration & Citizenship in the Gulf*, ed. Abdulhadi Khalaf, Omar AlShehabi, and Adam Hanieh (London: Pluto Press, 2015), 58.

[64] Interviews and conversations, December 2019, January 2020, January 2021; Khalfan Al-Badwawi, 'Laḥaẓat fī masīrat inahhā' al-istiʿamār: ʿashar sanawāt ʿalā intafāḍat Ṣuḥār', Al-Hamish, 2 March 2021, https://al-hamish.net/11522/.

environments'.[65] The millennial labour story is embedded within the longer story of Omani workers and economic life.

Furthermore, I intentionally engage the term Global Political Economy (GPE) instead of IPE to indicate my orientation to the field as transdisciplinary and interested in multi-scalar and multi-relational analysis.[66] I build on a new tradition of scholarship that views the region as neoliberal in its orientation and entrenched within global capitalism.[67] By understanding Gulf labour markets as global, we can offer more convincing explanations for their transformations and contradictions, the facilitation of particular labour regulatory regimes, and their embeddedness in global economic trends. It is the ghettoisation of Gulf studies, forged by a belief in their remarkable exceptionalism, that stymies theorising and explanations of social and economic processes that are possible through comparative analysis and transnational and global lenses. I galvanise this lens in the analysis of youth in the Omani labour market, which facilitates important insights on the development and consequences of the global labour market, capitalist class relations, and labour governance patterns.

The theme of employment took centre stage in my engagements with young people even before I began formally analysing them. When I first lived in Oman, I worked with college students for two years in my capacity as a lecturer. Engaging with young people is always future oriented, especially among students. Like the questions we ask about what they plan to do with their lives, they too are wondering, worrying, and dreaming about the future. In college, they often want to talk

---

[65] Jamie Peck and Nik Theodore, 'Labour Markets from the Bottom Up', in *Handbook of Employment and Society: Working Space* (Cheltonham: Edward Elgar, 2010), 91.

[66] Ronen Palan, 'New Trends in Global Political Economy', in *Global Political Economy*, 2nd ed. (New York: Routledge, 2012); Huw Macartney and Stuart Shields, 'Space, the Latest Frontier? A Scalar-Relational Approach to Critical IPE', in *Critical International Political Economy: Dialogue, Debate and Dissensus*, ed. Stuart Shields, Ian Bruff, and Huw Macartney (London: Palgrave Macmillan, 2011), 27–42, https://doi.org/10.1057/9780230299405_3.

[67] Hanieh, *Money, Markets, and Monarchies*; Hanieh, *Capitalism and Class in the Gulf Arab States*; Khalili, *Sinews of War and Trade*; Rafeef Ziadah, 'Constructing a Logistics Space: Perspectives from the Gulf Cooperation Council', *Environment and Planning D: Society and Space* 36, no. 4 (2018): 666–82, https://doi.org/10.1177/0263775817742916; Crystal A. Ennis, 'The Gendered Complexities of Promoting Female Entrepreneurship in the Gulf', *New Political Economy* 24, no. 3 (2019): 365–84, https://doi.org/10.1080/13563467.2018.1457019.

about this with others. I spent hours listening to young women and men talk about their dreams and their expectations about the future – including ideas of family, of love (and secret love), and, always dominating the conversation, jobs.

Realities on the ground challenge long-held scholarly evaluations of Gulf societies, politics, and economic change. Young people's views and dreams told me one thing. Media, consultancies, and policymakers (both foreign and local) report another. Young people are regularly referred to as 'lazy',[68] 'choosy',[69] and 'reluctant to take up jobs'.[70] Employers and foreign analysts habitually suggest that nationals are not 'ready to take over' jobs in the private sector.[71] At the same time, Omani youth complain that employers do not want to hire them and, when they do, do not give them meaningful work or any at all. I listened to many stories of jobs that require the employee to fill a seat at a desk while not having any work to do. This is what Steffen Hertog calls 'phantom employment' where a national receives a salary but is given nothing to do or is told to stay home.[72] However, the most persistent complaint is the difficulty of getting a foot in the door. There is a widespread perception that the private sector systematically discriminates against Omani young people and only those with the right connections can surmount this. This sense creeps into anti-immigration accusations that expatriates holding managerial positions privilege their nationality and recruit only friends or family members from their home country.

Jobs and labour market problems were persistent anxieties during my regular returns and periods living in the region since 2005. The global financial crisis that began in 2007 and the uprisings that rocked the wider Arab world in 2010 and 2011 pushed such concerns to the

---

[68] 'From Oil to Toil', *The Economist*, 10 September 2016, www.economist.com/middle-east-and-africa/2016/09/10/from-oil-to-toil.

[69] 'Gulf States Struggle to Shift Jobs to Choosy Locals', *Arabian Business*, 3 November 2011, www.arabianbusiness.com/gulf-states-struggle-shift-jobs-choosy-locals-428611.html.

[70] Sunil K. Vaidya, 'Oman Private Companies Find Youth Reluctant to Take up Jobs', *Gulf News*, 10 August 2012, https://gulfnews.com/world/gulf/oman/oman-private-companies-find-youth-reluctant-to-take-up-jobs-1.1060229.

[71] 'Gulf States Struggle to Shift Jobs to Choosy Locals'.

[72] Steffen Hertog, 'Arab Gulf States: An Assessment of Nationalisation Policies', GLMM – Research Paper (Gulf Labour Markets and Migration [GLMM], 2014), https://cadmus.eui.eu/bitstream/handle/1814/32156/GLMM%20ResearchPaper_01–2014.pdf?sequence=1&isAllowed=y.

forefront of the global imagination and heightened the empirical importance of understanding young people in the Gulf. When I first started my doctoral work in 2009, I was discouraged from focusing on the region's youth. By the time I returned to the Gulf for my field research, the Middle East was already in the throngs of the uprisings. But the so-called Gulf exceptionalism meant I should not centre on youth but instead on the rentier state and its policy measures. I therefore analysed policy spaces that were critical to the future of a youth-filled region – the development of an innovation-driven, knowledge economy. At the same time, I continued gathering data and engaging with millennials. This ultimately only formed one chapter of my dissertation, with the rest saved and analysed for this book project. Following my year of dissertation field research in 2011–2012, I spent approximately another twenty-five months in Oman between 2013 and 2020.

This book is concerned with taking Gulf labour seriously in development governance discourses. It is based on this multi-year field work including around two hundred open and semi-structured interviews, eighty responses to written digital surveys, focus groups, five-years of ethnographic observations over a period of thirteen years, and historical records in physical and digital archives.[73] I have made use of multiple methods to analyse these sources, including process-tracing, qualitative content analysis within a discourse analytic approach, and contrapuntal reading.[74] A discourse analytic approach is a more

[73] Pamela Cawthorne, 'Identity, Values and Method: Taking Interview Research Seriously in Political Economy', *Qualitative Research* 1, no. 1 (1 April 2001): 65–90, https://doi.org/10.1177/146879410100100104; Oisín Tansey, 'Process Tracing and Elite Interviewing: A Case for Non-Probability Sampling', *PS: Political Science and Politics* 40, no. 4 (1 October 2007): 765–72; George E. Marcus, *Ethnography through Thick and Thin* (Princeton, NJ: Princeton University Press, 1998); Robert Emerson, Rachel Fretz, and Linda Shaw, 'Participant Observation and Fieldnotes', in *Handbook of Ethnography*, ed. Paul Atkinson (Thousand Oaks: SAGE, 2001), 352–68; James P. Spradley, *Participant Observation* (Long Grove: Waveland Press, 2016).

[74] Alexander L. George and Andrew Bennett, *Case Studies and Theory Development in the Social Sciences* (Cambridge, MA: The MIT Press, 2005); David Collier, 'Understanding Process Tracing', *PS: Political Science & Politics* 44, no. 4 (October 2011): 823–30, https://doi.org/10.1017/S1049096511001429; Cynthia Hardy, Nelson Phillips, and Bill Harley, 'Discourse Analysis and Content Analysis: Two Solitudes?', *Qualitative & Multi-Method Research* 2, no. 1 (31 March 2004): 19–22; Andrew Bennett and Colin Elman, 'Complex Causal Relations and Case Study Methods: The

qualitative form of content analysis that alongside looking for patterns and consistency of words also embraces sensitivity to the meaning, usage, and context in which words are used.[75] This approach matches well with contrapuntal reading, and its emphasis on giving voice to multiple contexts and perspectives. Edward Said introduced contrapuntal reading as a method in literary analysis to account for different structures, ideas, and discourses that are silenced through the way literature exclusively privileges the perspective and experience of the coloniser or imperial power.[76] The term is borrowed from music and refers to the relationship between themes, the 'independent yet harmonious lines in a musical composition', which, when extended to social science analysis, proposes reading to connect multiple experiences, contexts, and scales.[77] That is, in this analysis, source material from multiple perspectives are analysed to understand the history and context behind policy, as well as the history and context of resistance over time. I explain my application of contrapuntal reading to GPE explicitly in Chapter 3's historical analysis.

Research participants can be organised in five broad categories: (1) millennials / youth; (2) government officials and policymakers; (3) entrepreneurship and employment initiative actors; (4) employers, recruitment agents, and human resource professionals; and (5) unions and labour and civil society actors. The first category of millennials, described in Section 1.3, sit at the heart of the inquiry. I held interviews, focus groups, and countless informal conversations with young people.[78] I also distributed a digital survey aimed at understanding perspectives and experiences on the labour market. I spoke with young people in colleges and universities across the country; jobseekers and

---

Example of Path Dependence', *Political Analysis* 14, no. 3 (20 June 2006): 250–67, https://doi.org/10.1093/pan/mpj020; Pinar Bilgin, '"Contrapuntal Reading" as a Method, an Ethos, and a Metaphor for Global IR', *International Studies Review* 18, no. 1 (2016): 134–46, https://doi.org/10.1093/isr/viv018; Geeta Chowdhry, 'Edward Said and Contrapuntal Reading: Implications for Critical Interventions in International Relations', *Millennium: Journal of International Studies* 36, no. 1 (2007): 101–16, https://doi.org/10.1177/03058298070360010701.

[75] Hardy, Phillips, and Harley, 'Discourse Analysis and Content Analysis', 20–21.
[76] Edward W. Said, *Culture and Imperialism* (New York: Vintage Books, 1993).
[77] Bilgin, '"Contrapuntal Reading" as a Method, an Ethos, and a Metaphor for Global IR', 139.
[78] As the project progressed, the youngest participants could include those that may popularly be referred to as Generation Z as they came of age.

also individuals in their early and mid career; aspiring entrepreneurs engaged in one of the many training, incubation, or other entrepreneurship promotion activities; and entrepreneurs themselves. I intentionally engaged across socio-economic classes, regions, and urban/rural divides.

Second, formal interviews, informal conversations, and participant observation (in the form of policy dialogue, conferences, workshops, and meetings) were held with active and retired, senior, and mid-level policymakers and bureaucrats in the various ministries and government bodies responsible for commerce and trade, labour, education, and economic planning. This category has significant overlap with the third: those who ran and implemented various entrepreneurship promotion initiatives from training and funding to incubating start-ups. Some of these are private and non-governmental, but many were connected to government bodies, educational institutions, or banks. The fourth category includes business owners and employers. This includes businessmen and -women from historic business families, chamber of commerce officials and committee members, established entrepreneurs, and other employers. Given the size of the state, each of these categories overlap and evolve as individuals move in and out of business and government or have one foot in the door of each. It also includes the human resource professionals responsible for recruitment, training, and retention in mid-sized and large companies. Finally, I spoke with unions, union members, civil society organisations, and labour rights activists and their networks.[79]

1.5 Reading the Book

The arguments presented at the start of the chapter are elaborated on and interwoven into the analysis throughout the chapters of this book. Together, the book weaves Omani labour market constituents into a wider tapestry of regional labour trends and the global labour market. It illustrates how the Omani labour market is globalised but also rentier and neoliberal and how it struggles with the path dependencies of its reliance on foreign labour and oil but also grapples like other labour markets globally with the pressures of global capitalism. It does

---

[79] In most cases, my participants will remain anonymous. The labour market remains a sensitive space.

this through a history of labour market policy and development planning, an exploration of sites of radical economic transformation, and examinations of labour market belonging and economic citizenship and of entrepreneurship and self-employment initiatives.

Akin to other labour markets wrestling with competitiveness and balancing meaningful, sustainable employment, workers in Oman's labour market confront varieties of exclusions and struggle to negotiate their belonging in various economic sectors. Citizens and non-citizens perceive their influence and privileges, and their exclusions and precarities in multiple ways. Such tensions give rise to economic nationalism. At the same time, millennial citizen expectations form out of an interaction between what society expects the government to provide through their governance of hydrocarbon revenues and what economic globalisation promises to young people globally. Comparison influences expectations, not just within domestic and regional contexts but from the interconnected hyper-global world as well.

In this work, I explore labour contestation among Omani citizens in a globalised labour space where *labour's power is not so much in the strength of its organisation but in the threat of its discontent.* Connecting domestic labour issues with global economic trends allows us to better interpret relevant changes in today's connected economies. It also offers new insights into the international political economy of labour.[80] Moreover, throughout the book, I explore the origins and conditions that have led to the governance and regulatory contradictions that have come to characterise Omani and Gulf labour markets. These inquiries lay the foundation for the two critical, overarching claims of the book.

First, I call for citizen labour to be brought into international political economy scholarship on the Gulf. By starting with labour rather than oil, we introduce new critical insights to understand the Omani and wider Gulf economy. It brings human beings back into our scholarship in places where they have been marginalised. Importantly, here it de-exceptionalises the 'Gulf citizen'.

---

[80] Harrod, 'Towards an International Political Economy of Labour'; Las Heras, 'International Political Economy of Labour and Gramsci's Methodology of the Subaltern'.

Second, I contend neoliberal capitalism has become an integral part of the Gulf development story.[81] That is, rentierism has gone to bed with neoliberal capitalism. It is not at all surprising that rentier states manifest authoritarianism when one considers how much state intervention transpires to create regulation to 'liberate' the market and facilitate patterns of accumulation.[82] The state wields its power on behalf of capital and the pursuit of profit through the way it regulates (and forcibly deregulates) economic activities. This view contrasts with prevailing literature on Gulf IPE where rentierism and neoliberalism came to be regarded as separate detached phenomenon until the recent turn's focus on capitalism in the Gulf. It is perhaps no surprise that this is the case. In classic literature on rent, all competing schools of thought, from neoclassical and Keynesianism to Marxism, agreed that rent was at most a residual phenomenon within capitalism and most agreed it was ephemeral.[83] In the march toward competitive market futures, manifestations and patterns of rentierism were going to dissipate. Yet as studies such as Piketty's *Capital in the Twenty-First Century* show, rent continues to be important in contemporary

---

[81] The terms neoliberal, neoliberalism, and the idea of something becoming neoliberalised runs into difficult definitional territory. The very idea of neoliberalism has been the victim of such wide concept stretching, it risks losing its analytical value. Here I engage two meanings of neoliberalism featured in academic debates. First, neoliberalism is an economic ideology associated with the privileging of free markets, growth, and private enterprise as represented by work such as that of Friedrich Hayek and Milton Friedman. This ideology emerged as a dominant political project by the 1980s and 1990s in the international political economy, advocating privatisation, deregulation, and liberalisation as generalisable strategies for development across the world (John Williamson, 'What Washington Means by Policy Reform' [Washington: Peterson Institute for International Economics, April 1990], www.iie.com/publications/papers/paper.cfm?researchid=486). Second, neoliberalism can be used to express a somewhat manufactured cultural consensus around markets and economic rationalities that is used by governments to galvanise support for policies and instil a sensibility for responsible citizens. See Ennis 'The Gendered Complexities of Promoting Female Entrepreneurship in the Gulf', 366–67; Andrew Barry, Thomas Osborne, and Nikolas Rose, eds., *Foucault And Political Reason: Liberalism, Neo-Liberalism and the Rationalities Of Government* (New York: Routledge, 1996); David Harvey, *A Brief History of Neoliberalism* (Oxford: Oxford University Press, 2005).

[82] Polanyi, *The Great Transformation*, 147.

[83] Brett Christophers, 'Class, Assets and Work in Rentier Capitalism', *Historical Materialism* 29, no. 2 (19 March 2021): 3–4, https://doi.org/10.1163/1569206X-29021234.

capitalism.[84] Definitions of rent include both those that consider income received by a landowner for letting out property and those that consider rent as excess profits more broadly. In this book, I follow Christophers' definition of rent as 'income derived from the ownership, possession or control of scarce assets and under conditions of limited or no competition'.[85] This definition is especially useful for three reasons. First, it includes all forms of assets, including not just land but also intellectual property patents. Second, it is built on a foundation in which market conditions exist through which rent income is realised. Third, it sufficiently incorporates rentier states without exceptionalising how rent functions within global capitalism.

Rent-seeking too is a key feature of neoliberal capitalism, as actors seek to earn wealth through extracting rent from resources, contracts, land, labour visas, patents, and the like. The centrality of neoliberal capitalism to Gulf development underlies regulatory tensions between the impulse of generous social welfare, on the one hand, and the logic of economic profit maximising, on the other. This tension becomes visible by a focus on the labour market and the various economic reform measures. This runs as a thread throughout this book. Rentier neoliberalism emerges as a form of 'authoritarian neoliberalism', where authoritarian statisms are clearly intertwined with neoliberal reforms.[86] Indeed, the embeddedness of the Gulf in global capitalist markets, in hydrocarbon trade but also in global production networks, entrenches the countries of the region within a global neoliberal logic that pursues profit and durability at all socio-political costs.

In Chapter 2, I lay the contextual groundwork substantiating my claim that the Omani labour market is global and subject to both neoliberal and nationalist forces. Development planning, economic ideologies, and regulatory frameworks interact, shape, and institutionalise economic structures and economic life. I unpack the Omani labour market, zooming in on its structure, demographics, organisation, and regulation. Through presenting the backdrop to the labour market, I detail its segmentations, structures, and challenges. I also explore the processes of class formation, the role of wages in a global

---

[84] Thomas Piketty, *Capital in the Twenty-First Century*, trans. Arthur Goldhammer (Cambridge, MA; London: Belknap Press of Harvard University Press, 2014).

[85] Christophers, 'Class, Assets and Work in Rentier Capitalism', 5.

[86] Bruff and Tansel, 'Authoritarian Neoliberalism', 239.

labour market, and the patterns of labour market regulation and reform. I pay specific attention to labour nationalisation and labour sponsorship regimes and how the regulatory regimes governing citizen and foreign employment interact.

Chapter 3 takes a step back to assemble the historical context around work in the modern history of Oman. Through re-reading development history by starting with labour, it explores both Omani modern work history and labour market governance. The chapter argues that the contemporary governance, regulatory, and resistance state of affairs in Oman has lineages in the past. These extend from the colonial and oil industry labour practices and discourses through the era of neoliberal reform to the present. In particular, the chapter sets up the backdrop to the regulatory frameworks that shape and constrain how citizens and non-citizens engage and have engaged in the economy over time and how their labour has been governed. Tracing the lineages of differentiation and resistance in the labour market reveals how segmentation, differentiation, discourses of workers, and labour resistance, as well as the pressures for both liberalisation and nationalisation have a much longer history than is usually told. It contradicts exceptionalist narratives of Gulf labour market governance and shows transnational and global historical connections with patterns of recruitment and employment. The politics of work and its regulation that began in the late colonial period in the wider region have continuities in present-day Oman. Earlier practices and patterns around employment and immigration governance have imprints on the structure, regulatory space, and collective memory of the Omani labour market today.

Chapter 4 explores sites and projects of radical transformation, focusing on Sohar and Duqm. These two cities offer examples of two extreme cases of economic transformation and social impact – one a location that is a population centre and another that is remote. Both cities became cornerstones of national development imaginaries in development plans, where the development of Special Economic Zones (SEZ) with logistics infrastructure like ports and major industrial activities are supposed to be key diversification drivers that will generate non-oil growth and private sector expansion. It begins with the city of Sohar, which rapidly transformed from a small coastal town to a city and national industrial hub in the 2000s. The promise of Sohar raised expectations yet its limited and uneven benefits shattered them. In the face of all of this growth and change, Sohar was at the heart of Oman's 'Arab Spring' in 2011. Ten years later, in May 2021, Sohar emerged again as the starting point of protests that continued for a few days in several cities. Economic disenfranchisement and a lack of opportunities for local youth were at the core of concerns. Duqm today epitomises the promise of economic development for the national future. It is undergoing radical transformation from a small fishing village to an enormous SEZ, with investment from China, India, Japan, Belgium, Kuwait, among others. Through the Sohar and Duqm accounts, I ground the argument about Oman's global labour market in empirical examples of spatial transformation. The case studies offer concrete examples of Oman's integration into global value chains and the material outcomes and ramifications of neoliberal policies and development plans. The chapter argues that the expectations of young citizens take shape in the interaction of the promises of economic development's trickle-down effect, of globalisation, and of government responsibilities for governing petrol wealth; and their reactions emerge from their perceived right to, or exclusion from, these returns. Continuing the patterns examined in Chapter 3, these cases also show how capital works to avoid labour disruption and therefore draws on the global labour market for both a supply of labour and also for an enhanced capacity to control workers and secure seamless operations.

Chapter 5 builds on the disconnect between economic promises and expectations to explore the construction of belonging and contestation of economic space among diverse Omani millennials. Centring on belonging, class, and social relations, it examines how forces of inclusion and exclusion play across both national and expatriate divides in Gulf economies. Nationals in Oman may have citizenship and permanence in the country but are marginalised in economic production by their weak representation in the private sector. Non-nationals, although comprising the majority of private-sector workers, in many ways 'belong' in different sectors of the private sector yet have no political claim on permanence in the country. The divisions within these groups construct different senses of belonging and not belonging, resulting in tenuous economic citizenship and practices of othering. I argue, first, that perceptions of belonging and unbelonging emerge from the structures of segmentation and the tension between neoliberal reform and labour protection, and second, that class is key to understanding these patterns. These findings not only shed light on the competing pressures in the governance of Gulf labour markets but also contribute to scholarly understandings of economic citizenship and Gulf labour-market complexities in a globalised context.

Chapter 6 focuses on entrepreneurship promotion among millennials and women – two overlapping constituents who are disproportionally represented among the jobless demographic. In Oman, like in neighbouring Gulf states, the promotion of entrepreneurship – small- and medium-sized enterprises – has been a key state strategy over the past decade as both a vital component of innovation policy and as an alternative career path for citizens. If you cannot get the market to hire the citizen, perhaps the citizen can make their own market. The proliferation of neoliberal growth discourse across rapidly developing economies is obvious in the promotion of entrepreneurship and celebration of individual enterprise. Oman's embrace of an entrepreneurial market discourse may seem peculiar next to the preponderance of the state in political and economic spaces. Yet it is perhaps this policy discourse that most clearly underpins the rentier-neoliberal marriage and the making of rentier neoliberalism. This chapter demonstrates how Omani youth and female entrepreneurs confront competing tensions within three intersecting political economy logics: the logic of the economic structure, the logic of development narratives, and the logic of socio-economic organisation. Rather than resolving labour market issues, this chapter shows how most forms of entrepreneurship reproduce the same dominant, segmented employment patterns in the wider economy. Meanwhile, new entrepreneurs are still subject to the same regional and global inequalities and patterns of capital accumulation.

By centring the margins of labour, the book responds to Adam Hanieh's call to study the Gulf within a view of 'capitalism as a social system' with attention to 'class relations in Gulf society'.[87] Following this, the Conclusion reflects on the lessons learned throughout this book. To take stock of its central claims, it identifies and reviews three intersecting vectors that run through the book – (1) the embeddedness of segmented labour markets within global structures and processes, (2) the key historical junctures shaping regional labour trajectories, and (3) the liberalising/nationalising dialectic in labour governance.

---

[87] Hanieh, *Capitalism and Class in the Gulf Arab States*, 12.

2 | *Making Global Labour Markets and National Dreams*

The major task, then, is to match the new economic and socio-political dislocations and configurations of our time with the startling realities of human interdependence on a world scale.[1]

—Edward Said

This chapter begins our journey of recentring labour in development accounts, sketching the making of Oman's global labour market and the construction of national dreams of what economic life should entail. It is concerned with framing the claim of this book that the labour markets of Oman (and, indeed, the wider Gulf region) are global. Following Peck and Theodore, my work is grounded in a 'heterodox vision' of the labour market. That is, I view the labour market 'as a site of conflicting power relations, enduring regulatory dilemmas, necessary (but problematic) forms of institutionalisation, embedded path dependences and systematic uneven development'.[2] This heterodox vision of Oman's labour market accounts for the regulatory incongruities and the competing, multi-scalar pressures toward economic reform. It demonstrates how both neoliberalising and nationalising pressures coincide to co-create and co-constitute the shape of, and outcomes in, the Omani labour market. By connecting the Omani case with the regional economic space and global labour market, we can understand the making of global Gulf labour. The transformations in the production and circulation of global labour impact the region, which is in turn impacted by it. This approach, furthermore, begins to unravel development planning and 'visioning' and the influence of these on the national imagination and citizen dreams, a thread that continues through this book.

---

[1] Said, *Culture and Imperialism*, 330.
[2] Peck and Theodore, 'Labour Markets from the Bottom Up', 87.

Most development accounts habitually articulate Oman's labour market as an object of development, a self-contained unit to be regulated and deregulated toward developmental ends, and a place for pursuing both individual prosperity and national developmental objectives. Development policy and academic discourse, in short, treat the labour market as a bounded, local space with enclosed, segmented social relations. In contrast to this development planning imaginary, this chapter argues that the labour market needs to be interpreted in global context and with a view of how regulation, labour, and social relations transpire within, between, and across segmentations. The labour market is a place in which you can clearly see the outcomes of global market pressures and the competing poles for labour's management and (de)regulation. These come from within but also outside national and regional boundaries. In combination, by looking from the bottom up, the labour market offers a space where we encounter humans in the economy and can more clearly visualise the human impact of economic transformations and choices. The chapter proceeds as follows. First, I sketch the structure of Oman's labour market and analyse the segmentations that characterise it. Next, I explain how this book understands class and how class formation unfolds. Third, I focus on wages and use wages and their determination to show how globally situated yet locally segmented labour markets are regulated (deregulated, and reregulated). The focus on wages further substantiates our understanding of class formation within global labour markets. Finally, I explore the patterns and processes of labour market reform and regulation by looking at the contemporary history of employment nationalisation and immigration policy. Together, the chapter shows how development planning, economic ideologies, and regulatory environments interact, shape, and institutionalise particular economic structures in the local and regional economy.

2.1 The Structure of the Omani Labour Market

Oman's labour market is characterised as 'segmented' or 'bifurcated' – reflecting dual labour market structures that are features of the regional political economy. Slightly over two out of ten employees in the country are Omani citizens, and these individuals primarily find work in the public sector.[3] Such are the most common segmentations

---

[3] Calculated from NCSI, 'Monthly Statistical Bulletin' (Muscat: National Centre for Statistics and Information, February 2020), 19–23, www.ncsi.gov.om/

described in Gulf labour markets – those between citizens and expatriates and between the public and private sector. In Oman, the separation is stark. Whereas over 76 per cent of employment available in the Sultanate is in the private sector, fewer than 13 per cent of working Omanis are employed there. The remainder work in the public sector. 10.5 per cent of work in the country is in the government, which represents fewer jobs than the household sector.[4] Expatriates primarily staff economic activities in the private sector. Figure 2.1 illustrates these segmentations.

The startling difference in scale of labour between citizenship status and sector brings attention to the immense social policy challenges embedded within these structures. It is extraordinarily difficult to compose and implement any labour market reforms, migration reforms, or unemployment responses given the organisation of labour in the economy.

Alongside divisions between citizenship status, several gendered dynamics are also immediately apparent in Figure 2.1. Omani women are concentrated in the public sector – holding 32 per cent of work in the civil service or 4 per cent of all available positions in the country. Omani women in the private sector only represent 8 per cent of all jobs. This is despite the fact that female labour force participation rates have been increasing each decade, going from 12.5 per cent of the female labour force in 2000 to 35 per cent in 2021.[5] The private sector, demographically dominated by expatriate males and certain types of (often manual) labour, is less hospitable to female employment than working for the civil service or in state-owned enterprises (SOE). Across the Omani labour market, men hold 83.8 per cent of total paid employment and women 16.2 per cent.[6]

Elibrary/. These figures do not include Omanis employed in security services. This data is not reported.

[4] The household sector refers to domestic services and includes occupations such as cleaners, child or elderly care givers, cooks, and drivers. NCSI, '2019 Statistical Year Book' (Muscat: National Centre for Statistics and Information, August 2019), 104–29, www.ncsi.gov.om/Elibrary/.

[5] This data corresponds to female labour force participation as a percentage of the female population aged 15+. Data on the female labour force participation rate of those age 25+ is even higher at 42.5 per cent in 2021. In the same period (2000–2021), the male labour force participation rate grew from 59.2 to 83.8 per cent of the male population. 'Labour Force Participate Rate by Sex and Age', Labour Force Survey, Labour Force Statistics, ILOSTAT (Geneva: International Labour Organization), accessed 12 December 2022, https://ilostat.ilo.org/data/.

[6] NCSI, '2019 Statistical Year Book', 105.

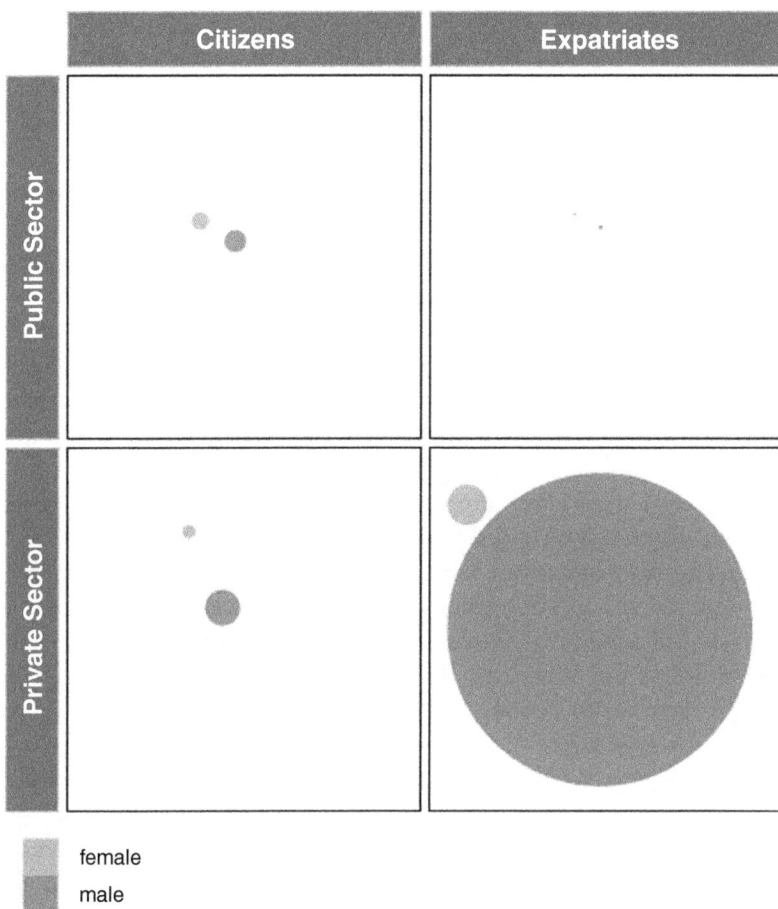

Figure 2.1 Omani workforce by citizenship, sector, and gender.
Source: Calculated from NSCI, Statistical Year Book 2019. Circle size reflects the number of workers, proportional to the size of the workforce. Official figures exclude military and security services.[7]

The highly segmented labour market illustrated here is positioned within the global labour market in particular ways and is able to

---

[7] It is estimated that 1.8 per cent of Oman's labour force are active armed forces personnel. This figure is higher than the global average of 0.8 per cent but lower than the MENA average of 2.3 per cent. The MENA average is higher than any regional share. International Institute for Strategic Studies, 'Armed Forces Personnel (% of Total Labor Force)', World Bank Data, 2017, https://data .worldbank.org/indicator/MS.MIL.TOTL.TF.ZS.

selectively draw from global supplies of low-, semi-, and high-skilled labour. The same forces that facilitate the mobility of capital within global value chains in search of cost effective, weak labour and environmental regimes have also fostered Gulf labour markets that look beyond borders in search of the cheapest available workers across skill levels. The 'cost' of expatriate labour is primarily determined by the market rate or regulatory practices of the labour-sending country. This has resulted in wages for low-skilled and semi-skilled occupations that are lower than the minimum an Omani citizen would be willing to work for, and frequently, below the cost of living.[8] As the required skill set and education level rises, the wage differential narrows and there is more possibility for job competition. One of the foundational institutions of capitalist social organisation is matching employers in search of employees with workers in search of a wage. Given Oman's position within a global labour market, this basic organising principal shapes recruitment practices but at a transnational scale drawing from Asia's 'continent of labour'.[9]

Gulf labour markets can best be understood as evolving alongside the development of a global capitalist system, with labour flows growing out of historical patterns of human mobility across and through the Indian Ocean world and West Asia. As a growing body of historical work has shown about earlier periods,[10] our understanding of labour and mobility is furthered with a view of the evolution of social relations within the Gulf as well as between the Gulf and the world market. Labour market patterns, the governance of migration and labour, and the social relations that evolve within labour markets are not produced in isolation in Oman or in the Gulf regional economic space. They are co-constituted by transformations within the global political economy and the relations between capitalist developments in the region, Asia, and globally.[11]

---

[8] Especially for low-skilled occupations, this is often below the minimum wage – an issue I turn to later in this chapter.

[9] Chang, 'From Global Factory to Continent of Labour'.

[10] See, for example, Fahad Ahmad Bishara, *A Sea of Debt: Law And Economic Life in the Western Indian Ocean, 1780–1950* (Cambridge: Cambridge University Press, 2017); Johan Mathew, *Margins of the Market: Trafficking and Capitalism across the Arabian Sea* (Oakland: University of California Press, 2016); M. Reda Bhacker, *Trade and Empire in Muscat and Zanzibar: The Roots of British Domination* (London; New York: Routledge, 1994).

[11] Adam Hanieh has done the most to further theorising on the Gulf regional economic space as part of the Global economy and essential to the making of it. Hanieh, *Capitalism and Class in the Gulf Arab States*; Hanieh, *Money, Markets, and Monarchies*.

Likewise, the governance of labour in Oman is tied to the neoliberalising propensities of the global political economy, with labour flows serving the demands of global capitalism and global value chains. Within hydrocarbon-dependent Gulf economies, such patterns have contributed to generating an addiction to foreign labour. The figure above reveals the present scale of this dependence, but this pattern has been long standing.

Policy concerns about this so-called imbalance are also not a new phenomenon. Oman's history of economic development planning throughout Sultan Qaboos bin Said's rule (*Qābūs bin Saʿīd*, 1970–2020) shows an acute cognizance of the imperative to reduce the country's dependence on not only oil income but also foreign labour. 'It is not wise, nor good policy, to be dependent on oil as a sole resource to finance our development', emphasised the Sultan in his national day speech on 18 November 1998.[12] Much earlier, in 1975, the government's Development Council articulated a development policy and issued a thirteen-point resolution defining its aims. This development policy was facilitated by oil income enabling investment in fundamental economic and social infrastructure. Yet it was also grounded in an acknowledgement that oil reserves would eventually be exhausted and that 'the wealth generated from it should be exploited in investments for the benefit and welfare of the present as well as future generations'.[13] While declaring the 'free economy' the basis of development policy, the resolution emphasised the necessity to develop new sources of revenue, rationalise the use of oil income, and give 'priority to income generating projects to supplement oil receipts'. Clearly acknowledging the imperative of diversification, the resolution explicitly calls this the 'duty and most important task of the Development Council'.[14] Moreover, an 'equally important' task highlighted in the top five points was protecting population centres 'against the dangers of mass immigration'.[15] Already, this early development

---

[12] Sultan Qaboos bin Said Al-Said, 'The Royal Speeches of His Majesty Sultan Qaboos Bin Said' (Muscat: Ministry of Information, 2015), 390, www.omaninfo.om/english/files/Book/royal-speech.pdf.

[13] Development Council, 'Resolution on Aims and Objectives of Economic Development Policy in the Sultanate (Issued at Its Meeting of Sunday, 9 February 1975)', in *The Five-Year Development Plan 1976–1980* (Muscat: Sultanate of Oman Development Council, 1976), 106.

[14] Development Council, 107.   [15] Development Council, 108.

Table 2.1 Private sector employment estimates (1975)

	Omani	%	Expat	%	Total labour	% of Total employment
Petroleum and mining	2,892	62	1,787	38	4,679	5
Manufacturing	825	38	1,374	62	2,199	2
Building and construction	18,640	25	56,596	75	75,236	81
Trade	923	33	1,841	67	2,764	3
Hotels	1,420	54	1,194	46	2,614	3
Transportation	2,286	74	794	26	3,080	3
Financial institutions	668	60	454	40	1,122	1
Services	348	27	954	73	1,302	1
TOTAL	28,002	30	64,994	70	92,996	100

Source: Calculated from Development Council, FYP 1976–1980

policy reveals the tension between the incentives and pressures of the free market and the awareness of the need to protect the interests of "local human resources" in the national economy. I return to this dialectic in the last section.

In the mid-1970s, the private sector already relied on foreign recruitment to staff its positions (Table 2.1). This was attributed to the shortage of 'trained Omani manpower' at the time, which investment in education and vocational training was to resolve.[16] Moreover, until the 1990s, slightly over half of Oman's population was in the dependent age group, with insufficient numbers reaching employable age each year to meet the national growth demands on the labour market.[17] It was already evident by 1975 that the building and construction sector constituted the largest share of the workforce. The idea was that this sector should be prioritised in vocational training. Indeed, over 81 per cent of jobs were in construction, with 75 per cent of these positions held by expatriates.

The picture has since remained constant and by some metrics worsened. In these early decades, the public sector quickly absorbed

[16] 'The Five-Year Development Plan 1976–1980' (Muscat: Sultanate of Oman Development Council, 1976), 48.
[17] Mohamed Bin Musa Al-Yousef, *Oil and the Transformation of Oman: The Socio-Economic Impact* (London: Stacey International, 1996), 100.

educated Omanis. Despite immense improvements in human development indicators in the country, education chief among them, Omanis continue to have a weak presence in the private sector even as unemployment persists. The private sector retains its preference for recruiting abroad, and citizens have both a preference and an expectation of public sector employment. The tension has persisted alongside a growing awareness in the public imagination that such patterns are unsustainable, exacerbated by growing job demand from young Omani nationals.

Across the decades, the government has tackled national job creation and the economic dependence on expatriates through two types of interventions. The first, demand side interventions, involve a combination of human capital investment through education and vocational training and direct labour market interventions like quotas where a designated percentage of a particular occupation is reserved for citizens. Together, these labour nationalisation policies are known as ta 'mīn or Omanisation. The second type of interventions are on the supply side of labour. Here the government targets the inflow of labour immigration by increasing visa fees for employers or by blocking foreign recruitment in selected occupations. Policies associated with Omanisation first started to be embedded in policy documents in the late 1980s; their history is explored in more detail later in this chapter. Yet despite ebbs and flows in labour nationalisation or liberalisation, the labour market structure remains largely fixed.

The percentage of positions held by Omanis in the private sector has only declined since the 1970s despite explicit objectives aimed at curtailing expatriate growth. In 1975, 30 per cent of private sector jobs were held by Omanis (see Table 2.1). With each oil boom, larger waves of migrant workers streamed to the Gulf to staff massive infrastructure projects. Simultaneously, demand for service labour grew. The rapid growth of the service industry is a shared feature of oil economies and the expanding consumption needs of the growing national middle class.

Figures 2.2 and 2.3 illustrate the organisation of the labour market in terms of its segmentation between citizen and expatriate, but also the distribution of workers by economic activity and the type of occupation. As shown in Figure 2.2, a majority of the work available in the private sector is in construction. It contributes the largest share of employment to the Omani labour market, but at least 89 percent of

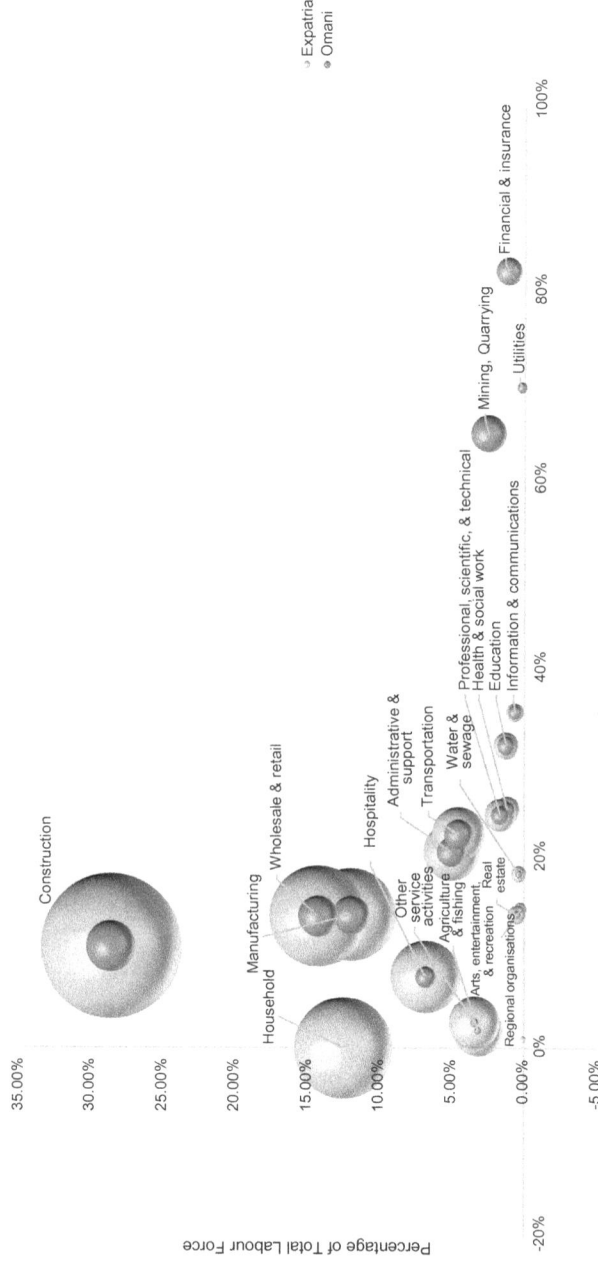

Figure 2.2 Labour distribution in the private sector, by economic activity.

SOURCE: Calculated from NCSI, Monthly Statistical Bulletin (January 2020). Bubble size corresponds to the number of workers.

42

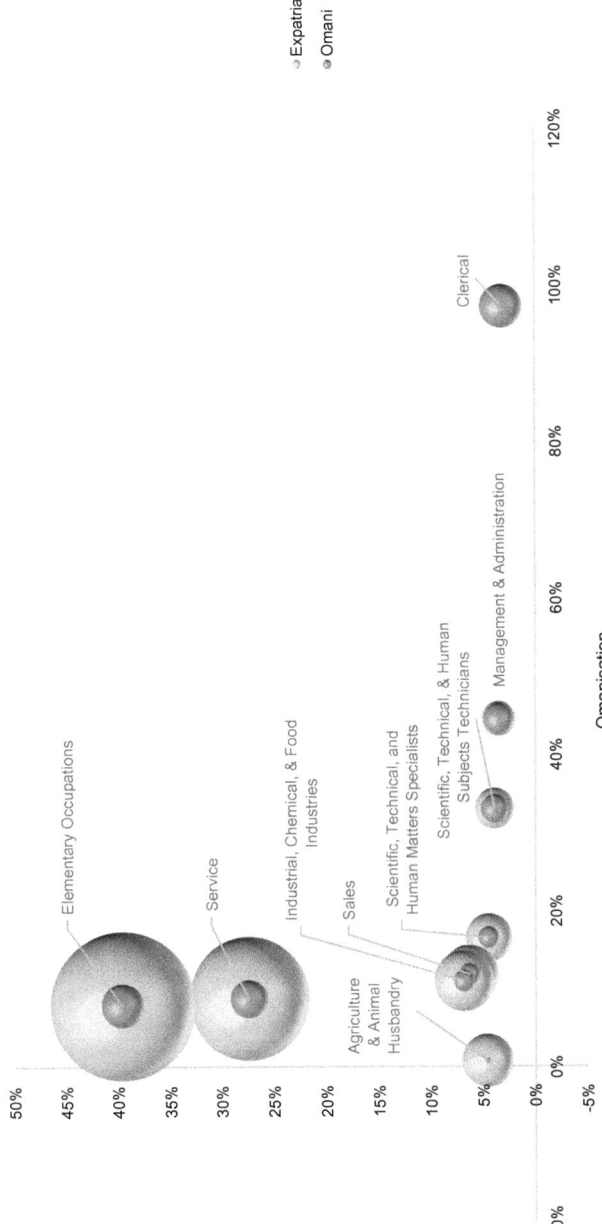

Figure 2.3 Labour distribution in the private sector, by occupational category.

SOURCE: Calculated from NCSI, Monthly Statistical Bulletin (January 2020). Bubble size corresponds to the number of workers.

43

jobs in the construction sector are held by foreign workers. Construction mainly delivers unskilled and semi-skilled occupations, and attracts labourers from South and South-East Asia who are willing to work for a fraction of the cost of the local minimum wage. Underlining this trend, Figure 2.3 clearly shows that elementary occupations constitute the greatest percentage of the total labour force and that these positions are primarily staffed by foreign workers.[18]

What we also observe in Figure 2.2 is that the economic activities with a majority of Omani labour are those in the lowest employment-generating sectors; that is, those sectors that hire the highest proportion of Omanis are those that constitute only a small portion of the total labour force. These economic activities include finance, insurance, utilities, and mining / quarrying. Employment data by occupational categories (Figure 2.3) renders an Omani presence even more difficult to detect. The glaring exception is clerical work: 97 per cent of clerical positions are held by Omanis, which was one of the earlier fields to be reserved for citizens. Banking has also been hugely successful in workforce nationalisation initiatives, which, according to the Central Bank of Oman archives already started in the 1970s. By 2019, according to an interview in the trade union magazine, nearly 94 per cent of bank employees across the country were Omani.[19] Omanis also have a stronger showing in administrative and scientific positions. It is evident that government efforts toward labour force nationalisation have been successful in the public sector, in activities that are capital rather than labour intensive like mining, and in occupations like those in the financial sector that are less labour intensive and more affordable to confine to citizens.[20]

---

[18] According to ISCO, elementary occupations are those jobs that 'consist of simple and routine tasks which mainly require the use of hand-held tools and often some physical effort'. These occupations can be found in sales and services, agriculture and fisheries, and in mining, construction, manufacturing and transportation. Tasks range from selling goods to providing services like cleaning or doorkeeping to performing simple farming or fishing, to assembling components, packaging, or simple manual tasks in mining, construction or manufacturing. 'ISCO: International Standard Classification of Occupations', International Labour Organisation, 18 September 2004, www.ilo.org/public/english/bureau/stat/isco/isco88/major.htm.

[19] Tahir Salim Al-ʿAmri, 'Ḥiwār ʿamal', *Majalat Sawaʿid Niqābīyya*, 2019, 12–14, www.gfow.om/?p=4333.

[20] For an earlier discussion of this trend, see Crystal A. Ennis and Raʾid Z. Al-Jamali, 'Elusive Employment: Development Planning and Labour Market

Where one works and lives alongside where employment is available also shapes social organisation. Figure 2.4 illustrates that the majority of jobs are concentrated in the most economically active regions of the country – the governorates of Muscat and Al-Batinah North topping the list. Unsurprisingly, expatriates are concentrated here. Likewise, 41.5 per cent of employed Omanis work in the Muscat governorate and 14.2 per cent in Al-Batinah North.[21] Such data explains the rural to urban movement in the country, where the working-age population across the various governorates are attracted to move to the capital area for work. Over recent decades, many Omani families have permanently moved their primary household to Muscat, retaining extended familial or land-based ties with their 'home' regions. Others spend the working week in the capital and return home on Thursday afternoon after work to spend the weekend with their families and communities.[22]

Across all regions of the country, Omanis form only a small percentage of the total labour force. Omanisation rates do not near half the labour force in even the least populated parts of the country (Figure 2.4). It is noteworthy that 49 per cent of all jobseekers are located in Al-Batinah North, Al Batinah South, and Dhofar.[23] These regions, along with Al-Sharqiyyah South, have the highest rates of unemployment in the country.[24] These were also regional pressure points in 2011, and it is not without consequence that Al-Batinah and Dhofar are also regions that have been targets of significant industrial development and host economic zones or ports – but little trickle down in terms of jobs.[25]

2.2 Class Questions

Understanding the making of Oman's global labour market requires connecting the demographic and structural features described above to

---

Trends in Oman', Research Paper (London: Chatham House, September 2014), www.chathamhouse.org/sites/files/chathamhouse/field/field_document/20140916ElusiveEmploymentOmanEnnisJamali.pdf.

[21] NCSI, '2019 Statistical Year Book', 114–15.

[22] Since 2013, the weekend in Oman is on Friday and Saturday. It was previously Thursday and Friday.

[23] NCSI, 'Khaṣāʾiṣ al-Bāḥthīn ʿan ʿamal', 32.

[24] NCSI, 'Khaṣāʾiṣ Al-Bāḥthīn ʿan ʿamal', 29.

[25] Chapter 5 addresses this phenomenon in detail.

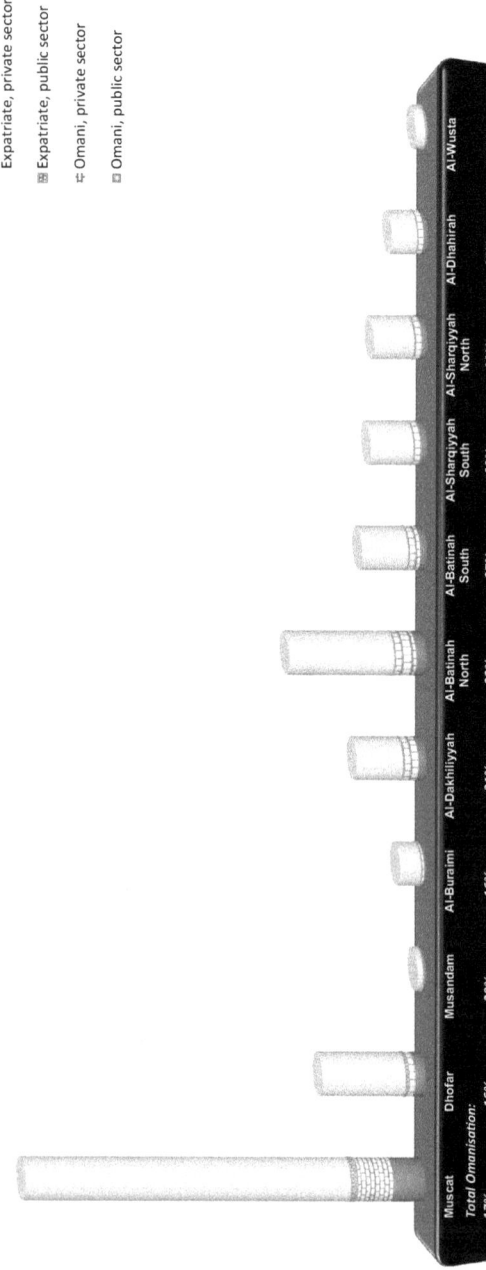

Figure 2.4 Omanisation and labour force size, by region.

SOURCE: Calculated from NSCI, Statistical Year Book 2019. The height of the cylinder proportionally corresponds with the size of the labour force in each region.

the global political economy. Doing so fortifies our understanding of class formation in the region, which is intimately connected to the global nature of the circulation of both capital and labour.

In this work, I take a causal, intersectional, and integrated approach to understanding class. By causal, I understand class as enormously significant in social explanations. However, I understand this causal factor *intersectionally*, that is, alongside other identities, relations, and experiences. This corresponds with Erik Olin Wright's definition:

Class is a powerful causal factor because of the way in which class determines access to material resources and thus affects the use of one's time, the resources available to pursue one's interests and the character of one's life experiences within work and consumption. Class thus pervasively shapes both material interests and capacities for action.[26]

The formation of this powerful factor intersects with various other identities and segmentations that are important to one's life experiences. In all societies, 'labour is necessarily social' and the social relations that emerge from this process are at the core of class formation.[27] This process is embedded within a global labour market that is especially visible in the Gulf. Migration to Oman (and the Gulf more broadly) links the development of social relations and class formation in Oman with the development of social relations and class in the home countries and regions of migrants.[28]

By integrated, I refer to an analytical approach advanced by Wright that integrates the three major approaches to class – a focus on the mechanisms of exploitation and domination rooted in Marxist political economy, a Weberian focus on opportunity hoarding, and

---

[26] Erik Olin Wright, 'Class Analysis, History and Emancipation', *New Left Review*, no. I/202 (1 December 1993): 27.

[27] Labour's social character as the development of social relations through the division of labour is central to Marxist theories of class. Hanieh, *Capitalism and Class in the Gulf Arab States*, 17.

[28] The 'spatial structuring of class' is at the core of understanding the broader structural features that draw workers to Oman from the global labour market. Employment relations form the primary axis of class differentiation, that is, the division between owners of capital and workers. Next, there are subsequent divisions of working classes as mediated by their possession of particular skill sets, levels of authority, and access to power and material resources. Employers in Oman benefit from the poorer conditions and opportunities in labour sending countries of Asia and the Middle East because it increases the surplus value they can extract. Hanieh, *Lineages of Revolt*, 126–27.

stratification's focus on individual attributes. While I lean heavily toward an approach that pays attention to power and exploitation, combining the three and viewing each as 'a key process that shapes a different aspect of class structure' helps explain various outcomes and dynamics in Oman's labour market elucidated throughout the book.[29] Moreover, an integrated approach allows us to understand 'mediated' and 'temporal' class locations, where social relations, educational opportunities, or career trajectories can influence changes in 'class' but still be embedded within power dynamics and structural features of the global economy.[30] Thus, we can focus on the mechanisms of exploitation and domination between capitalists and workers, as well as the sliding scales between them and relationships of oppression within them. A causal, intersectional, and integrated approach to understanding class offers tools to delineate and nuance mechanisms of exploitation, to understand historical change and the influence of identities and belonging, and to examine the mechanisms of co-option by the state, the impact of career promotions, and the impact of an influx of wealth.

Unpacking class in this way pushes beyond the simplification of class to a division between working class foreigner and Omani citizen. It nuances and enriches our understanding of class, offering insights into the nature, development, and governance of the labour market and the economy. While a major aspect of the formation of class evolves out of the bifurcation between expatriate and citizen, it is also mediated by identities, experiences, and the skills and educational level required in various occupations (as Section 2.1 illustrated). The Omani labour market is not simply segmented by public and private sector and by citizenship status, but it is also gendered, classed, and raced.[31] That is, the structuring of class among Omani citizens evolves in relation to migrant worker class formations while simultaneously

---

[29] Erik Olin Wright, 'Understanding Class: Towards an Integrated Analytical Approach', *New Left Review*, no. 60 (1 December 2009): 109.

[30] Wright, 'Class Analysis, History and Emancipation', 30–31.

[31] I use 'raced' instead of 'racialised' intentionally, following the idea that markets 'take their modern forms as raced', not as outcomes of rational capitalism subsequently distorted and racialised. David Roediger, 'Raced Markets: Prefatory Note', *New Political Economy* 23, no. 5 (3 September 2018): 531–33, https://doi.org/10.1080/13563467.2017.1417365.

evolving in relation to educational and social status.[32] This is part of a regional and global process of class formation.

Figures 2.2 and 2.3 clearly illustrate types of sectors and occupations where citizen labour coalesces and where it does not. The nature of the job, the financial incentive of working in it, and the value associated with it all matters to this story. Moreover, region of origin, region of living and working, and communal ties also intersect. One aspect of understanding regional intersections is grounded in the history of what John Wilkinson called Oman's 'fundamentally split personality'[33] – that is, the historical political divisions between Muscat and (coastal) Oman and the Imamate of the interior.[34] Both institutional differences and legacies of resistance are part of this differentiation, as well as the cultural experience associated with the cosmopolitanism and exchange of littoral societies. From a political economy perspective of today, it is not solely the legacies of political division and cultural experience that holds every day meaning. Whether you are primarily based in the capital area and tie and build your social capital there or whether you are primarily based in one of the other governorates in the country all matters to your economic life and opportunities. Geography, ethnicity, race, education level, community ties, gender, and occupation all intersect with class formation in Oman's development story.

The development of capitalist classes and what we can identify in Weberian terms as upper and middle classes in Oman emerged from a combination of pre-oil and post-oil socio-economic processes.[35] These included those that arose from various forms of pre-oil livelihoods and were well-positioned to build careers or businesses during the early period of oil-led development. This allowed some to enter a middle and upper class and others opportunities to begin to accumulate wealth. These groups include families with connections to Oman's history of overseas empire who built lives in Zanzibar and around the Indian

---

[32] The role and influence of race, caste, and gender is discussed at greater length below, and in Chapters 5 and 6.

[33] John C. Wilkinson, *The Imamate Tradition of Oman* (Cambridge: Cambridge University Press, 1987), 1.

[34] For a detailed discussion of the history, and politics of this division, read Wilkinson, especially 'Regional Divisions I: Muscat and Oman, and Regional Divisions II: Core and Periphery' in Wilkinson, *The Imamate Tradition of Oman*, 41–88.

[35] See Said Sultan Al-Hashimi, '*'Umān: 'an Masālat al-Ṭabaqa, wa fī musā'lat al-Wusṭā*', *Al-Mustaqbal Al-Arabi*, no. 495 (May 2020): 65–81.

Ocean rim who returned to Oman, those who found ways to leave Oman to pursue education abroad and then returned as an educated class, and the merchant families who first developed private educational opportunities in the country and those who benefitted from state contracts and foreign agency agreements, among others.[36] Some further benefitted immensely from the post-1970 era, moving into upper classes with the vast wealth they accumulated. From among these groups, and from the children of communities sustained by farming, fishing, and crafts, many found work as government employees in the civil or security services and others in the growing oil industry.

The roll out of rapid educational and economic development in post-1970 Oman facilitated a second phase of groups joining the middle class – primarily from the tribes across rural Oman (whether from mountainous areas, desert, or small coastal towns), that settled in the cities, and the many Omanis who studied on (government or oil company) scholarships abroad or in new colleges and universities across the country to become engineers, nurses, doctors, teachers, pharmacists, lawyers, and accountants among others. Together these disparate groups of Omanis reached certain levels of income and consumption power usually associated with a middle class. The record speed of this transformation, and the availability of employment within the state apparatus, built up an interwoven set of expectations of secure employment and certain standards of living.

The expansion of these middle classes grew alongside the development of a shared Omani national identity. Upon assuming power, Sultan Qaboos began fostering 'a feeling of belonging' and a 'timeless Omani' identity that was intended to supersede allegiances to tribes and local communities.[37] It was aimed at uniting a country fractured by insurgency and revolution against imperialism and divided by tribal politics and alliances.[38] While the port cities of Muscat and Matrah, as well as Sohar, already boasted a great deal of cultural, religious, and

---

[36] Al-Hashimi; Nasser Abdullah Salim Al-Saqri, 'Private Education in the Omani City of Maṭraḥ during the Reign of Sultan Saʿīd b. Taymūr (1932–1970)', *Arabian Humanities*, no. 12 (November 2019), https://doi.org/10.4000/cy .5429.

[37] Marc Valeri, *Oman: Politics and Society in the Qaboos State* (London: Hurst, 2009), 119.

[38] Takriti perceives the mechanisms of this identity construction as part of nurturing a 'Sultan's cult' for the loyal following and deference necessary to secure absolute rule and rapid decision-making. Abdel Razzaq Takriti, *Monsoon*

linguistic diversity, the expansion of economic development across the country provided more and more opportunities for expanding social relations.[39] Today 'social networks increasingly overlap' and 'identities transcend boundaries' as communities intermingle in spaces of education, work, and residence.[40]

Likewise, Said Al-Hashimi observes some levelling out of differences based on traditional cultural values, sectarianism, and tribalism toward a new shared sense of an Omani community.[41] However, he suggests Omanis still form solidarities along these identities before class-based ones.[42] The structural features of the economy, including both segmentation and embeddedness in a global labour market, make it difficult for class to become 'a compass of orientation' and a location of solidarity.[43] Such structural obstructions are not absolute but do remerge across time, as is evident in subsequent chapters. They limit the potential for widespread cross-identity, cross-segmentation solidarity with the 'exploited, oppressed, and disadvantaged in all their variety'.[44] Hence, labour mobilisation and activism often mirrors the broader labour segmentations.

Remarkably, very little scholarship on the Arabian Peninsula includes class as a meaningful unit of social analysis.[45] Even after the

Revolution: Republicans, Sultans, and Empires in Oman, 1965–1976 (Oxford: Oxford University Press, 2013), 198–206.

[39] Khalid Al-Azri, *Social and Gender Inequality in Oman: The Power of Religious and Political Tradition* (New York: Routledge, 2013), 12–14; Fredrik Barth, *Sohar: Culture and Society in an Omani Town* (Baltimore: John Hopkins University Press, 1983), 36–41.

[40] J. E. Peterson, 'Oman's Diverse Society: Northern Oman', *The Middle East Journal* 58, no. 1 (January 2004): 33, https://doi.org/info:doi/10.3751/58.1.12.

[41] Al-Hashimi's article is one of the few accounts focused explicitly on class. In his view, alongside this 'modernist' attempt at identity building, competing identities of local regionalism, tribalism, and community remain relevant. Al-Hashimi, ''Umān: 'an Masālat al-ṭabaqa, wa fī musā'lat al-wusṭā'.

[42] Al-Hashimi, ''Umān: 'an Masālat al-ṭabaqa, wa fī musā'lat al-wusṭā, 71–72.

[43] Göran Therborn, 'Class in the 21st Century', *New Left Review*, no. 78 (1 December 2012): 26.

[44] Therborn, 'Class in the 21st Century', 26.

[45] Adam Hanieh, Ahmed Kanna, and Michelle Buckley have led the way centring class in their research. Adam Hanieh, 'Khaleeji-Capital: Class-Formation and Regional Integration in the Middle-East Gulf', *Historical Materialism* 18, no. 2 (2010): 35–76, https://doi.org/10.1163/156920610X512435; Hanieh, *Capitalism and Class in the Gulf Arab States*; Ahmed Kanna, 'Class Struggle and De-Exceptionalizing the Gulf', in *Beyond Exception: New Interpretations of the Arabian Peninsula*, ed. Ahmed Kanna, Amélie Le Renard, and Neha Vora,

proliferation of modern wage labour with the beginning of the oil age, Oman, it is said, 'remained a tribal country'.[46] The 'fundamental distinction in Omani life patterns' continued to be that of *ḥaḍar* and *badū* (referring to the sedentary population in towns and nomadic peoples, respectively).[47] Such features seem to have been accepted as though that somehow renders class politics irrelevant. The emphasis on tribes and tribal structures, while important to understanding a great deal about social life, is largely blind to political economy divisions. If one would discuss class, it was simply a descriptor for the division between foreign worker and Gulf citizen. This reduction of class to one labour segmentation removes the diversity within and across these categories. It also imagines away the shared workplace of citizens and foreigners.

Identities and social relations form within a collective Omani identity and also across familial, ethnic, and religious ones. Tribalism like race, caste, and other identities are deeply intersected with class and shapes material interests, opportunities, and life experiences.[48] A picture of only one would be incomplete without the others. Hierarchical customs and legacies of tribal, racial, and caste divisions continue to inform social and legal relations within the country, including the heritage of being from an emancipated slave background, or from castes associated with servitude, peasantry, or mixed racial or

---

illustrated ed. (Ithaca: Cornell University Press, 2020), 100–22; Michelle Buckley, 'Locating Neoliberalism in Dubai: Migrant Workers and Class Struggle in the Autocratic City', *Antipode* 45, no. 2 (2013): 256–74, https://doi.org/10.1111/j.1467-8330.2012.01002.x.

[46] J. E. Peterson, *Oman in the Twentieth Century: Political Foundations of an Emerging State* (Routledge, 2016), 13.

[47] Peterson, *Oman in the Twentieth Century*, 23.

[48] The significance of caste divisions seem to decline with each generation, but the connotations of caste and racial identities remain persistent when it comes to questions of marriage. Family backgrounds of being servants (*khadam*) or slaves ('*abīd*) are still visible among older generations. Despite the growing distance, some social stigmas linger around being from certain communities like peasants or cultivators known as *bayādīr* or of mixed or unknown racial and tribal origin – *bayāsir*. Both of which were also usually considered *mawāla* (client group of a tribe). Some descendants remain affiliated with the tribes or families they depended on or served historically (*mawāla*), while others have worked hard to distance themselves and forge independent identities alongside embracing a shared Omani identity.

unknown genealogical origin.[49] At the same time, these intermix with education level and type of work, with distance and proximity to power, and with capacity for capital accumulation and level of income. Moreover, Omanis hold middle-class and upper-class jobs next to expatriate colleagues. Identity and class formation are influenced by, and in turn influence, the workplace and labour market structure.

The marginalisation of class as a unit of analysis is also common in political economy scholarship on the rentier state.[50] The argument being that in some modes of production, like rentier, distributive states, very little production occurs and thus class relations of production become less relevant.[51] In such countries, it is believed, class struggle is not an animator of politics,[52] and the 'Marxist emphasis on class does not apply because people do not identify themselves by their relation to means of production'.[53] Much scholarship thus claims that the 'more salient identities' include tribe, family, region, and religion.[54] While these works do not suggest abandoning class in analysis, this to a large extent occurred. Rather than studying other dynamics and identities that influence political economy alongside class, scholarship moved away from taking class formation seriously.

At the heart of this absence is the reliance of classic rentier state literature upon the assumptions of political apathy and of relative state autonomy to analyse state-society relations. The rentier state's policies for the redistribution of wealth are seen as purposely aimed at buying off dissent. In the words of Chaudhry,

Explicitly designed to depoliticize the population, these distributive policies forestalled the emergence of class conflict and public debate about the ends

---

[49] Mandana E. Limbert, 'Caste, Ethnicity, and the Politics of Arabness in Southern Arabia', *Comparative Studies of South Asia, Africa and the Middle East* 34, no. 3 (2014): 590–98; J. C. Wilkinson, 'Bayāsirah and Bayādīr', *Arabian Studies* 1, no. 1 (1974): 75–85; Al-Azri, *Social and Gender Inequality in Oman*, 12–14; Barth, *Sohar: Culture and Society in an Omani Town*, 43–49, 227; Peterson, 'Oman's Diverse Society', 48.

[50] Ehsani, 'Disappearing the Workers'.

[51] Jacques Delacroix, 'The Distributive State in the World System', *Studies in Comparative International Development* 15, no. 3 (1980): 3–21, https://doi.org/10.1007/BF02686463.

[52] Delacroix, 'The Distributive State in the World System', 18.

[53] Gwenn Okruhlik, 'Rentier Wealth, Unruly Law, and the Rise of Opposition: The Political Economy of Oil States', *Comparative Politics* 31, no. 3 (1999): 295, https://doi.org/10.2307/422341.

[54] Okruhlik, 'Rentier Wealth, Unruly Law, and the Rise of Opposition', 295.

of development and growth. In all cases, governments deliberately destroyed independent civil institutions while generating others designed to facilitate the political aims of the state.[55]

The state, here, is viewed as a distinct domain of political economy with a high degree of independence to carry out economic policy-making without the constraints of social pressure or a separate capitalist class. While such means of securing power and control are certainly visible, the rigid presentation of these assumptions were widely accepted as canon. Much work then overlooked and missed social dynamics that subsequent literature has only recently been addressing.[56] Part of the problem is how the state is viewed as detached from social and class relations.[57]

Socio-economic transformations are better understood through a view that sees the state as part of society and social relations occurring within the growth and transformation of capitalism. Such a perspective recognises the patterns of accumulation that interlink state and private capital.[58] It also facilitates cognisance of, and further insight into, mechanisms of power, accumulation, exploitation, and the forms of

---

[55] Chaudhry, 'Economic Liberalization and the Lineages of the Rentier State', 19.

[56] Michael Herb's work pushes beyond the exclusive oil centrism to focus on the relationship between the labour market and rentierism. In the extreme rentiers, he finds that the ability of the state to employ the majority of citizens without taxing them 'creates and unusual class structure' (15), breaking the link between capitalists and wage employees. In the UAE, the ruling families are the dominant capitalists and can pursue their economics interests almost unencumbered. Herb, *The Wages of Oil*. Steffen Hertog also untangles the simple rentier assumptions around state-society relations by examining the social relationships generated by rent distribution mechanisms. His insightful work on brokerage not only shows the social relations within the Gulf rentiers that occur within economic life but also shows types of class formation that have evolved in relation to oil's impact on economic structures. Steffen Hertog, 'The Sociology of the Gulf Rentier Systems: Societies of Intermediaries', *Comparative Studies in Society and History* 52, no. 2 (2010): 282–318, https://doi.org/10.1017/ S0010417510000058; Hertog, *Princes, Brokers, and Bureaucrats*.

[57] As Hanieh shows, shifting the analytical departure point from the relationship between state and society to that between capitalism and class offers a perspective of how the state is not 'an independent, separate feature of society, severed from the class structure that generates its character'. Hanieh, *Lineages of Revolt*, 8.

[58] Christian Henderson, 'Gulf Capital and Egypt's Corporate Food System: A Region in the Third Food Regime', *Review of African Political Economy* 46, no. 162 (2 October 2019): 602, https://doi.org/10.1080/03056244.2018 .1552583.

contestation that do occur.[59] This perspective underpins the relevance of my analytical focus on labour. State and society are co-constitutive.

In light of this understanding, the making of global Gulf labour markets becomes easier to comprehend. Oman's global labour market is not simply a national space with bifurcated spheres of citizen and foreign labour. Both the development and governance of labour is a multi-scalar phenomenon that occurs across geographic space and above and beyond national domains.[60] One aspect is that social reproduction occurs in the migrants' home country, where the labour force is reproduced and family and care of emigrant communities is centred. Oman and the region's position within a global market for labour led to the formation of the bulk of the working classes as foreign and precarious. This contributed to a spatial structuring of class bolstering the formation of Gulf capitalists. Another aspect, therefore, is how the redirection of wealth into and through the Gulf from the influx of oil receipts stimulated and expanded the process of Gulf capitalist class formation, expanding opportunities for people across the country, region, and wider Indian Ocean sphere.[61] This is not an 'accidental class structure that results from a lack of regulation' but is a 'direct consequence' of the transformation of capitalism that produced a global labour market and facilitated the processes of capital internationalisation in the Gulf.[62] Next to Gulf citizens, for example, some of the wealthiest capitalists in the region are Keralite entrepreneurs, several of whom appear in the regional Forbes billionaire lists.[63]

---

[59] But contestation does exist and is not all simply reducible to contestation over oil wealth. This is especially apparent in the middling rentiers. Ala'a Shehabi and Marc Owen Jones, eds., *Bahrain's Uprising: Resistance and Repression in the Gulf*, 1st ed. (Zed Books, 2015); Menoret, *Joyriding in Riyadh*; Okruhlik, 'Rentier Wealth, Unruly Law, and the Rise of Opposition'; Toby Matthiesen, *The Other Saudis: Shiism, Dissent and Sectarianism* (Cambridge: Cambridge University Press, 2014).

[60] Ennis and Blarel, *The South Asia to Gulf Migration Governance Complex*, 2022.

[61] Important to the contemporary examination of this process is the ownership of assets outside the means of production and how this shapes class within and beyond relations of employment; that is, the classic category of land ownership combined with newer forms of intellectual property and financial assets have continued to expand sources of wealth and introduced more granularity to class divisions across the world.

[62] Hanieh, 'Khaleeji-Capital', 55.

[63] Nicolas Blarel and Crystal A. Ennis, 'Contested Governance and Sovereignty in the Kerala-Dubai Migration Corridor', in *The South Asia to Gulf Migration*

This focus on Omani labour reveals more about the history of labour and class formation among citizens than the emphasis on the development of an elite capitalist class can capture. Not all citizens in the Gulf fall into the wealthy elite categorisation and their realities and struggles are easily lost in the conversation.[64] A further, and crucial, aspect of the multi-scalar nature of the development and governance of labour is how social relations unfold between Omani and non-Omani citizens in the workplace. In different forms of work, relations between Omanis and foreigners extend beyond the employer-employee one that transpires in much of construction and domestic labour. In many skilled and professional fields, Omanis and foreigners may work together, participating in the same team, and an expatriate may be just as likely to be a manager.

Even in sectors and occupational categories in Oman that almost exclusively draw on migrant workers, the global character of the labour market irrevocably mediates and shapes the ways in which Gulf labour of any citizenship performs labour and participates in economic activity. While all expatriates are temporary in legal terms, some white-collar workers spend their whole working lives in Oman, view their life centred within it, and raise their families there. The concern of their temporary status is, however, always present as their job requires their employer to renew their residency at given intervals. The condition of temporariness intervenes in all workplaces. The consciousness of a lack of job security and a sense of impermanence lingers in the background and affects multiple aspects of work life for both foreigners and citizens. The consequences of this insecurity problématique are unpacked in Chapter 5's discussion of inclusion and exclusion in the private sector.

Placing labour (and youth labour in particular) at the centre of this project furthers this productive direction integrating class and class formation into IPE analysis of the region. Class is thus a thread running in the background through the book. It brings to life critical elements of social relations, work, and youth expectations in the everyday economic life of Oman. What is already clear from the data examined in this chapter is that class intersects with tribe, community,

Governance Complex, ed. Crystal A. Ennis and Nicolas Blarel (Bristol: Bristol University Press, 2022), 150, https://bristoluniversitypressdigital.com/view/book/9781529221510/ch007.xml.
[64] see Figure 2.5 and discussion in Section 2.3.

and region just like it does with gender, race, and nationality. Crucially, class formation does not emerge in a vacuum but rather is built from the historical, political, and economic context.[65] Indeed, Chapter 3 shows the significance of pre-oil social disruption and the organisation of the labour market to patterns of class formation and the structure of the economy. Likewise, the empirical cases in Chapter 4 unpack this further, showing the emerging tensions around class transitions and expectation structures. These cases also speak to how identity markers do not occur in isolation.

Moreover, and significantly, perceptions and expectations of jobs emerging from the combination of class formation experiences and transitions frame desires, experiences, and struggles of belonging and not belonging in the labour market, as is explored in detail in Chapter 5. In interviews, some people clearly identify with being in a middle class, and many more identify themselves as being outside of an upper class – which variably includes the *tujār* (meaning merchants and referring to the trading or 'big' business families) and a Muscat elite of ministers and their perceived deep, intertwined state and economic interests. These feelings are very much evidence of identity markers of class even if not expressed using those terms. Chapter 6 too speaks to class dynamics by demonstrating their interaction with entrepreneurship promotion and entrepreneurial pursuits and especially how these intersect with being identified as 'youth' and / or 'female.' This causal, integrated and intersectional view of class encourages a nuanced and holistic understanding of work life in Oman's global labour market.

2.3 Wages in Global Labour Markets

Wages intersect with the governance and regulation of labour markets in interesting ways. As feminist political economy teaches us, wages

---

[65] Hanna Batutu showed this clearly in his immense investigation *The Old Social Classes of Iraq*. The text underlines the significance of looking at the history of the processes of commercial and political penetration from imperial powers, patterns of developing economic and social structures, and the history of oppression, dislocation, and social upheaval. Hanna Batutu, *The Old Social Classes and the Revolutionary Movements of Iraq: A Study of Iraq's Old Landed and Commercial Classes and of Its Communists, Ba'thists and Free Officers* (Princeton: Princeton University Press, 1978).

reflect how we value particular forms of work and also how the attribution of value is institutionalised through wages.[66] A view of wages uncovers certain patterns of work and class formation in Oman and how these processes occur in global labour markets. This lens also reveals the dialectic of neoliberal reform or the 'invisible hand' of market regulation in conflict with the 'visible' hand of state regulation in terms of labour protection and migration control. This tension sits at the heart of labour market governance in Oman and is a regulatory force running alongside and in between the various actors and institutions in multiple levels and spaces of governance.

The Omani labour market, as illustrated above, is organised and segmented by a complex interaction of economic and social forces that structure and regulate the labour market. These forces are connected to Oman's position in global value chains, its natural resources, and its place in labour flows. Oman's labour market is governed not only by a contestation between the state and market within its spatial boundaries but also by the home countries and regions of labour immigrants; by private actors like multinational companies (MNCs) that demand particular incentives to enter and remain in the economy; by international organisations through protocols, commitments, and reform recommendations; and even by pressure from below – from citizen labour and immigrant labour and the unions and civil society organisations that advocate on their behalf.[67] Wages in Oman, and a view of the labour market in general, reveals a complex and dialectical interplay between labour market structures, regulatory institutions, and global processes. Labour markets 'must be understood as an institutionalised and politicised arena which is systematically structured by social relations of

---

[66] V. Spike Peterson, *A Critical Rewriting of Global Political Economy: Integrating Reproductive, Productive and Virtual Economies* (London; New York: Routledge, 2003); Isabella Bakker, 'Social Reproduction and the Constitution of a Gendered Political Economy', *New Political Economy* 12, no. 4 (1 December 2007): 541–56, https://doi.org/10.1080/13563460701661561; Catherine Hoskyns and Shirin M. Rai, 'Recasting the Global Political Economy: Counting Women's Unpaid Work', *New Political Economy* 12, no. 3 (1 September 2007): 297–317, https://doi.org/10.1080/13563460701485268.

[67] Crystal A. Ennis and Nicolas Blarel, eds., *The South Asia to Gulf Migration Governance Complex* (Bristol: Bristol University Press, 2022).

production and reproduction and by immanent institutional forces'.[68] Oman is no exception.

This pattern is especially evident through the persistent administrative and policy differences between citizens and non-citizens.[69] One such foundational difference is that the minimum wage in Oman applies only to citizens. What such distinctions mean is that Omani and expatriate labour are in practice not easily substitutable. Labour market problems cannot be effortlessly solved by pushing Omanis into the private sector, especially in low and semi-skilled occupations where reservation wages of other nationalities are significantly lower than those for Omanis.[70]

Citizens and non-citizens are therefore essentially not competing for the same jobs, despite high levels of unemployment. For Omanis, wage levels, the terms of employment contracts, the frameworks for social security, and pensions are all determined by the Omani state for the Omani citizen. These are means of enabling the economic security of the citizens of the country. While migrant workers are still bound by rules that govern the domestic labour market, their work, their wage level, and their terms of contract are either left to the market or determined by a variety of other actors and processes involved in legal or social regulation.[71]

An interesting example of how actors other than Omani authorities are involved in social policy formation within Oman can be found through looking at the health care sector in Oman and the differentiation between citizens and non-citizens. Omani nurses have wages, pension schemes, and work conditions determined by the Ministries of Health and Labour. On the other hand, the wages of Philippine nurses (for example) are determined by the country of origin or sending state – the Philippines. Authorities and regulators within the Philippines, and the labour attaché in Oman, ensure contracts conform to a minimum salary level for Philippine migrant health care workers. They also specify benefits and living conditions required for their

---

[68] Jamie Peck, *Work-Place: The Social Regulation of Labor Markets* (New York: The Guilford Press, 1996), 261–62.

[69] Herb, *The Wages of Oil*, 35; Hertog, 'State and Private Sector in the GCC after the Arab Uprisings', 179–80.

[70] The term 'reservation wage' refers to the minimum wage that the worker requires in order to participate in the labour market.

[71] Labour law applies to everyone, regardless of nationality.

citizens working in the field.[72] The regulatory strength wielded by the sending country varies by country, and when its position is weak, wages and benefits are determined by market forces. This means different nationalities working in the same field and doing the same job are paid discriminatory wages, and this difference is determined by multiple actors and processes. The health sector highlights how social policy can be deterritorialised in globalised labour markets. It also indicates how incentives for employers will be shaped by the perceived ease of recruitment and regulation and the costs of recruitment and employment.

Wage levels and incentive mixes shape preferences of both employers and jobseekers and work against substitutability. Profitability in Oman's private sector is made possible not only by government contracts funded by oil money but also by the availability of cheap labour. As the extraordinarily high percentage of expatriates in the labour market indicates, there is demand for labour in the economy. Yet even when local labour is qualified for the position, the dual-wage structure has a two-pronged hindering effect. Citizens are more expensive to employ and difficult to fire. At the same time, private sector jobs are perceived as low paying, less secure, and offering fewer benefits than the public or oil sectors. Profit margins would shrink if there were a minimum wage for all that matched both a living and reservation wage.

Social status and salary levels intersect to inform class formation and play a role in social regulation and in shaping livelihoods. It is not such a simple delineation between poor working-class foreigner and wealthy Omani citizen. A breakdown of Omani salary levels reveals that Omanis find employment at a wide range of skill and remuneration levels (Figure 2.5). In fact, over half of Omani citizens working in the private sector earn less than 500 Omani rials (OMR), or $1,300 USD, a month, with 30 per cent earning around the minimum wage. The minimum wage for citizens is 225 OMR with an allowance of 100 OMRs, reaching a total of 325 OMR or $845.25 USD per month. Such salary levels would be insufficient for a single-income family unit. As more Omanis become urbanised and want independent households,

---

[72] Crystal A. Ennis and Margaret Walton-Roberts, 'Labour Market Regulation as Global Social Policy: The Case of Nursing Labour Markets in Oman', *Global Social Policy* 18, no. 2 (2018): 169–88, https://doi.org/10.1177/1468018117737990.

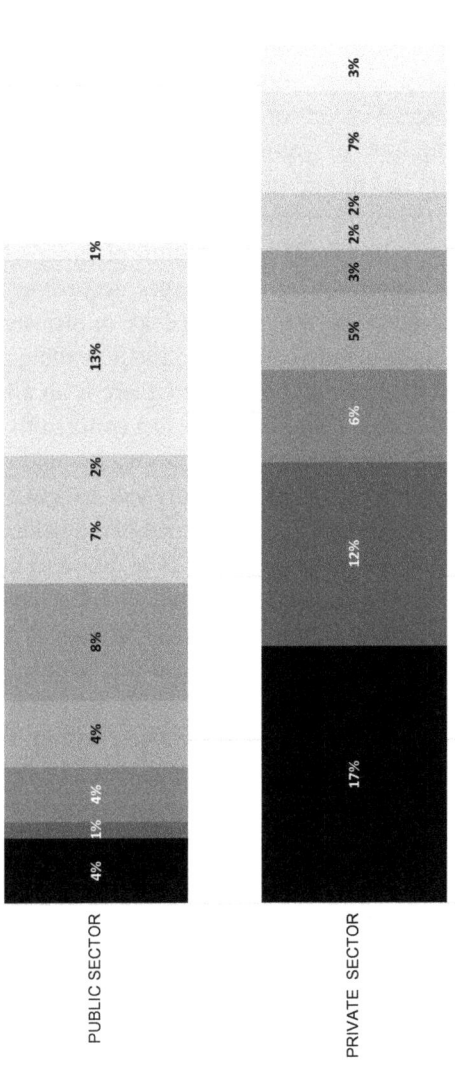

Figure 2.5 Monthly salary levels of employed Omani citizens (in USD).
Source: Calculated from NCSI, Monthly Statistical Bulletin (January 2020). 1 OMR = \$2.60 USD.

rather than traditional households shared with parents and siblings, the unattractiveness of working-class jobs or other minimum wage employment becomes apparent.

Increases in educational attainment also make minimum wage work less attractive. More and more young Omanis are achieving higher education yet finding that this does not pay off in the labour market. The unemployment rate for university diploma and degree holders is more than double that of high school graduates and dropouts.[73] Only with graduate degrees do employment prospects and salary levels look promising.

Within the working classes, non-citizens earn far less than the Omani minimum wage. Market forces primarily determine this, along with some bars imposed by labour-sending states. As mentioned above, the Philippines has minimum wages based on skill level institutionalised through their recruitment and employment processes. Similarly, the Overseas Indian Affairs division of India's Ministry of External Affairs has minimum referral wages according to occupational category, but these are not enforced as rigorously as by the Philippines. In fact, these mostly conform to the prevailing market rate especially in lower skilled occupations where there is an abundance of available labour. Studies indicate that there is a concern that a market rate below the referral wage for low-skilled sectors would result in the substitution of employment contracts on arrival, irregular migration where the state cannot intervene, or in the substitution of less expensive workers from other source countries.[74] The desire to not price the Indian working classes out of the Gulf labour market has resulted in referral wages that serve as a domestic political message demonstrating interest in protecting Indian nationals overseas but is meaningless in its effectiveness in structuring wages.

The income of the foreign working classes within Oman thus remains primarily determined by the global labour market. Constraints on this pattern emerge from protection pressures – pushing to reserve jobs for citizens or advocating for better wages and working

---

[73] NCSI, 'Monthly Statistical Bulletin', (2020), 25.

[74] S. K. Sasikumar and Seeta Sharma, 'Minimum Referral Wages for International Migrant Workers from India: An Assessment', ILO Decent Work Team for South Asia and Country Office for India (New Delhi: International Labour Organization, 2016), www.ilo.org/wcmsp5/groups/public/—asia/—ro-bangkok/—sro-new_delhi/documents/publication/wcms_538168.pdf.

conditions for non-nationals. A common supply-side intervention comes from the Omani state, which makes foreign labour more or less expensive for employers through the costs it imposes on visas and labour permits. This tension between the market and state is a strong current that I view as moulding the oscillating policy frameworks and responses in Oman.

The structuring of wage, class, and work highlights the role that migration plays in class formation in Oman. That there are more Bangladeshi and Indian citizens working in the economy than Omanis is already a significant feature (Figure 2.6). The type of work they do matters as well. Class formation and social regulation are informed by attributions of value derived from wage levels and perceptions of worth. The type of education required for a job naturally influences perceptions of value. Not only do skill, wage, and education levels matter but so do gender, race, and ethnicity, alongside developed social cues and sentiments toward the nature of work. An observable outcome of the sectoral and occupational divides is the tendency for certain occupations to become associated with particular ethnicities and genders. The pattern of value ascription is well known in scholarship on feminist political economy and on gender and migration.[75] Recruitment and regulatory actors within the migration process play a role in fostering these associations by framing and producing ideal migrant subjects, who are desired for certain occupations. For example, the Philippines has nurtured a stereotype of clean, English-speaking, well-educated, amiable employees well-suited to childcare or nursing.[76] These distinctions therefore both contribute to class

---

[75] E.g., Mary Borrowman and Stephan Klasen, 'Drivers of Gendered Sectoral and Occupational Segregation in Developing Countries', *Feminist Economics* 26, no. 2 (2 April 2020): 62–94, https://doi.org/10.1080/13545701.2019.1649708; N. Yeates, ed., *Globalizing Care Economies and Migrant Workers: Explorations in Global Care Chains* (London: Palgrave Macmillan, 2008); Shirin M. Rai, *Gender and the Political Economy of Development: From Nationalism to Globalization* (Cambridge: Polity Press, 2002); Erin Trouth Hofmann and Cynthia J. Buckley, 'Global Changes and Gendered Responses: The Feminization of Migration from Georgia', *International Migration Review* 47, no. 3 (2013): 508–38, https://doi.org/10.1111/imre.12035.

[76] Given the gendered nature of these occupations, it may come as little surprise that approximately 75 per cent of Philippine migrants are women. Likewise 73.6 per cent of Sri Lankans and 96.6 per cent of Ugandans working in Oman's private and household sector are women. Both nationalities tend to work in domestic services as cleaners and caregivers. Ennis and Walton-Roberts, 'Labour

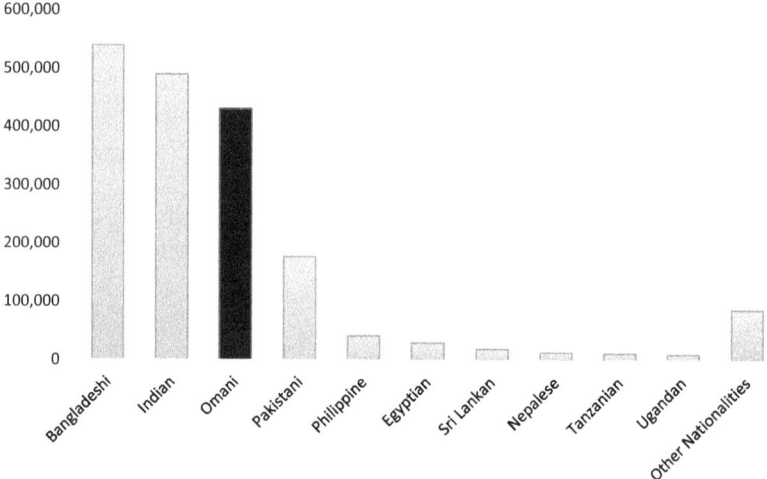

Figure 2.6 Labour force, by nationality.
Source: Calculated from NCSI, Statistical Year Book 2021 (August 2021).

formation and institutionalise particular segmentations and hiring preferences and practices.

The intersection of wages and migration in Oman informs class formation and structures social relations in other interesting ways too. One is through being colleagues in the workplace that are differentially paid.[77] Interviews and conversations with expatriates reveal a widespread belief that Omanis, by virtue of their citizenship alone, are always better paid than their Asian (that is, non-white/Western) colleagues.[78] On the other hand, my interviews with Omani employees suggest that many believe that wages are determined in accordance with experience and seniority. In some cases, especially among the unemployed, the perception that foreigners not only sit in jobs that could be filled by Omanis but also receive more pay for them is prevalent. Widely shared images on social media in 2011, resurfacing again in more recent campaigns for jobs, included photos of alleged

Market Regulation as Global Social Policy', 179. See Figure 2.5 for the nationality breakdown of the labour force; NCSI, 'Statistical Year Book 2021', 107.

[77] Other aspects of social relations in the workplace are treated in Chapter 5, on the labour market and belonging. Here, I restrict the discussion to the intersection of wages, and perceived wages.

[78] This was also clear in the health care sector in the results of a survey I conducted with M. Walton-Roberts. See Ennis and Walton-Roberts, 'Labour Market Regulation as Global Social Policy'.

employment contracts of South Asian employees with salaries higher than many of the unemployed could imagine.

A second way that social relations and class formation are shaped by the intersection of wages and migration is through the very act of giving a wage; this is, being a *kafīl* – a sponsor and the one responsible for giving the wage. The employer doubling as visa sponsor ties the right of the employee to work and stay in the country to the employer. This is a key feature of the guest worker programme known as *kafāla* in the region.[79] It encourages deferential labour relations and exposes migrants to the risk of exploitation. While skilled workers and knowledge workers often interact as colleagues across nationality lines, the interaction of low skilled migrant workers with Omani citizens are mostly limited to their sponsor and employer. In the words of a migrant worker advocate in Muscat, blue collar workers 'have some fear' generated by their precarity and non-integration in society. They are worried about losing their jobs and being deported.

They do not really interact with anyone in society. They only have this kafīl relationship and that is it! Many will only work for a short time. Some do stay for a long time. I've met people who have been workers for 15, 20, and 25 or more years. But they always think about returning.[80]

This form of labour relations and possibility for social relations is distinct. This pattern is no more apparent than in the household.

---

[79] *Kafāla* is the Arabic term for the sponsorship system common in many West Asian states. It means sponsorship, guarantee, or protective care. It derives from the Arabic root k-f-l, which alongside sponsor, can mean to guarantee, to be liable for, to vouch for, or to care for. *Kafīl* is the Arabic singular noun for sponsor, which in an employment relationship is the employer. To read more about the definition, history, and practice of *kafāla*, read Mohammed Dito, 'Kafala: Foundations of Migrant Exclusion in GCC Labour Markets', in *Transit States: Labour, Migration & Citizenship in the Gulf*, ed. Abdulhadi Khalaf, Omar AlShehabi, and Adam Hanieh (London: Pluto Press, 2015), 79–100, www.press.uchicago.edu/ucp/books/book/distributed/T/bo21636617.html; Omar AlShehabi, 'Policing Labour in Empire: The Modern Origins of the Kafala Sponsorship System in the Gulf Arab States', *British Journal of Middle Eastern Studies* 48, no. 2 (2021): 291–310, https://doi.org/10.1080/13530194.2019.1580183; Crystal A. Ennis, 'Networking through Kafala: Skilled Workers and Transnational Networks in the Governance of Health Care Migration in the Gulf', in *Global Migration, Gender and Professional Credentials*, ed. Margaret Walton-Roberts (Toronto: University of Toronto Press, 2022), 145–66; Noora Lori, *Offshore Citizens: Permanent Temporary Status in the Gulf* (Cambridge: Cambridge University Press, 2019), 133–44.

[80] Interview, Muscat, 27 March 2018.

Indeed, a significant but underexamined dimension of labour relations occurs in the space of domestic work. Approximately 17.1 per cent of formal labour immigrants in the country work in people's homes, as maids, cooks, nannies, and drivers.[81] Thus, a key space of class formation in Oman occurs in the private realm that is simultaneously workplace and that shapes the dynamics of employer-employee and sponsor-sponsee.[82] This mode of class formation, the very exercise of being a *kafīl*, shapes the view of and interaction with expatriates and limits the depth of relations and opportunities for community or solidarity building: the local boss – the foreign other. For the purpose of this discussion, what is most important is the way that this dependency, the relationship between sponsor and employee, wage giver and wage earner, shapes relations and produces class.

Oman's labour market is not a space of absent labour regulation. Rather, it is one in which there are complex layers of regulation and governance occurring at multiple scales. Differences between sectors, and between citizenship status, creates a complex regulatory web. Wages in the Omani economy provide a helpful space of analysis to illustrate this unevenness and examine both patterns of class formation and of labour market governance. At one level, wages serve as empirical indicators of how global and de-territorial forces interact with the national and, at another level, illuminate how differentiation and value perceptions intervene in processes of work and of class formation. Pay, like other regulatory differentiations, also works to segment solidarities. The spaces of legal and social regulation can be productively understood with a view of how (neo)liberalising forces and protection/constraining forces interact, as I highlight below.

2.4 Omani Jobs for Omani Workers

I hope that the state provides employment opportunities for citizens, that there is justice in their employment, and jobs given to everyone entitled to them.[83]

---

[81] NCSI, 'Monthly Statistical Bulletin', 21.

[82] Faisal Hamadah, 'Kafala and Social Reproduction: Migration Governance Regimes and Labour Relations in the Gulf', in *The South Asia to Gulf Migration Governance Complex*, ed. Crystal A. Ennis and Nicolas Blarel (Bristol: Bristol University Press, 2022), 173–89, https://bristoluniversitypressdigital.com/view/book/9781529221510/ch008.xml.

[83] Young Omani female jobseeker, Al-Buraimi, 7 July 2018.

Young Omanis today not only dream of fulfilling jobs but also feel they have a right to gainful employment in their country. They largely look to the government to meet these expectations, viewing the state as both job provider and labour market regulator. These feelings of national rights and state responsibility have emerged not only because of the presence of natural resources but also because of the way planning and discourse around the labour market have unfolded.

Two policy groups are the most visible in the regulatory sphere of the Omani labour market – that is *ta'mīn* and *kafāla*.[84] Together they garner the most attention in media and business and public circles. They shape recruitment and employment practices, hiring and firing, and immigration regimes. These bodies of policy are at the centre of tensions between liberalising and protecting the labour market and its participants. They encapsulate the classic political economy tensions of states and markets and the question *cui bono* – who benefits – from policy decisions.[85] Indeed, the history of policy-making on the Omani labour market illustrates the dialectic of neoliberal reform in conflict with labour protection.

Oman's post-1970s development planning and governance of the economy reflected the usual language of developmentalism with the goals of catching up, modernising, and meeting economic and social development needs. Qais Abdulmunim Al-Zawawi (who was the deputy prime minister and minister for financial and economic affairs) noted in his capacity as deputy chairman of the Development Council that the 'main objective' for the first five-year plan (FYP) (1976–1980) was 'to ensure the continued healthy growth and modernisation of the economy, to diversify the source of national income and to raise the standard of living of different population groups living in the various regions of the country'.[86] To do this, the targets of the first FYP included not just capital investment and diversified income generation but the encouragement of trade and 'a free economy in which the

---

[84] *Kafāla* was defined in the section above, and *ta'mīn*, or Omanisation, was defined and introduced in Chapter 1.

[85] *Cui bono* – who benefits – is the key question that drove and grounded Susan Strange's work on IPE, explaining and tracing power and outcomes in the international political economy. Susan Strange, *States and Markets*, 2nd ed. (London: A&C Black, 1994); Susan Strange, *The Retreat of the State: The Diffusion of Power in the World Economy* (Cambridge: Cambridge University Press, 1996).

[86] 'The FYP 1976–1980', ii.

private sector plays a leading role on the basis of free competition in a market clear of monopolistic practices'.[87]

While planning was regular, and occurred in five-year intervals, large parts of each plan were ideologically positioned on the principles of the free market following the Development Policy, discussed earlier.[88] The economic recession of the 1980s and oil price decline informed the third and fourth FYPs, and measures to strengthen the private sector were given more precedence. At the same time, concern was regularly expressed about the 'imbalance' between expatriates and citizens, and the importance 'to safeguard [citizen] communities from the danger of mass immigration'.[89] Two narrative threads thus weaved throughout the development plans – an economic growth narrative alongside an economic nationalist one.

Early in modern Omani development planning, particular processes shaped and governed the economy and labour. First, the realisation of oil wealth coincided with the onset of the neoliberal shift in Western economies. Not just the empirical transformation under intensifying globalisation but also the ideological transformation under neoliberal economic advice intersected with material realities of oil wealth and labour need. Such transitions operated within a global oil market and coalesced around particular patterns of trade and economic organisation. Economic (neo)liberalism was embedded in the policy advice Oman received from the British, the Americans, and the Bretton Woods institutions.[90]

Second, the young 'Qaboos state'[91] clearly positioned itself against communism as not only a major ideological challenger but also a very real security threat from the ongoing anti-imperialist resistance of groups like the Popular Front for the Liberation of Oman and the

[87] 'The FYP 1976–1980', 13–14.
[88] Development Council, 'Resolution on Aims and Objectives of Economic Development Policy in the Sultanate (Issued at Its Meeting of Sunday, 9 February 1975)', in 'The FYP 1976–1980', 106.
[89] 'The Third Five-Year Development Plan 1986–1990' (Muscat: Sultanate of Oman Development Council, 1987), 47; The phrase mirrors the one in the first development policy mentioned earlier in the chapter. The language of 'danger' continues to appear and is also present in the first and fifth FYP. 'The FYP 1976–1980', 13; 'The Fifth Five-Year Development Plan 1996–2000' (Muscat: Ministry of Development, 1997), 8.
[90] Oman became a member of the IMF and the World Bank on 23 December 1971.
[91] Valeri, *Oman*.

Arabian Gulf (PFLOAG).[92] Here the ideology of the free market confronted a discourse of socialist liberation. This socialist discourse specified liberation not only from colonialism and imperialism but also from tribal conflict, illiteracy, and economic 'backwardness' through education, economic development, and women's liberation.[93] Revolutionary publications emphasised the protection of national markets from the international capitalist market, the protection of citizens from exploitation, and the building up of an independent economy and educational sector toward these ends.[94] For the Qaboos regime, the discourse of liberation and the protection of the citizen could not be left associated with socialism. Different visions of freedom and development were thus articulated to the public from competing actors, coached in visions of capitalist or socialist potentialities.

Religion too was used by the State to both rally support against the 'evils of communism'[95] and to underpin the State's developmental narrative. The following excerpts from royal speeches on national day are indicative:

While we are waging a battle for building our country in various fields of development we are also waging a sacred and armed battle against the enemy of Islam and the country, supported by Marxist Aden.[96]

The struggle we are waging against atheism is a sacred duty which our religion imposes upon us.[97]

---

[92] Takriti, *Monsoon Revolution.*

[93] 'Documents of the National Struggle in Oman and the Arabian Gulf [trans. and ed. Gulf Committee]'; Arabic Original, Dar at-Talia, Beirut, 9th June Studies (London: Gulf Committee, 1974), International Institute of Social History (Az15 – Bro E 760 – Bro E 4898). See for example, pp. 11–12, 18, 29, and 58.

[94] See for example, 'National Democratic Working Plan: Peoples Front for Liberation of Oman and Arabian Gulf', Constituent Conference at Ahleesh (Dhofar), December 1972, Collection Documentation and Leaflets Great Britain, ARCH01732/468, International Institute of Social History; Faris Glubb, 'The Role of the Workers in the Struggle of British-Occupied Arabia', translation of a lecture delivered to the Arab Students Union by Faris Glubb, Secretary of the Committee for the Rights of Oman on the occasion of Occupied South Yemen Day (London: Omani News, 1966), Collection Documentation and Leaflets Great Britain, ARCH01732, International Institute of Social History.

[95] 'Speech of His Majesty at the Police Stadium' (11 December 1975), Al-Said, 'The Royal Speeches of His Majesty Sultan Qaboos Bin Said', 63.

[96] National day speech (18 November 1972), Al-Said, 22.

[97] National day speech (18 November 1973), Al-Said, 26.

Here we challenge and face communist infiltration – a more subversive and dangerous international movement which works to undermine our religion and our national prestige.[98]

The Communists spread hardship among their citizens. They open prisons and detention camps while we build schools and hospitals. They lay obstacles, sow thorns and choke the freedom of the people, while we remove obstacles and make the hardships of life easy, and we encourage public freedom provided that they do not impair the security of the State because the security of the State means, at the same time, the security of the citizen.[99]

The Omani state under Qaboos was promoted as a new era and the period referred to as *al-nahḍa* (the renaissance). *Al-nahḍa* was staged as a sharp break from the rule of Qaboos' father. It had to be seen to prioritise the Omani national. The nation building of *al-nahḍa* entailed modernity, unity, and a collective Omani identity to push back against liberation movements, regional splits, and tribalism.[100] This nation building was fuelled by oil abundance and forged under a discourse of economic growth. Material and ideological realities were instrumental and had governing power.

One way of demonstrating a commitment to the Omani national was through the labour market. 'Where is the benefit to the citizens of the country?' became a pressing question with the transformation occurring in the economy. Who was benefitting from job and financial growth? Such questions became a rallying point of the socialist liberation movements in Oman.[101] Central to removing imperialist control over the politics and governance of the country was strengthening the

---

[98] National day speech (18 November 1974), Al-Said, 32–33.

[99] National day speech (18 November 1975), Al-Said, 44.

[100] Valeri, *Oman: Politics and Society in the Qaboos State*; Al-Hashimi, "Umān: 'an Masālat al-ṭabaqa, wa fī musā'lat al-wusṭā.

[101] For example, a solidarity bulletin notes, 'Even new industries generally make no use of local potential or raw materials. Most factories are effectively controlled by Western corporations. The foreign technicians and supervisors receive inflated tax-free salaries and live in luxury. A desalinization plant recently built by a European company does not function. The builders sabotaged the plant, leaving it useless, and there are no Omanis who can run or repair it. This is just one example of the incredible waste and chaos which occurs under the guise of "industrial development." No attempt has been made to interconnect industries so that an integrated Omani economic base could be built to take the country past the oil boom.' 'Omani Regime: Dependency and Reform', *Gulf Solidarity: Bulletin on Oman and the Gulf*, 1977, International Institute of Social History (IISG ZK 35376).

control of 'the people' over their economy. The 'people's' access to the labour market was already perceived as being restricted by businesses prioritising foreign labour. The PFLOAG included labour as one of seventeen 'objectives of the revolution':

The passing of laws to guarantee the rights of workers and employees and to raise their standard of living. To accomplish this it is necessary to:

1. Abolish the present labour law imposed by the colonialist firms and adopt a progressive law guaranteeing the rights of workers and employees, which their representatives will participate in drafting.
2. Allow workers and employees to establish trade unions, to defend their rights and grant them the right to strike.
3. Ensure the participation of workers in running companies and factories through their representatives.
4. Establish vocational training institutes, and compel foreign firms and contractors to employ and then train Omanis for the assumption of higher responsibilities.
5. Ensure social and medical insurance for workers and employees and their families without discrimination on any tribal, racial or other basis.
6. Combat unemployment, guarantee a decent standard of living to all citizens, and create suitable conditions for Omani emigrés to return home; to provide the people with proper employment so that they will not emigrate and will contribute to the development of the homeland.[102]

In the lead up to 1970, the British mused that the slow pace of training and hiring Omanis provided fodder for labour agitation and political opposition movements.[103] At the same time, some officials expressed concern that rectifying this by offering worker's education, or forming Worker's consultation committees as was occurring in the young oil

---

[102] The People's Front for the Liberation of Oman and the Arab Gulf, 'National Programme of the People's Front for the Liberation of Oman', in Documents of the National Struggle in Oman and the Arabian Gulf [trans. and ed. Gulf Committee]', Arabic Original, Dar at-Talia, Beirut, 9th June Studies (London: Gulf Committee, 5 August 1974), 101–2, International Institute of Social History (Az15 – Bro E 760 – Bro E 4898).

[103] Stewart Crawford, 'Development in the Sultanate of Muscat and Oman', Confidential document for the Foreign Office and Whitehall Distribution, , 'Muscat Economic Affairs', Foreign and Commonwealth Office (London: The National Archives, 1967–1968), FCO 8/589, Arabian Gulf Digital Archives, www.agda.ae/en/catalogue/tna/fco/8/589.

industry elsewhere in the Gulf, would open a window for 'revolution-ary pan-Arab movements of subversive groups in the Gulf' to influence workers and link labour and political struggles.[104] Labour and labour rights were indeed explicitly tied to revolutionary objectives and were a recurring theme in resistance.

The idea of securing jobs for citizens was thus already a political question locally and regionally in the early 1970s.[105] This intensified within the context of navigating new oil wealth and the concomitant economic questions and choices it carried. The idea of Omani jobs for Omani workers grew with the expansion of the oil industry and the increase of foreign nationals recruited specifically to staff positions in the various economic activities popping up around the country. This was reflected in policy discussions quite early.[106] By 1973, a compre-hensive labour law was issued, which, at over twenty pages, stipulated rules around employment, work contracts, wages, leave and working hours, labour disputes, and penalties, among others. Articles 19–21 delineated the rules of regulating foreign employment, institutionalis-ing the idea that Omanis should be given priority for jobs and only when sufficiently qualified and trained Omani workers were not avail-able could an employer request a visa.[107] The foreign worker could only enter the country through the residency system with an approved visa from the ministry, and it was up to the minister to determine the ratio of foreigners to Omanis that would be permitted to an employer.

Some of the earliest direct references to the term Omanisation popped up at the beginning of the 1970s with regard to the Armed Forces. The records indicate pressure to Omanise security but also anxiety around the threat to the established power this could afford. The British held the reigns, and all senior posts, of all branches of the security services. Steps to Omanise seemed to be undertaken

---

[104] See, for example, the views of the First Secretary of Labour, R. L. Morris, 'Oil Industry: Comment on Personnel Policies', in 'FCO 8/589'.

[105] In Chapter 3, we will see how agitation around national rights to work and the economy unfolded.

[106] The British, too, tracked the number of expatriates and local labour hired by major companies like PDO and its contractors. 'FCO 8/2224: Economic Situation in Oman', Foreign and Commonwealth Office (London: The National Archives, 1974), NBL 5/2, Kew.

[107] Royal Decree 34/1973, 'Promulgating the Labour Law (Issued 15 November 1973, Published 1 Dec 1973)', Official Gazette 44, [author translations from Arabic], 1973.

reluctantly, and opposition papers described the British as 'keen on undermining the attempt at Arabising the army'.[108] British officials expressed quite some concern about the 'Omanisation of the Armed Forces', suggesting such moves would be risky[109] and 'could lead to political ambitions'.[110] They were no doubt pleased that in the early days of his reign the Sultan noted his intention to maintain British involvement in the military rather than replacing them with Arab officers. Of course, the British were central in the coup that brought him to power and remained indispensable in the ongoing efforts to suppress the revolution in Dhofar. At the same time, Qaboos expressed his wish 'to concentrate on a policy of direct Omanisation' and encouraged young people from the tribes to join the army.[111] And indeed the army's educational, literacy, and training programmes across Oman were successful parts of not just Omanisation but also the rural educational drive.[112] Omanisation of the police and armed forces thus occurred gradually, but it is noteworthy that the senior ranks of the Internal Security Services remained staffed by contracted or seconded British officers until 1992.[113]

Like the development policy, the first three iterations of the FYPs also noted the importance of training local labour and spoke about the need to 'rationalize reliance on expatriates'.[114] Of course, these

---

[108] Abdul-Hadi Bakker (17 February 1972), 'A New Bangladesh in Oman', Al-Sayyad in 'Political Situation in Oman', Foreign and Commonwealth Office (London: The National Archives, 1972), FCO 8/1844, Arabian Gulf Digital Archives, www.agda.ae/en/catalogue/tna/fco/8/1844.

[109] P. R. H. Wright (14 November 1974), 'The Anatomy of Oman', 'Political Situation in Oman', Foreign and Commonwealth Office (London: The National Archives, 1974), FCO 8/2215, Arabian Gulf Digital Archives, www.agda.ae/en/catalogue/tna/fco/8/2215.

[110] T. P. Hollaway (12 November 1974), 'The Anatomy of Oman', 'FCO 8/2215'.

[111] D. F. Hawley (15 October 1972), 'Calls on the Sultan on 8 and 11 October 1972', 'Political Situation in Oman', Foreign and Commonwealth Office (London: The National Archives, 1972), FCO 8/1845, Arabian Gulf Digital Archives, www.agda.ae/en/catalogue/tna/fco/8/1845; Bakker, in 'FCO 8/1844'.

[112] Dale F. Eickelman, 'Oman's Next Generation: Challenges and Prospects', in *Crosscurrents in the Gulf: Arab, Regional and Global Interests*, ed. H. Richard Sindelar III and J. E. Peterson (London; New York: Routledge, 1988), 168–69.

[113] Dale F. Eickelman and M. G. Dennison, 'Arabizing the Omani Intelligence Services: Clash of Cultures?', *International Journal of Intelligence and CounterIntelligence* 7, no. 1 (1 March 1994): 1, https://doi.org/10.1080/08850609408435235.

[114] 'The Third FYP 1986–1990', 98.

were oil boom years, and the primary focus was on infrastructural and developmental investment and capital formation. Ambitions around labour were mostly concentrated on developing the educational sector, with an emphasis on vocational training for workers.[115] In the mid-1970s, the Ministry of Social Affairs and Labour worked with the British Council and the Technical Education and Training Organisation for Overseas Countries (TETOC) to recruit an adviser for technical and vocational training and a 'manpower planning expert' to develop a national labour classification system and advise on issues of training.[116] Increasingly, the main economic periodicals were discussing the labour issue and emphasising the value of various vocational and technical training and educational initiatives.[117] Attention was given across sectors and ranks of authority. Noting the significance of having a 'pool of indigenous skilled labour', Ali Hassan Ali, the director general of vocational training, wrote in 1978 that 'Oman's future prosperity will depend largely upon the development of a skilled labour force whose productivity is the key to economic growth and whose ability to find rewarding employment is a cornerstone of social progress'.[118] By 1988, Omanisation was formally adopted in policy documents; and throughout 1989 and 1990, the state consultative council was involved in efforts at formulating the concept and policy.[119]

The consolidation of Omanisation in policy terms coincided with a focal shift to labour market reform and private-sector development during the contraction of the oil market in the mid-1980s. The fourth

[115] 'The Second Five-Year Development Plan 1981–1985' (Muscat: Sultanate of Oman Development Council, 1981), 105–6. Improvements in education and training were rapid and dramatic, and by the 1980s, the country was actively training students in nursing, banking, teaching, and public administration. 'The Third FYP 1986–1990', 95–96.

[116] 'BW 91/757: TETOC: Oman – General Correspondence', British Council Archives (London: The National Archives, Kew, 1974–1978), A/OMA/2, Kew.

[117] Riazuddin Alvi, 'The Need for an Effective Training Programme in the Sultanate of Oman', *Al-Markazi*, July 1976, Central Bank of Oman Archive; S. M. I. Mahmood, 'Training and Its Benefits to the Employees', *Al-Markazi*, September 1976, Central Bank of Oman Archive; 'Development of Skilled Labour in Oman', *Al-Markazi*, November 1978, Central Bank of Oman Archive; 'Industry in the Economy of Oman', *Al-Markazi*, November 1979, 11, Central Bank of Oman Archive.

[118] Ali Hassan Ali, 'Manpower Development in Oman', *Al-Markazi*, January 1978, 3, Central Bank of Oman Archive.

[119] Al-Said, 'The Royal Speeches of His Majesty Sultan Qaboos Bin Said', 236.

FYP reflected the new economic landscape and gave incredible prominence to labour market issues, as well as a louder push toward privatisation. By this stage, the segmentation of the labour force had grown deeper as its size multiplied. Between 1975 and 1990, the total labour force grew by 153 per cent, while Omanis in it by 53 per cent.[120] As the economy contracted, and the state capacity for providing jobs and benefits did as well, the pressures of job creation began taking greater prominence. The plan notes,

With an increase in the number of graduates and the inability of the government sector to absorb new workers, it has become necessary to find mechanisms to deal with the deficiencies of the labour market from the point of view of its composition (national/expatriate) and the occupational and sectoral distribution of the labour force, so as to increase the participation of the national labour force within an integral manpower planning framework that would reconcile the graduates of the various educational and training institutions with the needs of the labour market.[121]

This comment could easily be taken and placed in any policy document today attempting to deal with the sharp rise of jobseekers. This suggests the stickiness of labour market issues, indicating that the processes that fostered the regional labour market organisation are well embedded and difficult to shift. Their lineages, as we will see in Chapter 3, started even before the oil era.

This FYP embedded Omanisation, and its policy mechanisms, into development planning and policy. It allocated OMR 40 million ($104 million USD) to the Omanisation programme.[122] An entire chapter was dedicated to human resources, which described both the 'skewed structure' and the planned policies and measures to tackle it.[123] These included the supply and demand side measures noted earlier and also a variety of incentives to encourage the private sector to hire, train, and retain Omanis. Likewise, encouraging women to join the labour market was noted as a measure toward the goal of Omanisation.[124] Planning also included institutional reforms to support more robust policy and data analysis, including planning units, job classifications,

---

[120] 'The Fourth Five-Year Development Plan 1991–1995' (Muscat: Development Council General Secretariat, November 1991), 29.
[121] 'The Fourth FYP 1991–1995', 29–30.
[122] 'The Fourth FYP 1991–1995', 185.
[123] 'The Fourth FYP 1991–1995', 133.   [124] See Chapter 6.

and a social security system for the private sector. Implementation of these moved rapidly; a social security law was already issued by late 1991 to offer retirement security to permanent private-sector employees.[125]

Efforts to cap the increase of expatriates being added to the labour market and encourage more Omanis into the private sector demonstrated how difficult it was, even in times of austerity when the urgency was stronger, to push against the high demand for inexpensive foreign labour. While the size of the expatriate labour force increased by 12.8 per cent during this period despite the planned rate of 3.5 per cent, the Omani labour force did not meet its targeted growth rate.[126] Noteworthy at this time is that the rate of Omanisation of skilled and specialised jobs was lower than for semi-skilled and unskilled ones. For instance, at the time, the agriculture and fisheries sector was 81.2 per cent Omanised, even higher than government services, which was the next highest at 58.6 per cent.[127] By contrast, today agriculture and fisheries has approximately a 1.3 per cent Omanisation rate and the government sector 84.5 per cent.[128] The picture today is considerably different as skills and education levels have increased dramatically in the intervening decades. This too affects the type of work Omanis want to do.

What is especially interesting about this plan for our purposes is a very visible presentation that the neoliberalising and nationalising tensions underpinning the labour market also impact economic planning. While much of the plan concerned itself with private sector growth, identifying ways of reducing the role of government, and increasing its efficiency, an entire section was dedicated to policy mechanisms not just to protect and train nationals but to intervene in the market in such ways that were designed to encourage and/or force it to absorb Omani workers. This tension remains present throughout Oman's development policy-making.

The Fifth FYP was issued alongside Oman's first long-term economic vision in 1995 and built upon the precedents of the Fourth

---

[125] Royal Decree 72/1991, 'Promulgating the Social Security Law (Issued 2 July 1991, Published 15 July 1991)', Official Gazette 459, [author translations from Arabic], 1991; Salma Al-Lamki, 'Barriers to Omanization in the Private Sector: The Perceptions of Omani Graduates', *The International Journal of Human Resource Management* 9, no. 2 (1998): 384.
[126] 'The Fifth FYP 1996–2000', 111.   [127] 'The Fourth FYP 1991–1995', 149.
[128] NCSI, '2019 Statistical Year Book', 108, 118.

FYP in developing the labour force indigenisation policy measures we have become familiar with. A decade of deficits and a weak oil market made diversification, privatisation, and labour market reform clear needs in the minds of policymakers. It was within this context that Oman pioneered economic visions in the Gulf region, long before these became trendy, and developed its first long-term development plan, *Vision for Oman's Economy 2020.*

The World Bank was involved in economic advisement and technical cooperation with Oman during this period. Four years after Oman graduated from World Bank lending in 1987, it signed a framework agreement for annual technical cooperation. This cooperation included social policy expenditure reviews, advisory services to the Capital Market Authority, and supporting labour market reform and Small and Medium-Sized Enterprise (SME) development.[129] On the government's invitation, the World Bank produced a report, detailing the economic situation in the country and policy recommendations.[130] This 224-page document informed the development of Vision 2020. The FYPs that fit within the vision's twenty-five-year window were designed to achieve the vision's objectives in stages. The overarching goal was to transform the economy into one that would no longer be oil-dependent by 2020. To reach these aims, focus was not only placed on economic diversification and private-sector development but also on sustainable growth and human resource development.[131] As we saw in the figures and description of the labour market sketched above, the 2020 threshold has been crossed and much remains undone.[132]

Resolving labour market problems meant intensifying the emphasis on Omanisation and the means to achieving it. Among these, Vision 2020 proposed stripping away the advantages of public sector employment, including working hours and holidays. It also prescribed increases of Omanisation rates from 68 to 95 per cent in the public sector and 15 to 75 per cent in the private sector by 2020.[133] Within

---

[129] 'Oman Country Program', World Bank, 4 December 2016, www.worldbank .org/en/country/gcc/brief/oman-country-program.

[130] World Bank, 'Sultanate of Oman: Sustainable Growth and Economic Diversification' (World Bank, 31 May 1994).

[131] 'Vision for Oman's Economy – 2020: Long-Term Development Strategy (1996–2020), 2nd Edition' (Muscat: Ministry of National Economy, 2007).

[132] Oman has now moved into a new long-term vision, Vision 2040, that I will discuss in later chapters.

[133] 'Vision 2020', 94, 208.

ten years, Oman had already made such great strides in nationalising public sector employment while also reducing the size of the public sector workforce that the World Bank took note. Its 2004 report on employment in the MENA praised Oman's efforts in reducing employment in the public sector, pronouncing it the only GCC country to do so.[134] This reduction was partly the result of a determined cutback programme that retired one-quarter of Omani civil servants between 1996 and 1998.[135] Austerity measures and labour market reforms increase in intensity during weak oil market periods.

Efforts to Omanise the private sector have been far more difficult than in the public sector; and while Omanisation rates reached 22.5 per cent by 2005, it has gradually decreased since that time.[136] While this was largely the result of the significant increase in expatriates added to the private sector during the boom years of the 2000s, this trend points to the difficulty in rectifying nationalisation with the demands of economic growth and cost efficiency in globalised labour markets. Indeed, the 2000s were a period of neoliberal deepening across the Middle East.[137] Oman saw privatisation and economic liberalisation forces amplified in the lead up to joining the World Trade Organisation in 2000 and in signing the bilateral free trade agreement with the United States in 2009. Government reform efforts are pulled in opposing directions, between the gravity of the growing ranks of the unemployed and the pressure from the private sector to increase labour market flexibility and facilitate foreign recruitment by reducing costs and regulation. Incentive structures for private companies like labour levy rebate schemes to subsidise training and salaries of new Omani employees have come and gone.[138] New policy measures are introduced and amended, quotas for national employment are

---

[134] World Bank, 'Unlocking the Employment Potential in the Middle East and North Africa', 160.

[135] Cyrus Sassanpour et al., 'Labor Market Challenges and Policies in the Gulf Cooperation Council Countries', in *Financial Systems and Labor Markets in the Gulf Cooperation Council Countries* (Washington, DC: International Monetary Fund, 1997), 39, www.imf.org/external/pubs/FT/gcc/.

[136] 'Facts & Figures 2010' (Muscat: Ministry of National Economy, June 2011), 21; 'Seventh Five-Year Development Plan (2006–2010)' (Muscat: Ministry of National Economy, 2006), 185; NCSI, '2019 Statistical Year Book'.

[137] Hanieh, *Lineages of Revolt*; Laura Guazzone and Daniela Pioppi, eds., *The Arab State and Neo-Liberal Globalization: The Restructuring of State Power in the Middle East* (Cairo: American University in Cairo Press, 2009).

[138] Al-Lamki, 'Barriers to Omanization in the Private Sector', 383–85.

added and changed, and visa restrictions are put in place and removed. The seriousness with which the government tackles labour force indigenisation rises during oil lows when the state capacity to absorb employment is stretched. The susceptibility of labour market reform to diverse stakeholder pressures changes with the economic fortunes of the state.

The story of indigenisation in the private sector is certainly not all negative. As we saw in Figures 2.2 and 2.3, certain industries have been successful in labour force nationalisation, including banking and oil and gas. It is noteworthy that some of the first occupations to be fully nationalised in the private sector were low-skilled ones, including positions such as taxi and bus drivers, security guards, receptionists, and office clerks.[139] The latter were the result of explicit targets and concomitant policy measures. Each development plan filling the stages of Vision 2020 offered Omanisation targets on the basis of job categories, and it remains the Ministry of Labour (the Ministry of Manpower until 2020) that sets interval targets and regulates the implementation.

Omanisation finds few enthusiasts in the private sector. Many employers, especially foreign ones, view Omanisation as a necessary 'tax' of operating in the country. Others lament Omanisation audits by the authorities, 'That's what happened to me, I had no choice and I had to hire an Omani.'[140] 'Omanisation is one of the top three hindrances' to private sector development and entrepreneurship, noted a business reporter.[141] Some Omani business owners however attribute their successes with Omanisation to giving Omanis 'a real chance' and to having greater cultural understanding.[142] They indicated embeddedness in the local culture, a flexible work environment, and respect for workers can be key to successfully Omanising.

Differentially applicable labour regulation reinforces the segmentation it is meant to address. As per the issue of wages discussed previously, the application of a minimum wage that applies only to Omanis or rules that make it more difficult to fire a citizen further distorts the incentive structures. Minimum wage and job security measures are

---

[139] 'At a Crossroads', *Oman Economic Review*, September 2003, 18, 28–37.
[140] Interview, Omani SME owner, Muscat, 24 October 2011.
[141] Interview, business reporter, Muscat, 16 October 2011.
[142] Interviews, business owners, Muscat, 14 November 2011, 15 November 2011, 26 January 2019.

designed in the interest of protecting the citizen in the labour market and trying to balance the benefits between the public and private sectors. Yet these are two frequently cited excuses for resistance to Omanisation by employers – the difficulty to fire even with cause.[143] Absent policy recognition of the co-constitution of the labour market by Omanis and other nationalities, and absent a move that would offer shared and equal protections for all labour, these challenges will remain.

State-owned enterprises (SOE) in Oman have one foot in the private sector and another in the public and are positioned in a fuzzy in-between in terms of economic policy and recruitment.[144] While largely governed in line with the sectors and markets in which they compete, SOEs are more subject to interventions on national recruitment. This is because SOEs are productive assets of the Omani state, and even with consecutive revisions to make them more autonomous and efficient are prone to pressure to create employment. They frequently receive orders to hire citizens, control consumer prices, and face pressure to create social development schemes like training or leadership programmes. There is concerted pressure for state companies to lead the way in national employment outside the civil service. Omani SOEs can also be the target of popular mobilisation for jobs and economic justice. Demands on social media and newspapers agitate for direct recruitment and push for the government, or call on the Sultan, to make this happen. In the popular imagination, the role of the state continues to be welfare and job provider.

Regulations designed to secure jobs for, and protect, Omani workers do not occur in a vacuum. They are relational. Efforts to reserve positions for Omanis have implications for the *kafāla* system, because the protection of one in practice often means a limitation on another. Restricting a job to an Omani citizen means excluding a non-citizen. Precarity in segmentation is relational; the task of making the private sector employ national labour depends on amplifying the

---

[143] This was brought up repeatedly in conversations and interviews.
[144] While SOEs were once viewed as a relic of excessive state intervention and bloated bureaucracies, with the rise of the developmental state successes in Asia and elsewhere, there is a sense that SOEs can be managed efficiently and help stimulate private sector development. For a more extensive treatment of divergent paths and patterns that lead to success or failure in SOEs, see Hertog, 'Defying the Resource Curse'.

precariousness of non-citizens in the labour market and the country. That is, getting the private sector to hire Omanis often happens only when they are restricted from renewing the contracts of expatriate staff or prevented from obtaining labour permits to recruit from abroad. Likewise, the private labour market's organisation as an inhospitable or undesirable space for citizens is largely determined by a recruitment and sponsorship regime that is produced within a global market for cheap, flexible labour. And thus the two most visible labour policy groups, *kafāla* and *taʾmīn*, are mutually constitutive.

Two examples further illustrate this pattern: the re-institution and subsequent rescindment of the no-objection certificate (NOC) and labour brokerage. Both are outcomes of the interaction of a sponsorship regime with efforts to protect citizens in the economy. The NOC is an especially interesting case. It had been removed during the liberalisation period that saw restrictions ease around the mobility of labour in the 2000s. Then, the devastating decline of oil prices that began in 2014 prompted a wave of new policy measures in the intervening years. One was reintroducing the NOC in 2014. This requires an expatriate to acquire a letter from their employer when they leave or complete their contract in order to move to another employer. Failure to obtain an NOC results in a two-year visa ban.[145] The government's justification for this move was partly attributed to the idea that imposing difficulties on hiring expatriates by limiting their availability within the domestic market would encourage companies to hire Omanis and partly to the idea that this would safeguard the employers' investment in terms of visa, relocation, and training costs in foreign recruitment. Some employers exploit this leverage to retain employees, often justifying it in the interest of unfair competition and business secrets. According to one active member of the Chamber of Commerce,

The NOC is good. The private sector wants it. And even we want it for Omanis too – for example – guarantee that six months after leaving our business you cannot go and work for a competitor. You need this NOC. Otherwise, they will just leave and take all the clients and business secrets and work for your competition or start their own business and bring their

---

[145] Rejimon Kuttapan, 'Thumbs up for NOC Compromise in Oman', *Times of Oman*, 30 November 2016, https://timesofoman.com/article/97693/Oman/Thumbs-up-for-NOC-compromise-by–bosses-workers-and-government-bodies-in-Oman.

clients with them. This is only natural. If I leave [my partnership], I know all the business ways and have contacts with all the clients – and they know me and how I work. And if I move somewhere else I will also need to have a good performance. So what will I do? Of course I will call all my clients and will probably bring 70 to 90 per cent of them with me.[146]

In practice, these restrictions can also compel employees to endure unpleasant working conditions. Omani trade unionists have argued that the NOC and visa ban harms expatriates by keeping 'a worker bonded to the company'.[147] By December 2020, the government announced that in 2021 it would once again scrap the NOC in favour of more 'employee-friendly' policies.[148] Business owners were reportedly concerned about declining productivity by losing trained expatriates to their competitors. The government rationale for the policy reversal was also offered in terms of supporting Omanis in the labour market. It suggested the move might increase the level of competitiveness of Omani workers by shrinking the wage gap between citizens and foreigners who could both more easily change jobs. This case shows rather clearly how intertwined efforts to Omanise are with the regimes governing migration.[149]

Second, the large demand for foreign labour across the region has produced practices and governance gaps where citizens may earn income through acting as a labour broker.[150] Although illegal in practice, and increasingly difficult with regulatory efforts to limit its practice, this so-called free visa mechanism remains in practice.[151] Through

---

[146] Interview, Muscat, 26 January 2019.

[147] Hasan Shaban Al-Lawati, 'Minister of Manpower Backs 2-Year Visa Ban in Oman', *Times of Oman*, 16 January 2017, https://timesofoman.com/article/25809-minister-of-manpower-backs-2-year-visa-ban-in-oman.

[148] 'Scraping of NOC in Oman: Balancing Act for Employees and Employers', *Oman Observer*, 26 December 2020, www.omanobserver.om/noc-scrapping-balancing-act-for-employees-and-employers/.

[149] A similar tug-of-war is evident in Bahrain's history of labour market reform. Bahrain was a first-mover in the Gulf in removing the NOC and likewise faced pressure to reimpose employment mobility restrictions. Françoise De Bel-Air, 'Demography, Migration, and the Labour Market in Bahrain', Gulf Labour Market and Migration (GLMM) Programme, 2015, 4, https://cadmus.eui.eu/handle/1814/35882.

[150] Like the earlier discussions on wages, this pattern has a mutable impact on class formation.

[151] For a discussion of this mechanism in other Gulf countries, see Hertog, 'The Sociology of the Gulf Rentier Systems'.

a registered business, an Omani might apply for more labour permits than actually needed and once the workers arrive let them work as 'free agents' selling their own labour on a per-job or per-hour basis. The workers pay a monthly fee to their sponsor in exchange for this (illegal) labour mobility. Sometimes the employees do not realise this practice is against the law. This is a very precarious existence for the migrant, and one where they can easily fall into irregularity.[152] Yet the freedom afforded by this informal system is sometimes preferable even to the worker.[153] Sometimes this practice occurs more systematically, and a sponsor may send their sponsees to work for another company or under another occupational category where the employer encountered problems procuring visas. Labour brokerage, or trade in visas, serves as an unproductive way of making a living but is the outcome of the difficult employment situation, patterns of rent seeking, and the migration regulatory landscape that creates such opportunities. In this case, both citizen and expatriate are functioning outside the law and can be subject to penalties. Yet they are operating within a landscape facilitated by the combination of legislation, social regulation, and incentive structures.

One can observe that during times of high regulation of labour immigration, businesses pursue informal arrangements or tap into their personal bureaucratic connections to acquire exemptions from stringent regulatory demands. Measures to discourage foreign recruitment are often resisted by the private sector. Some of these measures include discouraging foreign recruitment through raising visa fees, regulating the quantity of workers through limitations on the number of work permits, or complete bans on foreigners taking up jobs in particular professions.[154] A 2018 ban of foreigners from

---

[152] For a discussion of how irregularity occurs in migration in the Gulf and Oman, see Philippe Fargues and Nasra M. Shah, eds., *Skilful Survival: Irregular Migration to the Gulf* (European University Institute and Gulf Research Center, 2017), and the chapter by Jihan Safar and Melissa Levaillant, 'Irregular Migration in Oman: Policies, Their Effects and Interaction with India', 115–33.

[153] Sandhya Rao Mehta, 'Contesting Victim Narratives: Indian Women Domestic Workers in Oman', *Migration and Development* 6, no. 3 (2 September 2017): 403–5, https://doi.org/10.1080/21632324.2017.1303065.

[154] The labour law allocates authority to determine such measures to the Minister of Labour. Royal Decree 35/2003, 'Promulgating the Labour Law (issued 26 April 2003, published 3 May 2003)', Official Gazette 742, 2003.

working in eighty-seven different occupations was particularly irksome to employers, who, like with many arrangements, seek ways to circumvent the regulation.

There's a problem with statistics because of the ban. For example, all the service guys and marketing guys are blocked. So if I want to bring a marketing guy, and I cannot, I will bring someone on a different visa. I will hire an engineer. He'll actually work as the marketing guy I need, but I will hire him under an engineer visa. Then when you go to request statistics, they are wrong. Maybe there are, for example, 300 of a certain type of engineer, but the statistics might show you 2000 – but actually many of them are working in different occupations.[155]

Not only do such practices have governance and data implications, they also aggravate the perception among jobseekers that the private sector is an unwilling employer and magnify allegations of corruption and privilege.

As we have seen, the regulatory toolkit for labour force nationalisation has been large in practice, targeting incentive structures for employers to recruit Omanis and to make the private sector more attractive to citizens. These are announced, amended, and rolled back at various times in response to competing pressures from stakeholders. Restrictive measures are criticised by consultancies and international organisations like the World Bank and IMF as 'counterproductive', instead suggesting measures that would 'improve market efficiency' such as determining wages and benefits based on the market, removing hiring quotas, and increasing labour mobility.[156] As O'Brien argues, 'regulations which assist in freeing market forces and increasing competition between private enterprises are seen as being economic, while those that might pose restrictions upon market forces are viewed as political'.[157] But in fact, both require regulatory choices. Such critiques and policy proposals from financial institutions illustrate the tensions facing policymakers between liberalising the labour market and protecting national labour. It also speaks to the core issue of differential

---

[155] Interview with the CEO of a shipping and transportation company, Muscat, 26 January 2019.

[156] World Bank, 'Unlocking the Employment Potential in the Middle East and North Africa', 162; Sassanpour et al., 'Labor Market Challenges and Policies in the Gulf Cooperation Council Countries', 26, 42–48.

[157] O'Brien, 'The Varied Paths to Minimum Labour Standards', 225.

regulation: efforts to protect only one community of workers exacerbate segmentation and impact class formation.

2.5 Conclusion: States and Markets in the Governance of Gulf Labour

The Omani case reveals on a micro-scale the making of global labour markets and its imbrication with national dreams of economic life and development. It shows how regional labour markets are segmented and socially constructed and how these labour market structures are tied to three groups of intersecting social processes: production and the associated structuring of labour demand and nature of work, social reproduction and the structuring of labour supply, and the forces of regulation.[158] The analysis in the chapter demonstrates all three. The first sections illustrated the nature and organisation of work, as well as the patterns of demand from international pools of labour. Second, the chapter implicitly shows how the labour market is supplied or reproduced. This partly occurs in the usual formula of reproduction and caregiving in the home, producing and replenishing the worker through mostly unaccounted female labour within the nation. In addition, in Oman a large part of social reproduction occurs through the sourcing of labour from abroad, meaning key functions of labour supply and caregiving have been outsourced. Third, the chapter presents how the forces of legal and social regulation mediate how citizens and foreigners participate in the labour market and form social relations.

The complicated relationship and tensions between states and markets is strikingly visible in the Omani labour market, with its multiple, competing regulatory frameworks. Thinking of labour in terms of market is one of the most problematic tendencies of economic analysis. As Polanyi well explored, even if the description of labour as a commodity is entirely fictious, it remains the principle on which actual labour markets are organised.[159] When we speak about states and markets in the economy, the usual framing of it as states versus markets is both unhelpful and historically inaccurate. The pretention of liberalised markets for labour were constructed, and the push back to provide protections and regulate this market occurred spontaneously and

---

[158] These processes have been identified by Jamie Peck in *Work-Place*.
[159] Polanyi, *The Great Transformation*, 76.

continues to re-emerge across time and place. As Polanyi said, 'Laissez-faire was planned, planning was not.'[160] Opening the Omani (and regional) labour market had to be planned and facilitated, and the reaction to protect (or privilege) different social actors emerges in response. We see this clearly in the recommendations of IFIs and in the mixture of national regulations that are aimed at facilitating the 'free' market, and others aimed at protecting labour from it. It is more fruitful to consider states and markets in economic governance, where there is a 'preference for governing rather than eliminating the market'.[161] It is usually some sort of power, often the state, that facilitates an unregulated or liberalised market. As Susan Strange noted, 'It is power that determines the relationship between authority and market. Markets cannot play a dominant role in the way in which a political economy functions unless allowed to do so by whoever wields power and possesses authority.'[162] Studying this balance and this tension in Gulf labour markets allows us to understand a great deal about the political economy of the region.

What the Omani labour market case therefore illustrates is that treating labour as a commodity, regulating work, or liberalising markets are choices carried by actors with power. The problem with accepting such 'fictions'[163] and policy advice is that the labour market, while exhibiting some competitive efficiencies, does not function like an idealised commodity market. Instead, we see very clearly that those participating in the 'market' do not enter as equals, and segmentation and differentiation continue to shape and characterise their participation. Social regulation intervenes. The competition is neither pure nor efficient. Rather, we see a race to the bottom to the cheapest labour market competitor. The visible segmentations and structure of the Oman labour market highlight these broader patterns in the global labour market.

---

[160] Polanyi, *The Great Transformation*, 147.
[161] Walden Bello, 'States and Markets, States versus Markets: The Developmental State Debate as the Distinctive East Asian Contribution to International Political Economy', in *Routledge Handbook of International Political Economy (IPE): IPE as a Global Conversation*, ed. Mark Blyth (London: Routledge, 2010), 186.
[162] Strange, *States and Markets*, 23.
[163] Polanyi, *The Great Transformation*, 75–76.

3 | Rereading Omani Work History and Labour Market Governance

The story of Oman's history and of development is the story of living and working. You want to understand the Omani story? Follow the workers.[1]

—Abbas Al-Zadjali

This chapter offers a critical rereading of Omani work history that foregrounds labour, flipping the perspective from the view of industry and capital to the human experience. Through examining the history of labour governance and resistance in Oman, I argue that the contemporary governance, regulatory, and resistance environment for labour have clear lineages in the past. The research presented in this chapter shows how the practices of recruiting, framing, and segmenting labour alongside the experiences of working and resisting have profoundly shaped the growth and organisation of wage labour in Oman and the region.

I retell development and labour policy and resistance history with labour at the centre. This retelling is essential to understanding both the global nature and policy landscape of the contemporary Omani and regional labour market today. Because the oil industry is the main industry today and it is capital rather than labour intensive, the story of work remains at the margins. What unfolds in this chapter is the reverse. Inspired by the words of my interlocutors, I begin at the margins, and centre on 'living and working' – I 'follow the workers'. Starting with labour offers natural connections between translocal historical analysis and contemporary global political economy.[2]

---

[1] Interview, Abbas Al-Zadjali, Muscat, 22 January 2020.

[2] I borrow the term 'translocal' from Ulrike Frietag and Achim Von Oppen's conceptualisation of 'translocality', which facilitates a study of transnational mobility, the 'movements of people, goods, ideas, and symbols which span distances and cross boundaries', with attention to local context. This term is useful here because it is more nuanced than simply referring to 'globalised' or 'internationally penetrated' spaces. Instead, it allows for global processes like the

Using process tracing and contrapuntal reading as methods of analysis, this chapter takes a journey through multiple archival and interview sources to trace the lineages of differentiation and lineages of resistance.[3] I further locate this analysis within feminist inquiry's emphasis on understanding how difference operates in historically contingent situations to shape not only the social but also the economic. Through a critical and feminist global political economy of labour, it becomes apparent how capitalist modes of development operate across the global economy and 'fragments the labour process across space'.[4]

The historical, labour-centred exercise contained in this chapter reveals a genealogy of practice and discourse underpinned by racial capitalism that has shaped work life in Oman and the Gulf more widely.[5] It provides a crucial backdrop to the labour market segmentations running across economic sectors in the country and region and provides a retelling of the forces and trajectories shaping Omani workers' and jobseekers' labour market experiences. A historical, labour-centred perspective uncovers how the discourses around the

---

impact of racial capitalism on Gulf labour markets discussed here, while also offering 'a more open and less linear view on the manifold ways in which the global world is constituted: through the trans-gression of boundaries between spaces of very different scale and type as well as through the (re-)creation of "local" distinctions between those spaces'. 'Translocality: The Study of Globalising Processes from a Southern Perspective', in *Introduction. 'Translocality': An Approach to Connection and Transfer in Area Studies*, ed. Ulrike Freitag and Achim Von Oppen (Leiden: Brill, 2010), 5–9.

[3] Contrapuntal reading is introduced in Section 1.4 and my application of it to GPE of labour analysis is explained below. Said, *Culture and Imperialism*; Bilgin, '"Contrapuntal Reading" as a Method, an Ethos, and a Metaphor for Global IR'; Chowdhry, 'Edward Said and Contrapuntal Reading'; Bennett and Elman, 'Complex Causal Relations and Case Study Methods'; Collier, 'Understanding Process Tracing'.

[4] Jennifer Bair, 'On Difference and Capital: Gender and the Globalization of Production', *Signs* 36, no. 1 (2010): 205, https://doi.org/10.1086/652912.

[5] Racial capitalism refers to understanding the role of racism in enabling capitalist development and how race 'permeates the social structures emergent from capitalism'. Racial capitalism, according to Bhattacharyya, 'operates both through the exercise of coercive power and through the mobilisation of desire'. That is, people are both forced to participate in selling their labour or other economic activities but also become keen to be included in these activities. Diamond Ashiagbor, 'Race and Colonialism in the Construction of Labour Markets and Precarity', *Industrial Law Journal* 50, no. 4 (2021): 510, https://doi.org/10.1093/indlaw/dwab020; Gargi Bhattacharyya, *Rethinking Racial Capitalism: Questions of Reproduction and Survival* (Rowman & Littlefield, 2018), ix–xi.

Omani labour market today became embedded in development plans and polices (written initially by outsiders) and accepted into the developmental consciousness in policy-making and private sector business practice. It also reveals how the pressures for both liberalisation and nationalisation illustrated in Chapter 2 have a longer history. I separate these into the lineages of differentiation and resistance.

Adopting this labour-centred approach, the chapter first traverses three key legacies of governing work and workers – the colonial modes of circulating, disciplining, and classifying labour; the oil industry's human resources recruitment and management practices; and the framing and management of labour in national economic development planning. Second, it traces discourses about workers and how these discourses and prejudices are persistent technologies of governance that influence practices and assessments of employment and development. Finally, it assembles these dynamics together and shows the ensuant contestation to and within them over time, including connections to antiimperialist movements and activism and various manifestations of worker mobilisation and protest.

3.1 A Contrapuntal Reading on Oman's Segmented Labour Market

Scholarship in the humanities, especially postcolonial studies, has long engaged with Said's development of the contrapuntal technique for literary criticism.[6] Less so in the social sciences. I apply it here to global political economy analysis, borrowing from Chowdhry and Bilgin's use of contrapuntal reading as method and methodology in international relations.[7] I suggest a contrapuntal reading in GPE means a grounded, multicausal reading of development outcomes. This grows out of Said's call

for 'worlding' the texts, institutions and practices, for historicising them, for interrogating their sociality and materiality, for paying attention to the

---

[6] Said, *Culture and Imperialism*; Edward W. Said, *Reflections on Exile and Other Essays* (Cambridge, MA: Harvard University Press, 2000).

[7] Chowdhry, 'Edward Said and Contrapuntal Reading'; Bilgin, '"Contrapuntal Reading" as a Method, an Ethos, and a Metaphor for Global IR'; Pinar Bilgin, 'How to Remedy Eurocentrism in IR? A Complement and a Challenge for The Global Transformation', *International Theory* 8, no. 3 (2016): 492–501, https://doi.org/10.1017/S1752971916000178.

hierarchies and the power-knowledge nexus embedded in them, and for recuperating a 'non-coercive and non-dominating knowledge.[8]

Beginning with a historical, labour-centred reading of Oman's economic development history demonstrates how developmental consciousness and policy planning has been informed by particular discourses and interpretations of Omani and Gulf labour.[9] It also provides a framework through which theory building on the global political economy of labour can be generated. As Bilgin has claimed, generating scholarship that is truly international involves 'rethinking the hierarchies among different kinds of knowledge'.[10]

Using contrapuntal reading as a method of studying political economy moves my analysis away from origins and a singular source for ideas or processes like oil's intervention into the Gulf development trajectory. In its place, it allows a reading of 'overlapping territories and intertwined histories' that shows how development paths and narratives are co-constituted by multiple ideas, materialities, beginnings, and relationships in the local, regional, and global economy. That is, it better allows for multicausality, complicating tidy narratives of oil's impact on economics, politics, and society. Critical, contrapuntal political economy analysis of historical processes can be layered and nuanced. Following Edward Said, 'we begin to reread it not univocally but *contrapuntally*, with a simultaneous awareness both of the metropolitan history that is narrated and of those other histories against which (and together with which) the dominating discourse acts'.[11] Policy documents by colonial authorities and theoretical literature on the rentier state are dominating narratives in this space. We do not discard these but read alongside and understand beyond their contextual and analytical scope.

---

[8] Chowdhry, 'Edward Said and Contrapuntal Reading', 105.

[9] I engage a combination of archival and ethnographic research. My sources include archival materials from the International Institute of Social History Amsterdam (IISH), Royal Dutch Shell, the British archives (Kew), the Qatar Digital Library, the Arabian Gulf Digital Archives, the archives of the Omani Ministry of Economy and Central Bank, and interviews with Omani citizens in various age categories and with diverse work life experiences.

[10] Bilgin, '"Contrapuntal Reading" as a Method, an Ethos, and a Metaphor for Global IR', 137.

[11] Said, *Culture and Imperialism*, 51.

With these tools, we can look at the records showing the organisation of modern wage labour, with its divisions between ethnicities and skill levels, and the history of labour market regulation in the country as more than a simply objective record. We can also interpret these as products of particular historic moments and colonial legacies and trace how labour market discourses emerged and became embedded in development planning and in the social consciousness. By overlapping official accounts with the experience of workers – and with the historical record of contestation, of difference, and fragmentation of labour – we are able to shed new light on what was always a contested development history.[12] Discourse and practice overlap to shape and re-shape types of development choices and impasses. The official Omani narratives of its modern development history, the records of the oil industry and its recruitment and training practices over time, and the British archives weaved together in scholarly accounts of oil-led development offer a univocal reading. Shifting the departure point to labour, and overlapping it with 'intertwined and interdependent, and above all overlapping streams of historical experience',[13] widens our frameworks and allows us to engage more closely with processes of socio-economic and socio-political significance.

3.2 Lineages of Differentiation

The segmentations characteristic of Gulf labour markets have lineages that stretch before the first oil boom that so rapidly and extraordinarily transformed economic life in the region. Omani work life, and the Omani worker, encountered change not only through the expansion of wage labour as a form of livelihood but also encountered the framing and categorisation of their work and work practices in particular ways. Certainly, this is a story that could start much earlier, but I will primarily begin around the early twentieth century. During this time, Omanis migrated to work abroad in pursuit of a better economic life. They often went to other Gulf countries like Bahrain, working in various development and industrial activities popping up around the burgeoning oil industry. They also worked on British infrastructural

---

[12] Takriti's book is a fine example of the value of overlapping and intertwining histories for offering new and critical insights to Omani and regional history. Takriti, *Monsoon Revolution*.

[13] Said, *Culture and Imperialism*, 312.

projects in the country and region, such as setting up an air field on Masirah island in the 1930s. By 'following the worker', we find present a long story of the pursuit of work opportunities. As another interviewee declared, 'Before 1970, the full power was with the Sultan. Employees were only chosen by loyalty or sheikh-wise. Simple. It was a big reason so many of us left to Zanzibar and other GCC countries – work.'[14]

In this section, I look at the heritage of legal and political divisions during the colonial period and the practices of racial division in the oil industry in Oman. By starting with the labour experience, we can trace the lineages of the patterns of differentiation that underpin the Omani labour market segmentations today. We can also better engage with the interconnected global reorderings, observing how 'the globalization of production is fundamentally about reorganizing the social geography of industry'.[15] By 'differentiation', I mean both the multiple segmentations within labour markets, as well as the patterns and practices involved in *producing* difference. To do so, I begin by looking at the heritage of colonial legal and political practices in the region, then turn to the specific human resource practices of oil companies and follow with a discussion of discourses about workers. Starting with labour allows a reading along and against the archival grain,[16] therefore, a *rereading* of development history including oil. This offers a critical backdrop to how the patterns of recruitment and differentiation took hold and became structurally embedded in how work and wage labour in Oman are viewed.

3.2.1 The Heritage of Colonial Legal and Political Division

By the end of the nineteenth and early twentieth centuries, Britain played a defining role in the Arabian Sea and Indian Ocean economic and labour space. Forms of work, labour, and the mobility of labour

---

[14] Interview with expert for economic research at OCIPED/Public Authority for Investment Promotion and Export Development (Muscat, 17 October 2011)

[15] Bair, 'On Difference and Capital', 205.

[16] Ann Stoler, *Along the Archival Grain: Epistemic Anxieties and Colonial Common Sense* (Princeton: Princeton University Press, 2010); David M. Gordon, 'Reading the Archives as Sources', in *The Oxford Encyclopedia of African Historiography: Methods and Sources* (Oxford: Oxford University Press, 2019).

were governed primarily through British colonial agents and industry men. Workers and labour markets were ordered and cast to the benefit of the commercial, military, and business interests of empire, the expansion of the oil industry, and the facilitation and maintenance of governing control. Evolving forms of differentiation shaped and facilitated political, legal, and economic governance directly through British rule and indirectly through the impact of their interventions in the political and economic space.

The transition in flows of manual labour during the abolitionary period offers insights into how financial and political incentives interact to shape development policy and practice. British efforts to curb and then abolish the Indian Ocean slave trade were a central part of their larger strategy to fortify their economic position in the region.[17] Prior to abolition, slave labour was integral to a great deal of economic activity in the Western Indian Ocean by Arab, Asian, and African traders, plantation owners, and merchants. Enslaved peoples accompanied ivory, spices, and various commodities from the interior of the African continent to its eastern coast and overseas. They were involved in multiple forms of labour in East Africa, Oman, and the wider Persian Gulf including date, spice, and coconut plantations, and pearl diving. They also served administrative, governance, and security functions as military leaders, regional governors, commercial agents, sailors, and artisans, among others, although productive labour surpassed these roles. The ports of Muscat and Sur were the principal destinations and ports of transit in the 1800s.[18] By the beginning of the

[17] Edward A. Alpers, 'On Becoming a British Lake: Piracy, Slaving, and British Imperialism in the Indian Ocean during the First Half of the Nineteenth Century', in *Indian Ocean Slavery in the Age of Abolition*, ed. Robert W. Harms, Bernard K. Freamon, and David W. Blight (New Haven: Yale University Press, 2013), 45–58; Benjamin J. Reilly, 'A Well-Intentioned Failure: British Anti-Slavery Measures and the Arabian Peninsula, 1820–1940', *Journal of Arabian Studies* 5, no. 2 (3 July 2015): 91–115, https://doi.org/10.1080/21534764.2015.1114735; Sultan Muhammad Al-Qasimi, *Omani-French Relations 1715–1900*, trans. B. R. Pridham (London: Forest Row, 1996); Bhacker, *Trade and Empire in Muscat and Zanzibar*, 32–44.

[18] Pedro Machado, *Ocean of Trade: South Asian Merchants, Africa and the Indian Ocean, c.1750–1850* (Cambridge: Cambridge University Press, 2014), 212–17; Bishara, *A Sea of Debt*, 46–50; Bhacker, *Trade and Empire in Muscat and Zanzibar*, 128–32; Matthew Hopper, 'Slaves of One Master: Globalization and the African Diaspora in Arabia in the Age of Empire', in *Indian Ocean Slavery in the Age of Abolition*, ed. Robert W. Harms, Bernard K. Freamon, and David W. Blight (New Haven: Yale University Press, 2013), 223–40.

century, however, Britain had already established itself as the dominant imperial power in Oman and was busy throughout the Indian Ocean world securing its trade and commercial interests in competition with regional and European powers.[19] Anti-slavery activities offered a convenient rationale for British interventions to manage labour flows just as it had provided them justification for dominating trade routes.[20] Moreover, ending slavery generated unremitting demand for Indian indentured labour.[21] On the one hand, the British praised their own efforts at fighting against and abolishing slavery in the Indian Ocean. On the other hand, they were crucially interested in maintaining access to 'secure a disciplined labour force' for their economic activities in their colonies and protectorates.[22] Scholarship on the period shows that 'the intense British opposition to slavery and outrage at the treatment of slaves by "Arabs" in the Indian Ocean at the time did not translate into British attention to or care for actual slaves'.[23]

---

[19] For example, the British signed a treaty with Muscat in 1798 to establish a fortified factory that forbade similar agreements with the Dutch and French. Omanis agreed to this treaty to protect their commercial interests with Indian Ocean ports already under British domination. However, this treaty signified the 'first nail in the coffin of Omani independence of action' and the 'first step towards the political and economic stranglehold that Britain was to exercise over Oman throughout the nineteenth and for the best part of the twentieth'. Bhacker, *Trade and Empire in Muscat and Zanzibar*, 33.

[20] This has been well documented. Abdul Sheriff, *Slaves, Spices and Ivory in Zanzibar: Integration of an East African Commercial Empire into the World Economy, 1770–1873* (Rochester: Boydell and Brewer, 1987), 223–44, www .cambridge.org/core/books/slaves-spices-and-ivory-in-zanzibar/ 8BBA2BA56875E3637C05D875E04280CD; Sugata Bose, *A Hundred Horizons: The Indian Ocean in the Age of Global Empire* (Cambridge, MA: Harvard University Press, 2006), 72–121; John C. Wilkinson, *The Arabs and the Scramble for Africa* (Sheffield; Bristol: Equinox, 2014), 81–82; Robert W. Harms, Bernard K. Freamon, and David W. Blight, eds., *Indian Ocean Slavery in the Age of Abolition* (New Haven: Yale University Press, 2013); Bhacker, *Trade and Empire in Muscat and Zanzibar*, 164–76.

[21] Hugh Tinker, *A New System of Slavery: The Export of Indian Labour Overseas, 1830–1920* (Oxford: Oxford University Press, 1974); Bose, *A Hundred Horizons*, 75.

[22] Nandita Sharma, *Home Rule: National Sovereignty and the Separation of Natives and Migrants* (Durham: Duke University Press, 2020), 5.

[23] Mandana Limbert, '"If You Catch Me Again at It, Put Me to Death": Slave Trading, Paper Trails, and British Bureaucracy in the Indian Ocean', in *Indian Ocean Slavery in the Age of Abolition*, ed. Robert W. Harms, Bernard K. Freamon, and David W. Blight (New Haven: Yale University Press, 2013), 120.

As Johan Mathew establishes, the abolition of slavery in the Arabian Sea and Indian Ocean world was more semantic than actual. It formed and governed a different system of unfree labour, replacing regional slave owners with the Empire as 'the manager and beneficiary of a massive trade in Indian "coolie" labour'.[24] It was a transition *from* trafficking slaves *to* a market for bonded labour, where the balance of beneficiaries of this new 'market' was tipped toward the British.[25] That is, the British used emancipation to drive flows of labour in their favour.

This new market for unfree labour regulated by the British grew alongside a slave trade that, while slowing, continued into the early twentieth century. Demand for controllable, cheap labour shaped labour regimes across the region – both indentured and enslaved – which was in turn structured by global economic forces. While the persistence of slavery in particular industries along the Arabian coast has often been explained as an outcome of some cultural or religious exceptionalism, the interests of capital offer a more compelling explanation. As Hopper cogently argues, 'Western countries increased demand for the commodities produced by slave labour in the gulf at the very moment they increased their pressure on the region to end the slave trade and slavery.'[26] Material motivations clearly underpin the continuities in the demand for exploitable labour in the transition from enslaved labour to indentured workers. The subsequent transition to flows of cheap, flexible labour to the economic activities of the region today represent the continuation of this pattern. With the collapse of the pearling industry in the Gulf and the intensification of the Great Depression, slavery did in fact end. But as the commercial dominance of the British Empire grew and prospects of oil intensified foreign interest, the patterns in demand and work governance regimes began to institutionalise.

British bureaucrats and diasporic merchants were able to reframe the understanding and practices of labour exploitation. Enslavement was unacceptable, but mobile populations of poor contracted labour

---

[24] 'Coolie' is a pejorative term used during the period to refer to South and East Asian low-wage workers that circulated around the British Empire as part of an indentured labour system that replaced the use of slavery in the colonies. Mathew, *Margins of the Market*, 54.

[25] Mathew, *Margins of the Market*, 52–81.

[26] Hopper, 'Slaves of One Master', 234.

were within the realms of regulatory permissibility. The exploited subclass of labour were no longer actual slaves, and their labour and migration could be explained and justified using racialised reinterpretations portraying such labour flows as purely the result of misfortune in some overseas space driving labouring bodies to seek work contracts elsewhere. The discursive shift from bodies *forced* to work to bodies who *wanted* to work alleviates responsibility for oppressive recruitment and regulatory structures that facilitate forms of bonded and exploited labour. This narrative continues to frame the pull-push factors account of labour migration today.[27] Accordingly, this transition to indentured labour already began to entrench a practice of a global market for manual labour in the region, where this labour was both contractually bonded, racialised, and underpaid.

Managing flows of both unskilled and skilled labour brought jurisdictional and regulatory questions, which in turn informed practices of differentiation and segmentation of residents in Oman. As early as 1867, the Muscat Order in Council began treating foreigners differently in judicial and legislative terms.[28] With this order, British subjects and protected persons in Muscat and Matraḥ were forbidden from petitioning the local authorities with complaints and instead had to appeal to the consulate or face a fine. Commercial treaties in 1891 and 1939 conferred even more extensive jurisdiction over British subjects and protected persons to the political agent.[29] M. Reda Bhacker's work problematises the 'distorted views' given by colonial agents and writers by 'their insistence on separating' Omanis, Indians, Swahilis

---

[27] Catherine Dauvergne and Sarah Marsden, 'The Ideology of Temporary Labour Migration in the Post-Global Era', *Citizenship Studies* 18, no. 2 (17 February 2014): 232, https://doi.org/10.1080/13621025.2014.886441; Marko Valenta and Jo Jakobsen, 'Moving to the Gulf: An Empirical Analysis of the Patterns and Drivers of Migration to the GCC Countries, 1960–2013', *Labor History* 57, no. 5 (19 October 2016): 627–48, https://doi.org/10.1080/0023656X.2016 .1239885; Stephen Castles, *The Age of Migration: International Population Movements in the Modern World*, 2nd ed. (Hampshire: Macmillan International Higher Education, 1998), 19–23.

[28] 'File 18/54 (A 89) Muscat Order in Council, 1867: New Regulations', British Library: India Office Records and Private Papers, 4 April 1911, IOR/R/15/1/ 297, Qatar Digital Library, www.qdl.qa/en/archive/81055/vdc_100023834010 .0x000012.

[29] 'Historical Summary of Events in the Persian Gulf Shaikhdoms and the Sultanate of Muscat and Oman, 1928–1953', British Library: India Office Records and Private Papers, 1953, 197, IOR/R/15/1/731(1), Qatar Digital Library, www.qdl .qa/archive/81055/vdc_100000000193.0x0002c1.

and others in the nineteenth-century Omani dominions and determining who was a subject of Britain.[30] This differentiation obscured the role and identity of various communities such as certain South Asian diasporas who 'regarded themselves as part of the Albusaidi Omani' by superimposing 'European notions of political organisation and demarcation'.[31]

By 1947, courts were reorganised to reflect the jurisdictional differences that had been gradually institutionalised. Still, ambiguous categories of 'foreigner' remained, leaving jurisdiction unclear. By 1949, a new Order in Council named the British political agent judge of the court, imbued with the powers of district magistrate, sessions judge, and district judge.[32] The separation of jurisdiction and legal regimes for different categories of residents persisted and strengthened. As the early decades of the twentieth century wore on, British officials expanded their jurisdictional reach over increasing categories of foreigners, delineating who was foreign and who was not – who belonged to the geoeconomic and political spaces and who did not.

In her work on the construction of citizenship regimes in the formation of the neighbouring United Arab Emirates (UAE), Noora Lori demonstrates how the grafting of the 'square peg' form of nation-state and citizenship regime 'onto the round hole of Gulf networks of merchant capital with its diasporic, eclectic, non-territorial logics led to the creation of a demographic boundary zone of ambiguous legal statuses'.[33] For Bhacker, these practices and patterns were part of the roots of British domination in Oman. His research not only documents the British financial motivations for demarcation but also the difficulty in differentiating among the racial, ethnic, and national categories of residents and determining who were or could be British subjects in the Omani dominions.[34] Such practices of differentiation sit uneasily in port cities like Muscat and Matraḥ with histories of residents from around the Indian Ocean littoral that preceded British influence in the space. This history also hints at what Fahad Bishara claims are the challenges scholars face 'when trying to reconcile fixed, territorial

---

[30] Bhacker, *Trade and Empire in Muscat and Zanzibar*, 117.
[31] Bhacker, *Trade and Empire in Muscat and Zanzibar*, 117 and 123.
[32] 'Historical Summary – IOR/R/15/1/731(1)', 198.
[33] Lori, *Offshore Citizens*, 51.
[34] Bhacker, *Trade and Empire in Muscat and Zanzibar*, 117–67.

notions of society – and of nation – with a history of circulation, entanglement, and imbrication with contending imperial projects'.[35]

According to Omar AlShehabi, these mechanisms of divided rule and co-sovereignty are forms and practices of governance in the region.[36] Co-sovereignty was a key theme in the governance of human mobility during this period in and out of Oman. While the Sultan was, as the British government perceived, 'in theory a wholly independent ruler', in practice, British influence was paramount.[37] The British considered Said bin Taymur (*Saʿīd bin Taymūr*), Sultan Qaboos' father, to be 'extremely jealous of his independence'. This lent to some contention over treaty relations, legal jurisdiction, and the delineation of who was a subject of Britain or the Sultan and who could determine whether a worker could enter Muscat and Oman.[38] The British were keen to maintain what they considered the Sultan's 'façade of independence' as a means of facilitating consultation, influencing his decisions, and remaining informed about his affairs.[39]

Classifications based on nationality became increasingly imbued in labour politics as British officials took more control over border and immigration controls. What began as jurisdictional differences expanded throughout the commercial and economic spheres as forms of employment legislation. Sponsorship systems, which continue to characterise foreign employment in the region today, were first applied by the British to control the migrant labour population in Bahrain. After the discovery of oil in Bahrain, this experience was used as a blueprint and applied in Oman and then elsewhere in the Gulf.[40] Sponsorship systems became embedded in the border control and labour recruitment practices of the region, and the practices of

---

[35] Fahad Ahmad Bishara, 'The Many Voyages of Fateh Al-Khayr: Unfurling the Gulf in the Age of Oceanic History', *International Journal of Middle East Studies* 52, no. 3 (August 2020): 398, https://doi.org/10.1017/S0020743820000367.

[36] AlShehabi insightfully details these processes in Bahrain. Omar AlShehabi, *Contested Modernity: Sectarianism, Nationalism, and Colonialism in Bahrain* (London: OneWorld, 2019), 13–33, 142–66.

[37] 'Historical Summary – IOR/R/15/1/731(1)', 172.

[38] This is observable across many of the British records, which include debates over granting certain groups or individuals permission to enter the country for projects, trading, or work, and discussions over whether or not Omanis abroad would be permitted to return to Oman

[39] 'Historical Summary – IOR/R/15/1/731(1)', 172.

[40] AlShehabi, 'Policing Labour in Empire', 303–6.

recruitment and sponsor-based employment evolved into the various *kafāla* systems known today across the region.[41] Such patterns were political from the beginning; and as the early twentieth century wore on, the decision of employing Omanis or other Arabs or South Asians became an increasingly contentious issue and increasingly entangled with nationalism and notions of national belonging.[42]

The practices of governing mobility and employment through sponsorship regimes began to take form in No Objection Certificates (NOCs) and the development of passport and visa regimes. NOCs were issued to ease travel to other Gulf ports, to facilitate exit and return of workers and traders between Iran and the Arabian Peninsula, to permit individuals to import arms and ammunitions, and to allow Indian employees of British policing and bureaucratic services to bring their families to join them.[43] Increasingly, NOCs became required for foreign employees, and by the late 1960s more countries in the region began using a NOC system to govern visas, labour contracts, and residency.[44] Immigrants who arrived for work would be sponsored by the contractors or parties responsible for their employment. The

---

[41] See Chapter 2 for a further definition and explanation of *kafāla*.

[42] The legal and jurisdictional regulation of migration and mobility described here refer to formal mobility – that is, migration that could be traced, managed, and therefore governed. It should be noted that informal population movements occurred then, as they do now. By staying below the radar, these migrants are able to escape some forms of governance whilst becoming subject to others. To read more, see L. Stephenson's work on regulations that targeted Iranians in Bahrain, which impacted mercantile communities more heavily than smaller communities, 'Rerouting the Persian Gulf: The Transnationalisation of Iranian Migrant Networks, c. 1900–1940' (Dissertation, Princeton University, June 2018), https://dataspace.princeton.edu/handle/88435/dsp016h440w16b; See also Ennis and Blarel, *The South Asia to Gulf Migration Governance Complex*, for discussions of irregular migration and governance gaps in the region.

[43] 'Coll 27/9(2) "Passports. British-Protected Persons. Travel Documents for Persons Proceeding to, and for Natives of, Certain British Protectorates and Arab States"', British Library: India Office Records and Private Papers, 1948 1939, IOR/L/PS/12/3370, Qatar Digital Library, www.qdl.qa/en/archive/81055/vdc_100000000602.0x00039a; 'File 29/7 I "Consular: Passport and Visa Regulations (Governing Bahrain, Muscat, Kuwait and Other Shaikhdoms)"', British Library: India Office Records and Private Papers, 1934 1929, IOR/R/15/2/1748, Qatar Digital Library, www.qdl.qa/en/archive/81055/vdc_100000000282.0x0001e3; 'Historical Summary – IOR/R/15/1/731(1)', 14; AlShehabi, 'Policing Labour in Empire'.

[44] Lori, *Offshore Citizens*, 112–14.

system tied both entry to the country and residency to labour contracts and increasingly privatised the governance of labour – offloading it to companies or individuals that served as employers. The visa system became based on local labour sponsors, who would be responsible to obtain the NOC from the authorities and then remain responsible for wages and repatriation.

Similar to earlier decades,[45] the difficulties associated with recruiting Omani labour make a regular appearance throughout reports in the 1950s and 1960s, with regard to the availability, training, training 'potential', and methods of recruitment. 'Local labour is only forthcoming in small numbers and the only jobs sought after are those of watchmen. So far no one has been recruited', bemoaned one report.[46] In fact, the recruitment of labour was always discussed by ethnicity and nationality. For example, during the exploration at the Fahud site in the 1950s, the drilling works plan notes,

As the only labour available in the area are completely unskilled Bedouin Arabis, all skilled workers of every kind will be brought in. When the operations are in full swing these will consist of –

British	20
American	6
Indian	24
Arabs	30
Total	80 [sic].[47]

British commercial and oil interests described the recruitment of skilled and unskilled labour as a difficult exercise, with reports lamenting 'the poor material available from which to recruit, owing to the flight of so

---

[45] See, for example, 'Historical Summary – IOR/R/15/1/731(1)', 180–81: 'The story of development in Muscat is a sad one. A number of surveys have been carried out and reports written but nothing has been done partly because of the difficulty of finding qualified experts to serve in Muscat on salaries which the State can afford and partly because of the lack of resources to implement the proposals which have been made. The Sultan has said he does not want any more experts who will only look at the country and write reports; what he requires is somebody who can suggest and implement small practical schemes and teach his people improved methods.'

[46] 'File 15331: Oil Exploration', Foreign Office (London: The National Archives, 1954), 291, FO 1016/330, Arabian Gulf Digital Archives, www.agda.ae/en/catalogue/tna/fo/1016/330.

[47] 'FO 1016/330', 22.

many people to established oil fields in the Gulf'.[48] In fact, Omanis did not only have a history of migration to East Africa but also of searching for wage labour elsewhere outside of Oman. During the Said bin Taymur era, many Omanis left the country (often illegally) to find work or in pursuit of an education. Many men especially from across Northern Oman found employment opportunities in the new oil economies around the region, starting with Bahrain in the 1930s.[49] During the first half of the twentieth century, it was common and relatively easy for nationals of Muscat and Oman to migrate to Bahrain in search of work,[50] and some estimated that as many as 10,000 Omanis may have been working in Kuwait alone by 1970.[51] Other estimates claimed that in northern Oman 'no fewer than 74% of the adult males aged 14–39 years were away working' in 1974.[52] Despite the practice of labour emigration during the period, the difficulty of recruiting local labour and the stock of untrained or unavailable labour within Muscat and Oman was used as a rationale for continued foreign recruitment for cheap low-skilled labour, skilled labour, security work, and others.[53]

Moreover, how to govern labour was also determined in large part by racial, ethnic, and nationality-based considerations. It is clear from the records that pay, as well as the conditions of work and living like food and accommodation, were determined first and foremost by nationality. The British determined who needed to be treated better, and this varied over the decades as certain ethnicities became associated with certain skilled or unskilled professions at various times. The division of labour into categories of nationality prompted within-group agitation to discriminatory policy. We see a notable example

---

[48] 'FO 1016/330', 235–36.

[49] Al-Yousef, *Oil and the Transformation of Oman*, 22; Roderic W. Dutton, *Changing Rural Systems in Oman: The Khabura Project* (London: Kegan Paul International, 1999), 11.

[50] Reportedly, Bahraini authorities did not wish to restrict the migration of Gulf nationals while there was demand for unskilled labour. One account estimated that 9,075 immigrants from Oman and the Trucial coast entered Bahrain for work in 1952–53. David Finnie, 'Recruitment and Training of Labor: The Middle East Oil Industry', *Middle East Journal* 12, no. 2 (1958): 129.

[51] Terence Clark, *Underground to Overseas: The Story of Petroleum Development Oman* (London: Stacey International, 2007), 77.

[52] Dutton, *Changing Rural Systems in Oman: The Khabura Project*, 13.

[53] This pattern of complaints bears striking resemblance to contemporary ones frequenting policy discussions in the country.

through an article by an Indian migrant in Kuwait, published in a paper for Indian welfare, which complained of ill treatment and differentiation based on his nationality and race. He described Kuwait's oil fields as a 'hell hole for Indian employees', who were mistreated by 'the white staff' known as 'Senior Staff'.[54] Similarly in Oman, complaints emerged in reaction to this differentiation. By the 1950s, there was a widening sense among the British that Arab labourers needed to be treated better than South Asian ones because of a perceived linguistic and cultural affinity. One letter laments a British officer who had dismissed seventeen Adenese who dared complain about their living conditions and food rations. The letter, from Brigadier Robert Baird, goes on to say that 'Arabs and Sudanese must be treated differently' and be provided 'suitable and sufficient' food and accommodations because 'these officers are an important cog in the wheel'.[55] Discipline and governance was organised to ensure productivity.

Economics and politics were both at the forefront of choices around employment and two sides of a coin: on the one face, the pull of cheap labour and, on the other, the pull of political control and the preservation of the status quo. These continue to underline policy choices until the present. Discussions of labour in the colonial records reveals the tension inherent in maintaining political and economic power in 'development' policy in the Gulf. For example, a working paper from the British Foreign Office sent to the Cabinet's Middle East Committee in December 1949 showed how, on the one hand, the British mused about the importance of encouraging further education, especially to facilitate a small pool of locally trained labour, to a Sultan they described as reluctant to do so. On the other hand, they expressed considerable anxiety that further education risked creating 'a class of unemployed effendis' who could 'poison' the political atmosphere like in Egypt and Iraq.[56] There was an awareness of the importance of economic inclusion to mitigate disenfranchisement and a fear of the risks in educating a working class. Education could offer more tools

---

[54] 'File 13/5 "Foreign Consular Representation in Kuwait (and Persian Gulf)"', British Library: India Office Records and Private Papers, 1 November 1933, IOR/R/15/5/315, Qatar Digital Library, www.qdl.qa/en/archive/81055/vdc_100000000831.0x000166.

[55] 'FO 1016/330', 223.

[56] 'Coll 30/232 "Arab Sheikdoms of the Persian Gulf"', British Library: India Office Records and Private Papers, 1949, IOR/L/PS/12/3974, Qatar Digital Library, www.qdl.qa/archive/81055/vdc_100000000648.0x000224.

for mobilisation and effective collective action. In the 1950s and 1960s, the British grew increasingly worried that workers' education across the Arabian Gulf would lead to 'labour subversion' and be influenced by 'extremist pan-Arab groups' and 'infiltrated by the communists'.[57] British interests were very much wrapped up in the maintenance of their imperial reach and economic benefit, especially in the context of the contractions of the post-war period and the rising anticolonial movements around the world.

It comes as no surprise then that decisions of employment and recruitment were determined by security and oil interests. These interests run in the foreground with the tensions to 'discipline and contain'[58] labour underpinning policy concerns across the colonial record. First, the objective of securing a supply of cheap, compliant labour is present in the margins of many records. This sentiment was visible in the 1940s when the British were preoccupied with the quality and quantity of landing strips for the increased air traffic into the Persian Gulf as security and oil company operations expanded.[59] Labour had to be recruited for these projects. For example, in a series of correspondence on the development of the landing ground and aerodrome in Muscat for the Royal Air Force (RAF), a request indicates a need for approximately '150 coolies to carry out this work' and asks the British political agent to 'please obtain same in the usual manner from Contractor at the lowest possible rates [sic]'.[60] As such records indicate, British officials were involved in the sourcing of cheap, accessible labour for trading companies and contractors bidding for such projects like Khimji Ramdas, Nassib bin Mohamed and Son, and Haji Bhacker and Brothers (see Figure 3.1). Local contractors could bid for the work and help source materials, and British officials could tap into their networks of labour brokers to source low-wage workers. In this way, local trading companies were engaged in economic projects while creating distance between labour practices and their source. That is, the use of agencies and subcontracting for labour-intensive

---

[57] 'Report on Labour, Social and Industrial Developments', (5 December 1967), 'Labour Relations', Foreign and Commonwealth Office (London: The National Archives, 1968), 78–83, FCO 8/70, Arabian Gulf Digital Archives, www.agda.ae/en/catalogue/tna/fco/8/70.

[58] Sharma, *Home Rule*, 25.   [59] 'Historical Summary – IOR/R/15/1/731(1)'.

[60] Repairs to Landing Ground 'File 2/21 R.A.F. Landing Ground at Beit al Falaj (Petrol Store at Muscat)', British Library: India Office Records and Private Papers, 17 February 1938, 2 January 1945, IOR/R/15/6/99, Qatar Digital Library, www.qdl.qa/en/archive/81055/vdc_100000000831.0x0002eb.

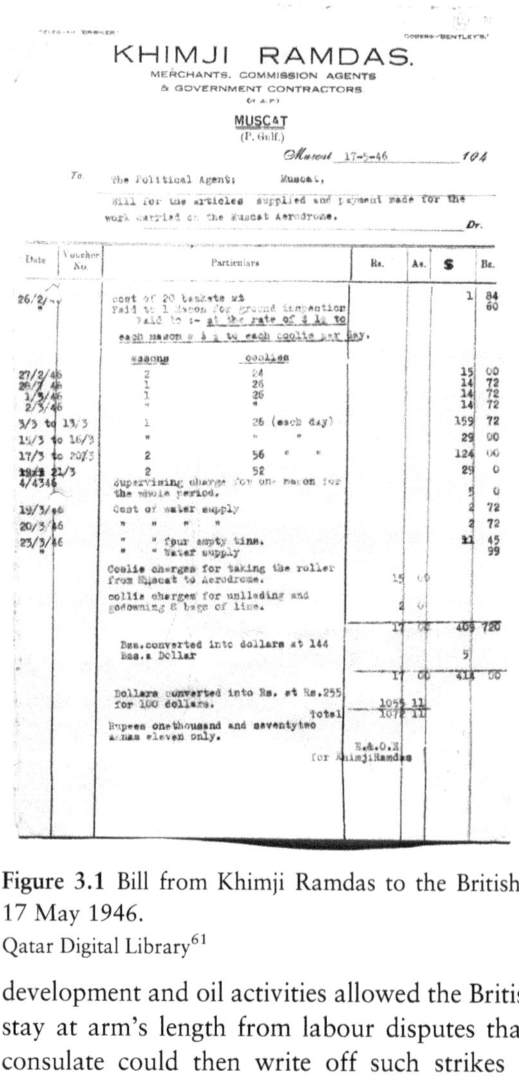
KHIMJI RAMDAS.
MERCHANTS, COMMISSION AGENTS
& GOVERNMENT CONTRACTORS
MUSCAT
(P. Gulf.)

Muscat 17-5-46 194

To. The Political Agent; Muscat,

Bill for the articles supplied and payment made for the work carried on the Muscat Aerodrome. Dr.

Date	Voucher No.	Particulars	Rs.	As.	$	Bz.
26/2/46		cost of 20 baskets at			1	84
"		Paid to 1 Mason for ground inspection				60
		Paid to :- at the rate of $ 1½ to each mason & $ ½ to each coolie per day.				
		masons coolies				
27/2/46		2 24			15	00
28/2/46		1 26			14	72
1/3/46		1 26			14	72
2/3/46		" "			14	72
3/3 to 13/3		1 26 (each day)			159	72
15/3 to 16/3		" " "			29	00
17/3 to 20/3		2 56 " "			124	00
21/3		2 52			29	0
4/43/46		Supervising charge for one mason for the whole period.			5	0
19/3/46		Cost of water supply			2	72
20/3/46		" " " "			2	72
23/3/46		" " four empty tins.			11	45
"		" " Water supply				99
		Coolie charges for taking the roller from Muscat to Aerodrome.	15	00		
		collie charges for unlading and godowning 8 bags of lime.	2	0		
			17	00	409	720
		Bzs. converted into dollars at 144 Bzs. a Dollar			5	
			17	00	414	00
		Dollars converted into Rs. at Rs.255 for 100 dollars.	1055	11		
		Total	1072	11		
		Rupees onethousand and seventytwo annas eleven only.				

E.&.O.E
for KhimjiRamdas

Figure 3.1 Bill from Khimji Ramdas to the British Political Agent, Muscat, 17 May 1946.
Qatar Digital Library[61]

development and oil activities allowed the British and oil companies to stay at arm's length from labour disputes that emerged. The British consulate could then write off such strikes as occurring 'amongst employees of companies working on contract for' the oil company.[62]

[61] Khimji Ramdas Group, File 2/21 R.A.F. landing ground at Beit al Falaj (Petrol Store at Muscat) 'File 2/21 - IOR/R/15/6/99' www.qdl.qa/en/archive/81055/vdc_100076684101.0x000088.

[62] 'Commercial Export of Oil', Foreign and Commonwealth Office (London: The National Archives, 1967–1968), FCO 8/600, Arabian Gulf Digital Archives, www.agda.ae/en/catalogue/tna/fco/8/600.

Second, the concerns about the supply of cheap labour were weighed with concerns about unrest among local labour. Balancing the maximum profitability with political feasibility quietly underpins the running discourse. Over time, political authorities agonised that the presence of oil would add fuel to the fire of antiimperialist agitation, and the revolutionary movement in Dhofar. Correspondence in the 1960s are filled with debates between British officials and Shell employees on 'the labour problem'.[63] These express anxieties about recruiting Omanis working in oil fields abroad back to Oman who might 'have become infected with undesirable ideas'.[64] They were likewise concerned about recruiting politicised Arabs from elsewhere in the region versus 'Indians and Pakistanis who are readily available'.[65] Both British officials and the Sultan were wary of the spread of radical political ideologies and labour solidarities.

As the 1960s wore on, securing oil and access to oil became a paramount goal. Tension within the ranks of colonial officials and within Shell and Petroleum Development (Oman) suggest a lack of consensus on whether educating and training the local unskilled workforce would be positive and what form of labour organising to facilitate or quash. The ultimate hope was stated explicitly – that oil wealth would 'make its pacifying influence felt'.[66]

Similar sentiments emerge as a source of concern in leftist anti-imperialist publications, which associate rentier patterns of wealth distribution with technologies of governance to de-radicalise populations. The regime was using its wealth to attempt creating 'new social classes' through offering 'bribery of a fat job' in government.[67] Rather than educating citizens, the opposition bemoaned, the regime wanted to 'ensure the loyalty of a certain sector of the population, and form a new privileged class with a stake in the regime' where 'Oman gained a stooge, but lost an engineer'.[68]

This dialectic between how to both facilitate work but also discipline labour are a pattern of logics observed by Mongia in her work on the

---

[63] R. S. Crawford (6 March 1964), 'Shell Operations in Oman', 'Oil Prospecting', Foreign Office (London: The National Archives, 1964), 25, FO 371/174573, Arabian Gulf Digital Archives, www.agda.ae/en/catalogue/tna/fo/371/174573.

[64] J. S. R. Duncan (24 March 1964), 'FO 371/174573', 30.

[65] J. S. R. Duncan (4 April 1964), 'FO 371/174573', 34.

[66] W. Luce, Correspondence (16 November 1964), 'FO 371/174573', 101.

[67] 'Omani Regime', 3.   [68] 'Omani Regime', 3.

colonial genealogy of Indian migration and border regimes. She calls these the *logic of facilitation*, which aims to enable the flow of workers, and the *logic of constraint*, which looks for ways to regulate and restrict labour.[69] Both are clearly influenced by market versus state ideologies that compete on how best to facilitate capitalist growth. They are also immersed within a justification of protection. This is visible in the Omani case and is a pattern observable globally. During the colonial period, constraining forces were proffered as a means not only to facilitate but also to protect indentured labour. Later, border immigration controls were rationalised as an instrument for protecting migrants from poor recruitment regimes or, increasingly, as a means of protecting citizens and, importantly jobs for citizens, from migrants.[70] We saw this tension in Chapter 2 and will continue to see this pattern surface throughout the book, underscoring the legacy of differentiation and regulation on both policy and resistance until today.

The division and differentiation of labour has been even more marked than jurisdictional differentiation alone and reflected similar logics: logics of who belonged under which type of rule and who belonged to which type of work, alongside capitalist and governmental logics of who were the cheapest and most flexible workers, best trained, and easiest to govern. The lineages of labour segmentation can be seen in the processes noted above – processes of abolition, demarcating jurisdiction, and regulating the border – as well as the circulation of workers and organisation of industrial projects across the Indian Ocean and British Empire. Practices of differentiation became more conspicuous with the onset of the oil age, next to the growth and institutionalisation of wage labour, outmigration for wage labour, and rising employment in infrastructural projects.

3.2.2 The Legacies of the Oil Industry Human Resource Policies

The beginning of exploration and the growth of the oil industry established particular practices around labour and human resources that have persisted. As shown above, the political and legal practices of

---

[69] Radhika Mongia, *Indian Migration and Empire: A Colonial Genealogy of the Modern State* (Durham; London: Duke University Press, 2018).

[70] In chapter 3, Sharma shows how immigration controls globally have been engaged under a justification of protection. Sharma, *Home Rule*.

ethnic and national differentiation, and the policing of the border, were intertwined with questions of power and oil. The story of work – including when employment was offered, to whom it was offered, where the work was, and who ultimately worked – unpacks our understanding of labour in oil economies and how development unfolded. With the oil age came the expansion of modern wage labour in Oman and also the institutionalisation of particular patterns of dividing, recruiting, paying, and training workers. As we learn from Vitalis, despite oil companies being more capital than labour intensive, *labour matters* in how firms and states transformed the global oil economy.[71] Peeking into this historical moment offers important insight into the lineages of segmentation and the regulation of labour today.

The export of oil from Oman was much later than its neighbours, and the first shipment left Oman on 27 July 1967 on a tanker bound for Japan. This entry into the international oil market was half a year earlier than intended, as geopolitical events in the region and beyond increased the urgency for Shell International Petroleum (hereafter Shell) to export crude from one of its newest markets. The 1967 war between Egypt, Jordan, Iraq, Syria, and Israel in June and the onset of a civil war in Nigeria the next month put pressure on Shell's international market commitments.[72]

Even before oil was discovered in Oman, it began to impact human resource practices through the experiences of 'oil men' and colonial officials managing operations in the Kuwait Oil Company, Qatar Petroleum Company, Aramco, and others. These experiences were directly used to draw comparative lessons on how best to manage, pay, house, and discipline labour in the various Omani contexts.[73] This occurred not only through exchanged notes but also through shared management structures. Petroleum Development Oman was administered by Petroleum Concessions Limited in Bahrain until 1952 and was then managed by the Qatar Petroleum Company, with a local representative only appointed in 1954.[74] Labour relations were also informed through the experiences of Omanis who travelled to

---

[71] Vitalis, *America's Kingdom*.   [72] Clark, *Underground to Overseas*, 2–3.
[73] R. L. Morris (20 February 1968), 'Labour Relations', Foreign and Commonwealth Office (London: The National Archives, 1967–1968), 7–8, FCO 8/588, Arabian Gulf Digital Archives, www.agda.ae/en/catalogue/tna/fco/8/588; 'FO 371/174573', 33.
[74] Clark, *Underground to Overseas*, 31.

Bahrain, Kuwait, Qatar, and elsewhere in the Gulf to work for oil companies. Omanis who returned for work were therefore not only familiar with working in the industry but also acquainted with its practices of racial segregation.

Oil explorations in Oman had started earlier in the century but had borne little fruit initially. The British government secured an agreement with Sultan Taymur bin Faisal (*Taymūr bin Fayṣal*) al-Busaidi in 1923 that granted Britain exclusive rights for exploration in the territories under the control of the Sultan. Under this agreement, D'Arcy Exploration Company Limited, the exploration company by that time under the Anglo-Persian Oil Company, signed an accord with Taymur bin Faisal on 18 May 1925 for a two-year license to explore Oman, with an option for a two-year extension.[75] This was 'the period of maximum British involvement in the affairs of the Sultanate', and the British political agent had the right to determine where exploration could occur.[76] Often this meant expanding the reach into the territories of the Imamate and other tribal federations. It also meant recruiting local guides, and security men, to accompany these expeditions and negotiations. The exploration teams faced opposition from communities suspicious of their intentions and resistant to claims on their territories from foreign powers and the Sultan. George Lees, leader of the survey expedition, described the communities around Duqm and along the coast as 'jealous of their independence', suggesting their expedition was greeted with unease – 'Our welcome could not be described as cordial, nor were any regrets expressed at our departure.'[77] Given fairly pessimistic resource and feasibility assessments by the end of the 1920s, exploration stalled for roughly a decade.

With renewed interest in oil prospects, the next decade under Sultan Said bin Taymur, saw Oman remerge as a site of geopolitical contestation within the Arabian Peninsula, which continued over the next several decades.[78] Sultan Said was especially interested in

---

[75] Clark, *Underground to Overseas*, 10.

[76] Robert John Alston and Stuart Laing, *Unshook Till the End of Time: A History of Relations between Britain & Oman 1650–1970* (Fulham: Gilgamesh, 2012), 264.

[77] Lees cited in Clark, *Underground to Overseas*, 13.

[78] For a more detailed discussion of the oil competition and rivalry of the period and how this influenced local, regional, and international politics, see Jeremy Jones and Nicholas Ridout, *A History of Modern Oman* (New York: Cambridge University Press, 2015), 100–31; and Michael Quentin Morton, *Buraimi: The*

encouraging oil exploration to enhance the economic prospects of the country and also help expand and secure his rule over a unified Omani state. He grew impatient with the slow progress and stagnation during the war years. As well, he had some tensions with the British over how labour should be treated, who should be recruited, and who would be permitted to staff various operations. The reasoning for both parties' choices were generally political and aimed, as explained above, at reducing the possibility of resistance and discontent. What is important for our story as we re-read the known oil history is understanding the predominance of the British in exploration, in setting up operations, and in staffing them. This perspective highlights the role of capital and power in shaping the trajectory of labour market organisation.

Such patterns were already visible in the 1937 agreement, which offered exclusive license to a British-registered company Petroleum Development (Oman and Dhofar) Limited, a branch of the Iraq Petroleum Company (IPC) that managed its Oman operations. The license terms extended to any directly related company registered in the British Empire. After IPC terminated the Dhofar concession in 1950, it was eventually renamed Petroleum Development (Oman) – or PD(O).[79] By 1960, Shell increased its ownership of PDO to 85 per cent and took over operation of the company.[80] The jurisdictional differences discussed in Section 3.2.1 were similarly reflected within the concession agreement. The Company was given degrees of authority over criminal and residency proceedings that made its integration into the British power structure quite evident even though the British officials tried to maintain an image of separation between the private company and the British government's interest. For example, PD(O) employees who committed an offence and were a subject of the Sultan would be dealt with by local laws. However, if a foreigner committed an offence, the Sultan could 'apply to the company to send the person

---

Struggle for Power, Influence and Oil in Arabia (London; New York: I. B. Tauris, 2013).

[79] 'Historical Summary – IOR/R/15/1/731(1)', 191; Alston and Laing, *Unshook Till the End of Time*, 266–67.

[80] Clark, *Underground to Overseas*, 34; For simplicity and style, I will use PDO. However, PD(O) only officially changed from Petroleum Development (Oman) Ltd or PD(O) to Petroleum Development Oman, L.L.C, an Omani-registered company, in May 1980. 'PD(O) Becomes PDO', *Al-Markazi*, May 1980, 5, Central Bank of Oman Archive.

concerned . . . out of the Sultanate'.[81] This striking language highlights the enmeshment of private authorities in governing work migration.

Oil companies retained the economic power, backed up by political power, to determine employment policies within their operation and even played a role in managing the migration and residency of foreign staff. Although human resource policies were the subject of negotiation and contention, both between employees from various nationalities and between the Company and the Sultan, the Company wielded significant influence. It played a key role in shaping the labour market landscape. It did meet some political pressure to hire citizens. Most Gulf governments had 'insisted on the inclusion in the concession agreements of clauses giving priority to local labour'.[82] In Oman, moreover, the dialectic of enabling worker movement and disciplining labour is clearly visible within the negotiations and textual evolution of oil exploration contracts. Even as early as the 1937 agreement, Article 16 indicates pressure to show a desire for local employment, while embedding the right to recruit from abroad. It states:

The Company shall employ subjects of the Sultan for all work for which they are suited under the supervision of the Company's skilled employees, but if the local supply of labour should in the judgement of the Company be inadequate or unsuitable the Company shall have the right to import labour, preference being given to labourers from neighbouring Arab countries who will obey the local laws. The Company shall also have the right to import skilled and technical employees. The Company shall pay to the workmen it employs a fair wage, such wage to be decided and stated by the company at the time the workmen are engaged.[83]

The negotiations around, and drafting of, the PD(O) concession agreement in the mid-1960s, which was ultimately signed in 1967, similarly crafted regulation that facilitated the right for foreign recruitment, while also noting a desired percentage of Omani

[81] 'Oil in Muscat and Oman', Foreign Office (London: The National Archives, 1963), 10, FO 371/168719, Arabian Gulf Digital Archives, www.agda.ae/en/catalogue/tna/fo/371/168719.

[82] Finnie, 'Recruitment and Training of Labor', 129.

[83] 'Sultanate of Muscat and Oman: Petroleum Concessions Ltd.: Agreement, Dated 24th June, 1937, Relating to Sultanate Exclusive of Dhofar', Oil in Muscat and Oman, Foreign Office (London: The National Archives, 1963), FO 371/168719, Arabian Gulf Digital Archives, www.agda.ae/en/catalogue/tna/fo/371/168719.

employees in the workforce.[84] The idea of aspirational labour quotas for citizen employees was embedded within the draft text and mark early appearances of what became known as 'Omanisation' policies (introduced in Chapter 2). Article 6 reads:

1. The Company shall train and employ subjects of the Sultan as far as practicable for all work in the management and conduct of its operations hereunder for which they are suited. As far as practicable 70 percent of its personnel within the Sultanate shall be subjects of the Sultan. Subject to the aforesaid:
   (i) If the local supply of labour should, in the judgement of the Company, be inadequate or unsuitable, the Company shall have the right with the approval of the Sultan (which shall not be unreasonably withheld) to recruit other labour employees and bring them into the Sultanate.
   (ii) The Company shall also have the right to recruit and bring into the Sultanate skilled and technical employees.[85]

The article further affords the Company the right of terminating and possibly deporting Company employees who are not 'a subject of the Sultan' for misconduct, public disturbance, or who 'otherwise render himself undesirable'. It further promises not to employ persons 'undesirable to the Sultan for political or security concerns'.[86] The entanglement of the public and private governance of security, migration, and work is discernible.

Such texts already indicate an awareness of the need to employ and train local citizens and the risk associated with a failure to do so. In the early oil days, recruitment of locals was ad hoc and driven by equal parts necessity and politics. Exploration teams, camps, and early operations all required some degree of local knowhow and support. In the interior, PDO, often with the support of a trained 'Arabist', would liaise with Bedouin communities and with local sheikhs to recruit

[84] 'FO 371/168719', 1963; 'Oil', Foreign Office (London: The National Archives, 1965), FO 371/179828, Arabian Gulf Digital Archives, www.agda.ae/en/catalogue/tna/fo/371/179828.

[85] 'The Draft Revision of the P.D.(Oman) Concession Agreement and the accompanying Tax Degree which were handed to the Sultan on the 21 November in Salalah', BC 1531/19 (7 December 1965), 'FO 371/179828', 56–126.

[86] 'FO 371/179828', 72.

Table 3.1 *Staff composition PDO, 1960*

Level	Number	Description
PDO senior Staff	44	mainly British
Monthly-rate staff	95	only 1 Omani
Daily-rate staff	624	418 Omani

SOURCE: Data from Clark, Underground to Overseas, p. 59

drivers and guides, as well as camp and well guards and kitchen help. It seems that hiring was mostly but not exclusively focused on males, but the PDO history recalls, for example, that the senior well guard at Afar in Wadi Halfayn was female. Well guards and day labourers for construction projects were recruited through the sheikhs of the areas where the well or construction was taking place, providing some employment within the affected regions. Along the Omani coast, in contrast, labour needs were filled through labour contractors.[87]

By the 1960s, some reports indicate that unskilled workers were 'entirely national', which is quite the contrast with later decades.[88] In PDO's account, before Shell took over operations in 1960, day labourers were largely Omani, but the further up the ranks of junior and senior staff one went the more expatriates were employed (see Table 3.1).

Likewise, the American contractors responsible for laying the pipeline running from Fahud to Sayḥ al-Māliḥ, the William's Brothers, employed a workforce of which 700 of 1,150 were Omani. By the end of 1970, 62 per cent of PDO staff were Omani – almost all in general labour or junior staff positions. All but 3 of the 210 senior staff members were expatriates.[89]

The concession agreements also underline the importance foreign capital gave to the right to recruit labour from abroad. Shell's global experiences informed practices of employee management, training and career development, operations management, and of contracting and outsourcing works. The company recruited, dismissed, and managed its labour in particular ways – akin to practices in oil companies and by

---

[87] 'FCO 8/589'; Clark, *Underground to Overseas*, 37–47.
[88] R. L. Morris, 'Muscat and Oman: Report on Social, Labour and Industrial Developments' (30 January 1968), 'FCO 8/589'.
[89] Clark, *Underground to Overseas*, 59.

British officials across the region. As opposed to American oil companies who built on their domestic experiences, with a legacy of Jim Crow laws visible in how Aramco organised labour in Saudi Arabia, Shell's experiences did not grow out of the experiences of the presence of oil in one of its 'home' countries. In contrast, 'its first access to crude oil came through the British and Dutch colonial empires'.[90] This difference did not mean it was any less obvoluted in racial capitalism. Rather, its labour practices took shape through the imbrication of colonial rule and power, and it only began to change when anticolonialism confronted it with a sudden political urgency to hire locals within national contexts.[91] Shell in Oman remained very much postcolonial in the Stuart Hall sense where 'everything still takes place in the slipstream of colonialism and hence bears the inscription of the disturbances that colonization set in motion'.[92]

In the global context after the Second World War and the rise of anticolonialism, Shell began to adopt a human resource policy it called 'regionalisation'. Regionalisation was known in its early days as 'local for local' in Shell circles and laid the foundation of ideas of labour force localisation. It essentially meant facilitating ways of reducing the ratio of expatriate employees to local people in a given region. Prior to this, other than in the United States, Shell only trained local employees for managerial posts when required to by national legislation. It was not until the 1950s that Shell started to engage regionalisation in some of its international locations. Moreover, the impetus of maintaining and expanding its corporate reach during the collapse of European colonies forced it to find ways to enlarge its cadre of internationally mobile managers. Shell's adoption of 'local for local' did not arise out of the 'goodness of the Group's heart' but 'to accommodate rising local desires for participation'. In fact, Shell 'held out against such pressures until managers felt that they had to accept in order to protect the

---

[90] Keetie Sluyterman, *Keeping Competitive in Turbulent Markets, 1973–2007, A History of Royal Dutch Shell*, vol. 3 (Oxford: Oxford University Press, 2007), 5.

[91] It is important to note that Oman was neither a formal colony nor a protectorate of Britain like many of its neighbours. Rather, there were a series of treaties that prescribed the relationship between the two.

[92] Stuart Hall, *The Fateful Triangle: Race, Ethnicity, Nation* (Cambridge, MA: Harvard University Press, 2017), 101.

business'.[93] As Dietrich traces, 'histories of petroleum colonization' linger throughout the debates and struggles for sovereign rights and nationalisation.[94] In labour market organisation, racialised divisions and the struggle for job nationalisation linger longer.

In Oman, they were especially slow but, as I discuss later in this chapter, not without pressure to forward nationalisation and enhance labour rights. British correspondence suggested the practices of contract workers and racial segregation were at fault, despite being the architects of these practices. 'It is difficult to apply such progressive management techniques in the Sultanate of Muscat and Oman', noted the labour attaché R. L. Morris, 'Over half of the labour engaged is employed by contractors, whilst the Company's own labour force is split into three racially distinct groups corresponding broadly with levels of skill.'[95]

The sense of segregation was palpable. More than once I was told, 'We used to call PDO little Johannesburg in the 1960s.'[96] The division of Dutch and Europeans, Omanis, and other non-white expatriate staff was not just in the labour force but also in access to canteens, restaurants, and social clubs. 'In 1969', noted one interlocutor, 'we were not even allowed to have meals with Indians. The junior staff were Omani, the senior staff were Indian and other South Asians, and higher management were white'.[97] Junior and senior staff were provided separate facilities, and it was not until the late 1990s that 'comingled messing was introduced in the Interior and recreation clubs were progressively opening up to all staff'.[98] In May 1968, PDO started a monthly newsletter called PDO news, which they named in Arabic *akhbār sharikatunā* (my company news). Poignantly, an Omani employee reacted 'It is not "Our Company"; it belongs to the foreigners for

---

[93] Stephen Howarth and Joost Jonker, *Powering the Hydrocarbon Revolution, 1939–1973, A History of Royal Dutch Shell*, vol. 2 (Oxford: Oxford University Press, 2007), 133.

[94] Christopher R. W. Dietrich, *Oil Revolution: Anticolonial Elites, Sovereign Rights, and the Economic Culture of Decolonization* (Cambridge: Cambridge University Press, 2017), 89–123.

[95] R. L. Morris (30 January 1968), 'Muscat and Oman: Report on Social Labour and Industrial Developments', 'FCO 8/589'.

[96] Most recently in an interview with former PDO employee, Muscat, 6 January 2020.

[97] Interview with retired PDO employee, Muscat, 22 January 2020.

[98] Clark, *Underground to Overseas*, 109.

whom the Company builds houses, provides meals etc!'[99] Likewise, Abdullah al-Lamki noted, 'I also found PDO very "colonial". There were few Omani senior staff: only two on the technical side – Samir al Kharusi and I. The Company really did not cater for senior Omanis: it was all designed for the expatriates.'[100]

As late as the early 1960s, Shell identified Arab countries as being difficult to plan for regionalisation and internationalisation given objections by some countries to employing foreign Arabs.[101] In Oman, this was blamed on the Sultan who, the British suggested, wanted to 'treat [PDO] as a separate community'[102] Such characterisations were contested, however, by those who noted such images of the Sultan were 'tragically inaccurate'.[103] Still the view was widely held and, as noted earlier, Said bin Taymur was reportedly resistant to hiring Arab managers and advisers, reflecting the shared British concern about antiimperialist mobilisation in the wider Arabic-speaking world. Shell began training some Omanis in the 1960s in line with its regionalisation policies but noted that 'there is no pressure on P.D.(O) to replace expatriates by local personnel, but we are training and upgrading Muscatis and Omanis and will continue to do so'.[104] By February 1970, PDO formed a section aimed at replacing expatriate staff with 'Omani staff of equal ability' and appointed an employee to tour other Arab countries in search of Omanis working away from home.[105] In fact, labour mobilisation incentivised these moves (as I discuss in more detail later). This period of contestation and human resources reform was viewed by a retired Omani PDO employee as 'the start of labour rights'.[106]

Senior staff across Shell's international operations were not very keen on integrating non-Europeans into managerial structures and senior staff – which was mostly synonymous with white staff. This

[99] Clark, *Underground to Overseas*, 59.
[100] Abdullah bin Mohammed al Lamki quoted in Clark, *Underground to Overseas*, 114.
[101] Howarth and Jonker, *History of Royal Dutch Shell*, 2:126–36.
[102] W. C. Luce (5 April 1965), 'FO 371/179828'.
[103] Comments by P.D.(Oman) ltd on individual paragraphs of the report of the labour attaché, British Embassy, Beirut, 'FCO 8/589'.
[104] Comments by P.D.(Oman) ltd on individual paragraphs of the report of the labour attaché, British Embassy, Beirut, 'FCO 8/589'.
[105] Clark, *Underground to Overseas*, 77.
[106] Interview with retired Omani PDO employee, 21 January 2020.

experience was not limited to Oman. Shell's own historical account called a segment of its British and Dutch international employees 'old-fashioned expatriates' and characterised them as not viewing regional-isation kindly.[107] Despite this, Shell eventually pursued its local for local and international training policies. In the Omani context, the regionalisation process was also resisted by senior staff and took longer. 'Not all PDO staff found it easy to come to terms with what they saw as the erosion of their privileged status. Some were unhappy', for example, when the Ras al Hamra residential area was open to the wider Omani community and when the PDO hospital became public in 1974.[108] Indeed, the privileged practices of differentiation throughout the British presence in the Gulf embedded the expectation of elite white exceptionalism in the Company's expatriate consciousness.[109]

Transitions in human resource practices were not only forced by changing domestic political conditions and decolonisation, which made international oil companies adapt to maintain market access, but also by geopolitical changes in the oil industry itself. During the wave of nationalisation of strategic resources, and with the rising strength of OPEC, nations across the region nationalised their oil companies. While Oman did not fully nationalise PDO, it acquired a 60 per cent ownership stake in 1974 after a period of negotiation. It left the remainder to foreign shareholders, among which Shell remained the largest at 34 per cent.[110] Acquiring a larger stake gave the government its first formal role at the table in determining PDO's exploration and production activities. Two Omanis were thus appointed to the board of directors, and a joint management commit-tee was created to oversee operations.[111]

According to Mohammad Musa Al-Yousef, former Minister of State for Development Affairs, this arrangement was taken to align with three considerations: Oman's market-friendly development policy, neo-classical economic perspectives on the role of multinationals in

[107] Quite the euphemism for racism. Howarth and Jonker, *History of Royal Dutch Shell*, 2:133.
[108] Clark, *Underground to Overseas*, 81.
[109] AlShehabi demonstrates this clearly in the context of Bahrain. One telling example is how British protected subjects were exempt from local taxation and subject to different legal regimes. *Contested Modernity*, 142–45.
[110] Sluyterman, *History of Royal Dutch Shell*, 3:31, 181.
[111] Clark, *Underground to Overseas*, 86.

'Third World' economic development, and the belief that foreign capital would be 'complementary to local capital rather than displacing it'.[112] Even this oil agreement reflected the tension between economic liberalism and nationalisation in the country. That is, both the necessity of state intervention to mobilise resources for economic development and to enact policies to protect national interests within it were constantly in tension with pressure for liberalisation, privatisation, and the adoption of 'pragmatic orthodoxy in macroeconomic management'.[113] While Al-Yousef characterises Oman's development strategies and policies as 'very eclectic',[114] they represent the structural tension underlying economic policy in the country.

Labour divisions in Shell's history in Oman clearly show not just continuity from British imperial practices but how much it was part of the development and shape of capitalism in the country and region. By relying on and producing labour that is socially differentiated, Shell and its human resource practices were a key part in producing racial capitalism and in the 'production of difference'.[115] The history of Shell and the evolution of its human resource policies in Oman are very much integral to the foundations and orderings of the labour market. Changes in Shell's international recruitment and human resource practices were strategic calculations to try to move with the times, and the integration of various nationalities and races at different historic moments reflected these patterns. Such changes were deemed necessary to maintain market access and productivity across its many international operations. Capitalist governance advances 'through a process of differentiation and hierarchical re-ordering of the global proletariat'.[116] By changing ways of incorporating and evaluating labour, the company could try to depoliticise its practices of racial sorting.

Ways of categorising work and evaluating labour eventually became systematised. Key in the bureaucratisation and depoliticisation of

---

[112] Al-Yousef, *Oil and the Transformation of Oman*, 27–30.

[113] Al-Yousef, *Oil and the Transformation of Oman*, 56.

[114] Al-Yousef, *Oil and the Transformation of Oman*, 108.

[115] David R. Roediger and Elizabeth D. Esch, *The Production of Difference: Race and the Management of Labor in U.S. History* (New York: Oxford University Press, 2012).

[116] Satnam Virdee, 'Racialized Capitalism: An Account of Its Contested Origins and Consolidation', *The Sociological Review* 67, no. 1 (1 January 2019): 22, https://doi.org/10.1177/0038026118820293.

human resources practices was the introduction of a job classification system in the 1960s. The classification system used numbered and lettered categories to help recruitment planning, to systematise performance assessments, and forecast future achievement potential for individuals. Shell later developed the current estimate potential (CEP) appraisal system, based on research at Utrecht University in the Netherlands, and used this to shape company personnel development policies, shape managerial incentive structures, and even to inform staff how far they were expected to be promoted within the organisation.[117] CEP continues to be used in PDO.[118] Such developmental practices and discourses 'focus on individuals' through addressing individual attributes and behaviours but 'have as their aim populations that are disciplined and productive'.[119]

Shell's programme to develop expatriates through its regionalisation and internationalisation policies became part of a formation and disciplining of a particular corporate culture that was intended to supersede cultures present in its international locations. It is no wonder that Shell embraced Geert Hofstede's cultural taxonomy of world regions and imagined its 'rational analysis' was useful for predicting cultural differences and planning its international operations.[120] Hofstede's survey research of IBM subsidiaries across forty countries in the late 1960s and 1970s was used as a basis to build organisational theory for multinational corporations and has informed management education in business schools, corporate training, and even cultural sensitivity and diversity training within organisations.[121] The separation of cultural dimensions – power distance, uncertainty avoidance, individualism, and masculinity – systematised and rationalised belief systems, values, and practices and grouped countries into cultural areas.[122]

---

[117] Howarth and Jonker, *History of Royal Dutch Shell*, 2:157–58; Sluyterman, *History of Royal Dutch Shell*, 3:242–60.

[118] Saleh Al Alawi, Yaqoub Al Mufargi, and Ikhlas Al Waili, *Oil and Gas Dictionary* (Muscat: Petroleum Development Oman, 2014), 28 and 109.

[119] Simon Philpott, 'The Natural Order of Things? From "Lazy Natives" to Political Science', *Inter-Asia Cultural Studies* 4, no. 2 (1 January 2003): 259, https://doi.org/10.1080/1464937032000112980.

[120] Sluyterman, *History of Royal Dutch Shell*, 3:263–65.

[121] Geert Hofstede, *Culture's Consequences: International Differences in Work-Related Values* (Thousand Oaks: SAGE, 1984).

[122] Geert Hofstede, *Culture's Consequences: Comparing Values, Behaviors, Institutions and Organizations Across Nations*, Second (Thousand Oaks: SAGE, 2001).

It made technologies of labour governance seem natural and rational and helped institutionalise discourse and business practice in seemingly apolitical procedural terms. Returning to Hall is insightful here:

> Capitalist modernity has always advanced as much by way of the production and negotiation of difference as it has through enforcing sameness, standardization, and homogenization ... it is the exploitation of difference – the taking advantage of differentials, and not the standardization of economic variables – that pushes the story of capitalist modernity remorselessly onward.[123]

In practice, Shell used Hofstede in its training and planning to homogenise and rationalise its business and human resource protocols, while justifying and institutionalising a culture of differentiation[124]

The PDO experience follows this pattern. Initially, as indicated, the separation of PDO employees into staff categories largely corresponded with racialised ones. Later, PDO grades continued to correspond with ethnic divisions but were always explained through sanitised job readiness, training, and educational reasons. The transformation of blatant racial differentiation into the post-war period attention to 'rethink its training policy and ensure that staff from outside Shell's traditional employment pools in Britain and the Netherlands would get an equal chance to get into programmes and succeed'[125] both bureaucratised and depoliticised the legacies of differentiation across Shell's locations including Oman. It allowed similar practices to continue with much more digestible, pragmatic explanations. On paper, everyone could be described as welcome to work, and when they did not succeed it could be blamed on experience and education. As Kunz finds elsewhere, Shell's postcolonial expatriate 'codified shifting racialised and gendered labour hierarchies'.[126] Expatriates further 'became theoretically unhinged from geographical origin yet acquired internal fault lines that evidenced the ongoing relevance of imperial power-geometries in corporate management'.[127] Policy and language changes reproduced the similar patterns and

---

[123] Hall, *The Fateful Triangle*, 118–19.
[124] Sluyterman, *History of Royal Dutch Shell*, 3:263–65.
[125] Howarth and Jonker, *History of Royal Dutch Shell*, 2:159.
[126] Sarah Kunz, 'A Business Empire and Its Migrants: Royal Dutch Shell and the Management of Racial Capitalism', *Transactions of the Institute of British Geographers* 45 (2020): 278, https://doi.org/10.1111/tran.12366.
[127] Kunz, 'A Business Empire and Its Migrants', 384.

expectations as Western expatriates continued to comprise the bulk of internationally mobile managers and carried with them certain expectations of treatment and conditions abroad. Change was therefore gradual but latent in the old.

As Shell's attention shifted to local staff development, and PDO to training and development of select Omanis, these updated human resource policies served the dual purpose of image recovery. PDO public relations wrote in late 1978 in the central bank's monthly journal, Al-Markazi, that the management 'sees regionalization, i.e. the process of replacing expatriates with Omanis, as an essential part of their duty'.[128] In that year, PDO reported spending time on staff training initiatives, sent sixty Omani staff overseas on educational or training assignments, and had the first three of its scholarship students graduate from the United Kingdom and return to work.

While continuing to reify foreign expertise and management, this shift did facilitate PDO into something of a first mover in Omanisation initiatives, training, and local content policies. These categories all fit under the umbrella of what have been called in-country value (ICV) schemes since 2012.[129] Indeed, PDO HR policies, and the ICV programme it pioneered in Oman, have been informative and instrumental in shaping broader labour policies and training practices in the country. At a minimum, PDO is looked to as an example for training and hiring practices. In the 1980s and 1990s, PDO improved its training opportunities and started sending more graduate trainees to Britain and awarding scholarships to a select number of high school students for their university education abroad.

Omanisation likewise accelerated in PDO in the late 1990s.[130] Part of this occurred due to internal social pressure. For example, the Shaikh of the *Durū'*, Maṭar bin Muhammad al Dur'ay, had complained that the community were not benefitting from the oil industry within their tribal area.[131] Instead of hiring *Durū'*, PDO contractors along the coast were primarily recruiting expatriates. To respond to

---

[128] PDO Public Relations, 'PDO's Training Efforts', *Al-Markazi*, December 1978, 2, Central Bank of Oman Archive.
[129] 'Annual Report 2012' (Muscat: Petroleum Development Oman, 2012), 27.
[130] Clark, *Underground to Overseas*, 95–96, 106.
[131] The spelling Shaikh Matar bin Muhammad al Dur'ee was used in the book. Clark, *Underground to Overseas*, 106. I retained the above for consistency in later uses.

this, PDO introduced the Local Community Contractors (LCCs) scheme in 1998, which created two kind of contractors, Al Ahliyya and private. LCCs established companies where any member of the tribe could become part owner. Al Ahliyya could accept oil and gas contracts in any of PDO's concessions, whereas private LCCs were limited to the geographical space connected to the tribe.[132] Al Ahliyya businesses were referred to internally as class A and B, referring to the scale and type of the operations. Class B, for instance, received contracts for jobs like cleaning, sand sucking, and renting buses. Initially, these contracting opportunities started with the *Durū'* and *Janaba* tribes; but as time went on, communities in the north of the country complained that the opportunities were only going to a few.

In a few years it worked well. It was easy to start. But then people complained in the north that these opportunities belong only to a few and they benefit only these tribes but it should benefit everyone. Everyone should be able to be a shareholder. There were big complaints that went up to all levels of government, and the diwan also got involved.[133]

Partially as a result of this, PDO developed a super LCC format, which were formalised in the mid-2000s. These were more structured, could include more shareholders, and operated with fairer rules overseen by a government committee.[134] LCCs were much more successful in employing Omanis than other contractors, reaching around 80 per cent. Companywide, by the 1980s, 'the replacement of expatriates by Omanis at all levels within the company became official company policy. In 1988 half of the staff were Omani and by 2000 this had risen to 84 percent'.[135] Local content became the developmental order of the day, and the company provided not only training programmes for local staff but also a local purchase policy to support local businesses.

PDO reflects the wider labour market transitions, both continuities and change. It has been a constituting force of labour market structures and among the most successful organisations in training, nationalising, and local content initiatives. It is likewise noteworthy that moments of transition were preceded by pressure from below for that change.

---

[132] Clark, *Underground to Overseas*, 106–9.
[133] Interview with member of PDO's LCC development team, 16 July 2021.
[134] Interview with member of PDO's LCC development team, 12 March 2020
[135] Sluyterman, *History of Royal Dutch Shell*, 3:181.

Thus, like with the government's economic and labour market policies, public pressure or concerns about potential public pressure have prompted policy change.

3.2.3 Tracing Discourses about Workers

It is also possible to trace discourses about Omani workers woven throughout the history relayed above. Many of these, which are regularly repeated today – (un)productivity, (un)readiness, and (un)motivation – have been long present in the public sphere around Omani labour. Here Aihwa Ong's assertion that 'the organization of capitalist production is embedded in and transformed through cultural discourse/practices'[136] is instructive. This assertion can be extended beyond her application to the factory floor to include how the discourses and practices of differentiation are produced and reproduced with the organisation, mobility, and framing of the labour market. Systems of labour relations in the early days of the exploitation of oil in Oman followed practices in the region determined by Western oil men and colonial agents. Their impression of the value, worth, productivity, and 'readiness' of labour for particular economic functions shaped how Omani economic life was incorporated into modes of domination based on skill level, perceptions of work ethic, and productivity. Well-rehearsed stereotypes of local labour justified hiring practices and the organisation of labour in the country, which have continued to the present.

One can not only trace the lineages of discourses about workers through colonial narratives and development planning but also observe how they have been internalised in both national politics and academic debate. Value judgements and descriptors of labour are visible in the theoretical building blocks of rentier state literature. In this tradition, an impact of rentierism on societies is the so-called rentier mentality based on a positivist, liberal economic assumption concerning a causal relationship between hard work and financial reward as a natural outcome in a meritocratic, production-oriented

---

[136] Aihwa Ong, *Spirits of Resistance and Capitalist Discipline: Factory Women in Malaysia*, Second Edition (New York: State University of New York Press, 2010), 155, http://muse.jhu.edu/book/1369.

economy.[137] I am not disregarding evidence from institutional political economy that highlights the importance of incentives on economic behaviour. As I show throughout this book, economic structures and incentives play a large determining role. However, it is important to interrogate the foundations for some of the claims used in rentier state literature and rethink the causal chains and origin stories we examine. A longer historical view shows that such characterisations and discursive differentiations of workers have been presented as cultural fact in the development discourse that predates the rentier state. That is, in the history we are re-reading in this chapter, we see regular descriptions of Omani citizens as untrained, ill-prepared, unproductive, and entitled. These descriptions run throughout colonial, oil industry, business sector, and leftist internationalist histories and critique and remain so present today that they are taken for granted in analysis of labour market outcomes.

An article by David Finnie on recruitment and training in the oil industry that appeared in the Middle East Review in 1958 captures the essence of this discourse. These identify the training and preparedness of the Gulf citizen as the major challenge facing local employment possibilities. As Finnie notes, 'The question of hiring local labour is closely linked to the problem of training; for untrained men can be put into responsible jobs only at the jeopardy of the efficiency of the organization.'[138] The argument of training certainly had some salience in the days before the oil age thrust the economies of the region into larger scale modern wage labour. Yet, as the article reveals, the reluctance to hire was less about training than about the orientalism and racism embedded in Western political and economic projects.

At the other extreme is the firm but only privately expressed conviction on the part of many Western oil men, including some who know the Middle East well, that training in a 'myth', in the sense that it is impossible to raise a backward people to a level of industrial competence in less than two or three generations. This feeling persists especially among job supervisors who must cope with trainees after they finish their courses. Anecdotes abound . . . .

---

[137] Martin Hvidt, 'The State and the Knowledge Economy in the Gulf: Structural and Motivational Challenges', *The Muslim World* 105, no. 1 (2015): 24–45, https://doi.org/10.1111/muwo.12078; Benjamin Smith, *Market Orientalism: Cultural Economy and the Arab Gulf States* (Syracuse: Syracuse University Press, 2015), 83, 122–27.

[138] Finnie, 'Recruitment and Training of Labor', 137.

Is this sort of thing the result of faulty training? Or of something inherently 'non-industrial' in the makeup of the worker involved, which no amount of training can change? Company supervisors are not sure, but are sometimes inclined to show little confidence in their own men, even when they are trained at great effort and expense by the company. Since for the most part the Western supervisors are sincerely dedicated to the efficiency of the operations on which their jobs depend, perhaps one should not be too quick to accuse them of hypocrisy.[139]

These views bluntly capture the biases and raced modalities embedded in justifying labour market practices from recruitment to training and promotions.[140] They construct an image of 'lazy' local in contrast with the protestant ethic/capitalist Western man who is inherently hardworking.[141]

Such constructions and discourses were widespread in international business circles and embedded within their operational practices. Returning to Hofstede, discussed above, we can see that his 'scientific' division of cultural areas systematised long-held racialised beliefs. In his preface to *Culture's Consequences*, Hofstede himself suggests an internalisation of these: 'multicultural readers and those who have earlier gone through one or more culture shocks in their lives may find that the book expresses in formal terms much that they already intuitively knew'.[142] The whole model is established on racialisation conveyed as cultural difference. Corporate adoption of models like Hofstede's 'revivified earlier modernizing discourses concerning

[139] Finnie, 'Recruitment and Training of Labor', 141.

[140] These discourses combined with the practices of classification evidence a broader trajectory whereby race is a 'mode of classifying, ordering, creating and destroying people [and] labour power'. Lisa Tilley and Robbie Shilliam, 'Raced Markets: An Introduction', *New Political Economy* 23, no. 5 (3 September 2018): 537, https://doi.org/10.1080/13563467.2017.1417366.

[141] A large amount of the political economy of development research deconstructs the image of the 'lazy native', especially in the context of South and South East Asia. See, for example, Ziauddin Sardar, 'Development and the Locations of Eurcentrism', in *Critical Development Theory: Contributions to a New Paradigm*, ed. Denis O'Hearn (London: Zed Books, 1999), 45; Charles Hirschman, 'The Making of Race in Colonial Malaya: Political Economy and Racial Ideology', *Sociological Forum* 1, no. 2 (1 March 1986): 330–61, https://doi.org/10.1007/BF01115742; Syed Hussein Alatas, *The Myth of the Lazy Native: A Study of the Image of the Malays, Filipinos and Javanese from the 16th to the 20th Century and Its Function in the Ideology of Colonial Capitalism* (London: Routledge, 2013).

[142] Hofstede, *Culture's Consequences*, 8.

'native' indiscipline, the problems of regulated and consistent labor, and the difficulty of producing of subjects fitted to the multifarious demands of capitalist modernity'.[143] The presentation in rational and scientific terms seems to justify both scholarship and forms of governing that reproduce past patterns and prejudices.

The dichotomous presentation of Western efficiency and Eastern non-productivity or 'lazy native' characterisations are entrenched. Oil companies' personnel services in the interior regions interpreted the unwillingness of many *badū* who had been hired as guards and watchmen to 'remain in isolated posts for long periods of time with no task other than to be physically present' as confirmation of laziness instead of confirmation of the importance of having work to do.[144] Stereotypes continued through the decades and evolved into expatriate versus local characterisations. The way private sector employers have operated within this space and navigated contracts and labour recruitment is indicative. Reporting on Wimpey's, a major infrastructural contractor, in 1975, D. E. Tatham at the British Embassy in Muscat recalled,

We discussed labour relations, and he told me that his company [Wimpey's] had managed to reduce the Omani proportion of their work force in Muscat from 60% to 15%. This made life a lot easier as Indian and Pakistani workers were not only better qualified but also far more amenable and accepted lower rates of pay.[145]

Discourses become entangled in structural and regulatory realities, reproducing and reinforcing the other. For example, a USAID-funded training assessment conducted by Ernst & Young in 1990 found that private sector managers were reluctant to hire Omanis because of their perceived lack of appropriate skills, inappropriate work attitudes (including a lack of commitment, insubordination to authorities, unwillingness to perform undesirable tasks and slow work pace), the

---

[143] Philpott, 'The Natural Order of Things?', 259.
[144] Dawn Chatty, 'Bedouin Economics and the Modern Wage Market: The Case of the Harasiis of Oman', *Nomadic Peoples* 4, no. 2 (December 2000): 74, https://doi.org/doi/10.3167/082279400782310593.
[145] D. E. Tatham, 'Wimpeys in Oman', (10 July 1975), 'Economic Situation in Oman, Part C', Foreign and Commonwealth Office (London: The National Archives, 1975), 153, FCO 8/2465, Arabian Gulf Digital Archives, www.agda .ae/en/catalogue/tna/fco/8/2465.

high attrition rate of Omanis, and their higher comparative salary requirements.[146]

Such depictions remain present today among employers and in the workplace. Even with the extraordinary improvements in educational and training attainment, the rationalised discourse of training and productivity concerns are used as explanations for the low levels of labour market nationalisation. As an expatriate health care worker who had been working in Oman for a decade felt:

Working with Omanis is fine. We work together well. You know, in fact, the Omani people are very nice. They talk to you, have respect. They are very nice people. The problem is they are lazy or they get tired very quickly. It is not their fault though. They are not used to working. They never had to work hard in their life. The government gives them everything.[147]

Likewise, an Omani manager suggested there was 'a mentality challenge. Omanis are not willing to work everywhere . . . . We are suffering from a syndrome of spoon feeding – a spoon feeding mentality."[148] Some Omani employers also point to training and productivity narratives to explain problems in Omanisation.

When people are not trained or experienced, they become a nuisance in the trade. Then you find they don't report to work or they don't come on time and leave much before time because they don't see they have to have work ethic. One has to admit, culture, education, business ethics, and behaviour – all these things are related to a very young country. Forty years is not much to make a complete shift to become very practical, promising, and productive. It is not an easy thing; You can build beautiful buildings and streets but people development takes longer.[149]

The same manager admitted that turnover and work ethic were fine among Omanis if they had good training opportunities, a future career path, and proper pay. 'Paying a low salary affects the productivity of the job – if the manager doesn't know that, he's shooting himself in the foot.'

---

[146] Ernst & Young, 'Oman: Private Sector Training Needs Assessment' (Bureau for Private Enterprise, US Agency for International Development, December 1990), http://pdf.usaid.gov/pdf_docs/pnabh460.pdf.
[147] Interview, Muscat, 19 June 2014.
[148] Interview, Muscat, 2 November 2011.
[149] Interview with Omani business owner, Muscat, 9 May 2010.

The discourses of productivity and work ethic are clearly difficult to unlink from economic incentives, the structural organisation of the economy, social regulation, and the production of class as detailed in Chapter 3. Controllability and governability become key here. Omanis are presented as having a weaker work ethic in contrast to the foreign worker who appears more willing to work overtime and in some cases under less safe and harsher work conditions. With different governing regimes over Omani labour and foreign labour, incentives and discourses on work ethic become entangled. As one general manager of a group of companies noted, 'you can control expats better. Omanis will leave'.[150] The private sector business model is then not only based upon profitability but the expectation of an unempowered, flexible, and malleable workforce. A chief executive officer of a major industrial project put it bluntly:

Another huge problem with the workforce is the labour law …. As long as they do not change this law it becomes difficult to want to hire Omanis. They are four times more expensive and one half as efficient. They risk strikes, and you almost cannot fire them. The courts always rule in favour of the employee.[151]

Changing hiring patterns is difficult given structural segmentations. An Omani business manager went even further, 'I believe that people used to slave labour will not be in a position to change for Omanisation to satisfy the national interest.'[152] Whether blue or white collar, the expatriate worker's stay in the country is completely tied to his employment fostering an acute sense of precarity. Being fired often means deportation, and this offers clear motivation for responding agreeably to employer demands. It is clear that *kafāla* and *ta'mīn* (Omanisation) have complicated interactions, made all the more so by the separate regulatory regimes.[153] Discourse, incentives, and structural realities become very closely linked to labour regulation and social regulation.

This tension and embeddedness of discourse permeates national policy circles too and extends to royal speeches. In these speeches, we

---

[150] Interview, General Manager, group of companies of approximately 300 staff, Muscat, 8 May 2010.
[151] Interview with CEO of major industrial project, 7 January 2020.
[152] Interview with Omani business manager, Muscat, 9 May 2010.
[153] See the discussion on *kafāla* and *ta'mīn* in Section 2.4.

can see an acceptance of the discourse of unproductivity, lack of training, and sense of entitlement, and, perhaps even more interestingly, both nationalistic and neoliberal undertones offered as remedy to these challenges. On the one hand, the speeches push against these narratives, declaring 'We are a society that is used to hard work and it is not our style to be lazy or negligent, but to responsibly and honestly carry out our obligations. This is the only way we can achieve progress.'[154] Yet through the years, there are also a great deal of paternalistic advice on working hard, where 'discipline and work, on the part of the individual'[155] is defined as 'right' and 'duty',[156] and Omanis are told they are required to 'roll up' their sleeves because 'the great ambitions of nations and people ... are achieved by self-reliance, hard work, creative efforts, wholehearted and responsible participation'.[157]

This nationalistic motivation, toward building the nation and taking part in its developmental achievements, is combined with an emphasis on the individual role. Like the broader developmental discourse, the speeches also responsibilise the individual for the labour market segmentation and employment problems.

We believe in the role of Omani youth in building the country, we call upon them to set a good example in adopting a responsible sense of duty and in seeking perfection in their work. They must be prepared to participate in all sectors. They must not accept a future of merely obtaining certificates of qualification – they must be prepared to work in all fields regardless of the type of that work. Thus will they perform nobly for our country and people. Moreover, we shall never be able to reduce our dependence on foreign labour in most of the unskilled professions unless our people show their interest and capability to take over. God said: 'Man will receive the fruits of his work which are seen. He will be rewarded in full.'[158]

It offloads the responsibility of the failures of the market and the national economy onto the shoulders of the individual, who should have worked harder and been more willing to work for less under various conditions. The following excerpt from Sultan Qaboos' speech

---

[154] Sultan Qaboos bin Said (18 November 1992), National Day Speech, 'The Royal Speeches of His Majesty Sultan Qaboos Bin Said', 286.
[155] National Day Speech (18 November 1992), Al-Said, 287.
[156] Speech before the Council of Oman (13 November 2012), Al-Said, 550.
[157] National Day Speech (18 November 1990), Al-Said, 258.
[158] National Day Speech (18 November 1986), Al-Said, 187.

given at the conclusion of his meet-the-people tour of the country on 30 January 1995 is informative.

The Government wishes to see its citizens employed and, likewise, it is the citizens wish that they should have employment. But when there is work in several sectors, we hear people say the salary is insufficient. There is nothing called sufficient salary or insufficient salary. But there is the productive human being who works to earn his wages gradually, with the help of his efforts and efficiency.

The citizen should not refuse to accept work when there are job opportunities in various sectors – particularly in the private sector which is full of job opportunities – and which still depend upon the expatriate workforce. The work is there, but some people do not like to work or use the excuse of the small salary, or that the employer prefers foreign labour as he thinks, unfortunately, [foreign labour] is cheaper and profitable and willing to work for longer hours. Yes, he may work for longer hours but will the proceeds go to the employer? The worker does this for his own benefit and not for his employers. Has the citizen thought of this? Is it better to engage a foreign worker or someone from his own family, people or society and encourage them to work and be satisfied with a small return and wait for better to follow?

These comments highlight the segmentations of the labour market as well as the internalisation of an individualist explanation for the difficulty citizens face during job seeking. That this speech was delivered in the mid-1990s also underlines the continuity and persistent salience of labour market issues over the decades. The medicine, then like now, prescribes individual effort and responsibility with a view of the broader national goals. The speech continues in the same vein:

The citizen serves himself first and by doing so, he serves his country. If he is an active, productive member of his society, he benefits himself and his society. And if he is unproductive and unemployed, he harms himself and his society. Moreover, he will become a burden on the community and will depend on others. This is a matter which we reject totally. Any talk of unemployment in this country at the present time, is talk of artificial unemployment and not real unemployment . . .. Where is the unemployment in a situation where there are half-a-million expatriate workers and 30,000 citizens seeking jobs, if the citizen really wanted to work? But if he makes excuses, then it is a different matter.[159]

---

[159] Speech (30 January 1995), Al-Said, 332.

Speeches do not only speak to individual responsibility alongside the narrative of productivity but also tap into neoliberal solutions to the labour market and economic development. The Sultan urged citizens 'to enlighten your children on these matters so that they can feel responsibility towards themselves and towards serving their country'.[160] As Chatty demonstrates in her study of bedouin communities in Oman, Oman's development paradigm drew on the strategies of international development agencies aimed at modernising and monetising rural society using, as she says, the catch phrase of 'make the poor of the world economically productive people'.[161] By the 1990s, this slogan was 'just beginning to be sounded out in government corridors in the Sultanate and applied to its nomadic pastoral people' under beliefs that viewed the value of communities as tied to their ability to be 'productive contributors to the country's gross national product'.[162] This pattern reifies the market as liberator, alongside the growth and transformation possibilities brought by oil.

Likewise, religion is invoked to both encourage hard work and reinforce the government's developmental narrative and neoliberal economic advice. In a speech to the Chamber of Commerce and Industry members, the Sultan pointed to 'the teachings of our religion which calls for serious work and self-reliance to overcome hardships'.[163] In other speeches, work is defined as 'noble', 'a sacred duty', the values of which are called upon by our Islamic religion where religious teachings 'urges the individuals to work'.[164]

The true Muslim must be a productive force in the service of society. Almighty god has said in the Holy Quran, 'And when the prayer is ended, then dispense in the land and seek of God's bounty.' There are endless sayings from the Holy verses of the Quran and sacred utterances of the Prophet which elevate the value of work and of workers.[165]

---

[160] Speech (30 January 1995), Al-Said, 332.
[161] Dawn Chatty, *Mobile Pastoralists: Development Planning and Social Change in Oman* (New York: Columbia University Press, 1996), 178.
[162] Chatty, *Mobile Pastoralists*, 178–79.
[163] Speech (18 February 1990), Al-Said, 'The Royal Speeches of His Majesty Sultan Qaboos Bin Said', 242.
[164] National Day speech (18 November 1986) and speech at conclusion of the meet-the-people tour (30 January 1995), Al-Said, 186–87, 335.
[165] National Day speech (18 November 1992), Al-Said, 287.

The use of religious justification, nationalist discourse, and the internalisation of stereotypes and cultural othering underline the complex constitution and tensions inherent to labour governance regimes.

This section has illustrated how a selection of discourses – on productivity, readiness, and motivation – were reproductions of 'lazy native' narratives merging into those of the unwilling worker that have been embedded within the very essence of labour market organisation and development plans. Like the other sections re-reading the history of labour, in the discussion of discourse too, we see the centrality of neoliberal capitalism to Gulf resource-led development. Neoliberalism is part and parcel of a longer trajectory of the Gulf's integration into global capitalism. Its entwinement with authoritarian statism and rentierism has produced rentier neoliberalism as a form of authoritarian neoliberalism where we see the state and capital push to forge neoliberal subjects and cast these efforts in national developmental goals.[166]

3.3 Lineages of Resistance

Labour markets have a tendency to produce contentious politics. This element has been marginalised in Gulf political economy with a few exceptions.[167] Yet the politics of work, who has the right to work, and under what conditions, also sit just below the surface in Oman and have a history of seeping over. At the heart of contestation is the right to employment as well as resistance to the organisation of production discussed earlier as being divided along ethnically defined skill lines. The labour market differentiation we have been describing has never been fully accepted. There has always been resistance to its implementation. Still, as national identity strengthened across and within Omani society, this at times reinforced a politics of difference, an internalisation of stereotypes, and a normalisation of 'racism in which political separations and segregations are seen as the natural *spatial* order of

---

[166] Bruff and Tansel, 'Authoritarian Neoliberalism'; Jones, 'Seeing Like an Autocrat', 33.

[167] Omar AlShehabi's work has been pathbreaking. See, for example, his tracing of contentious politics and labour markets in Bahrain in 'Divide and Rule in Bahrain and the Elusive Pursuit for a United Front: The Experience of the Constitutive Committee and the 1972 Uprising', *Historical Materialism* 21, no. 1 (1 January 2013): 94–127, https://doi.org/10.1163/1569206X-12341267.

nationally sovereign states'.[168] Thus, resistance often assumes nationalist undertones.

With the advent of the oil age and the build-up of industrial development across the country, the problem of how to manage labour unrest, mobilisation, and the politicisation of the population were strong governance priorities of British officials, Omani authorities, and multinational commercial interests. As discussed, there was a great deal of concern around the potential of unrest from return Omani migration, the rise of an educated class, and the potential for sharing experiences of unionisation and labour agitation. It was 'unrealistic to think', Morris wrote in his capacity as first secretary of labour at the British Embassy in Beirut, that revolutionary pan-Arab movements of subversive groups in the Gulf would not make attempts to influence the new oil workers in Muscat and Oman'.[169] He was especially worried by the 'close connection between the oil companies of Muscat and Qatar' and the resemblance of demands presented by the Workers' Consultative Committees in Qatar. In managing discontent, he advised against PDO adopting a similar system of joint consultation because it would, in his view, 'inevitably be infiltrated by political groups seeking to overturn the Sheikhly regimes in the Gulf'. He goes on to say that the 'interests of the Company' would be best served by adopting the practices of Aramco in Saudi Arabia by having 'progressive industrial and public relations and by avoiding any attempt to organise the workers'.[170]

These concerns were not unwarranted, and the history shows the transnational flows of people and of ideas inevitably did influence political mobilisation, the organisation of workers, and the creation of activist organisations like clubs, underground political parties, and unions.[171] As Al-Rashoud has shown, Omanis educated abroad, and those benefitting from educational scholarships from sponsors like Kuwait, were key members of the anticolonial group *al-Ittiḥād al-*

---

[168] Sharma, *Home Rule*, 4.

[169] R. L. Morris (30 January 1968), 'Muscat and Oman: Report on Social, Labour and Industrial Development', 'FCO 8/589'.

[170] R. L. Morris (30 January 1968), 'Muscat and Oman: Report on Social, Labour and Industrial Development', 'FCO 8/589'.

[171] John Chalcraft, 'Migration and Popular Protest in the Arabian Peninsula and the Gulf in the 1950s and 1960s', *International Labor and Working-Class History*, no. 79 (2011): 28–47.

'Umānī (the Omani Union), which supported the armed uprising of the Imamate against Sultan Said bin Taymur and the British.[172] The Omani Union was established in 1952 initially to secure scholarships for Omani students to Arab countries and raise patriotic awareness among the Omani diaspora. It was later in the 1950s that it aligned with the Imamate movement, which was, at the time, increasingly not perceived in religious terms alone as an Ibadi-specific movement but rather one that was synonymous with broader anti-imperialism and national liberation struggles.[173] Elsewhere, Al-Rashoud has argued that the Omani Union was the first modern political group, and its ideas drew on Arab nationalism and Third Worldist socialism, reflecting the members' experiences in exile in Karachi, Cairo, Kuwait, and Bahrain.[174]

Likewise, the later movements in Dhofar during the revolution (1965–1976) 'were fed by circular migration' and many of the involved actors were informed by the experience of having been emigrant workers elsewhere in the Gulf.[175] Poverty, drought, and politics had driven many Dhofaris abroad in the 1940s and 1950s. Alongside others, many were influenced by the struggle for popular sovereignty, Nasserism, and the revolutionary moment in 1956. Dhofaris in Kuwait formed the Dhofar Charitable Association (DCA) to raise funds and recruit youth for the revolution.[176] Eventually, DCA was dissolved as its membership was absorbed into the Movement of Arab Nationalists (MAN). A later split recreated the DCA, but by 1964 the Dhofari MAN and DCA were dissolved to form the Dhofar Liberation Front, the forerunner to the PFLOAG.[177]

---

[172] Talal Al-Rashoud, 'From Muscat to the Maghreb: Pan-Arab Networks, Anti-Colonial Groups, and Kuwait's Arab Scholarships (1953–1961)', *Arabian Humanities*, no. 12 (November 2019), https://doi.org/10.4000/cy.5004.

[173] Amal Sachedina, *Cultivating the Past, Living the Modern: The Politics of Time in the Sultanate of Oman* (Ithaca: Cornell University Press, 2021), 89.

[174] Talal Al-Rashoud, 'The Omani Union (1952–1965): Would-Be Vanguard of the Imamate's Uprising' (Arab Nationalism and its Legacy in the Gulf States Workshop, Princeton University, 2019).

[175] Chalcraft, 'Migration and Popular Protest', 35–36; Fred Halliday, *Arabia without Sultans* (London: Saqi Books, 1974), 362; Takriti, *Monsoon Revolution.*

[176] Takriti, *Monsoon Revolution,* 49–56.

[177] Chalcraft, 'Migration and Popular Protest', 36; Takriti, *Monsoon Revolution,* 67; 'Documents of the National Struggle in Oman and the Arabian Gulf [trans. and ed. Gulf Committee]'.

Popular resistance to British imperialism had been present for decades, according to opposition sources, rather than emerging with the Imamate uprising in the 1950s.[178] The Treaty of Sīb in 1920, which granted sovereignty over Muscat and Oman to the Sultan while granting the Imamate autonomy over the interior, failed to completely quell discontent. There was already significant antiimperialist sentiment. These sources further suggest there were several uprisings in these early decades spurred both by a worsening economic situation and opposition to foreign influence.

Further, in the 1940s, there were a number of strikes notable enough for the British to mention. In September 1942, the Muscat infantry at Bait al-Falaj went on strike to protest the cancelling of rations. Sayyid Shihab bin Faisal Al-Busaidi (Shihāb bin Fayṣal) had ordered that a small payment would be made in lieu of rations but the infantry rejected this idea, and while still standing guard, they refused to perform certain duties like attending parades and wearing fatigues.[179] To respond to this act of protest, the authorities dismissed 119 men, including trained gunners and signallers, from their work. The British political agent suggested they could easily find men to replace these, and the political agents and commanding officers spent several months trying to prevent the fired strikers from enlisting in the Royal Air Force and other security divisions. The names of the dismissed men were circulated as far as Gwadar where it was believed several men may have reenlisted under assumed names.[180]

---

[178] See, for example, M. Fathalla El-Khatib and Issam Kabbani, 'British Aggression against the Imamate of Oman', in *British Imperialism in Southern Arabia*, Information Papers 6 (New York: Arab Information Center, 1958), 43–57.

[179] Sayyid Shihab, and uncle of the Sultan Said bin Taymur, was Minister of External Affairs from 1939 until he was removed from his post in 1945. During this time, he acted in the Sultan's stead when he travelled. The police force and harbour guards under the direction of the military advisor were under his auspices from 1940. 'Administration Reports of the Persian Gulf, 1939 to 1944', British Library: India Office Records and Private Papers, 1939–1944, IOR/R/15/1/719, Qatar Digital Library, www.qdl.qa/en/archive/81055/vdc_100000000193.0x0002b5; 'Coll 30/9(2) "Admin. Reports of the Persian Gulf – 1945–"', British Library: India Office Records and Private Papers, 1945, IOR/L/PS/12/3720A, Qatar Digital Library, www.qdl.qa/en/archive/81055/vdc_100000000648.0x00011b.

[180] 'File 8/72 Muscat State Affairs: Muscat Levies Strike; Muscat Customs Strike', British Library: India Office Records and Private Papers, 1942–1944, IOR/R/15/6/266, Qatar Digital Library, www.qdl.qa/en/archive/81055/vdc_100000000831.0x000166.

Opposition writings identify a labour strike in Muscat in 1944 as the most important.[181] The British too believed this to be 'Muscat's first attempt at an organised strike'.[182] It was seen as particularly significant and worrying to the authorities, because it was a strike of government employees. The British records note that customs employees in both Muscat and Matrah had gone on strike, demanding an increase in wages and amendments to certain regulations in their department.[183] A petition demanding wage increases was presented to the director general of customs on 24 August. After the protestors demands were rejected, they declared a strike starting on the 26th. It is particularly salient that the British account illustrates their attempt at breaking up collective action by advising the protestors to individually ask to settle their grievances. They refused. Eventually, the Sultan and the British agreed to put down the strike and do whatever was necessary to avoid it spreading. Ringleaders were put in detention in Jalali prison, with an extra harsh approach suggested for one, Khamis Abdu, whom the British described as 'notorious'. Khamis was also identified as a dismissed employee of the Bahrain Petroleum Company (BAPCO). Strike action eventually ended on the 31st of August although not all issues were settled until later in September.[184]

According to a speech by Faris Glubb, there was also a notable labour strike in 1948, although this date is disputed.[185] The Muscat harbour workers had set up a trade union and were mobilising for workers' rights. Suppression of labour agitation in these periods was harsh. The political authorities crushed the strike action, prompting its

[181] Opposition sources differ on whether this strike occurred in 1944 or 1945, however the British records date the strike in 1944. al-Ghazālī, ʿAbdulmunʿim, *al-ʿUdwān al-briṭāniyy ʿalā ʿUmān wa-l-Yaman* (Cairo: Dār Al-Fikr, 1957), 31–32; Fayṣal ʿAlī. Fayṣal, *al-Qaḍiyya al-"Umāniyya* (Dār al-Hanā', 1960), 32; 'File 8/72 Muscat State Affairs: Muscat Levies Strike; Muscat Customs Strike'.

[182] 'Chapter VIII: Administration Report of the Political Agency, Muscat, for the Year, 1944. p. 3' in 'Administration Reports - IOR/R/15/1/719'.

[183] Perhaps collective action should not have come as such a surprise. Food prices had been increasing so dramatically during the war years that by the end of 1942 the British commented that 'the poorer classes were very near to famine conditions', 'Administration Report of the Political Agency, Muscat, for the Year 1943' in 'Administration Reports – IOR/R/15/1/719', 9.

[184] 'File 8/72 Muscat State Affairs: Muscat Levies Strike; Muscat Customs Strike'; 'Administration Reports - IOR/R/15/1/719'.

[185] The absence of other documents to corroborate the year suggest the date may not be accurate and may in fact be referring to the 1944 strike discussed above.

leader Muhammad Amin ʿAbdullah to flee to Pakistan to escape arrest and a possible death sentence.[186] ʿAbdullah continued to be involved in activist organisations like the Omani Union in exile.[187] Like ʿAbdullah, many exiles involved in activism had early memorable experiences of economic deprivation and of struggles for work or education. They experienced first hand the consequences of the combined governing effects from British and commercial interests alongside the Sultan's imposed national isolation and tight political control.

Anticolonial agitation and dissatisfaction were high in the 1950s with the expansion of oil interests into the country. These were amplified by the Buraimi crisis, the Sultan's cancellation of the Treaty of Sīb, and abolishment of the Office of the Imamate in 1955.[188] Competing nationalist projects, opposition to imperialism, and labour protests occurred both separately and in conjunction. Tellingly, PDO had employees from various tribal groups who would report on any 'plotting' of anticolonial or labour agitation among their communities.[189] In fact, Eickelman and Dennison describe PDO as maintaining 'a de facto intelligence capability' from the 1950s to the 1970s. Within this context, PDO's labour relations officers would liaise closely with the Sultan's armed forces during crises like the Jebel al-Akhdar War. The general manager would lobby the Sultan to adopt policies in PDO's commercial interest and the 'country's stability', which were understood as interlinked.[190] So, while political authorities were described as 'totally unprepared and unequipped'[191] to deal with industrial labour problems, and especially unwilling to permit trade unions, oil company intelligence in a sense filled the gap.

Clearly, the governance of labour in Oman was very much imbricated with the interests of capitalism and the oil industry. A strike in 1967 of Pakistani employees of Williams Brothers, an American company building the pipeline for PDO, is revealing. The employees initially went on strike to oppose the trial of Pakistanis who had been

---

[186] Glubb, 'The Role of the Workers in the Struggle of British-Occupied Arabia', 8–9.
[187] Al-Rashoud, 'From Muscat to the Maghreb.'   [188] Morton, *Buraimi*, 199.
[189] For example, a report names residents of Khaluf who had reported on anti-British propaganda and plans to cause trouble for the oil company. 'FO 1016/330', 166.
[190] Eickelman and Dennison, 'Arabizing the Omani Intelligence Services', 5.
[191] 'FCO 8/70', 130.

involved in a fight with Iranian co-workers that resulted in the death of an Iranian. To stop the strike, the employees were warned that they would be fired if they did not return to work within two days. One hundred thirty employees did not return to work but remained on strike and Williams Brothers began procedures for their repatriation. While all strikers wanted to return to work after the sentencing, Williams Brothers only accepted sixty-seven and allowed the rest to be deported as per PDO's wishes. What is remarkable about this incident is that these were employees of an American company, and yet the British consulate in Oman not only leveraged their powers to reduce protest by removal and border control, they also produced a no-hire blacklist of all the strikers that they sent to the political agents across the Gulf, the Royal Air Forces at Masirah, the Arabian department, Communications department, the labour attaché in Beirut, and the High Commission in Rawalpindi and Karachi.[192]

As shown, migrants too contributed to forms of contestation.[193] While these strikes were often within communities like the story above, a taxi strike in 1963 indicates that not all worker mobilisation was along ethnic lines. According to opposition sources, authorities had fired Arab Omani employees and recruited instead from the Persian Omani community in an attempt to fragment the taxi drivers' collective mobilisation. Instead, both Arab and Persian workers reportedly went on strike together.[194] Khalili's account of labour protests in the peninsula also recounts Omani labourers coming out in support of striking Pakistani and Indian workers in Muscat in 1965.[195] Attempts at solidarity within movements to strengthen the claims of labour were pushed back against by governing patterns. The British practices of divide and rule that dominated and fragmented labour accentuated ethnic, race, and class differences within the citizenry and between citizens and foreigners. Over time, we see that both economic growth and the survival and stability of the system were mutually reinforcing goals and the practices in earlier periods of regulating, governing, and segmenting the population and labour market participants remained

---

[192] Confidential letter from the British Consulate General Muscat (27 February 1967), 'FCO 8/600'.

[193] Chalcraft, 'Migration and Popular Protest'.

[194] Glubb, 'The Role of the Workers in the Struggle of British-Occupied Arabia', 10–11.

[195] Khalili, Sinews of War and Trade, 206.

central pillars of governance. The patterns, or the outcomes of these patterns, have continued to characterise labour contestation in the country.

This section shows how there has been some documentation of labour agitation in each decade from the 1940s through the 1970s, increasing as more wage labour became available and the processes of economic development and urban drift sped up.[196] British official correspondence in the 1950s and 1960s regularly complained about local and foreign recruitment problems and the tensions and agitation around conditions of work. There are regular notes pointing to labour unrest due to differences in pay between nationalities, the type of housing offered, the segregation of mess halls, and the quality of food provided.[197] In the spring of 1954, for example, labourers employed by Muscat-based contractor Khimji Ram Das went on strike in the Duqm area to protest that they received lower rates of pay than PDO employees.[198] The Shell and PDO histories also hint at discontent among the local population about the special expatriate housing, the highly securitised guarding of these accommodation compounds, the separate company social clubs, and separate food catering.[199] The feeling of segregation and prejudice in the Omani workplace was palpable and the departure point for much discontent.

There was an intensification during the late 1960s and early 1970s. Along the coastal areas in 1967, there was 'resentment by nationals that Indians and Pakistanis occupy the better jobs and receive free messing and accommodation'.[200] When their requests for similar allowances were rejected, Omanis organised a boycott of the celebrations planned for the first shipment of oil from Oman. An Omani employee quoted in the PDO history recalled how unhappy Omani staff were with their poor working conditions and with the arrangement that segregated the celebrations by senior and junior staff – where senior staff celebrated with guest dignitaries while junior staff and Omanis were 'in the Indian camp'. Khalfan Nasser al-Wahaibi added,

---

[196] See also, 'Oman: Report by the deputy overseas labour adviser, FCO', 'LAB 13/ 2740 Gulf States Labour Reports', British Council Archives (London: The National Archives, Kew, 1973), 4/OS192/1973, Kew.

[197] 'FO 1016/330'.   [198] 'FO 1016/330', 166.

[199] Sluyterman, *History of Royal Dutch Shell*, vol. 3; Howarth and Jonker, *History of Royal Dutch Shell*, vol. 2; Clark, *Underground to Overseas*.

[200] 'FCO 8/589'.

'There was a feeling of resentment at the fact that, while expatriate junior staff had their club, the Omanis had nowhere where they could eat their lunch and had to sit in available shade.'[201] The racialisation of workers was simultaneously endemic and resisted.

The trajectory continued even after the political transition that saw the British orchestrate a coup where Sultan Qaboos deposed his father and assumed leadership. Dwarfed by political unrest and the Dhofar revolution during this period, labour agitation has escaped much attention in the literature.[202] Halliday notes that there were strikes in August 1970 in towns across the interior, including Nizwa, Rustaq, and Ibri. He suggests that rapid economic transformation inescapably politicised construction labourers working for foreign companies across the country.[203] Then on 25 August, oil workers went on strike at two locations in the country. One site was Mina al Fahal, which is now subsumed in the greater Muscat area but was at the time some distance from old Muscat. The other was at Fahud, a PDO oil field located in the Al-Dhahirah region in the interior of Oman.[204] The workers 'wanted an eight-hour day, the right to organize unions, higher wages and equal rights for Omani and foreign workers'.[205]

These oil strikes finally prompted PDO to overcome their earlier reluctance and organise a format for labour relations consultation between management and junior staff. Eventually, as a retired employee recalls,

PDO allowed junior staff to form a committee. The senior staff were then jealous and started their own. Eventually these associations took on a role of union. It was the start of labour rights. PDO realised in the end they had to give us rights – our country, our oil – and then Omanisation began in the company with a very few better positions. This was because of the strikes. The government interest was really interested in the business side, not so much the employee side.[206]

Labour agitation forced the company to reassess its profitability potential with a view of its employment practices. A forum for consultation

[201] al-Wahaibi quoted in Clark, *Underground to Overseas*, 8.
[202] For a full account of the Dhofar revoluion, read Takriti, *Monsoon Revolution*.
[203] Halliday, *Arabia without Sultans*, 296.
[204] Clark, *Underground to Overseas*, 69.
[205] Halliday, *Arabia without Sultans*, 296.
[206] Interview with retired Omani PDO employee, 21 January 2020.

was viewed as the best way to get in front of labour grievances, with the hope that the airing of perspectives would defuse unrest. PDO formed Omani Junior Employees Representative and Advisory Committees on the coast and in the interior and throughout the year that followed increased wages and improved access to allowance schemes. These measures, however, did not prevent labour agitation.

In the first quarter of 1971, there were again a number of strikes both at PDO and among various local and foreign construction con-tractors.[207] Yet it was the labour protests and general strike in the capital region at the start of September 1971 that gained the full attention of authorities and the international press. On the first and second of September, several thousand protestors, many workers attached to PDO and to various contractors, took to the streets in Muscat and Matraḥ to protest their economic conditions, wage differ-entials between foreign and local staff, precarious and insecure employment, and the increasing numbers of South Asian workers arriving to take up jobs. By mid-day the strike spread in the public and private sectors.[208] It was described as a diverse Omani strike that cut across ethnic, tribal, and class lines.[209] The protest seemed to have been organised as an inclusive Omani 'us' in contrast to a foreign worker 'other'.

The two days of protests were characterised as 'a violent uprising'[210] in some accounts, as workers blocked the roads to the airport, threw stones at cars, and prevented people from going to work or opening businesses. Agitation rose throughout workers' camps in Ruwi.[211]

---

[207] 'Development Projects in Oman', Foreign and Commonwealth Office (London: The National Archives, 1971), File 10a, FCO 8/1683, Arabian Gulf Digital Archives, www.agda.ae/en/catalogue/tna/fco/8/1683.

[208] 'FCO 8/1848 Annual Review of Oman for 1971', Foreign and Commonwealth Office (London: The National Archives, Kew, 1972), File NB/M14, Kew; 'Oman Inquiry Ordered into Rioters' Grievances', *The Times*, 4 September 1971; Halliday, *Arabia without Sultans*, 295–96; Clark, *Underground to Overseas*, 69–71.

[209] PDO's intelligence gathering the day before the strikes indicated that individuals from over sixty different tribes were joining the demonstrations, and other reports point to members of various coastal communities, including many young members of the Khoja community, participating as well. *Oman: A Class Analysis*, translated from Arabic, originally published by 9th June Studies, Beirut, 1973. (London: The Gulf Committee, 1974), 20; Clark, *Underground to Overseas*, 70.

[210] Halliday, *Arabia without Sultans*, 295–96.

[211] Takriti, *Monsoon Revolution*, 220.

Airport personnel were also said to be on strike, forcing the airline to suspend flights.[212] While the late 1960s strikes and boycott are remembered as being 'resolved peacefully', 1971 'got ugly. The police used force and gas cannisters. Protesters burned cars and trucks'.[213] 'Abdullah al-Ṭā'iyy, who was the minister of labour and social affairs at the time, drew particular ire from the protesters.[214] Some demonstrators marched from Matraḥ to the palace in Muscat. The government declared a state of emergency, imposed a curfew, and used tear gas to disperse rioters. Many participants, and even bystanders, were arrested and imprisoned.[215]

The worry about the possibility of this labour resistance to spill over, and the Dhofari revolution to expand to other regions, was so high that the British engaged officials who had previously worked in the East African colonies and were involved in massive suppression of rebellions. In early 1971, Colonel d'Silva, who had formerly served in the Tanzania police, became the deputy commandant of the police. After the strike, he was promoted to Commandant and then to Commissioner for his role in identifying the strike leaders.[216] By 1972, Ray Nightingale became director of intelligence. He was known for his counterinsurgency experience, both for his role in the Mau Mau uprising in Kenya and for organising the Ugandan intelligence service.[217] After the protests, the government prohibited all demonstrations and strikes.[218]

Pressure did not evaporate but often took other forms. For example, critique lodged against the company in the local newspaper *Al Waṭan*

---

[212] Diplomatic Staff, 'Curfew Quells Disorders in Omani Towns', *The Times*, 2 September 1971.

[213] Interview with someone present during the labour unrest, Muscat, 22 January 2020.

[214] 'FCO 8/1844'.

[215] 'Oman Inquiry Ordered into Rioters' Grievances'; Halliday, *Arabia without Sultans*, 295–96.

[216] 'FCO 8/2215'.

[217] Eickelman and Dennison, 'Arabizing the Omani Intelligence Services', 11.

[218] Clark, *Underground to Overseas*, 71. Peterson too recounts this strike, although through the British and regime security lens. This reproduces the narrative that the strike was solely prompted by 'agitators from abroad', rather than also part of longer lineages of labour contestation. Both Peterson and Takriti discuss the totality of suppression of this resistance, which required the Sultan's Armed Forces (SAF) alongside the police. J. E. Peterson, *Oman's Insurgencies: The Sultanate's Struggle for Supremacy* (London: Saqi Books, 2007), 280–83; Takriti, *Monsoon Revolution*, 220–21.

prompted PDO to purchase more domestically and find other ways to support local markets. Likewise, complaints about access to medical services facilitated the Company's medical staff to extend care beyond Shell employees and include Omani, Indian, and Pakistani staff of PDO and its contractors.[219] What these forms of protest also indicate is an expectation for certain types of economic life and certain conditions of work. There were, and continue to be, expectations that economic development should bring particular outcomes and that these should be reflected in wages, benefits, and future prospects.

The story of resistance in and around the oil industry has often been overlooked because the oil industry is capital intensive. The weaker position of labour vis-à-vis capital is said to reduce the intensity and potential for labour agitation. Despite the lower quantities of workers relative to other extractive industries, the discovery, extraction, and processing of oil and its by-products is dependent on both manual labour and expertise of people working in numerous capacities. Moreover, oil spawned a variety of other development projects, with employment in infrastructure and also in downstream activities. Globally, and in Oman too, labour and class relations have been contentious as a result of their political importance (local and geopolitical), market pressure to reduce costs, and harsh working and living conditions in some of its sectors. It has also been political given the propensity of oil companies to employ human resource strategies to reduce the chances of unionisation and collective action.[220]

Indeed, there has been a long-standing myth that social agitation and by extension labour agitation has been missing from the history of modern Oman. This section clearly contradicts this narrative. Such characterisations can only be perpetuated by the naive or for politically cynical reasons. Each form of contestation in Oman is always described as surprising and aberrant. Certainly, Oman is a peaceful and safe country, but failing to acknowledge a longer history of the contentiousness of labour markets obscures fulsome understandings of history and hinders the ability to address the failures evident in the

---

[219] The company's history also suggests that Sultan Qaboos' more open position in comparison with his father was a factor. Clark, *Underground to Overseas*, 72–76.

[220] Touraj Atabaki, Elisabetta Bini, and Kaveh Ehsani, eds., *Working for Oil: Comparative Social Histories of Labor in the Global Oil Industry* (Cham: Springer, 2018); Dietrich, *Oil Revolution*; Mitchell, *Carbon Democracy*.

labour market. As is shown in later chapters, resistance to policies and discontent with labour market practices and outcomes remains present. In this view, 2011, while the scale was surprising, is part of a larger story of struggle for employment and better economic futures. In 2011, outside observers also expressed surprise by the influence of protests, ideas, and aspirations in other parts of the wider Middle East on domestic political consciousness and aspirations. Yet evidence that such flows of ideas, aspirations, and ideologies occurred in earlier decades demonstrates a continuity of circulation and identification with wider regional and global struggles. While this circulation has certainly heightened with new technologies, the manner in which younger generations connect domestic labour market concerns with global points of struggle for justice and equality highlights a pattern rather than a departure.[221]

3.4 Conclusion

The opening quote of this chapter was an unprompted statement during my interview with Abbas al-Zadjali, who had just shared his own story of employment, training, and struggle in the early years of the last major transition in Oman's modern work history. It encapsulates well the argument of this chapter and the aim of this book. This book takes this notion, of *following the worker*, as the departure point for understanding Omani economic life. Tangible stories of development and perceived development can best be told through the human story of work in its many forms. The pursuit of work and of secure economic futures for individuals and families has shaped migrations in and out of Oman for centuries. This chapter thus historicises the situation of the labour market and economic life experienced by Omani millennials in the present by assembling the particular historical context around work in the modern history of Oman. The politics of labour and employment that began in the late colonial period in the wider region has reverberations in Oman today.

Taking a longer view of modern work history provides important contextual underpinning to the contemporary governance of labour

---

[221] This was even more strongly visible in the May 2021 job seeking demonstrations, where there were some recognitions of global protest movements like the Palestinian struggle and US racial justice campaigns.

and labour resistance in the country. As this chapter has shown, we can trace recruitment, employment, regulatory, and governance practices and developmental discourses from the period of British imperialism in the region, through the development of the oil industry, and across the decades of economic development planning and reform. There is much continuity. Likewise, the record of resistance reveals that labour agitation today is part of a longer account of resistance to racialisation, segmentation, and marginalisation. In traversing this history, it is evident that these earlier patterns have imprints on the regulatory landscape and collective memory of the labour market today.

The official narratives around Oman's economic development, and those in the British and oil archives and reified in scholarly accounts of development, offer one stable reading of Gulf economic development that mostly marginalises the story of work, treats workers as 'lazy natives', or dismisses them as having a 'rentier mentality'.[222] Yesterday, such characterisations were justified on the condition of underdevelopment, today they are explained as an outcome of wealth and accepted at face value. Reading along and against the archival grain becomes essential. By overlapping these accounts with the experience of workers, and with the historical record of contestation, of difference, and fragmentation of labour, a more fulsome, multi-causal explanation becomes possible. Such a narrative not only accounts for the patterns of market behaviour and state intervention that has structured labour markets, but also the reification of stereotypes and internalisation of these patterns into the developmental and business discourse. Taking a contrapuntal reading offers further insights and complicates conventional narratives. As Said tells us,

we must be able to think through and interpret together experiences that are discrepant, each with its particular agenda and pace of development, its own internal formations, its internal coherence and system of external relationships, all of them coexisting and interacting with others.[223]

The practices of labour segmentation, citizenship, *ta'mīn*, and *kafāla* that characterise labour governance and the experiences of workers in the region have been normalised in the region and exceptionalised in the international discourse. Their legacies and trajectories are far from exceptional and can better be understood in conversation with past

---

[222] Smith, *Market Orientalism.*   [223] Said, *Culture and Imperialism*, 32.

and present global processes. Understanding of the lineages of the governance and differentiation of labour in the region requires looking beyond the national and regional space to the transnational and global – embracing translocality. It is not only in the present that national labour markets are influenced by endogenous and exogenous patterns and pressures.

4 | *Promising Dubai in Sohar*
Radical Transformations and Job Creation from Sohar to Duqm

'Sohar is the next Dubai!'

'Sohar is coming!' 'Sohar will be the new Dubai!' These were common refrains in northern Oman in the mid-2000s. Al-Batinah was buzzing with talk of the possibilities. The refinery, the port in Liwa, the Sohar Industrial Estate – these were all major industrial developments promising dramatic economic growth for the country and for the greater Sohar area and its inhabitants. New job opportunities would become available, and the wealth would trickle down. The promise was constantly likened to Dubai, where changes over the previous decade were so dramatic they felt a world away despite being just a two-hour drive down the highway. Expectations were high. The government was investing in productive sectors in downstream activities, and this would lead to more investment and, critically, jobs. Higher education institutions opened in the vicinity to train Omanis from the area, including Sohar University (2001), Shinas College of Technology (2005), and Sohar College of Applied Sciences (2007), which was converted from the College of Education.[1] In the region, a new cadre of young Omanis could be trained in the new and revised education institutions to fill mid and senior level posts. The economic plans and developments resulted in an explosion of job vacancies for manual labour but also for technical and managerial roles. A majority of these posts were filled through foreign recruitment.

Ultimately, Sohar's transformation was dramatic. It went from a small coastal town in the mid-2000s to a city today that is almost unrecognizable. The promise of Sohar raised expectations and, unfulfilled for many, shattered them. Sohar was the heart of the Omani Spring in 2011, reflecting the wider uprisings that shook the Arab

---

[1] Royal Decree 62/2007, 'Organising the Colleges of Applied Sciences (Issued 3 July 2007, Published 15 July 2007)', Official Gazette 843, [author translations from Arabic], 2007.

146

world that year. The shortage of economic opportunities for local youth were pivotal grievances. Ten years later, in May 2021, Sohar was again at the centre of some of the largest street protests Oman has seen since.

Similarly now, Duqm holds the promise of the future. Although it has never been a population centre like Sohar, it has become a cornerstone of development imaginaries in the country's vision and development plans. It is undergoing radical transformation from a small fishing village to an enormous special economic zone (SEZ), with investment from China, India, Japan, Belgium, Kuwait, among others. Despite projects like Duqm promising a multitude of opportunities, jobseeker agitation persists across the country. The development of logistics infrastructure like ports, and SEZs in places like Sohar and Duqm are key diversification drivers that are supposed to generate non-oil growth and greater private sector involvement.[2] Mega logistics and industrial hubs alongside internationalisation and economic liberalisation policies are supposed to promote growth and jobs, but this growth is highly uneven.

By looking at Sohar and Duqm, this chapter grounds the overall argument of the book about Oman's global labour market in material cases of spatial transformation. This concretises our understanding of the material forms neoliberal policy takes and the integration of Oman into global value chains through which both commodities and labour circulate. I argue that millennial citizen expectations take shape in this environment, from the interaction of ostensible outcomes of economic globalisation, neoliberalism, and government responsibilities of governing hydrocarbon windfalls. Their reactions emerge from their perceived right to, or exclusion from, these returns. I further substantiate two points through these cases. First, both neoliberal reform and oil wealth explicitly or implicitly make promises to populations about an improved economic life, which, when unrealised, results in disenfranchisement and discontent. Second, capital needs labour and pursues supplies from the global labour market not only because it is cost effective but deliberately because it is both flexible and controllable. Capital seeks to avert potential labour disruption and hence relies on the global labour market for more than simply a supply of

---

[2] Ziadah, 'Constructing a Logistics Space'; Robert Mogielnicki, *A Political Economy of Free Zones in Gulf Arab States* (London: Springer Nature, 2021).

workers but also the capacity to control workers and secure seamless operations. Together, these findings show the power of labour through the threat of its resistance and the ways through which Omani labour organises. This shows continuity with the patterns examined in Chapter 3.

Both cities are examples of two extreme forms of transformation and social impact – that within a population centre and that which is far from one – and how they both fit within national development imaginaries and global circulations. The promise of drastic economic change that only delivers uneven benefits stirs the consciousness of labour. However, as we will see, it falls short of developing global labour solidarity. The analysis here draws from a combination of ethnographic, interview, and archival materials.[3] This combination allows for a reading from the top down and the bottom up, where the ethnographic texture in particular reveals the anticipation and context of change.

The chapter unfolds an examination of radical transformations in the overlapping spatial, demographic, and economic spheres and interrogates the nexus of economic development planning and the build-up of youth socio-economic expectations. First, it explores the case of Sohar – initially centring on the lived experiences of young people in Sohar and the region during the transformative period and then exploring the record of economic planning around Sohar's modern development. It then unpacks labour and protest developments, shedding light on the politics of labour and union development in the country. Next, it redirects its attention to Duqm and the redesign of its coastline into a critical port and special economic zone more thoroughly situating Oman within the global political economy, global logistics infrastructure, and, importantly, linking up with China's Belt and Road Initiative (BRI). Finally, the chapter closes with reflections on job seeking and labour control within hyperconnected, global spaces of job creation. This is a story that is just as much about global capitalism as it is about rentier states. A focus on the human side of radical transformation through the lens of globalised labour markets

---

[3] Archival materials include Omani government development visions, plans, records, and reports held in different periods in different physical and digital archives and libraries housed at (on a varying basis) the Ministry of Economy (and its various predecessors), the Chamber of Commerce and Industry, and the National Centre for Statistics and Information.

offers fresh insights for the international political economy of labour and for scholarship on Gulf economies.

4.1 The Promise of Sohar

It was early 2006. I was sitting with the women in my neighbourhood of Sohar. There were between five and ten of us at any given time, as women in the neighbourhood passed by to say hello and have some fruit, coffee, and dates. Like most of the communities outside the town centre, on the inner side of the main highway away from the coast, most families lived in a large family home or a small collection of homes, often attached. Brothers of the family would have a separate space with their wife and children, and the larger family would share common living spaces. A shared kitchen would be a separate structure, and, beyond the inner walls, a *majlis* for men's gatherings.[4] The homes were often surrounded by the family farm – plantations of banana, date palms, and lemon. Other times there were small fences or walls around the home structure, which was then surrounded by the plantations or simply used for privacy to separate the plot from that of the neighbours. Most families had goats; many also had cows, chickens, and camels. Much of greater Sohar was semi-rural.

Ahmed entered our female gathering, the husband of one of the three Fatima's sitting with us.[5] He had news – he had finally gotten a job in the army. He could leave his poorly paid position as a driver for a few private companies in the growing Sohar industrial estate. Yes, it would mean he would spend the week away from home in Muscat and elsewhere; but he would come home for weekends, and he would have a regular, secure salary. He was elated, as was his wife. Fatima had a university education – the only one in the family she married into. She was a schoolteacher who worked the morning shift. Demand for classroom space meant most primary schools had a morning and an afternoon shift. None of the other women in this household were employed, and most of the men either tended to the family farm or had irregular, minimum wage employment as gate attendants or drivers in the industrial area. Some of the luckier men of the

---

[4] As more men and women built independent modern homes for their nuclear family, and the city urbanised, the *majlis* would be in the main home structure, usually with a separate entrance.
[5] Names have been changed in all personal stories.

neighbourhood had work across the border in the United Arab Emirates (UAE), working in the police. Gone were the days when work in the UAE armed forces was a feasible alternative to working in the Omani military for those with only secondary education or lower. This door was closed by Mohamed bin Zayed when he became Deputy Crown Prince of the UAE and then Deputy Supreme Commander of the armed forces after his father passed away in 2005; although, the space for this had already been shrinking over the preceding decade.[6] Previously, especially for Omanis living in communities near the borders, working in the armed forces of the UAE was an attractive, and often more lucrative, employment option.[7]

Many of the communities in Sohar, like the one Ahmed was from, were connected to such tribes as the Maqābil (Al-Maqbālī), Banī Ghayth (Al-Ghaythī), Shabūl (Al-Shiblī), and, largely concentrated in Liwa, Banī ʿAmr (Al-Maʿmarī), who had cultural practices somewhat distinct from the town centre and coastal communities.[8] These were the settled, for some generations, sedentary badū.[9] Barth described this division in the 1970s, between the 'settlements along the beach and those inland from the belt of date orchards', as the fundamental division within Sohar.[10] This continued to hold true in the mid-2000s but was rapidly changing. With the plans for the development of the coastal highway connecting the Al-Batinah coast with Muscat, family homes were marked for demolition by the authorities and families offered compensation in the form of a home in the inland settlements. By the end of the 2000s, many of these primarily homogenous neighbourhoods were interspersed with families that had once lived along the beach and had somewhat different living practices. One of my former neighbours remarked in 2012, 'Things have changed so much.' She explained that the people from the seaside communities had

---

[6] Marc Valeri, 'So Close, So Far. National Identity and Political Legitimacy in UAE-Oman Border Cities', *Geopolitics* 23, no. 3 (3 July 2018): 600, https://doi .org/10.1080/14650045.2017.1410794.

[7] Eickelman and Dennison, 'Arabizing the Omani Intelligence Services', 20.

[8] Coastal communities also included the ʿAjam and Balūch.

[9] Marc Valeri, 'The Ṣuḥār Paradox: Social and Political Mobilisations in the Sultanate of Oman since 2011', *Arabian Humanities. Revue Internationale d'archéologie et de Sciences Sociales Sur La Péninsule Arabique/International Journal of Archaeology and Social Sciences in the Arabian Peninsula*, no. 4 (12 January 2015): 8, https://doi.org/10.4000/cy.2828.

[10] Barth, *Sohar*, 68.

come to live among them, with new homes provided by the government. Coastal communities were viewed as more *maftūḥīn* (open). She was referring to perceptions of liberal versus conservative social norms. She explained, 'It changed our culture. Now we women can take a walk together and visit our neighbours after sunset. It is no longer ʿayb (shameful).' This was not the only change. Next to farms and neighbourhoods, small apartment blocks were erected to house the increasing numbers of expatriates moving into Sohar to staff the expanding economic activities.

Ahmed felt lucky to have this chance in the army. At the time, unskilled young men had few options available to them. A position in the army or police would be ideal, while other options included working as gate attendants at the entrances to the new industrial sites or work as private drivers or taxi drivers. College students fared little better. Over the years, data show them faring worse. Unemployment among college graduates has risen compared to school leavers. Data from 2016 illustrates this trend well with a view of the registered unemployed Omanis. It shows that 56 per cent of active jobseekers were college or university educated (Table 4.1). The 2019 unemployment rate for university graduates fluctuates between double and triple the unemployment rate of those with only a high school diploma or lower.[11]

That university education does not necessarily guarantee you a better economic future adds to the malaise among young people. It has been fairly common to find young men using college as a holding place until a job in the police, army, or elsewhere in the government comes though. Students receive a very marginal monthly stipend to help offset school expenses, and this is sometimes viewed more favourably than being unemployed or working as unskilled labour for a pittance.[12] Indeed, minimum wage for citizens in the 2000s only reached 140 OMR (364 USD) at its highest.[13] Other young men studying in regional colleges really wanted to work as engineers or technicians when they graduated but were regularly rejected from jobs

---

[11] 'Monthly Statistical Bulletin' (Muscat: National Centre for Statistics and Information, January 2019), 23; 'Monthly Statistical Bulletin', 24.

[12] This was common among my students at Shinas College, and educators in the various college systems report this remains prevalent. Interview, Omani lecturer at Higher College of Technology, Muscat, 20 January 2019.

[13] Ennis and Al-Jamali, 'Elusive Employment', 12.

Table 4.1 *Unemployment by education level*

Educational attainment	Percentage of total jobseekers
Below General Education	13
Secondary School	31
College Diploma/University Degree	56
Graduate Degree	0

Calculated from NCSI 2017[14]

in the industrial area. There was a growing perception that jobs, on-the-job training to improve skills and experience, and knowledge transfer were being blocked by expatriates holding key positions in the various companies.

English language skills were required to study in most fields of higher education and for working in most professions.[15] Many students from small towns and villages attending local colleges like Shinas, especially the young men, would struggle to learn or improve their English in the foundation year offered at most institutions and would require more time. Despite English classes in school, for rural communities it was hardly a lived language. Arabic was naturally the primary means of communication and social life, and in some communities other local, minority languages too. Another outcome of diverse workplaces is the reliance on foreign languages, primarily English, as a medium of communication. This means that much of the skilled work in the country cannot be carried out in the local language alone, further adding barriers both to attain higher education and to work in skilled fields.[16] Companies in the developing industrial areas regularly used language and quality of education as one of the excuses for their limited hiring and absence of internship opportunities for college students and graduates.

Skilled and unskilled alike increasingly felt sidelined and mistreated as industrial activity grew up around their neighbourhoods. The feeling was already present in the mid-2000s but compounded as the decade wore on. In the early and mid-2000s, economic hardship

---

[14] 'As-Shabāb wa al'Amal', 4.
[15] Law, Arabic literature, and religious studies are among the few fields that remain Arabic taught.
[16] This was also an added difficulty for unskilled occupations in the private sector.

among young Omanis was allayed with the promise of a vibrant economic future. The growing Sohar Port, the oil refinery, and the many factories – petrochemical, aluminium, and others – being established in the Sohar Industrial Estate were just at their beginning. Sohar did not yet even have a large supermarket; and the main shopping was at the market in the town centre, 'food stuff' shops, or a small supermarket called Safeer.[17] Lulu Hypermarket, a chain run by the Keralite mogul Yusuf Ali, only opened in late 2006. And when it did, Lulu seemed to encapsulate the winds of change blowing into Sohar: a large hypermarket, and soon to follow inside its walls, the first Western-style café in the city. Together these introduced a new, modern meeting place, and new job opportunities for men and women without post-secondary education.

Soon, I was told, the young men would no longer have to go to Dubai or Muscat to find good work. Sohar was growing. It was growing fast, and it would bring jobs – industry, factories, hypermarkets, and even malls. Sohar was going to be the next Dubai – the Dubai of Oman.

4.2 A Decade of Radical Transformation

Sohar underwent a radical transformation during the 2000s. This transformation was both spatial and demographic. I borrow Omar Alshehabi's articulation of radical transformations as occurring in 'the spatial and demographic spheres over the geographic landscape' in a way which alters both physical and social relations.[18] In the late twentieth century, Sohar was a small, sprawling town with a primarily semi-rural population. The same was true of the surrounding communities in North Al-Batinah. In the first two decades of the new millennium, the population of the *wilāya* (state) of Sohar more than doubled in size from 107,203 in 2000 to 233,349 in 2020. In fact, the entire Al-Batinah population expanded rapidly – especially visible in the increase

---

[17] Safeer is a part of a hypermarket chain owned by J.P. Kalwani's Al Safeer Group (Indian capital) based in the UAE. It expanded first into Oman and then the wider region, and includes malls, stores, real estate, and manufacturing companies.

[18] Omar AlShehabi, 'Radical Transformations and Radical Contestations: Bahrain's Spatial-Demographic Revolution', *Middle East Critique* 23, no. 1 (2 January 2014): 42, https://doi.org/10.1080/19436149.2014.896596.

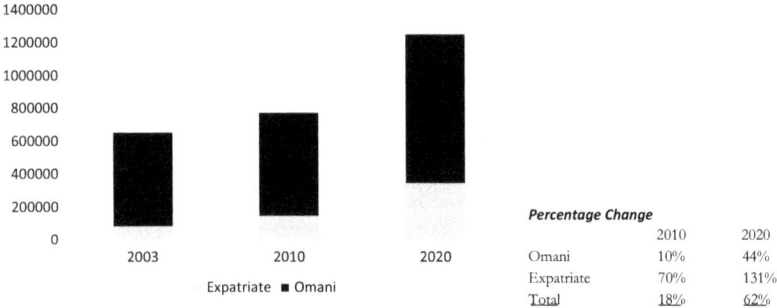

Figure 4.1 Population growth in Al-Batinah (North and South).
Calculated from Oman Census 2010, 2020[19]

in the population of foreigners by 70 per cent in the 2000s and by 131 per cent in the 2010s (see Figure 4.1). The second oil boom allowed the state to maximise investment opportunities and push forward a rapid development agenda. It liberalised the economy to attract foreign capital and emphasised privatisation and public-private partnerships. This all occurred from the top-down, with little consultation or citizen input into the process. But the promise was there – Sohar would be an economic hub. It would bring growth. The region knew what rapid growth looked like, as a neighbour of Dubai.

National development was so dramatic that, by the end of 2010, the UNDP lauded Oman as among the top ten development miracles of the world.[20] Certainly, natural resources had allowed this to happen, but changes were fused with an elite embrace of neoliberal economic growth advice. The promise of trickle-down economics was vivid in the public imagination. A tension arose between expectations of what economic growth should offer but also what the state's responsibility toward citizens were. Such tensions emerge across national economies and become especially apparent in the labour market.

[19] 'General Census of Population, Housing, and Establishments 2010' (Muscat: Census Administration, National Centre for Statistics and Information, 2010); 'al-Mūʾashirāt al-raʾīsiyya li-natāiʾj al-taʿdād al-iliktrūnī li-lsukān wa-l-masākin wa-l-munshāʾat' (Muscat: E-Census Government of Oman, December 2020), www.ncsi.gov.om/Elibrary/; 'Taʿdād 2020'.
[20] 'Human Development Report 2010: The Real Wealth of Nations: Pathways to Human Development' (New York: United Nations Development Programme, November 2010), www.hdr.undp.org/sites/default/files/reports/270/hdr_2010_en_complete_reprint.pdf.

This section traces economic development in Sohar and the Al-Batinah area to shed light on radical transformations in oil economies in connection with global economic changes and the tension between neoliberal reform and the push back for socio-economic protection. AlShehabi demonstrates how the

discourse that emerges around such [transformations] – that mix of viewpoints, opinions and memory that shapes the public and social outlook, although based on the material conditions on the ground, may not correspond exactly to them, and indeed is susceptible to shifting, altering and completely changing. It intersects with what media outlets report, previously held beliefs in society, and the general interactions and developments that happen on a social and political level.[21]

While AlShehabi was writing of neighbour Bahrain, we too see this 'mix of viewpoints, opinions, and memory' and intersections with beliefs, media, and interactions manifestly at play in Sohar. Social and public outlook, put otherwise as perceptions and expectations, grew out of the promises and spatial changes in Sohar and the wider Al-Batinah region. While viewpoints and perceptions are subjective interpretations of change, they are significant informers of experience and political behaviour. This section demonstrates what radical transformations can mean for political economies in terms of discourse and expectations, offering comparative insights for other countries in the global south.

4.2.1 Record of Development Planning in Sohar

This story is focused on Sohar's development in the period known locally in Oman as *al-nahḍa* – the renaissance – a period associated with the reign of Sultan Qaboos bin Said since he assumed the throne in 1970.[22] The adoption of *al-nahḍa* in curricula and common parlance was a centrally promoted narrative to emphasise a manufactured break with the pre-1970 period and especially with the rule of Qaboos' father, Said bin Taymur.[23] This period also coincides with the exploitation of oil revenues to develop the economy. One should be mindful, however, that Sohar itself has a lengthy known history with

---

[21] AlShehabi, 'Radical Transformations and Radical Contestations', 42.
[22] See discussion of *al-nahḍa* in Section 2.4.
[23] See Takriti, *Monsoon Revolution*; Valeri, *Oman*.

multiple historic moments where it served as a dynamic port along the coast. For various stretches in the medieval period, Sohar was the principal entrepôt connecting Oman with Western Indian Ocean trade routes.[24] The visibility of this history faded with the political decline of the Omani Empire in the nineteenth century; and by the twentieth century, Sohar had little of the cosmopolitan dynamism characteristic of Indian Ocean port cities. By the 1970s, foreign observers described Sohar as 'a backwater'.[25]

Serious attention to Sohar's economic development did not begin until the fifth five-year plan (FYP) (1996–2000) and only intensified by the sixth FYP with the start of the 2000s.[26] In the first three FYPs, investment in Sohar was mostly limited to basic development infrastructure like the construction of dams, connecting the Al-Batinah region to electricity grids and providing potable water, constructing roads, schools, and hospitals, and some investment in social housing. Funding was allocated to building the Sohar Development Office, the administrative wing to oversee developments and urban planning in the *wilāya*, and the building of mosques.[27] By the third plan, there is the first mention of establishing an industrial area in Sohar and funding to the Omani women's association branch in the region. Industrial development ideas had a long incubation period, starting at least in the late 1980s.[28] Yet it is not until the fifth plan that details about developing the Sohar Port and activity in the industrial area like the aluminium smelter plant were formulated in greater detail.

As introduced in Chapter 2, the FYPs articulate nation-wide development plans, which, after the publication of Vision 2020 in 1995, were geared to bring Oman in intervals toward the development goals laid out in this long-term vision for Oman's future. The fifth FYP was the first step toward Vision 2020. While nation-wide projects and those in the capital area received the bulk of investment attention, by

[24] Calvin H. Allen, *Oman: The Modernization of the Sultanate* (London; New York: Routledge, 1987), 29–42.
[25] Unni Wikan, *Behind the Veil in Arabia: Women in Oman* (Chicago: Universty of Chicago Press, 1982), 27.
[26] See Chapter 2 for further discussion of development plans on the national scale.
[27] 'The FYP 1976–1980'; 'The Second FYP 1981–1986'; 'The Third FYP 1986–1990'.
[28] 'The Third FYP 1986–1990'; discussion with retired minister 4 January 2020.

Table 4.2 *Regional distribution of total investment programme in the 2000s (%)*

Governorate	Sixth FYP (2001–2005)	Seventh FYP (2006–2010)
Muscat	10.2	19.3
Al-Batinah	48.5	65.7
Musandam	0.5	0.6
Al-Dhahirah	1.1	1.1
Al-Dakhiliyyah	2.7	6.7
Al-Sharqiyyah	7.9	3.6
Al-Wusta	0.9	1.0
Dhofar	3.8	6.9

Data from Sixth and Seventh FYP[29]

the sixth FYP several regions outside the capital area were targeted for more economic development attention – Al-Batinah chief among them. In fact, 65 per cent of the total public sector investment in major industrial projects was concentrated in Al-Batinah in the sixth FYP; 72 per cent of which was to be financed by foreign borrowing.[30]

Attention to Al-Batinah grew over the 2000s, with a significant investment jump from previous plans (see Table 4.2). In the fifth FYP, for example, Al-Batinah was slated to receive just 9.5 per cent of total investment.[31] This increased to 48.5 per cent in the first half of the decade and to 65.7 per cent in the latter half. These levels dwarfed all other regions, including Muscat. The Sohar Port, an oil refinery, and the Sohar Industrial Estate, including an aluminium smelter plant, methanol gas project, and a polypropylene project, among others, were all under development or in early stages of operation.

Investment in the sixth FYP moved in tandem with a doubling down of the privatisation drive (first approved in Vision 2020). This period coincides with what Hanieh has characterised as the intensification phase of privatisation in the wider MENA.[32] Despite not being subject to structural adjustment on the basis of IMF conditionality, Oman's foreign borrowing and development pursuits prompted its

---

[29] 'The Sixth FYP 2001–2005, Vol I', 131; 'The Seventh FYP 2006–2010', 350. Al-Buraimi was not included in the source data.
[30] 'The General Framework of the Sixth Five-Year Development Plan 2001–2005, Volume I' (Muscat: Ministry of National Economy, February 2002), 150.
[31] 'The Fifth FYP 1996–2000', 429.   [32] Hanieh, *Lineages of Revolt*.

commitment to creating attractive markets. IMF article IV consult-
ations, advice from the World Bank, and recommendations from
global consultants all coalesced around the idea not only of diversify-
ing the economy but creating more space for privatisation that would
stimulate growth in the new industrial areas.

Sohar was a petri dish, an intensified concentration of radical transformation in a condensed period. In the sixth FYP, 46.3 per cent of the
private sector investments in Oman were targeted at the Al-Batinah
region, more than double the next closest region (Dhofar). By the
second half of the 2000s, the plan was for private sector investment
in national projects to reach 56.4 per cent of all targeted investment;[33]
81.6 percent was directed at Al-Batinah, primarily because of the mega
industrial projects concentrated in the greater Sohar area.[34] Al-Batinah
was targeted for growth but growth of a particular kind –
private-sector led.[35] National development planning was putting in
motion the advice it had been receiving from international financial
institutions over the previous decades.

This push toward liberalisation and privatisation had been encouraged in the World Bank report that formed the research basis underpinning Vision 2020[36] and spurred by the adoption of the privatisation
policy in the commercial law (Royal Decree 42/96).[37] The privatisation
policies detailed the gradual privatisation of productive and service
activities like electricity, sewage, and post. Foreign investment and
participation in this process was encouraged. Altogether, it was
believed that increasing privatisation would usher in sustainable development, increase rates of growth, and distribute developmental outcomes across all regions and segments of society.[38] Nineteen ninety-
eight was named the 'year of the private sector' in the lead up to joining

---

[33] 'The Sixth FYP 2001–2005, Vol I', 162.
[34] 'The Seventh FYP 2006–2010', 367–68.
[35] Including, and primarily, multinational companies and MNCs in conjunction
    with state-owned enterprises, public-private partnerships (PPPs), and large
    regional and local companies and contractors. This private sector–led agenda is
    therefore less connected to the family enterprises in the wider national
    private sector.
[36] World Bank, 'Sultanate of Oman'.
[37] Royal Decree 42/1996, 'Approving the Privatisation Policies and Controls
    (Issued 8 June 1996, Published 15 June 1996)', Official Gazette 577, [author
    translations from Arabic], 1996.
[38] Royal Decree 42/1996.

the World Trade Organisation (WTO) in 2000.[39] This period was also marked by the formation of the Greater Arab Free Trade Agreement, the Indian Ocean Rim Association, and the development of the Gulf customs union within the GCC.[40] Capping it off, in 2006 Oman signed a Free Trade Agreement (FTA) with the United States, which came into effect in 2009. Oman is one of two GCC countries, and one of five Middle Eastern countries among a global total of only twenty nations that have a bilateral FTA with the United States.[41] By the middle of 2011, Oman was lauded as leading the region in the reform and privatisation of electricity and water sectors and was called a 'pioneer of private power in the GCC'.[42]

The government remained aware of the possible negative repercussions of privatisation and liberalisation on the population and attempted to design some regulations that would ameliorate these. This caution was present in policy language concerning the importance of developing export-oriented areas (like Sohar Port), which were careful to mention the indirect returns from forward and backward linkages from investments in major industries within Sohar.[43] The focus on softening the blow of privatisation and liberalisation was more loudly discernible in Omanisation efforts aimed at securing jobs for the local workforce, but there were others as well. For example, to respond to the status of Omani workers affected by privatisation processes in the electrical power generation and desalination activities, the government crafted recruitment regulation and legislated

---

[39] Al-Said, 'The Royal Speeches of His Majesty Sultan Qaboos Bin Said', 390.
[40] 'The Seventh FYP 2006–2010', 125; Anja Zorob, 'Intraregional Economic Integration: The Cases of GAFTA and MAFTA', in *Beyond Regionalism? Regional Cooperation, Regionalism and Regionalization in the Middle East*, ed. Cilja Harders and Matteo Legrenzi (Farnham: Ashgate, 2008), 169–83; Fred H. Lawson, 'Geo-Political Complications of US Free Trade Agreements with Gulf Arab Countries', in *Shifting Geo-Economic Power of the Gulf: Oil, Finance and Institutions*, ed. Matteo Legrenzi and Bessma Momani (Farnham: Ashgate, 2011), 199–210.
[41] 'Free Trade Agreements', Office of the United States Trade Representative, accessed 13 July 2021, https://ustr.gov/trade-agreements/free-trade-agreements; Nadira Lalji, 'Labor Law Matters', *Harvard International Review* 28, no. 3 (Fall 2006): 12–13.
[42] 'Oman Leads Gulf States in Reform and Privatization of Electricity and Water Sectors', *Power Engineering International*, 30 June 2011, www .powerengineeringint.com/news/oman-leads-gulf-states-in-reform-and-privatization/.
[43] 'The Sixth FYP 2001–2005, Vol I', 132.

employment transfer rights from the government to successor entities. This stipulated that salaries, allowances, and other privileges should not be less than those working for a government body prior to transfer.[44] This marks a trend that would continue, where the government introduces an economic reform and then when confronted by dissent either rolls it back or creates new, costly measures to temper its socioeconomic impact.[45]

The emphasis that 'the private sector should be the main source of securing rewarding employment opportunities for citizens' intensified over time.[46] The fifth five-year plan projected 93,000 job opportunities for Omanis in the private sector but by the end of the plan period only 21,700 opportunities materialised.[47] The period covered by the sixth five-year plan had more success. The new employment opportunities for citizens increased to 104,400 compared to the planned 99,000 (an increase of 5.5 per cent). However, the rate of Omanisation remained below the target as the number of expatriates added to the labour market continued to expand with the growth in the economy.[48] Thus, the sense that economic growth was not correspondingly benefiting nationals persisted. It was in this space that privatisation was also linked with promoting the creation of small- and medium-sized enterprises and entrepreneurship among Omanis. SME promotion was explicitly tied with job creation and Omanisation in the 7th plan.[49] This mechanism of developing self-employment is discussed at greater length in Chapter 6.

The promise of these ambitious plans raised expectations but ultimately faced a grimmer reality. Within a global economy and a global labour market that draws on international pools of labour, economic outcomes are not bound within a national space. Inputs and interests from multiple spheres of governance and finance impact how economic

---

[44] Royal Decree 78/2004, 'Promulgating the Law for the Regulation and Privatisation of the Electricity and Related Water Sector (Issued 20 July 2004, Published 1 August 2004)', Official Gazette 772, 2004.

[45] Crystal A. Ennis and Said Al-Saqri, 'Oil Price Collapse and the Political Economy of the Post-2014 Economic Adjustment in the Sultanate of Oman', in *Oil and the Political Economy in the Middle East: Post-2014 Adjustment Policies of the Arab Gulf and Beyond*, ed. Martin Beck and Thomas Richter (Manchester: Manchester University Press, 2021), 79–101.

[46] 'The Seventh FYP 2006–2010', 461.

[47] 'The Sixth FYP 2001–2005, Vol I', 50.

[48] 'The Seventh FYP 2006–2010', 184.   [49] 'The Seventh FYP 2006–2010', 427.

development occurs and how and whom it impacts. Just like in earlier historical moments discussed in Chapter 3, the tensions of economic change of the early twenty-first century in Sohar played out in the labour market. The governance of labour, likewise, continued to be shaped by political actors and economic interests internal and external to Oman.

4.2.2 Fall of Expectations, Spring of Discontent

The radical transformation of the greater Sohar area was extensive, even if it never ultimately reached Dubai forms of change. The economic indicators looked good for Oman. The seventh FYP assessed the progress of the prior period positively – pointing out its annual GDP growth (4.7 per cent) exceeded the target rate (3 per cent) – and this growth was based primarily on growth in non-oil industries.[50] From a policy perspective, employment outcomes were improving in terms of Omanis joining the private sector in various low-skilled professions like security gate attendants, drivers, and in production or general services. This was quite visible across Al-Batinah in the 2000s, where one was just as likely to encounter an Omani fuel pump attendant or cashier as an expatriate. During this period, Amal Sachedina observed the same pattern in the interior city of Nizwa. She notes 'Oman was different' alluding to comparisons with some of its wealthier neighbours where these occupations were uncommon among citizens.[51] Yet the low pay and weak benefits neither inspired long-term commitment to such jobs nor quelled feelings of missing out on the benefits of growth. Minimum wages could not support marriage and independent family living.

Sohar Port and Freezone emerged as a crucial site of the transformation of the greater Sohar area and North Al-Batinah more broadly. The construction of this massive zone of economic development within the larger industrial area created growth and opportunities. Yet it equally generated massive expectations and frustration with the limits to the breadth of beneficiaries. Sohar Port, which was initially established in 2004 as a joint venture between the Omani government and the Port of Rotterdam, officially became Sohar Port and Freezone by

---

[50] 'The Seventh FYP 2006–2010', 18.
[51] Sachedina, *Cultivating the Past, Living the Modern*, 3.

royal decree in late December 2010.[52] This created a liberalised space governed under a separate regulatory framework, offering corporate tax exemptions, full foreign ownership, no duties or income tax, low capital requirements, and lower levels of Omanisation. The principal objective is creating an attractive business and investment environment that supersedes wider national requirements. Labour is one such space with relaxed regulations. In all sectors within the freezone, investors may hire up to 85 per cent of their employees from abroad but are incentivised by a longer tax holiday should they achieve higher levels of Omanisation.[53] The crafting of the port guidelines are marked by undertones of the liberalisation-protection tension. That is, a majority of the measures look for ways to liberalise and privatise activities, but limited measures are instated to protect sensitive categories like national labour and the environment. In general, the protective-aimed regulation seems weak and performative and often wrapped up within corporate social responsibility (CSR) initiatives. Corporations around the world espouse CSR as a way to give back to local communities but are widely critiqued for using CSR to 'wash' negative records and/or images of their irresponsibility.[54]

Vital to the Sohar story being told here is the disconnect between the promised outcomes of such massive spatial transformation and the lived experience of unemployment and underemployment in the region. A package of social, economic, and environmental costs are visceral parts of this lived experience of change. There are several powerful

---

[52] Royal Decree 123/2010, 'Establishing the Free Zone in Sohar (Issued 20 December 2010, Published 1 January 2011)', Official Gazette 926, [author translations from Arabic], 2011.

[53] Unlike some other ports in the region, the Sohar Port and Freezone was still subject to Omani labour law and had rules around wages and positions reserved for Omani nationals. 'Sohar Freezone Investor Guide (Version 1)' (Sohar Port/ Freezone, 2019); 'Sohar Freezone LLC Guidance Notes on Labour and Visas' (Sohar Port/Freezone, 2019); 'Sohar Port Information Guide' (Sohar Port/ Freezone, 2021), https://soharportandfreezone.com/PDF/Sohar%20Port% 20Information%20Guide%20V9_single_page.pdf.

[54] Charles Kang, Frank Germann, and Rajdeep Grewal, 'Washing Away Your Sins? Corporate Social Responsibility, Corporate Social Irresponsibility, and Firm Performance', *Journal of Marketing* 80, no. 2 (1 March 2016): 59–79, https://doi.org/10.1509/jm.15.0324; Rosie Walters, 'Varieties of Gender Wash: Towards a Framework for Critiquing Corporate Social Responsibility in Feminist IPE', *Review of International Political Economy* 29, no. 5 (3 September 2022): 1577–600, https://doi.org/10.1080/09692290.2021 .1935295.

examples that manifest the contentious politics and disenfranchisement prompted by this transformation –namely, unemployment and under-employment – and environmental degradation, land reclamation, and dispossession. These examples further illustrate the ways through which privatisation and economic disembeddedness are equally parts of radical spatial and economic transformations.

The citizens of Liwa provide a vivid illustration (Map 4.1). The town is situated along the coast just north of, and contiguous with, Sohar. It partially encompasses the Sohar Port and Freezone. Just inland from Liwa sits the Sohar Industrial Estate in Majan, which notably houses, among other industrial operations, the Oman Aluminium Smelter, which was established in 2004 and exported its first shipment in July 2008.[55] Life in Liwa was disrupted by the port and freezone's construction, expansion, and concomitant environmental outcomes. In the mid-2000s, many of the inhabitants of the greater Sohar area, and certainly most of those involved in the port and industries in the Industrial Area, heard of the complaints and campaigns of the residents who lived along the coast. They protested the pollution that would wash ashore as companies dumped chemicals and waste too close to shore. They protested emissions, water and air quality, and there were discussions of increases in cancer cases and of forced displacement. They advocated for stricter enforcement of environmental regulation while complaining about the impact on the health, livelihood, and lifestyles of their communities connected to the sea. The concerns received more widespread attention by 2009 and 2010, when local complaints were reported nationally on TV, radio, and social media.[56]

---

[55] Oman Aluminium Smelter was set up in 2004. It is a joint venture between what is now called OQ (an Omani state-owned investment company that is an umbrella company that integrated Oman Oil, Orpic, Oman Oil Company Exploration and Production, Oman Gas Company, Duqm Refinery, Salalah Methanol Company, Oman Trading International, OXEA, and Salalah Liquified Petroleum Gas), Abu Dhabi National Energy Company PJSC-TAQA, and Rio Tinto, an Anglo-Australian multinational.

[56] Guests Musalam Al-Shahri and Habiba Al-Hinai interviewed by 'Barnāmaj nuqṭat niẓām ḥawl qaḍiyat talawuth'. idhāʿat al-wiṣāl, May 2010), www.youtube.com/watch?v=0B16jA0xrA0; Habiba Al-Hinai, . 'Silsilat Anīn al-Jidrān: Ghaḍafān taʿin'. Omani Association for Human Rights. Anīn al-Jidrān (blog), 8 April 2010, https://omanhr.org; Valeri, 'The Ṣuḥār Paradox'.

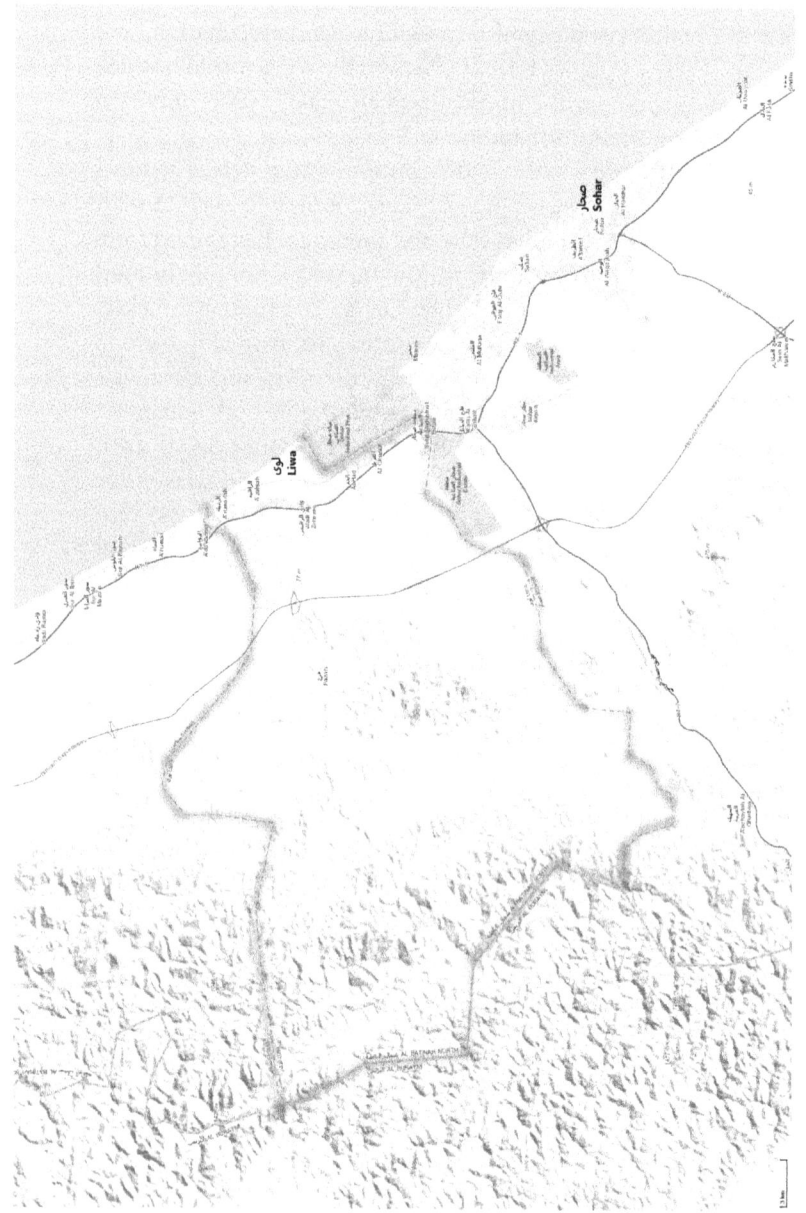

Map 4.1 Liwa in relation to Sohar Port and Freezone. Indicative boundaries of the *wilāya* of Liwa.

164

Map 4.2 Map of Sohar Port and Freezone
Sohar Port and Freezone (2023)
Used with permission. https://soharportandfreezone.com

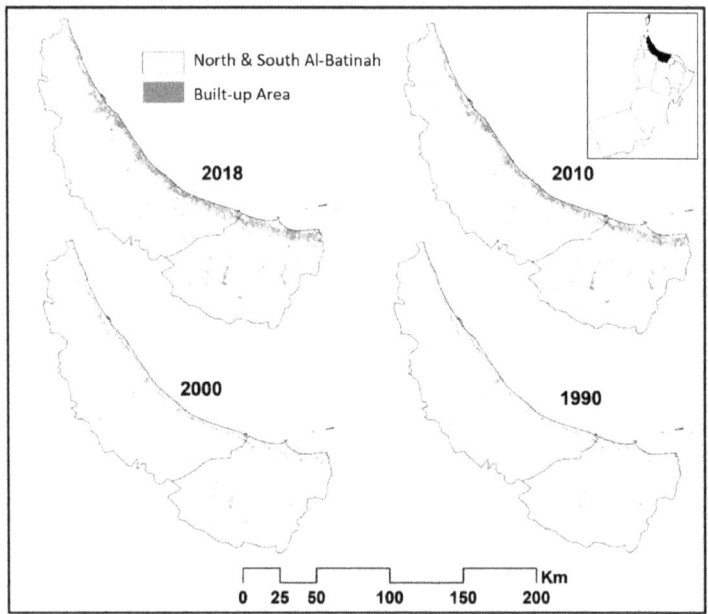

Figure 4.2 Urban transformation in the governorates of North and South Al-Batinah (1990–2018).
Adapted from Abulibdeh et al., 2021[57]

Increasingly, studies have confirmed the legitimacy of these concerns, showing that the rapid economic development and increased urbanisation has had significant impacts on the environment and health across Al-Batinah North (Figure 4.2). Some studies have documented an increase in adverse acute health effects in those living near Sohar industrial zone.[58] Other research identifies growing agricultural change and environmental vulnerability of coastal Al-Batinah to development projects.[59] There has reportedly been a

[57] Ammar Abulibdeh et al., 'Spatiotemporal Mapping of Groundwater Salinity in Al-Batinah, Oman', *Groundwater for Sustainable Development* 12 (1 February 2021): 100551, https://doi.org/10.1016/j.gsd.2021.100551.
[58] Adil Al-Wahaibi and Ariana Zeka, 'Health Impacts from Living Near a Major Industrial Park in Oman', *BMC Public Health* 15, no. 524 (2015), https://doi .org/10.1186/s12889–015-1866-3.
[59] E.g., B. S. Choudri et al., 'Relative Vulnerability of Coastal Wilayats to Development: A Study of Al-Batinah North, Oman', *Journal of Coastal Conservation* 19, no. 1 (2015): 51–57.

large reduction in traditional cropped landholdings, usually fruit trees and date palm plantations, in coastal Al-Batinah between 2004 and 2013 at the same time that greenhouse vegetable production has increased.[60]

Pollution and chemical discharge are regulated in Oman, and the 2001 royal decree on the conservation of the environment and preservation of pollution explicitly banned pollution and dumping.[61] By June 2005, a ministerial decree regulated the costs and procedures for acquiring permits for marine waste discharging.[62] Yet in the early years of port operation, there were no available facilities for industrial wastewater treatment, sewage treatment plants, or process streams. Waste was mostly discharged through the cooling water return channel, which was designed to accommodate the discharge of cooling water and brine from desalination units. Estimates suggest that approximately 90 per cent of hazardous industrial waste in Oman is generated in the Sohar area, and there are a lack of disposal options available.[63] A majority of industrial waste is stored in the industrial estates.[64]

There were a variety of initiatives in this period to try to get companies to follow protocols and demonstrate official responses to environmental concerns. By May 2008, the Port of Rotterdam announced

[60] Kathiya Al-Aufi et al., 'Analysis of Crops Cultivation Trend: A Shifting Scenario in a Coastal Wilayat, Oman', *Environment, Development and Sustainability* 22, no. 3 (1 March 2020): 2685–98, https://doi.org/10.1007/s10668-019-00309-4.

[61] Royal Decree 114/2001, 'Promulgating the Law on the Protection of the Environment and the Prevention of Pollution (Issued 14 November 2001, Published 17 November 2001)', Official Gazette 707, [author translations from Arabic], 2001.

[62] Ministry of Regional Municipalities, Environment, and Water Resources: Ministerial Decision 159/2005, 'Promulgating Regulation for the Discharge of Liquid Effluents into the Marine Environment (Issued 19 June 2005, Published 2 July 2005)', Official Gazette 794, [author translations from Arabic], 2005.

[63] Conrad Prabhu, 'Major Industrial Hazardous Waste Treatment Project Planned in Liwa in Oman', *Zawya*, 10 May 2015, www.zawya.com/mena/en/business/story/Major_industrial_hazardous_waste_treatment_project_planned_in_Liwa_in_Oman-ZAWYA20150510051307/; 'Briefings from Oman Waste Management' (Ithraa: The Public Authority for Investment Promotion and Export Development, December 2016), https://ithraa.om/portals/0/IthraaPDF/Brochures/PDF/ithraa_briefings_waste_engAW.pdf.

[64] By 2013, a sewage treatment plant and a wastewater effluent collection and treatment system were being constructed. And from July of that year all waste discharge was to be banned and permits stopped except for brine and cooling water.

that an Omani ministerial delegation signed an agreement with the Environmental Protection Agency Rijnmond (the Netherlands) to set up an environmental protection agency in Sohar.[65] To help companies manage the evolving environmental regulations, the Sohar Port and Freezone offered guidance notes to companies in their premises, including guidance notes on chemical substances (2011), environmental performance reporting (July 2011), requirements for environmental impact assessments, statements, and safety reporting (January 2011), waste management (October 2010), Environmental Review for Sohar Freezone Companies (April 2011), Industrial safety (February 2011), handling turtles in Sohar Industrial Port (August 2009), metal scrap (May 2013), General Environmental Regulations (May 2013), incident reporting to the Sohar Environmental Unit (March 2013), industrial waste storage (January 2012), Flaring (September 2011), and Water Management (April 2012) with details on discharge procedures.[66]

This moment also led to a flurry of CSR initiatives around both the environment and 'in-country value' (ICV).[67] Local environmental and employment protection serve as as packaged areas to exhibit national impact. For example, Vale and the Ministry of Agriculture and Fisheries cooperated on a project to increase marine life along the coast of Liwa by installing artificial reefs in coordination with local fishermen.[68] Marawid, the largest private mining company in Oman, won the Oman Green Innovation Award in June 2011 for its Tailings

---

[65] 'Rotterdam/Oman Environmental Protection Service', GreenPort, 12 May 2008, www.greenport.com/news101/europe/rotterdamoman-environmental-protection-service.

[66] Sohar Environmental Unit, 'Omani Environmental Regulations International References Documents SEU Guidance Notes', Advanced Regulatory Wiki Application (Sohar: Ministry of Environment and Climate Affairs, July 2013), www.soharportandfreezone.com/PDF/Complete%20pack%20Omani%20Environmental%20Regulations,%20International%20References%20Documents%20and%20SEU%20Guidance%E2%80%A6.pdf.

[67] ICV is a form of local content policy, pioneered by Shell in Oman, which is discussed in Chapter 3. ICV is often used invoked by companies in relation to local hiring, rather than a wider comment on a reliance on local inputs (products and services) being sourced in the country.

[68] Vale, 'Partnership between Vale and the Ministry of Agriculture & Fisheries Generates Positive Results to the Fishing Community in Liwa', *Press Release*, 30 June 2014, www.vale.com/oman/EN/press/releases-local/Pages/partnership.aspx.

Storage Facility in Liwa, which was designed to recover processed water for reuse and thereby reduce dependence on external water consumption and avoid contaminating the underground water table.[69] The same company likewise won an award for its Omanisation efforts in 2010 and again in 2012, in acknowledgement of its recruiting and training practices. Like many other companies, Marawid includes Omanisation as a CSR initiative. Forms of Omanisation 'success' such as this are loudly lauded in the media to generate attention to places where the employment of citizens does occur amid the many complaints about their absence. Omanisation thus becomes part of CSR washing.

Such initiatives around the environment and employment coincided with the increasing articulation of grievances, and the growth of pressure from below. Like environmental issues, frustration around the availability of jobs and working conditions were simmering. Meanwhile, the 2006 legalisation of trade unions and peaceful strike action within collective bargaining opened up a space for public labour mobilisation.[70] Debates around unionisation, threats of strikes, and of strike action in work places ranging from Al Ghubra Desalination Plant in Muscat in 2008 to Salalah Port throughout 2007, 2008, and 2010 filled threads on the popular local online discussion forum Sabla Oman.[71] In April of 2008, employees of the Oman National Electric Company (ONEC) working in Sohar, Saham, and Al-Khaboura in Al-Batinah went on a strike that lasted over a week. The year prior, they staged a shorter, three-day strike and lodged a complaint at the Ministry of Manpower. After a year with no progress, they turned again to strike action.[72] They stopped their work of distributing utility bills to residential and commercial properties and tendered their

---

[69] Marawid, 'Marawid Press Releases', 2013 2010, www.mawaridmining.com/press.html.
[70] Royal Decree 74/2006, 'Amending Some Provisions of the Labour Law (Issued 8 July 2006, Published 15 July 2006)', Official Gazette 819, [author translations from Arabic], 2006.
[71] See, for example, www.s-oman.net/avb/showthread.php?t=35917 , www.s-oman.net/avb/showthread.php?t=910375, www.s-oman.net/avb/showthread.php?t=256462, and www.s-oman.net/avb/showthread.php?t=221041. Sabla, in the name of the once popular virtual discussion forum, refers to community gatherings.
[72] 'Employees of ONEC Branches Continue Strike', The Free Library / Al Bawaba, 30 April 2008.

resignations en masse to protest their low and stagnant salaries, lack of incentives, and the inability to cover basic living expenses with their wage levels. These limited yet varied labour activities suggest a trajectory of discontent building up.

In early 2011, as the uprisings were taking off across the MENA, Sohar became one of the centres of Oman's own 'Spring', where the articulation of grievances around a lack of employment became even more pronounced and impossible to ignore. The first significant demonstration started in Muscat a mere three days after Zine al-Abidine ben Ali fled Tunisia amid the revolution attributed with igniting the regional protest flame. Many of these Omani protests and marches were focused on anti-corruption and the desire for greater political voice through publicly-accountable ministers, freedom of the press and association, and greater legislative powers. Protestors also called for jobs, wage increases, and labour law changes. Sit-ins and marches in Muscat continued pushing for demands that had become public the previous summer, with a document containing a range of political demands signed by fifty individuals, but merged with the pressing anti-corruption, jobs, and justice momentum building. Just a week after the first marches in the capital, massive protests erupted in Sohar.[73] There were also notable protest centres in Sur and Salalah and smaller solidarity protests and various wildcat labour strikes in multiple locations.

Sohar found its voice in this movement first through unemployed young people. It started with a small group of whom went to the Sohar branch of the Ministry of Manpower to protest the lack of jobs available to them. They were met with a security response and evacuated from the premises. They moved the protest to Sohar's main roundabout – known then as *dawār al-ʿālam* and *dawār al-kurat al-ārḍiyya* (and as the globe roundabout in English) due to the giant globe decorating its centre. Following overnight arrests, the next day some protestors also gathered at the police station to call for the release of those arrested. Tear gas and rubber bullets were used on

---

[73] Said Sultan Al-Hashimi, 'The Omani Spring: Towards the Break of a New Dawn?', Arab Reform Brief (Arab Reform Initiative, November 2011), www .arab-reform.net/publication/the-omani-spring-towards-the-break-of-a-new-dawn/; Ra'id Zuhair Al-Jamali, 'Oman, Kind of Not Quiet?', *Foreign Policy*, 7 November 2011, http://mideast.foreignpolicy.com/posts/2011/11/07/kind_of_ not_quiet.

the gatherings, and reportedly one or two protestors were shot dead. After this, more people convened at the roundabout which became known as *dawār al-iṣlāḥ* (reform roundabout) and sometimes maydān *al-iṣlāḥ* (reform square). While the majority of protests were peaceful, the disenfranchised reacted strongly to the early violence used against the protestors. The sense of shock and injustice combined with the feeling of despair at joblessness and unrealised dreams of a better economic future as growth popped up all around them. Lulu Hypermarket, adjacent to the roundabout, was set on fire and looted, several government offices were blocked and forced to close, and the police station and the office of the *wālī* were set on fire. Outside of these incidents, most of the protests were peaceful. Since the roundabout was located along the main highway at the time, connecting Muscat to the cities of Al-Batinah and the UAE, the protests blocked an important traffic route. Moreover, protestors organised several blockades of the port and industrial area to make their grievances heard at centres of economic power. Detailed overviews, reflections, and analysis of the stream of events during the 2011 uprising in Sohar and across Oman can be read in works of Al-Hashimi and also Valeri.[74] In contrast with the demonstrations in Muscat, which Khalfan Al-Badwawi, an activist from Shinas, defined as organised by the educated elite who focused on the demands of the urban middle and upper classes, a majority of Sohar's protestors belonged to the city's dominant class – the unemployed.[75]

Protests largely emerged from communities suffering from massive inequality and environmental destruction due to the region's transformation into the country's mega-industrial area. At the same time, there were numerous wildcat strikes in sectors ranging from oil and banking to health and education.[76] These strikes, combined with the

---

[74] Said Sultan Al-Hashimi, ed., *al-Rabī' al-'Umānī: qirā'a fī al-siyāqāt w-al-dalālāt.* (Beirut: Dār al-Farabī, 2013); Al-Hashimi, 'The Omani Spring: Towards the Break of a New Dawn?'; Valeri, 'The Ṣuḥār Paradox'.

[75] Al-Badwawi, 'Laḥaẓat fī masīrat inhā' al-isti'mār: 'ashar sanawāt 'alā intafāḍat Ṣuḥār'.

[76] Consider, for example, strikes in the financial sector during the protests, which included separate strikes for better wages in Bank Muscat, Oman Investment Bank, and Oman Investment Finance Company (OIFC). Saleh Al-Shaibany, 'Oman Sultan to Cede Some Powers after Protests', *Reuters*, 13 March 2011, www.reuters.com/article/us-oman-idUKTRE72C1WH20110313.

demands for work from jobseekers – sometimes as a mass of unemployed and sometimes as mobilisations of graduates from specific sectors – illustrates the mobilisation of *labour as a category* that took off at this time. It also provides examples of what Schlaumberg has called 'the ability of the working class to spontaneously self-mobilise'.[77] This account is not meant to ignore or diminish the other political and social grievances aired during 2011 and the very real demands for political change. What it does do is focus on the economic and labour-oriented ones. These, especially in the Sohar area, formed the bulk of motivation and inspiration that drove young people to protest.[78]

Unfortunately, workers and protestors in Oman are regularly dismissed as fragmented and disorganised. This is partly because the segmented nature of the labour market often fragments solidarities, which hinders the development of a wider labour movement. The interests of citizens and expatriate workers seem to contradict at the surface level, an issue I return to later. Furthermore, unions appeared to be absent from the large-scale protests in 2011 that centred around jobs and economic justice. Unions might respond that their mandate requires the presence of labour relations to engage. Despite this, as we see later, unions became more active and their membership expanded dramatically after 2011. Fundamentally, the isolated understanding of the Sohar protests as populated by the 'unskilled' and labour mobilisation as 'unorganised' is dismissive of the agency and experiences of those involved. This tendency also reflects elitist internal and external characterisations of protestors' demands, sometimes used politically to marginalise their meaning and write them off as opportunistic. Importantly, it misses an opportunity to more fully think through labour and class in Oman.

In contrast to these tendencies, local poet and writer Fatima Al-Shidi characterised the protestors by their awareness, enthusiasm, and desire

---

[77] Heike Schaumberg, '"Disorganisation" as Social Movement Tactic: Reappropriating Politics during the Crisis of Neoliberal Capitalism', in *Marxism and Social Movements*, ed. Colin Barker et al. (Leiden: Brill, 2013), 378, https://doi.org/10.1163/9789004251434_019.

[78] Jessie Moritz likewise found that youth protestors in Sohar indicated primarily material motivations like unemployment as the reason for protesting. 'Reformers and the Rentier State', 49.

for change. She juxtaposes this with the response of the security services, which she describes as one that

did not deal with [the protestors] with an awareness that corresponds with their awareness, or a sophistication that corresponds with their sophistication, or a humanity that accommodates their dreams and desires for change, reform, and the fight against corruption and the corrupt.[79]

Her description resonates with the lived knowledge and experiences that drive people to protest to begin with. Moreover, college and university students and graduates joined hands with school leavers – together making up the unemployed. While, like with many protests, grievances can sometimes be targeted inappropriately manifesting in intercommunal, class, and nationality tensions,[80] young peoples' social, economic, and political awareness should not easily be dismissed.

Elites and analysts speak about labour's lack of agency and capacity to capture state power as evidence of both its weakness and its need to be viewed as, and organised into, a national labour development initiative from the top town. Top-down organisation of labour offers a pretence of labour organisation and can be expeditious in pre-empting agitation. Consider the example discussed in Chapter 3 when oil companies organised worker committees to provide an opportunity for workers to air their complaints with the aim that such conversations would forestall labour action. This penchant persists in labour relations. Oman and its neighbours are not isolated cases of 'organising disorganisation' as a way for authorities to get ahead of labour disturbances.[81] Evidence from Argentina shows that the practice of organising disorganisation can be 'a method of domination employed by the country's political elites to quell the revolutionary potential of the working class'.[82]

Forms of formal labour organisation have been expanding. The General Federation of Omani Workers (GFOW) was, as mentioned,

---

[79] Fatima Al-Shidi, al-Mara'a al-ʿumāniyya w-al-Rabīʿ: bayn al- ḥuḍūr al-rāfil w-al-taghyīb al-muʾaṭar'. In *al-Rabīʿ al-ʿumānī: qirāʾa fi al-siyāqāt w-al-dalālāt*, ed. Said Sultan Al-Hashimi (Beirut: Dār al-Farabī, 2013), 56, author's translation.

[80] I return to these tensions in Chapter 5.

[81] Heike Schaumberg employs the concept of 'organising disorganisation'. In unpacking disorganisation as a tactic and strategy, she also suggests that disorganisation can also be 'a sort of "weapon of the weak"' - drawing on James Scott. '"Disorganisation" as Social Movement Tactic', 379 and 385.

[82] Schaumberg, '"Disorganisation" as Social Movement Tactic', 385.

notably absent from the 2011 unrest, and much of the active labour contention just described had not been organised formally through them. They preferred, according to Louër, to be viewed as a 'stabilising actor at times of crisis' and to serve as a mediator between various interests.[83] Thus, when one union within a company or sector announces the possibility of strike action, the GFOW may mediate between the union, government, and corporate interests. This can partially be explained with a view of how the formal organisation of labour politics in Oman has been top-down in a space where labour and political organisation had been prohibited and/or tightly controlled since the Dhofar revolution. The prior absence of formal labour organisation does not equate with the absence of labour politics itself, as shown. However, it was not until the 2003 labour law that workers had the legal provision to organise 'representative committees' within their workplaces.[84] These appear modelled on this history of representative committees in oil companies discussed in Chapter 3. Amendments in 2006 legalised trade unions, set the structure and legal independence of a supra-union body, the GFOW, and enshrined the freedom to organise activities.[85] Perhaps ironically, these amendments were required by Chapter 16 of the US-Oman FTA signed at the beginning of the year. Articles 16.1–16.7 covered labour, and both parties were committed to follow the ILO Declaration on Fundamental Principles and Rights at Work and its Follow-Up. This included 'internationally-recognised labour rights' such as the right of association and the right to organise and bargain collectively.[86]

It was not until 2010 that the GFOW held their founding conference, which was attended by representatives of the forty-five registered

---

[83] Laurence Louër, 'The Arab Spring Effect on Labor Politics in Bahrain and Oman', *Arabian Humanities. Revue Internationale d'archéologie et de Sciences Sociales Sur La Péninsule Arabique/International Journal of Archaeology and Social Sciences in the Arabian Peninsula*, no. 4 (12 January 2015), http://cy.revues.org/2865.

[84] Articles 108 and 109, Royal Decree 35/2003, 'Promulgating the Labour Law (Issued 26 April 2003, Published 3 May 2003)'.

[85] Royal Decree 74/2006, 'Amending Some Provisions of the Labour Law (Issued 8 July 2006, Published 15 July 2006)'.

[86] 'Final Text of the U.S.-Oman FTA', United States Trade Representative, 1 January 2009, http://ustr.gov/trade-agreements/free-trade-agreements/oman-fta/final-text; Nadira Lalji, 'Labor Law Matters: Trade Liberalization in Oman', *Harvard International Review* 28, no. 3 (22 September 2006): 12–14.

unions at the time.[87] This transpired at an opportune time for the federation. Workers increasingly began to take notice of the existence of the GFOW and use their unions, and the GFOW, as a place to put forward some of their demands and grievances. This trend is highlighted by the rapid increase in the number of registered unions to 310 by 2021.[88] Louër views the successes of the GFOW as stemming from their top-down endorsement rather than bottom-up labour politics and at least partly inspired by outside pressure and agreements with the ILO. This has allowed the federation to act as a mediator of disputes and to negotiate with government bodies for labour law changes in favour of workers. It has kept them in a subtle role, viewing quiet discussion and negotiation as more productive and effective than loud confrontation.[89] The GFOW and the Port of Salalah trade syndicate has openly claimed that the 'main role of the labour confederation is to address the manifestations that may hamper production ... to ensure meeting the public and social interests and enhancing the union in the national development process'.[90] The federation, however, despite mediating successfully, can hardly move beyond being a subordinate partner to state and capital in the development process.[91]

The onset of the unrest in early 2011 prompted a number of responses from the government with the aim of diffusing and then stopping the dissent. Key to this initial response was the announcement of a series of economic proposals including the abrupt creation of 50,000 government jobs; an increase of the minimum wage from 140 to 200 OMR; the establishment of a monthly unemployment benefit of 150 OMR; raising the living allowance, pensions, and social security allowances for government employees; and creating a consumer protection agency, among others.[92] Just under two years later,

[87] 'al-Itihād al-ʿām l-ʿumāl salṭanat ʿUmān. "'An al-Itihād al-ʿām l-ʿumāl salṭanat ʿUmān, n.d., www.gfow.om/?page_id=2877.

[88] 'Āl-Itihād al-ʿĀam l-ʿAmāl Salṭanat ʿUmān', 2021, www.gfow.om/.

[89] Interviews in January 2020 with GFOW gave this impression, which was also a finding of Louër, 'The Arab Spring Effect on Labor Politics in Bahrain and Oman'.

[90] 'Role of Labour Unions, Members in Focus', *Oman Daily Observer*, 23 January 2012, http://main.omanobserver.om/node/80476.

[91] Chang, 'From Global Factory to Continent of Labour', 38.

[92] Sunil K. Vaidya, 'Heavy Security Prevents Friday Protests in Sohar, Oman', *Gulf News*, 8 April 2011, http://gulfnews.com/news/gulf/oman/heavy-security-prevents-friday-protests-in-sohar-oman-1.789074; Al-Hashimi, 'The Omani Spring', 5–6.

the minimum wage for the private sector was again increased to 325 OMR per month.[93] In an interview in early 2012, a senior government official in the then de-commissioned ministry of national economy explained,

The government basically did this to freeze the problem so as to avoid a Tunisia situation. But listen, 61,000 high school students will sit for their final exams this year. Many of those won't move on to college or university and will need jobs – but the government will not be able to accommodate them ... it was a short-term solution.[94]

He accurately foresaw that this issue would continue to re-emerge. Along with economic measures, there was also a shakeup of cabinet, with the reshuffling or removal of ministers in key economic posts who had been viewed by the protestors as embodying corruption. A mid-level official at the Ministry of Manpower in 2012 wryly critiqued such changes, suggesting that the removal of ministers and changing of undersecretaries was 'mostly superficial in response to protestors' demands. What they have done is really just shift embedded people around and they are still there, mostly untouchable!'[95] Another royal decree (39/2011), viewed at the time as quite a significant political reform, granted legislative and oversight powers to the Council of Oman.[96] Finally, repression tactics were also used to try to end the dissent – including measures such as increasing the power of the police, detaining those viewed as vocal protest leaders, introducing *lèse-majesté* and cyber-crimes laws, and ramping up a very visible security presence in Sohar.[97]

---

[93] 'Council of Ministers / Statement', *Oman News Agency*, 2 February 2013, www .omannews.gov.om/ona/english/newsDetailsPrint.jsp?newsID=160144 See also Figure 2.5 and discussion of the minimum wage in Chapter 2.
[94] Interview, Muscat, 15 January 2012.
[95] Interview, Muscat, 2 February 2012.
[96] Royal Decree 39/2011, 'Granting the Council of Oman Legislative and Oversight Powers (Issued 12 March 2011, Published 15 March 2011)', Official Gazette 931, [author translations from Arabic], 1991; Al-Hashimi, 'The Omani Spring', 5.
[97] To read more about repressive measures, see Valeri, 'The Ṣuḥār Paradox'; Peter Salisbury, 'Insulting the Sultan in Oman', *Foreign Policy*, 19 October 2012, https://foreignpolicy.com/2012/10/19/insulting-the-sultan-in-oman/; Vaidya, 'Heavy Security Prevents Friday Protests in Sohar, Oman'; 'Oman: Drop Cases against Online Activists "Defaming the Sultan" Sentences Part of Wider Repression Campaign', *Cairo Institute for Human Rights Studies* (blog), 21 July 2012, https://cihrs.org/oman-drop-cases-against-online-

The economic policy responses were especially interesting in the context of this chapter. First, responses such as creating jobs and raising wages delivered the message that social pressure can result in policy change. In some ways, it was empowering. Despite the crackdowns, it demonstrated that there is voice in mobilisation and that social demands can lead to some (especially economic) concessions.[98] Second, these measures in part reinforced existing employment preferences and expectations for public sector employment. The measures countered the Omanisation gains achieved over the 2000s, especially in encouraging Omani participation in the private sector. As data show, after the announcements of governments jobs, there was an initial decrease in Omanisation rates as Omanis resigned from positions in the private sector in hopes of acquiring one of the new spaces opened up in the government. Omani participation in the private sector then flattened for several years.[99]

Even if there were antecedents to 2011, Al-Shidi's impression that 2011 was the beginning of a stage of change seems appropriate.[100] The sense of change combined with a bolder willingness to discuss socioeconomic and political grievances publicly was palpable, even amid the tightening of this space after 2012. Agitation, especially around jobs and working conditions, has continued since, physically and online. Employees in the oil and gas sector have been particularly active. Around 300 PDO employees protested for better wages outside the Muscat headquarters in 2011; and one year later, several thousand workers working for contracting companies for PDO and Oman Oxy went on strike in the Fahud oil fields. Activists who went to document and raise awareness of this strike were arrested,[101] and yet even a new

activists-'defaming-the-sultan'-sentences-part-of-wider-repression-campaign/?lang=en; 'The Sultanate of Silence ... Full Scale Crackdown on Omani Democracy Activists', *Cairo Institute for Human Rights Studies* (blog), 18 December 2012, https://cihrs.org/the-sultanate-of-silence-full-scale-crackdown-on-omani-democracy-activists/?lang=en.

[98] This claim is also supported in Chapter 2.

[99] Ennis and Al-Jamali, 'Elusive Employment', 12–13.

[100] Al-Shidi, 'al-Mara'a al-ʿumāniyya w-al-Rabīʿ: bayn al- ḥuḍūr al-rāfil w-al-taghyīb al-muʾaṭar'.

[101] 'Oil Workers Strike for Wage Increases', *Ahram Online*, 15 March 2011, https://english.ahram.org.eg/NewsContentP/3/7769/Business/Oman-oil-workers-strike-for-wage-increases.aspx; 'Rights Activists Held over Oil Field Strike in Oman', *Gulf News*, 1 June 2012, https://gulfnews.com/world/gulf/oman/rights-activists-held-over-oil-field-strike-in-oman-1.1030409.

government ban on strikes in essential services like oil companies, refineries, ports, and airports has not prevented their occurrence.[102]

In evidence of increasing labour organisation, in October 2015, trade unions in the oil and gas sector threatened to strike to protest the massive layoffs in the sector starting on national day, 18 November. The strike was called off only two days prior after a negotiation between union representatives and ministers resulted in satisfactory industry concessions.[103] Further labour solidarity and the strengthening of organisation can be observed through the Octal Petrochemicals Company strike in early 2014. The Octal syndicate announced on 5 February that it would strike on the 26th for better pay and working conditions, increased Omanisation, and for the reinstatement of their dismissed union leader. During the strike, which continued into April before an agreement was struck, some other unions supported Octal workers and decided to share salaries with the striking workers.[104]

Other sectors continued to mobilise too. Public school teachers held a four-week strike in fall 2013, which included approximately 35,000 teachers and affected 740 of 1,047 schools. Reports indicated that by the second week, hundreds more schools joined. Demands included the harmonisation of teacher salaries with other parts of the public sector civil service, the creation of a union to represent their collective interests, and improvements to curriculum and study conditions.[105]

---

[102] 'Oman Bans Strikes in Essential Services', *Gulf News*, 11 November 2013, https://gulfnews.com/world/gulf/oman/oman-bans-strikes-in-essential-services-1.1253912; Ministry of Manpower: Ministerial Decision 294/2006, 'Regulating Collective Bargaining, Peaceful Strikes, and Closures (Issued 29 October 2006, Published 2 December 2006)', Official Gazette 828, [author translations from Arabic], 2006.

[103] Fahad Al-Mukrashi, 'Omani Oil and Gas Unions Threaten Strike amid Oil Slump', *Gulf News*, 29 October 2015, https://gulfnews.com/world/gulf/oman/omani-oil-and-gas-unions-threaten-strike-amid-oil-slump-1.1609750; 'Oman Strike Called Off', *The Energy Year*, 16 November 2015, https://theenergyyear.com/news/oman/.

[104] 'Octal Employees Continue to Strike in Oman', *Gulf News*, 6 March 2014, https://gulfnews.com/world/gulf/oman/octal-employees-continue-to-strike-in-oman-1.1300525 More details can also be read on Octal Syndicate's Twitter account: https://twitter.com/octalsyndicate.

[105] Simeon Kerr, 'Oman Gets Tough with Striking Teachers in Revival of Unrest', *Financial Times*, 24 October 2013, www.ft.com/content/5bc595a5-5491-3874-a93f-1a8cade2fe8b; 'Oman Teachers Strike', *Teacher Solidarity* (blog), 14 October 2013, https://teachersolidarity.com/blog/oman-teachers-strike.

In addition to traditional physical protest, teachers mobilised the use of social media and especially WhatsApp messaging to communicate with the wider public and garner widespread social support and, importantly, student support.[106]

There were also considerable numbers of protests by expatriates, especially in the construction sector. Consider the thousands who went on strike at the new airport construction site to demand better safety conditions for workers in March 2013, the thousands of employees of a large construction company who protested pay and work conditions in September 2013, and the 3,000 workers who went on strike over unpaid wages when the pinch of the oil price collapse hit the labour market hard in 2015.[107]

It is notable that labour mobilisation tends to be divided along citizen and expatriate lines, and cross-national solidarity has been rare (but not absent). This is in spite of the fact that migrant workers have the right to join unions. It does, however, reflect patterns in other welfare states with high immigration where unions are discursively committed to all workers but in practice fear competition from migrants in the labour market.[108] In Oman, this corresponds partly with the sectoral segmentation of citizens and foreigners across occupations. For example, when construction workers strike, it is usually an expatriate strike since few citizens make their living as general construction labourers. This tendency also reveals the role segmentation plays in fragmenting workers and class interests. Jobseeker protests and labour mobilisations are occurring within the context of a

---

[106] Najma Al Zidjaly, 'WhatsApp Omani Teachers: Social Media and the Question of Social Change', *Multimodal Communication* 3, no. 1 (1 June 2014): 107–30, https://doi.org/10.1515/mc-2014-0007.

[107] Aarti Nagraj, 'Thousands of South Asian Workers Strike at Oman Airport', *Gulf Business*, 12 March 2013, https://gulfbusiness.com/thousands-of-south-asian-workers-strike-at-oman-airport/; 'Workers Strike in Oman over Pay and Conditions', *Construction Week*, 8 September 2013, www.constructionweekonline.com/appointments/article-24155-workers-strike-in-oman-over-pay-and-conditions; Joseph Benny, 'Oman: Over 3,000 Workers of Construction Firm on Strike Demanding Unpaid Wages', *Muscat Daily / Business Human Rights*, 20 December 2015, www.business-humanrights.org/en/latest-news/oman-over-3000-workers-of-construction-firm-on-strike-demanding-unpaid-wages/.

[108] Alexandre Afonso, Samir Negash, and Emily Wolff, 'Closure, Equality or Organisation: Trade Union Responses to EU Labour Migration', *Journal of European Social Policy* 30, no. 5 (1 November 2020): 528–42, https://doi.org/10.1177/0958928720950607.

growing climate of citizens who perceive foreigners as crowding them out of employment opportunities (a topic I return to in Chapter 5). Indeed, labour protests – companies going on strike and jobseekers demonstrating for work – have increased since the oil price crash in the last half of 2014 tightened the economy and labour market even further.[109]

Likewise, the environmental protests in Sohar and Liwa were not sudden but rather part of an ongoing process of complaints – to industrial actors, to the *wālī*, to their member of the *majlis al-shūrā*, and, ultimately, to the streets. The trend continued. In October 2012, around 200 Liwa residents protested pollution and what they believed were associated respiratory and cancer incidents due to their proximity to the industrial activities that surround the town. They began seeking relocation.[110] Again in August 2013, men, women, and children from Liwa protested in front of Sohar industrial gate worried about health risks and industrial pollution associated with a petrochemical complex and industrial estate.[111] Security forces reportedly fired tear gas to disperse the crowds and later arrested Talib Al-Mamari, the majlis al-shūrā representative from Liwa, a known activist and leader of demonstrations in the area. Activists condemned the outsized security response on residents simply demanding their right to a healthy life. Likewise, a UN Special Rapporteur and the International Parliamentary Union expressed alarm and concern at the arrest of a parliamentarian and the suppression of rights to peaceful assembly. Al-Mamari was initially given a seven-year prison term, reduced in a retrial to four years.[112] This was not the end of dissent, however.

---

[109] Ennis and Al-Saqri, 'Oil Price Collapse and the Political Economy of the Post-2014 Economic Adjustment in the Sultanate of Oman'.

[110] Fahad Al-Mukrashi, 'Liwa Residents Protest against Pollution, Want Relocation', *Times of Oman*, 7 October 2012, www.pressreader.com/oman/times-of-oman/20121007/page/1; Fahad Al-Mukrashi, 'Port Pollution Irks Liwa Residents', *Times of Oman*, 7 October 2012, www.pressreader.com/oman/times-of-oman/20121007/281522223312253.

[111] Linah Alsaafin, 'Omani Parliamentarian Remains Imprisoned amidst Crackdown on Dissent', *Middle East Eye*, 13 February 2015, www.middleeasteye.net/news/omani-parliamentarian-remains-imprisoned-amidst-crackdown-dissent; 'Tear Gas Used on Protesters in Oman', *Gulf News*, 23 August 2013, https://gulfnews.com/world/gulf/oman/tear-gas-used-on-protesters-in-oman-1.1223268.

[112] 'OMN/01 – Talib Al Mamari: Decision Adopted Unanimously by the IPU Governing Council at Its 195th Session', in *Results of the 131th Assembly and*

Statistics for 2014 indicate that complaints continued to pour into the relevant governmental bodies about the growing gas and effluent emission rates and the environmental and health outcomes.[113] With continuing complaints, the government announced the development of a housing project to relocate affected Liwa residents in 2017. These were tendered in 2019; and by October 2020, the government announced that 3,500 homes and facilities like schools, health care centres, and parks would be provided.[114]

The May 2021 resurgence of employment protests in Sohar and the re-occupation of the space that was previously the Globe roundabout (razed to make way for a highway overpass and exchange) highlights Al-Badwawi's characterisation of the 2011 Sohar uprising as a 'rebellion against stagnation'.[115] Soharis once again rose up in large numbers only ten years later in a massive showing that stagnation is not an acceptable outcome to the community. Such a recurrence was 'expected since 2011. There is nothing strange about that', commented Ibrahim bin Said.[116] Indeed, 2020 statistics indicate that 23 per cent of youth jobseekers live in North Al Batinah.[117] The demonstrators

Related Meetings of the Inter-Parliamentary Union (Geneva: Inter-Parliamentary Union, 2014), 105–8, http://archive.ipu.org/conf-e/131/results .pdf.

[113] Within just one year, 527 irregularities and complaints were submitted to the General Directorate for the Conservation of Nature, 51 environmental complaints to the Environmental Inspection and Control Department, 30 to the Environmental Planning Department, and 19 to the Pollution Operations Monitoring centre. Syed Ali Naveed Arshad and Maria Mariam Rabeaa Petrou, 'Major Projects: Environmental Risks in Oman: Overview' (Thomson Reuters Practical Law, 1 May 2017), https://uk.practicallaw.thomsonreuters .com/w-008-2712?transitionType=Default&contextData=(sc.Default) &firstPage=true#co_anchor_a118297.

[114] Arshad and Petrou, 'Major Projects'; Sushmita Sarkhel, 'Oman Tender Board Awards Contracts Worth over 724 Million Rials in 2019', *Oman Economic Review Live*, 18 August 2019, www.oerlive.com/economy/oman-tender-board-awards-contracts-worth-over-724-million-rials-in-2019/; Angitha Pradeep, 'New 3,500 Home Residential Community for Project Announced for Liwa in Oman', *ME Construction News*, 11 October 2020, https://meconstructionnews .com/43791/new-3500-home-residential-community-project-announced-for-liwa-in-oman.

[115] Khalfan Al-Badwawi, 'Human Rights: My Personal Experience', The Omani Centre for Human Rights, 18 December 2018, https://ochroman.org/eng/2018/ 10/event1/.

[116] Ibrahim bin Said, '‘Awdat al-i'itiṣāmāt: Wājib al-Kalima', *Alfalq*, 25 May 2021, www.alfalq.com/?p=24654.

[117] 'al-Shabāb wa sūq al'amal', 9.

protested that nothing significant had changed since 2011 and called for jobs, the benefits of economic development, and the dismissal of the Minister of Labour and the undersecretary. When local media ignored the movement, they also called for the dismissal of the Minister of Information.[118] Even with an almost immediate large security presence, smaller solidarity protests erupted across the country – *Saham taḍāmun* (Saham solidarity), *Al-Kabourah taḍāmun, Salalah taḍāmun, Nizwa tastajīb* (Nizwa responds)– read the Twitter hashtags alongside *Sohar tantafiḍ* (Sohar rises up). The economic growth, transformation of life, and the promise of the Dubai-like dream certainly elevated expectations – and when the limited aspiration of gainful, respectful employment went unfulfilled for many, Sohar raised its voice. Sohar embodies the idea that 'human beings cannot help but organise, both for resistance and the social reproduction of life'.[119]

Local writers and social media keep asking, Why Sohar? In an editorial, Anissa Al-Hutiya mentions the employment, economic, and demographic features Sohar has in common across the country and wonders why – even in the high heat of summer (May is one of the hottest months in coastal Oman) – are Sohari young people the ones to go out to demand their right to work again? She finds no answer by the end of her article but beseeches the government to productively tap into the energy and take advantage of the wealth of the country's youth. The time of promises is over, in her view, now is the time to build belonging and create jobs to occupy youth constructively.[120]

The story of Sohar and neighbouring towns like Liwa demonstrates how 'the logistics revolution remains an unfinished and contested process' as Ziadah adeptly notes.[121] The dispossession of communities along coastal Al-Batinah for the coastal highway connecting Sohar with Muscat unsettled lifestyles and livelihoods. In the mid-2000s, homes were already marked for dispossession and by 2011 many communities had been provided new homes in land – several kilometres from the sea. A process of demolition and relocation that is

---

[118] 'Ṣuḥār: Limādhā tuthīr al-iḥtijājāt wa al-mūājahāt fī 'Umān al-makhāwif min tikrār aḥdāth 2011?', *BBC News Arabic*, 24 May 2021, www.bbc.com/arabic/trending-57231803.

[119] Schaumberg, '"Disorganisation" as Social Movement Tactic', 378.

[120] Anissa Al-Hutiyya, 'Limādhā Ṣuḥār?', *Al-Roya*, 24 May 2021, https://alroya.om/p/282725.

[121] Ziadah, 'Constructing a Logistics Space', 668.

ongoing.[122] These processes mirror similar ones in neighbouring countries like Bahrain, where land is accumulated and repurposed for capital and growth narratives with clear economic winners and losers.[123] The reclamation of land to build the container terminal at Sohar port, the built environment and its encroachment on coastal and agricultural spaces of Liwa and Sohar, and the Al-Batinah Coastal Highway project are all powerful examples of how radical transformations of space and economic development are part of wider shifts – those of expanding infrastructures, of privatisation, but also of contestation. Radical economic transformations create the potential for strong macroeconomic outcomes and benefit certain parties among international and domestic capital. While creating some opportunities for new forms of business and livelihood, these also disrupt other ways of living and being. The economic wins sit in contrast with the losses among affected communities.

4.3 Conjuring Duqm

There are important similarities but also differences with the radical transformation of Duqm. It is similar in how the promises of transformation, growth, and economic opportunities are used and wrapped into a national interest poetic. The largest of differences are geographic and demographic. Unlike Sohar, Duqm is remote and sparsely populated. It is approximately 500 kilometres from Muscat, in the least populated and developed governorate of the country – Al-Wusta (see Map 0.1). Prior to the project's start, the area was home to an estimated 3,000 people – mostly communities of fishermen and semi-nomadic *badū*. In the early stages of its development, the media

[122] Conrad Prabhu, 'Construction Work to Resume on Batinah Coastal Road Project', *Oman Daily Observer*, 29 September 2019, www.omanobserver.om/article/23818/Business/construction-work-to-resume-on-batinah-coastal-road-project; 'MoHUP Reissues Tenders for Demolition Works in Al Batinah Coastal Road Project', *Oman Daily Observer*, 26 January 2021, www.omanobserver.om/article/4478/Front%20Stories/mohup-reissues-tenders-for-demolition-works-in-al-batinah-coastal-road-project.

[123] Omar Hesham AlShehabi and Saleh Suroor, 'Unpacking "Accumulation By Dispossession", "Fictitious Commodification", and "Fictitious Capital Formation": Tracing the Dynamics of Bahrain's Land Reclamation', *Antipode* 48, no. 4 (2016): 835–56, https://doi.org/10.1111/anti.12222.

dubbed it 'the city rising from the sand'[124] and a 'plug and play city for everyone',[125] yet there were many questions and concerns about the feasibility and practicality of this massive project. There was much murmuring in the public space concerning infrastructure connectivity given the floundering GCC rail network plans, the ability to find Omanis willing to work in Duqm despite its distance from their homes, and the nascent state of facilities and entertainment.

This section shows that Duqm, like Sohar, demonstrates various implications of the radical transformation of the built environment. These have spatial, environmental, livelihood, and lifestyle impacts resulting from dispossession and the repurposing of the area for economic growth.[126] It also illustrates how the promises–expectations gap may be more politically manageable in a distant location, where the threat of discontent is initially more diffuse and possibly easier to pre-empt and control. Yet the Duqm project has national implications in the promises it offers, especially for the country's many jobseekers. Importantly, this case further reveals the stickiness of certain embedded patterns in labour market organisation and regulation even in a new, constructed city far from urban centres.

The seventh FYP (2005–2010) did not yet focus on Duqm, only mentioning the plan to construct its airport. Rather, the plan paid explicit attention to the Sohar and Salalah ports and to a strategy to expand the overall capacity of the country's ports, the logistics and linkages between them, and their global connectivity. It specifically aimed to establish freezones to compete with the ports of neighbouring

---

[124] Wade Shepard, '"Five Years Ago There Was Nothing": Inside Duqm, the City Rising from the Sand', *The Guardian*, 6 August 2018, sec. Cities, www.theguardian.com/cities/2018/aug/06/five-years-ago-there-was-nothing-inside-duqm-the-city-rising-from-the-sand-oman-city-sand-luxury-hotels-housing.

[125] Mohamed Issa Al Zadjali, 'Duqm: A Plug and Play City for Everyone', *Times of Oman*, 14 July 2019, https://timesofoman.com/article/1607880/Oman/Duqm-A-Plug-and-Play-City-for-everyone.

[126] In other regions too, extractive capitalist systems target specific spaces for development, deeming them of public or national interest, and pursue economic growth through dispossession and suppression of discontent. Antulio Rosales, 'Venezuela's Deepening Logic of Extraction', *NACLA Report on the Americas* 49, no. 2 (3 April 2017): 132–35, https://doi.org/10.1080/10714839.2017.1331794; Christian Henderson, 'Land Grabs Reexamined: Gulf Arab Agro-Commodity Chains and Spaces of Extraction', *Environment and Planning A: Economy and Space* 53, no. 2 (1 March 2021): 261–79, https://doi.org/10.1177/0308518X20956657.

states and established a task force to prepare a strategic plan for ports development.[127] Yet in the midst of the period of the seventh FYP, the legal and financial foundations of Duqm's development began to be laid.

It was not until October 2011 that the Special Economic Zone Authority at Duqm (SEZAD) was established by royal decree.[128] Its announcement coincided with a big political push to create buzz around the government's steps to generate growth and economic opportunities given the heated start of the year. All the subsequent buzz since came with promises of specific radical development that would generate massive growth and, crucial in all the signalling, jobs and business opportunities for Omanis. The creation of the SEZ Duqm follows the pattern of economic liberalisation in Oman that was the result of political choices – state-directed liberalisation. The Freezones in Duqm and Sohar are two of four dispersed across the country, including also Al-Mazunah and Salalah in Dhofar. In 2020, these were all reorganised under a singular administrative body – the Public Authority for Special Economic Zones and Freezones.[129] Together, these are part of 'the specific spatialization' of freezones in the country, which Mogielnicki suggests 'illustrates how freezones are intimately connected to broader political and socioeconomic tensions in Oman'.[130]

Duqm has become synonymous with its massive special economic zone covering an area of approximately 2,000 square kilometres with a coastline extending 90 km along the Arabian Sea. It is organised into three industrial zones (light, medium, and heavy industries), a fisheries harbour, and a tourism zone. At its heart is the Port of Duqm, which is one of the largest in the Middle East, and consists of commercial, oil, and government berths, the latter for security and logistics services for governments. It is also home to several major operations like Oman Drydock Company, which is an international ship repair yard as well as manufacturer for ships and steel works for the petrochemical

---

[127] 'The Seventh FYP 2006–2010', 287, 303, 408, 468–70.
[128] Royal Decree 119/2011, 'Establishing the Special Economic Zone Authority at Duqm and Issuing Its System (Issued 26 October 2011, Published 29 October 2011)', Official Gazette 949, [author translations from Arabic], 2011.
[129] Royal Decree 105/2020, 'Establishing the Public Authority for Special Economic Zones and Free Zones and Defining Its Terms of Reference (Issued 18 August 2020, Published 19 August 2020)', Official Gazette 1353, [author translations from Arabic], 2020.
[130] Mogielnicki, *A Political Economy of Free Zones in Gulf Arab States*, 92.

industry; Duqm Refinery and Petrochemical Industries Company, which is a joint venture between Oman's parent oil and energy investment company (OQ) and Kuwait International Petroleum Company; and Sebacic Oman Refinery, which produces acid from castor oil and is a joint venture between Oman and India. Another large Indian investment is a tourism project called 'Little India', which includes residential villas and apartments with sea views as well as hotels, restaurants, and malls. Duqm also attracted attention from China's maritime silk road, with the Sino-Oman Industrial City being developed by Oman Wanfang, a consortium of Chinese companies from Ningxia. The Sino-Oman Industrial City is expected to host around thirty-five projects in heavy and medium industries. Duqm SEZ also has projects like the Karwa Motors bus manufacturing plant that is a strategic partnership between Oman Investment Authority and Mowasalat Qatar.

Among its incentives, the SEZ has in-house support for labour and environmental permits and can help ease and speed up the recruitment process for Omanis and foreigners. It is able to help manage all the labour recruitment and visa issues by having a Ministry of Labour representative as part of the authority. Like in Sohar, Duqm SEZ is a liberalised space governed by a separate regulatory framework that offers specific incentives for operating within the area designed to attract investment. It allows full foreign ownership, full repatriation of capital and profit, usufruct agreements for up to fifty years and renewable beyond. It also offers up to thirty years of tax exemption from the start date, which is renewable for another thirty years, no currency restrictions, no minimum capital requirements, and a lower Omanisation rate than the rest of the economy (only 10 per cent). Even with the expansion of foreign ownership options in the rest of the economy in 2019, these liberalised prospects are attractive.[131]

Importantly, for all the employees it will attract, it is Renaissance City that holds accommodation units for various skill classes of employees, massive canteens, socialising halls, and laundry (Figure 4.3). Renaissance is an Oman-based multinational company that operates in sixteen countries. One of its main branches of activities are 'accommodation solutions' and catering contracts for the oil and

---

[131] Royal Decree 50/2019, 'Promulgating the Foreign Capital Investment Law (Issued 1 July 2019, Published 7 July 2019)', Official Gazette 1300, [author translations from Arabic], 2019.

Figure 4.3 Renaissance City accommodation.
Photo by author (27 January 2020)

gas sector, education, hospitals, and military. It already had five other 'Renaissance Villages' in Oman's interior oil-fields, with Renaissance City in Duqm as its sixth. It started with 16,000 beds and is expanding to 31,435 to keep up with accommodation demand. These house Omani and expatriate staff, with the number of beds per room (1, 2, 4, and 6) determined both by the skill class of labour and the willingness of employers to pay. The general concept, however, is to have basic but clean and well-maintained accommodation with the idea of 'healthy housing'. This seems to serve as a point of marketing for SEZAD, which emphasises its attention to good housing and catering for all who work in the area. In fact, SEZAD suggests that it does not allow low-end 'worker camps' in Duqm, and there is legislation that prohibits worker housing in the zone without SEZAD approval.[132]

---

[132] SEZAD Decision 22/2020, 'Amending Some Provisions of the Regulation of Urban Planning and Building Licenses in the Special Economic Zone at Duqm (Issued 10 February 2020, Published 23 February 2020)', Official Gazette 1330, [author translations from Arabic], 2020.

I did, however, observe two makeshift worker accommodations next to construction sites during my visit in January 2020. Upon inquiry, a SEZAD employee expressed surprise and informed me that these were contrary to regulations and should not be there.

As in the case of the Sohar Port and SEZ, Omani port projects like Duqm heavily rely on concessionary agreements and joint ventures with, in most cases, European port operators. The Port of Duqm is a joint venture with the consortium Antwerp Port Company (Belgium). The ship repair yard that integrates Duqm Port and the Drydock Complex was developed under the oversight of Daewoo Shipbuilding and Marine Engineering (DSME), a South Korean company under a ten-year agreement between 2006 and 2016. The Oman Drydock Company then entered into a joint venture with Babock International (UK).[133] Salalah Port too is jointly owned by the government of Oman, APM Terminals (Netherlands), and a mix of institutional and private investors. These joint ventures allow international port operators access to the Gulf market and directly compete with DP World and Jebel Ali Port in the UAE (Figure 4.4).

According to Ziadah, Oman is unique in the region through how it facilitates privatisation by public-private partnerships (PPPs) through the use of concession / lease, or Build, Operate and Transfer (BOT) agreements.[134] It is intended that through these PPPs, Oman's ports are connected with international networks of global market-based port operators. Moreover, these forms of privatisation make it conveniently difficult to contest market logics. The overlapping role of state and capital in the projects mean identifying responsibility for various functions, activities, and outcomes can be challenging.[135]

4.3.1 Situating Duqm in the Story of Development

The promise of Duqm is in tremendous economic growth or, in the optimistic words of its mayor, Ahmed bin Salim Al-Mahruqi, the

---

[133] 'About Oman Drydock Company', Oman Drydock Company, 2021, www .omandrydock.com/about_us.html; Gye-Man Kang and Hyo-jin Kim, 'DSME, Hyundai Heavy Win String of Crude Carrier Orders', *Maeil Business Newspaper*, 18 January 2019, sec. english, www.mk.co.kr/news/english/view/ 2019/01/38110/.

[134] Ziadah, 'Constructing a Logistics Space', 677.

[135] See discussion in Hanieh, *Lineages of Revolt*, 54–56.

Figure 4.4 Shift change at the Port of Duqm.
Photo by author (27 January 2020)

possibility it 'could become the future capital of Oman'.[136] It is partly because it is the largest free trade zone in the MENA and among the biggest in the world that it so captures the imagination even while it initially raised considerable scepticism. Mohammad Al-Zadjali's column captures the sensation:

When I hear the word Duqm, I think of economic growth. I think of families moving to the city to start the first generation of businesses. I envision trading routes and large ships coming into the dock to bring trade and goods. I can almost feel the cool breeze of the Salalah monsoon dance across my face as I close my eyes and imagine what His Majesty has in store for us... it can only grow and prosper and eventually become the new city of the future.[137]

---

[136] Sebastian Castelier and Quentin Mueller, 'Oman's Duqm, a New Port City for the Middle East?', *Middle East Eye*, 10 February 2019, www.middleeasteye .net/news/omans-duqm-new-port-city-middle-east.
[137] Al Zadjali, 'Duqm'.

In addition to generating national income, its promise includes the creation of thousands of jobs for Omani citizens as well as opportunities for SMEs with clear ICV programmes.[138]

The roots of developing Duqm this way extend earlier than the creation of SEZAD, to when the framework for transforming economic life along Al-Wusta's coast through expropriating and accumulating land for 'the public interest' was set. In 2006, a royal decree allowed the seizure and development of facilities and land for the 'future of the Omani economy' – and the ideas for developing a regional centre for heavy industries, including the commercial port, dry dock, international airport and freezone – were enshrined.[139] The legal foundations were available in the 1978 law of expropriation for the public interest, which allows large scale development projects to move forward in spaces determined valuable for developmental purposes.[140] This law was amended nine years later to include the condition that fair compensation has to be given for land and real estate expropriated for public interest.[141]

Thus, like along the Batinah coast, land in Duqm had to be rezoned and repurposed. It was certainly less difficult given its limited population but not entirely uncontentious. The life of both fishing and nomadic communities was interrupted and changed (Figure 4.5). Fisheries in general have been targeted in development plans for modernisation, commercialisation, and internationalisation,[142] that is, to upscale the sector away from small-scale fishing and to expand exports from transportation by cars and small trucks to neighbouring Gulf

[138] Chapter 3 has already introduced ICV schemes, which were pioneered in Oman by PDO. These were in turn picked up by other large companies and projects in the country, where ICV is viewed as both a local content initiative and a mode of CSR.

[139] Royal Decree 85/2006, 'Determining the Character of the Public Interest for the Duqm City Development Project in Al-Wusta (Issued 25 July 2006, Published 1 August 2006)', Official Gazette 820, [author translations from Arabic], 2006.

[140] Royal Decree 64/1978, 'Promulgating the Law of Expropriation for the Public Interest (Issued 24 December 1978, Published 1 January 1979)', Official Gazette 161, [author translations from Arabic], 1978.

[141] Royal Decree 75/1987, 'Amending Some Provisions of the Law of Expropriation for the Public Interest (Issued 14 October 1987, Published 1 November 1987)', Official Gazette 370, [author translations from Arabic], 1987.

[142] L. Zaibet et al., 'Internationalization of Oman Fisheries Firms after the European Union Ban', *Agricultural and Marine Sciences* 9, no. 2 (2004): 1–6.

Figure 4.5 Small-scale fishing for export.
Photos by author (Duqm, 26 January 2020)

countries (Dubai being the largest export market). With its long coast-line, Oman is the largest fresh fish exporter in the GCC, and this feature naturally draws attention to its development.[143] A World Bank report in 2015, which identifies the coastal region encompassing Duqm as one of the country's major fishing areas, assessed Oman's fisheries sector as follows:

Fishing is not economically productive and aquaculture in Oman is in its infancy. It is conservatively estimated that Oman is forgoing 2.4 billion Omani Rials (OMR) [6.2 billion USD] from fisheries under current manage-ment of the sector. Many fishers are not involved full time in fishing, and despite significant subsidies, remuneration is often low. There is a need to improve economic management of the fisheries sector and create viable and sustainable employment opportunities.[144]

As part of this upscaling, Duqm's fishing harbour, completed in October 2021, is the largest in the country and among the largest in the region and includes an integrated processing and export zone that contains facilities for sea food processing, packaging, raw material storage, and deep freezers.[145]

Reports indicate that the Duqm fishing community were not entirely happy about the promise of this transformation. The head of the fish-ermen's union in Duqm reportedly raised concerns about the potential for overfishing because of the large boats the harbour could host, while

---

[143] 'Briefings from Oman: Agriculture & Fisheries' (Muscat: Ithraa: The Public Authority for Investment Promotion and Export Development, December 2016), 4, https://issuu.com/ithraaoman/docs/ithraa_briefing_agriculture_eng_aw.

[144] 'Sustainable Management of the Fisheries Sector in Oman: A Vision for Shared Prosperity', World Bank Advisory Assignment (Washington, DC: World Bank Group and Ministry of Agriculture and Fisheries Wealth, December 2015), 1, https://documents1.worldbank.org/curated/en/901371480601979449/pdf/110678-WP-Summary-Oman-Fisheries-PUBLIC.pdf.

[145] 'Oman Developing Eight New Fishing Harbours and Ports', *Zawya*, 25 December 2016, www.zawya.com/mena/en/business/story/Oman_developing_eight_new_fishing_harbours_and_ports-ZAWYA20161225041102; Gemsheer Mon Chalil, 'The New Investment Wave into Aquaculture in Middle East Countries: Opportunities and Challenges', GLOBEFISH – Information and Analysis on World Fish Trade (Food and Agriculture Organization of the United Nations), accessed 11 December 2021, www.fao.org/in-action/globefish/fishery-information/resource-detail/en/c/338614/; 'Construction of Oman's Largest Fishing Port Completed in Duqm', *Muscat Daily*, 20 October 2021, www.muscatdaily.com/2021/10/20/construction-of-omans-largest-fishing-port-completed-in-duqm/.

the means of the small-scale fishermen he represented were too modest to invest in the project. Concerns were perhaps worsened by the fact that while the harbour works were ongoing, the fishermen were restricted to a smaller, isolated beach.[146] Fishing communities have been offered a variety of recompenses by the state for the disruption, including new housing when needed and better integration into local, regional, and international fish markets.

Moreover, in vision documents, news releases, and reports such as the World Bank assessment quoted above, employment is always highlighted as one of the beneficial outcomes of the development of the sector. This despite that the same report suggests that Omani young people are reluctant to pursue fishing as a career.[147] Like fishing communities globally, the sector's precarity and low pay make it an unattractive option. Furthermore, fishing went through a major labour transformation in the past several decades. As mentioned previously, whereas over 80 per cent of agricultural and fisheries workers were Omani in the early 1990s, today Omanis comprise under 2 per cent of workers.[148] While efforts to re-Omanise the sector have been ongoing and integrated with sectoral modernisation and development efforts, small-scale fishing continues to rely on foreign workers. Technically, it should only be on the larger boats where recruiters can bring up to 70 per cent of their staff from abroad, while the small-scale, local fishing, as a traditional industry, should remain in the hands of local fishermen. Despite legislation that restricts official immigration in this sector, fishing is heavily dependent upon migrant workers. Many of these fishermen come from Bangladesh, the majority of whom arrive through irregular channels and live a rather precarious life where deportation is an ever-present reality.[149] Yet their de facto presence,

---

[146] Sebastian Castelier and Quentin Muller, 'Omani Fishermen Swept up in Belt and Road Wave', *Asia Times*, 11 January 2019, https://asiatimes.com/2019/01/omani-fishermen-swept-up-in-belt-and-road-wave/; Castelier and Mueller, 'Oman's Duqm, a New Port City for the Middle East?'

[147] 'Sustainable Management of the Fisheries Sector', 16.

[148] 'The Fourth FYP 1991–1995', 149; NCSI, '2019 Statistical Year Book', 108, 118.

[149] For more on Bangladeshi fishermen in Oman, see Marie Percot, '"We Sent Our Sons across the Seven Rivers": Tracing the Migratory Network and the Risky Migration of Bangladeshi Fishermen to Oman', in *The South Asia to Gulf Migration Governance Complex*, ed. Crystal A. Ennis and Nicolas Blarel (Bristol: Bristol University Press, 2022), 125–43.

and the reliance of boat owners and coastal communities on this labour, also means wages are drastically lower than the cost of Omani labour. An added ambition of development efforts is thus that by increasing the technological capacity, form, and scale of fisheries as a whole, new types of more attractive jobs would materialise. Yet lower Omanisation rates required for economic activities in freezones raise questions about these objectives. Again, the balance of investment attractiveness against protection measures are in tension.

Nomadic communities in the Duqm area, primarily the *Janaba* (*Al-Junaībī*, singular), also faced disruption, which seems reminiscent of the uprooting of life and livelihoods of Bedouin communities in Oman's interior documented by Dawn Chatty.[150] SEZAD officials informed me that the *badū* of the area had to be moved, and they built a neighbourhood specifically for the affected *Janaba* tribe. These were nice, middle-class looking homes, similar to ones one would find in Muscat and elsewhere in the country. In 2020, several SEZAD employees remarked that the homes given in compensation remained vacant, and some seemed perplexed by the unwillingness of the community to move into what they perceived as nicer accommodation. Many of the community were uninterested in this form of settled life, with properties right next to the neighbours and no space for livestock. Chatty wrote about similar housing units built in the desert for populations of mobile pastoralists in her 1996 book, remarking that

> they are, without much exception, tightly packed units of twenty to thirty two-story town houses that require substantial adjustment for a villager to comfortably occupy, let alone a nomadic pastoralist. No concession is made for livestock, small or large, in the patch of land between the house and the walls of the garden. Only when selected recipients refuse to move into these units are questions raised as to what might be lacking.[151]

Nearly three decades later, it seems as though a similar pattern unfolded. During my visit, I could see that many units remained vacant. Of the few units I noticed were occupied, it appeared as though the families had somewhat retrofit the exterior of the home to have a

---

[150] Dawn Chatty, 'Petroleum Exploitation and the Displacement of Pastoral Nomadic Households in Oman', *Center for Migration Studies Special Issues* 11, no. 4 (1994): 87–106, https://doi.org/10.1111/j.2050-411X.1994.tb00799.x; Chatty, *Mobile Pastoralists*.

[151] Chatty, *Mobile Pastoralists*, 189.

Figure 4.6 Homes built for the local *badū* community.
Photo by author (Duqm, 26 January 2020)

space for a few of their camels and to have a shaded area for themselves to enjoy outside. The style and size of the houses, and in particular the very limited outdoor space, clashes with the living norms of the community (Figure 4.6).

The reason for the reluctance to take up homes provided by the state in earlier episodes was partly attributed to the centrality of livestock, and the migrations necessary for their maintenance, as 'the organizing principle of social life' for Bedouin communities.[152] Many continue to interpret the reluctance for settling as part of an overall desire for maintaining a mobile lifestyle. For example, the *Janaba* move to and from the sea during certain fishing and agricultural seasons. The movement of mobile pastoralists has, however, already declined dramatically given several changes over the preceding decades, among which were the wider availability of water with modern wells drilled by oil companies. Furthermore, Duqm received its first school, primarily for the *Janaba* community, by the early 1980s and, like in the rest of the

---

[152] Dawn Chatty, 'The Bedu and Al-Badiyah in Oman', *PDO News*, 1991, 14.

country, the expansion of education offered new possibilities for wages, work, and lifestyles.[153] The reluctance and challenge of the housing project is therefore part of a wider pattern. Chatty argues that there is often a disconnect between policy-makers in urban spaces who are so remote from mobile lifestyles they frequently do not know how best to 'bring development' to the communities. Even when projects like the one in Duqm aims to be people-centred, the disconnect continues. SEZAD, PDO, and various companies within the zone like the Port of Duqm have hired liaisons with the aspiration of connecting with local communities and improving such outcomes.

Certainly, some within rural settled and mobile communities benefit from the new educational and economic opportunities available to them through and after such changes. The government has regularly paid attention to ensuring educational access and economic opportunities throughout the history of various changes impacting rural Oman, even if they are not always in the form most fitting local desires.[154] Yet economic transformation based on spatial reconfigurations necessarily creates disjunctures and questions about who benefits and how they benefit from these projects.

4.3.2 Recruiting and Working in the Zone

As the Duqm project accelerated, and especially after the jobseeker issue continued to resurface throughout the 2010s, the discussion of the massive development of Duqm nearly always coincided with the promise and capacity of this project to bring jobs. It became a cornerstone of messaging, like most of the national development initiatives. Yet early questions circled around how a remote, constructed city could attract and retain Omanis. The country has always struggled to staff distant locations, including recruiting teachers and nurses for remote posts.[155] In the early stages of Duqm's planning, it felt the

---

[153] Chatty, 'Bedouin Economics and the Modern Wage Market', 79.

[154] Chatty, 'Bedouin Economics and the Modern Wage Market'; Dawn Chatty, 'Boarding Schools for Mobile Peoples: The Harasiis in the Sultanate of Oman', in *The Education of Nomadic Peoples: Issues, Provision and Prospects*, ed. Caroline Dyer (Oxford; New York: Berghahn Press, 2006), 213–31.

[155] Chatty, 'Boarding Schools for Mobile Peoples'; Basu Ghosh, 'Health Workforce Development Planning in the Sultanate of Oman – a Profile (1991–2009)' (Muscat: Directorate General of Planning, Ministry of Health, 28 October 2009), MOH Library.

same way. The human resources departments of several of the major industrial projects were keenly aware of these concerns and trialled several approaches to working schedules. Some settled on those modelled after the oil and gas sector, with staff rotations such as two weeks of full-time work and one week off to allow employees to return to their home regions and families. Initially, offices kept their headquarters in Muscat and only flew into Duqm for purpose-specific meetings and supervision. Gradually, more companies are moving there.[156] One manager noted that the overwhelming number of Omani jobseekers in the country means these earlier location concerns have not become an issue, 'The jobs situation is on our side. Omanis are willing to travel if it means work.'[157]

Within the zone, some authorities suggest 'there is no tension around Omanisation', while some managers think it remains a difficult issue area.[158] Some cite well-rehearsed complaints of education and job-readiness, while others suggest that Omanis are just as good of employees as others. Some companies think the authorities listen well to their requests for lessening regulations around other issue areas like the frequency of surveillance and customs inspections but claim that Omanisation was different. 'I do feel like they listen to me and they did a lot, but there is one exception, with labour laws they are not listening.'[159] Further liberalisation of the employment space in the SEZ was a key desire. In a conversation with Yahya Al-Jabri, then chairman of SEZAD, he noted,

We started with a low Omanisation percentage of only 10 per cent, but the average is 24 to 26 per cent now. Some companies are much higher, like the refinery. These numbers are likely to decline as employee numbers rise, but they will continue to meet the set percentage. Everyone has met these percentages with two exceptions. The problem is there are incentive problems with cheaper labour.[160]

---

[156] By May of 2021, the Port of Duqm completed the move of its headquarters from Muscat to Duqm and transferred all remaining staff there 'All Port of Duqm Employees Relocated from Muscat', *Oman Daily Observer*, 29 May 2021, sec. Oman, www.omanobserver.om/article/1101497/oman/labour/all-port-of-duqm-employees-relocated-from-muscat.

[157] Interview, manager of a Duqm-based company, 7 January 2020.

[158] Interviews, Muscat and Duqm, January 2020.

[159] Interview, director of large industrial project at Duqm, Muscat, 7 January 2020.

[160] Interview, Yahya Al-Jabri, chairman SEZAD, 8 January 2020.

Mirroring the rest of the economy, the global market pressures based on the availability of cheap labour means indigenisation efforts in the labour market are expensive and difficult to digest.

Like company executives spoken with in Muscat and Duqm, Al-Jabri also indicated that there was a lot of focus on training initiatives. There was training in English among the local community, training on health and safety, and training with the Ministry of Education and the German University of Technology in Oman. Importantly, many companies were sponsoring students for further education. For example, based on an MOU, 1,000 students were being sent to China for training at Ningxia Polytechnic College by Oman Wangfang as part of a two-year training programme that combined academic and vocational training for various technological fields required in the Sino-Oman industrial city. In June 2018, thirty-nine students completed this training and returned for their internships.[161]

Given the low required rates of Omanisation within the zone, many of the recruitment and training efforts are either packaged as part of CSR initiatives and good citizenship signalling from companies to the wider country. The lower Omanisation rates are part of the attractive bargain of the zone, which, however low, many of my interlocutors in various businesses prefer not to have at all.

In general, human resource managers view regulation in Oman as having a pro-labour bias.[162] A member of the Chamber of Commerce committee on nationalisation and the labour market noted, 'For the Chamber, our focus is first on business. We say, "without business there are no jobs". But they want us to focus on jobs first. They think it's the opposite - give jobs and business will follow. But no, it is the opposite! You need strong business and then jobs will follow.'[163] Moreover, I regularly heard complaints that hiring an Omani was too much of a commitment because firing was nearly impossible. Despite all the petitioning from the Chamber of Commerce and

---

[161] 'Spotlight: Belt and Road Generates Growing Passion for China among Middle East Youths', *People's Daily Online*, 12 September 2018, http://en.people.cn/n3/2018/0912/c90000–9499750.html; Bitwize-, 'Omani Students Undergo Training at Chinese Centre', *Times of Oman*, 14 July 2018 edition, accessed 13 December 2021, https://timesofoman.com/article/138105/Oman/Omani-students-undergo-training-at-Chinese-centre.

[162] This finding is also shared by Louër, 'The Arab Spring Effect on Labor Politics in Bahrain and Oman'.

[163] Interview, Chamber of Commerce member, Muscat, 26 January 2019.

Industry members in the wider economy and even complaints from within SEZs, if a labour issue went to court, the perception was that the court would always rule in favour of the employee. The pressure points from jobseekers and Omanis in the labour market is a delicate one. With the overhaul of the labour law, the incremental addition of regulation to make the private sector more attractive to Omani labour, and the legalisation of unions, companies face a more empowered workforce that advocates for labour's interests.

The same segmentations that make expatriates on limited visas more flexible and easier to fire thus also increases their attractiveness even in skill levels when their wages may equal or exceed national ones. This creates a unique set of disciplinary tools and governing incentives for companies, which is well encapsulated in the following anecdote recounted by an expatriate executive at a company operating in Duqm.

Honestly, we took a risky approach. We started with a very, very highly Omanised workforce ... what I found was that Omanis work very well. All the stories and the things we were warned about were not true. When you have all Omanis, they work hard, they do what they need to do. Maybe they're not like 100 per cent or something, but really they're good. But ... well .... We had a problem and we ended up changing this .... We started very Omanised. I wish they hadn't made those promises. Better to start low and build up than raise expectations and get a lower and lower Omanisation percentage. But this, the real unwritten practice – everyone does it but cannot say it – we had to take a strategic decision to diversify the workforce. Because there was a premise of a strike. And you know .... We can't have a strike here. The way they deal with it in this part of the world is different, and commercially I cannot risk a strike. So to avoid a shutdown we decided we need foreign staff. So we hired Indians.[164]

The 'unwritten practice' the executive refers to clearly illustrates the reliance on foreign recruitment not just for the cost effectiveness but also for the disciplinary possibility. A diverse workforce is preferred not for diversity's sake but because it reduces the possibility of solidarity and weakens the threat of strikes. Likewise, an Omani business owner described one of the keys to his success, 'Break the lobby. Have mixed ethnicities! I have Omani and Indian and Sri Lankan and from the Philippines and China and from many places.'[165] While a diverse

---

[164] Anonymous interview, company operating in Duqm, January 2020.
[165] Interview, large business owner, Muscat, 26 January 2020.

workforce is sometimes viewed as a net positive for productivity, in the context of global Gulf labour markets, diversity is also pursued as a way to fragment solidarities or keep collective bargaining in check. Such fragmentation is exacerbated by the rather different conditions under which employees are hired and their legal connection to the country. It is worth recalling here that foreign employees' right to stay in the country is tied to their employer.

This is therefore another example of how the pursuit of competitiveness and productivity, keystones of neoliberal adjustment, actively disorganises working-class movements and institutions.[166] Freezones and international ports as liberalised and globalised spaces are situated in a global production network dynamically part of a global labour market space. As the examples of recruiting in Duqm illustrates, they are actively and explicitly shaped by pressures to deregulate, increase flexibility, and expand productivity and international competitiveness.

4.4 Conclusions on Job Seeking and Creation in Spaces of Radical Transformation

The cases of Sohar and Duqm highlight the contested impact of radical development on communities in general and labour in particular. In the Sohar case, we see that while the scale of 2011 protests was the largest and most sustained social mobilisation since the Dhofar revolution, and while it took local officials and outside observers by surprise, it was neither without precedent nor without antecedents. Viewing the Sohar uprising as an anomaly disconnects it from a longer reading of socio-economic mobilisation and contentious politics in Oman. The story of Duqm also reveals the disjunctures and disruption caused by the radical transformation of space, economy, and society. While, on the one hand, its local social contentiousness is significantly reduced by its location remote from major population centres. On the other hand, it carries with it the promise of jobs, and these need to be delivered to a much further dispersed community of active jobseekers. It is thus part of a larger national story promising the benefits of globalisation and liberalisation.

---

[166] Schaumberg, '"Disorganisation" as Social Movement Tactic', 379.

We can draw several conclusions from this chapter. First, radical transformations face associated contestations.[167] The two cases suggest an alternative reading of labour and its mobilisation in Oman, one that demonstrates the possibilities of studying Gulf labour as a category and a central mover in contestation. This contrasts with the persistent views of civil society as 'weak or irrelevant in Gulf rentier states',[168] which has contributed to the negligence of theory building on labour in the region. Labour (and job seeking) has become a key space of mobilisation. It has been said that the absence of an ideological underpinning to labour issues in Oman since the crush of the radical left in the 1970s results in a weakness in organisational or political resistance in Oman.[169] Despite this, we see that labour still matters both as an object of development and as a protagonist of change. That is, we see that rentier states are reactive and do respond to public pressure and even the prospect of social unrest. This is especially visible through the Sohari story.

Second, expectations, both their construction and their management, matter. The welfare benefits associated with rentier states build expectations among citizens that are arguably louder albeit similar to social expectations in welfare states elsewhere. These converge with expectations from the promises of economic liberalisation and comparisons with economic outcomes in neighbouring states and from comparisons with peer groups globally whose economic, social, and political life are more visible and comparable given social media pervasiveness. The promises of economic development projects made in this context heighten the expectations for tangible benefits from economic growth.

Third, and interrelated, the cases discussed in this chapter reveal the endemic tension between economic openness and growth, on the one hand, and social protection, on the other. Similar to the pendulum of liberalisation and regulation unpacked in Chapter 2, both cases demonstrate the pull between liberalising the market and the push aimed at protecting Omanis from the negative repercussions of it. While some

---

[167] AlShehabi, 'Radical Transformations and Radical Contestations', 49.

[168] Moritz, 'Re-Conceptualizing Civil Society in Rentier States', 136.

[169] See Louër's important comparison between Bahraini and Omani labour politics to better understand the role of ideology (or de-ideologisation) in labour politics. Louër, 'The Arab Spring Effect on Labor Politics in Bahrain and Oman'.

certainly benefitted, and lifestyles and dreams for the future changed, the benefits were uneven. At the same time that this unevenness is combatted with job nationalisation policies as a key social protection measure, both capital and the state pursue practices to forestall or suppress labour agitation and mobilisation. The recruitment and employment practices in the SEZs of Sohar and Duqm also reveals tactics of pre-empting and managing labour agitation (and pressure from below more broadly), from employers.

Finally, the cases highlight that the labour market is one of the crucial ways the region is integrated into the global political economy and where the impact of neoliberal capitalism has especially complex relationships with welfare pressures. The labour market allows us to illustrate this complexity clearly, and, by bringing the Gulf region into conversations on the impact of global capitalism on the wider Middle East and developing world, allows us to draw comparative lessons. Despite all the scholarship that describes the Gulf region as exceptional, many global economic trends are in fact visible in the economic transformations over the past several decades.

5 | Constructing Belonging and Contesting Economic Space

Why won't they hire me? My GPA in my bachelor was high, my English is great. I didn't just sit around at home before. I applied to every single job last year. I don't have much experience ok, but I had internships, I volunteered. I'm hardworking. I really tried all year, but this last month I just got too depressed about it.[1]

— Shamsa

For many Omani young people, the labour market is a space of struggle and a site of contestation. Despite possessing political citizenship and seeming like those who should belong and benefit most, many Omanis encounter multiple exclusions in their economic citizenship and feel marginalised in the private sector. Experiences of belonging and not belonging in the labour market are co-constitutive and occur below and between everyday social and class relations. In my interactions with citizens and expatriates – young and old – labour is a prominent feature of conversations and stories, which regularly concern the pursuit of work, pursuit of promotion, or the everyday experiences of working.

Belonging and *not* belonging in the Omani labour market takes different shapes and manifests in different ways. Perceptions of belonging are influenced by who has access to jobs, income, and legal status, as well as who feels they should have access to jobs, income, and legal status. The productivity stereotypes discussed earlier in the book hang heavily over Omani work life. While many studies of belonging in the region focus on foreign workers and the circumstances that determine the conditions, duration, and rights of their work and life,[2] Gulf citizens are assumed to be universally privileged actors due

---

[1] Shamsa, Muscat, July 2015.
[2] See, for example, Zahra R. Babar, 'The Vagaries of the In-Between: Labor Citizenship in the Persian Gulf', *International Journal of Middle East Studies* 52, no. 4 (November 2020): 765–70, https://doi.org/10.1017/S0020743820001075;

203

to the power and access their passports provide.[3] Yet economic and political inclusions and exclusions go beyond the question of who has what passport. Omanis certainly benefit from particular privileges by virtue of their citizenship when compared with other members of society. The depth of privilege varies by class, gender, race, and access, as discussed in Chapter 2. Yet feeling restricted from economic engagement or economic belonging powerfully informs social relations and regulation as well as economic choices and life. Perceptions, therefore, have implications not only for social and labour relations but also for state-society relations.

In this chapter, I explore economic belonging in Oman, foregrounding the ways Omani millennials explain, question, and navigate their place and opportunities in economic life. This exploration allows me to make two arguments. First, I argue that the construction of economic belonging (and not belonging) takes shape in the economic structures of segmentation, tied up within the dialectic of neoliberal reform and labour protection. The structure of the labour market is usually presented as an exceptional political economy feature of the region. Yet segmentation is not unique to the Gulf even if the sheer scale of foreign labour dependence remains distinctive. Furthermore, Oman's segmented labour market is inserted within a global market for labour that is classed, gendered, and raced, whereby Oman's labour market both benefits from and is shaped by broader global transformations that situate economies in particular positions in global value chains. As we have seen thus far, this structure emerges from 'the twin processes of capital formation and demographic management for political and social control'.[4] Labour takes 'complex forms of subordination' to capital in the global labour market, from wage and family labour to labour that is indentured and forced, but these 'different forms are

Neha Vora, 'From Golden Frontier to Global City: Shifting Forms of Belonging, "Freedom", and Governance among Indian Businessmen in Dubai', *American Anthropologist* 113, no. 2 (2011): 306–18, https://doi.org/10.1111/j.1548-1433.2011.01332.x; Deepak Unnikrishnan, 'The Hidden Cost of Migrant Labor', *Foreign Affairs*, 11 February 2020, www.foreignaffairs.com/articles/india/2020-02-07/hidden-cost-migrant-labor; Vora, *Impossible Citizens*; Gardner, *City of Strangers*.

[3] Neha Vora and Natalie Koch, 'Everyday Inclusions: Rethinking Ethnocracy, Kafala, and Belonging in the Arabian Peninsula', *Studies in Ethnicity and Nationalism* 15, no. 3 (2015): 540–52, https://doi.org/10.1111/sena.12158.

[4] AlShehabi, 'Radical Transformations and Radical Contestations', 36.

socially constructed (and resisted) and politically regulated'.[5] This line of argument reveals how regulation and reform, alongside engagements and entanglements within Oman's global labour market, are socially constructed, resisted, and regulated. Developing this understanding is only possible by listening to and engaging with those who experience everyday life in the region.

Second, I argue that class is central to understanding economic belonging and citizenship in the Gulf. Class cannot only be reduced to a simple division between a citizen population that is privileged and a migrant population that is subordinated through an exploitative labour relationship. Labour, as Sachedina notes, is 'the generative site among Omanis to claim rights of citizenship and sameness and by addressing the social and economic inequalities'.[6] Relations of inclusion and exclusions reveal how the politics and practice of difference in global capitalism produces particular tensions and perceptions of power and value that influence labour relations and reproduce class. This chapter thus buttresses the book's causal, intersectional, and integrated approach to class through unpacking the levels, layers, and influence of identities and belonging that impact labour market experiences. The dynamics producing perceptions of belonging and class also generate resistance and contestation around the boundaries of inclusion and exclusion. These dynamics accordingly help understand forms of resistance and help explain the ebbs and flows in the successes and failures of policies like Omanisation.

Theorising class in the Gulf has been a slow but growing effort. Scholars like Adam Hanieh, Ahmed Kanna, and Michelle Buckley have led the way in centring class in the study of Gulf economies. Hanieh, for example, focuses attention on the processes of Gulf capital class formation, which, despite some rentier specificities, remains 'fully capitalist'.[7] His scholarship shows that labour exclusion is embedded in the spatial structuring of class. It facilitates the formation of Gulf capitalists and is a form of social control that was necessary to underpin the region's rise to become a core zone in the global economy. The argument is that if workers were granted equal labour and citizenship

---

[5] Gurminder K. Bhambra and John Holmwood, 'Colonialism, Postcolonialism and the Liberal Welfare State', *New Political Economy* 23, no. 5 (2018): 579, https://doi.org/10.1080/13563467.2017.1417369.

[6] Sachedina, *Cultivating the Past, Living the Modern*, 20.

[7] Hanieh, *Lineages of Revolt*, 123.

rights it would challenge the 'inherent structure of the system'.[8] That is, the production of a foreign labouring class is intimately tied to the production of a *khalījī* capitalist class.[9] Meanwhile, others scholars have begun to unpack the layers of class within migrant communities, foregrounding foreign labour as central to biopower development in the region while at the same time showing how skilled and professional expatriate classes too are implicated in systems of exploitation.[10] The type of politics, and ways of agitating, are very much influenced by the workplace and the arrangement of households. For example, Buckley writes how the sequestering of construction workers in the workplace and in the 'mass-worker household' fostered the development of labour politics and facilitated strikes.[11]

Building from this path-breaking research, this work contributes to this scholarship by also interrogating class *within* citizen populations and between economic actors. The remainder of this chapter is organised as follows. In Section 5.1, I discuss the perceptions of exclusion millennials relate both at work and in seeking work. At one level, I show how two forms of government policies – one set aimed at nationalising job categories and another set aimed at making citizens neoliberal private sector actors – are both framed as responses to labour market challenges. These seemingly contradictory policy directions coalesce around the idea of the importance of pushing citizens into a largely uninviting economic space. At another level, Omani millennials embrace the rhetorics of both job-creating and entrepreneur-making in their imagination of belonging in a dynamic private sector. At the same time, the promises of these initiatives raise expectations and contribute to a growing malaise around perceived labour market exclusions. In Section 5.2, I show how Omani millennials, despite their legal belonging vis-à-vis citizenship, face multiple exclusions in their economic citizenship. Perceptions and reactions to

---

[8] Hanieh, *Lineages of Revolt*, 127; See also, Ahmed Kanna, 'The Arab World's Forgotten Rebellions: Foreign Workers and Biopolitics in the Gulf', *South Asian Magazine for Action and Reflection (SAMAR)*, 31 May 2011, http://samarmagazine.org/archive/articles/357.

[9] Hanieh, 'Khaleeji-Capital'.

[10] Ahmed Kanna, 'A Politics of Non-Recognition? Biopolitics of Arab Gulf Worker Protests in the Year of Uprisings', *Interface* 4, no. 1 (May 2012): 146–64; Kanna, 'Flexible Citizenship in Dubai'; Vora, 'From Golden Frontier to Global City'; Vora, *Impossible Citizens*.

[11] Buckley, 'Locating Neoliberalism in Dubai', 266.

rising unemployment range from collective (physical and virtual) job creation demands and protests, to accusing authorities of poor planning, corruption, and nepotism, to blaming foreigners for crowding the private sector labour market or companies for being biased against Omanis or favouring foreigners. Speaking about economic life in terms of belonging makes the missing nuances of class and labour market realities in the Omani economy more accessible. It affords understanding to the social side of the construction of belonging, relations, and regulation, further helping us appreciate how perceptions matter despite their subjectivity. This approach further addresses employment precarities and policy responses to them, unfolding how policy responses can trigger fluctuating senses of vulnerability within belonging. For example, measures aimed at enhancing the job security of citizens can heighten feelings of insecurity among the country's many noncitizens.

5.1 Job Hunting Anxieties and Exclusions

Especially over the years since 2011, *malaf al-tawẓīf (the employment file)* remains a familiar pressure point and draws considerable attention from various platforms.[12] So, in May of 2021, when Sohari residents once again occupied the space beneath an overpass that had previously been the site of the Globe roundabout and a centre of 2011 protests, the jobseekers' demands resonated with young people across the country (see Chapter 4). They felt *qaḍiyyat al-tawẓīf* – the employment issue – intensely and personally. Young men were again calling for work and this time in the context of the weak economic outcomes of the past half decade that were being compounded by the pandemic depression. The immediate and outsized security presence on the roads of Sohar drew quick ire on social media while tweets, posts, and comments expressed understanding and support of the issues. Small towns across the country held (albeit small) solidarity demonstrations. When local news outlets initially failed to report on the events, they were mocked and had to offer some coverage. The employment file was no secret and the protests could not simply be ignored. Feelings of exclusion from job opportunities and alienation from the private sector

---

[12] Muḥammad ʿAwaḍ al-Mashīkhī, 'Ilā ayn Ddahibūn fī idārat malaf al-Tawẓīf?!', *Al-Roya*, 31 May 2021, https://alroya.om/post/283134.

have been a large feature of my private conversations over the years. These impressions have become increasingly visible on social media. Old guard tactics of dismissal, suspicion, or suppression are hardly effective in the long run.

The unemployment issue had not disappeared in the decade after the 2011 uprisings, and in fact most new jobs added to the economy during this period continued to be filled through foreign recruitment. Ann al-Kindi characterises this unemployment problem as 'a strange type'.[13] It bewilders many young Omani jobseekers who observe no shortage of vacancy ads but still face joblessness. Trending social media hashtags over the last half decade regularly include *'Umānīyūn bilā waẓā'if* (Omanis without jobs) and *bāḥthūn 'an 'amal yastaghīthūn* (Jobseekers are calling out), alongside occupation-specific demands for employment or promotion possibilities. Many tweets marked with such hashtags are simply petitioning for jobs, while others share failed recruitment experiences. Yet others display screenshots of job ads posted in their field where they have been unable to find work, pointedly noting that the ad exclusively targets expatriates.

Malaf al-tawẓīf is not a new issue and neither are the associated contentions around belonging, but these were austerity times. Belt tightening began with the oil price downturn in 2014; and over the course of the intervening years, the government had attempted to implement a variety of austerity measures like energy and fuel subsidy reductions to help service ballooning debt and reign in public expenditure.[14] Public sector salaries were harmonised, allowances cut, ministries and SOEs reorganised. Omanisation was again high on the agenda as demands from jobseekers continued.

Amid these already financially tight times, 2020–2021 had been especially full of change. The COVID-19 pandemic struck the globe no fewer than two months after the death of Sultan Qaboos and the transition of power to his cousin Haitham bin Tariq. The economy contracted, businesses closed, and over 200,000 expatriates left the country between the Marches of 2020 and 2021 as jobs dried up and

---

[13] Ann Al-Kindi, 'Muqāwamat al-'Aqaliyya al-rī'iyya', 5 November 2017, https://annalkindi.net/archives/2030.
[14] Ennis and Al-Saqri, 'Oil Price Collapse and the Political Economy of the Post-2014 Economic Adjustment in the Sultanate of Oman'.

borders closed.[15] A long delayed value-added tax (VAT) was rolled out in April 2021. Some cutbacks were combined with protection mechanisms but ones that also cost the individual. For example, a social security system came into effect in January 2021 that required a contribution of 1 per cent of the monthly wage from both the employer and employee.[16] This security scheme applies to the civil, military, security, and the private sectors and is characterised in Public Authority for Social Insurance (PASI) reports as cross-sectoral 'social solidarity'.[17] Many felt the immediate impact of increased expenses and reduced take home income more than they considered the long-term prospect of contributing to a new source of social safety net.[18]

Economic woes combined with hope of more space for political and social debate and critique when, in January 2021, the Sultan announced the new basic statute of the state, which enshrined freedom of expression and freedom of the press (Articles 35 and 37).[19] Disappointment ensued when it quickly became clear that limits remained in place and both traditional and social media voices were uncertain where the boundaries were. Some advocated for protection of this enshrined right, and it was tabled for discussion at the *majlis al-shūrā*.[20] This disappointment merged with a perception that the state

[15] '218,000 Expatriate Workers Left Oman in the Past 12 Months', *National Centre for Statistics and Information*, 23 May 2021, www.ncsi.gov.om/News/Pages/NewsCT_20210523131776647.aspx.

[16] Royal Decree 121/2020, 'Promulgating the Value Added Tax Law (Issued 12 October 2020, Published 18 October 2020)', Official Gazette 1362, 2020; Royal Decree 50/2021, 'Ratifying the Unified Agreement for Value Added Tax for the States of the Cooperation Council for the Arab States of the Gulf (Issued 7 July 2021, Published 11 July 2021)', Official Gazette 1399, 2021; Royal Decree 82/2020, 'Promulgating the Employment Security System (Issued 17 August 2020, Published 19 August 2020)', Official Gazette 1353, 2020.

[17] On top of the 1 per cent contribution from employer and employee, a 5 per cent charge is applied to the cost of each labour permit (initial or renewal) for foreign workers. 'PASI Annual Report 2021' (Muscat: Public Authority for Social Insurance, 23 February 2023), 38, www.pasi.gov.om/?page_id=15396&lang=en.

[18] Within just one year, nearly 10,000 people began drawing on the fund, 81.7 per cent of whom were between 21 and 40 years of age. Moreover, 70.1 per cent of the beneficiaries received less than 300 OMR ($780 USD) per month. 'PASI Annual Report 2021', 77–78.

[19] Royal Decree 6/2021, 'Promulgating the Basic Statute of the State (Issued 11 January 2021, Published 12 January 2021)', Official Gazette 1374, 2021.

[20] Muḥammad ʿAwaḍ al-Mashīkhī, 'Ḥuriyyat al-Taʿbīr fī Zaman al-Samāwāt al-Maftūḥa', *Al-Roya*, 27 December 2021, https://alroya.om/post/293656.

was taking – taxes, contributions, fees – but giving nothing else in return. A friend in Sohar informed me, 'Still there are few jobs for *al-shabab* [young men]. Life has become hard. My salary is lower. The basic salary is there, but they cancelled all allowances. I get 200 rials less every salary. My colleagues' salaries are also lower, and they have huge loans. How can they pay?'

In 2020, the government also announced a mandatory retirement for around 70 per cent of its long-serving employees, akin to the retirement in 1990s, to reduce the public wage bill and make way for jobseekers.[21] In practice, people who were retired but still in their forties or fifties then also went on the private sector job market. A friend pushed into early retirement shared that she planned to apply to some advertised positions in a new company, but several people already told her 'not to bother. They will only consider an expat for this role'. I suggested she seemed perfectly suited for the advertised role and asked whether she could consider setting up a meeting to show that she has the skills, qualifications, and experience. 'I'll try', she claimed, 'but I've been told it's unlikely to work. Another friend has applied to three different positions there with no luck.'

When we take a view of changes in the global labour market and global political economy, it becomes clear that this ongoing employment struggle cannot simply be written off as an outcome of a bloated public sector and segmentation. The difficulty Omanis face in the private sector is also tied to Oman's embeddedness in global circulations of labour, grounded in years of neoliberalisation in the global political economy. As Chapters 2 and 4 unpack, alongside oil revenue, it is a flexible, controllable, and low-income workforce that underpins the regional development model. Flexibility encompasses a description of workers who are legally expendable and easily dismissed. Under the

---

[21] Sassanpour et al., 'Labor Market Challenges and Policies in the Gulf Cooperation Council Countries', 39; Royal Decree 33/2021, 'Regarding the Systems for Retirement and Social Security (Issued 7 April 2021, Published 11 April 2021)', Official Gazette 1387, [author translations from Arabic], 2021; International Monetary Fund Middle East and Central Asia Dept, 'Oman: 2021 Article IV Consultation-Press Release; Staff Report; and Statement by the Executive Director for Oman', IMF Staff Country Reports 2021, no. 206 (12 September 2021), www.elibrary.imf.org/view/journals/002/2021/206/article-A001-en.xml; '3601 Retired from Oman's Civil Government Bodies in 9 Months', *WAF*, 17 November 2020, https://wafoman.com/2020/11/17/3601-retired-from-omans-civil-government-bodies-in-9-months/?lang=en.

demands of creating an attractive investment and business environment, capital's thirst for cheap labour has nurtured an Omani labour market that is global and adept at looking beyond its borders to draw on global supplies of workers. This is a structure from which it is incredibly difficult to break.

Labour market governance is clearly a contested space where the government is caught between conflicting pressures: (1) to liberalise the private sector and deregulate the labour market to enable easy access to low-cost, flexible foreign labour and (2) to protect the interests of Omani workers through measure such as *ta 'mīn*. Within these opposing pressure poles, the private sector demands that labour market reforms, which aim to encourage Omani hiring, should include both reducing their cost and easing dismissal possibilities.[22] Rather than improving the social and economic frameworks that govern migrant workers to put citizens and foreigners on a more similar playing field, the private sector suggests reducing the costs and obligations associated with hiring citizens: make them cheaper and more flexible to make them more attractive. Yet already the overall economy's weaker performance and rising costs associated with various liberalising reforms make economic life for lower-income Omanis even more precarious. This furthers the backlash to policy change, raising demands from national labour for more opportunities and more security.

Labour market reforms aimed at easing or restricting access to foreign recruitment or aimed at protecting or flexibilising local labour impacts workers governed under different regimes unequally. That which supports one, harms another – keeping the interests of foreign and local labour divided. This pattern is clearly illustrated during the jobseeker mobilisation that began in late 2017, which culminated in a few small physical protests in the latter part of the year. The government responded quickly with a similar promise of job creation used to quell protests in the 'Omani Spring'. Rather than 50,000 jobs, this time the government said it would create 25,000 new positions within just six months. It soon became obvious that there was one fundamental difference – these were not all government jobs. The government simply pointed to the private sector. It pleaded publicly for private sector enterprises to 'take the initiative and shoulder their national

---

[22] A sentiment regularly repeated in interviews over the years.

responsibilities' to employ Omanis.[23] A few larger companies like PDO even received long lists of jobseekers from the national registry to select specific numbers of candidates from. Furthermore, the government announced a temporary freeze on issuing expatriate visas in 87 different occupations during the first half of 2018. By the month of May, 161 companies received fines for failing to hire even one Omani citizen.[24] The pressures continued as the financial crisis dragged on and the economy slid toward scarcity. January 2019 brought renewed jobs protests, prompting the government to establish the National Centre for Employment.[25] Media reports emerged toward the end of 2019 that more than 2,200 Omanis had been laid off from a number of large industrial and construction companies.[26] More and more Omanis joined the ranks of the unemployed over the next few years under similar situations as the job space for both citizens and foreigners contracted. The visa ban continued to be extended and amended throughout 2019 and 2020, with new occupations added to the list.[27] Foreign worker visas in construction and cleaning were added to the moratorium, and by early 2020 the MoM said they would no longer renew visas of expat sales representatives and purchasers to make way for Omanis. It was now the early months of the pandemic, and by

[23] '25,000 Jobs for Omanis in Public, Private Sectors', *Ministry of Foreign Affairs*, 5 October 2017, www.mofa.gov.om?p=10333&lang=en.

[24] Times News Service, '161 Companies Penalised for Violating Omanisation Law', *Times of Oman*, 14 May 2018, http://timesofoman.com/article/134058.

[25] 'Omani Government Promises to Address Unemployment after Nationwide Protests', *Middle East Eye*, 3 January 2019, www.middleeasteye.net/news/ omani-government-promises-address-unemployment-after-nationwide-protests; Royal Decree 22/2019, 'Establishing the National Centre for Employment and Issuing Its System (Issued 28 February 2019, Published 3 March 2019)', Official Gazette 1283, [author translations from Arabic], 2019.

[26] Times News Service, 'More than 2,200 Omanis Laid off in 2019', *Times of Oman*, 2 December 2019, https://timesofoman.com/article/2320658/oman/ more-than-2200-omanis-laid-off-in-2019.

[27] 'Visa Ban on 87 Jobs in Private Sector Extended: MOM', *Muscat Daily*, 4 February 2019, https://muscatdaily.com/Archive/Oman/Visa-ban-on-87-jobs-in-private-sector-extended-MoM-5cyh; Ministry of Manpower: Ministerial Decision 47/2020, 'Regulating the Practice of Some Professions (Issued 29 January 2020, Published 2 February 2020)', Official Gazette 1328, [author translations from Arabic], 2020.

April, state-owned enterprises were directed to replace expatriates with Omanis.[28]

The underlying policy logic motivating the restriction of access to foreign labour is that if fewer expatriates can attain work visas, perhaps more Omanis can fill these jobs. However, such moves serve to offload further precarity onto the labour market participants who are already the most flexible and vulnerable. The tension and social polarisation between national and migrant labour in local labour spaces is a function of the global labour market and a feature of immigration-dependent economies more broadly. In comparative perspective, policymakers make 'scapegoats' of migrants during crises.[29] Historically, in Oman, such measures barely inhibit labour inflow; and when the economy recovers, restrictions are quickly relaxed. Nonetheless, the mere announcement of these types of policy measures ties the economic circumstances of one community on the margin to another.

It is within this perceived rivalry over economic rights where national chauvinism and anti-immigration sentiments can fester. Sharma positions it clearly,

Nativeness is neither an essence nor an analytic tool. It is, instead, a racialized idea and political category allowing some to make claims against others. All autochthonous discourses are also relational. They *produce* Migrants as the negative others of National-Natives. By articulating Nativeness with 'nationness' and claiming that only National-Natives have rightful political claims to power, autochthonous discourses count on the subordination of Migrants.[30]

In Oman, policy responses to job creation demands normalise a discourse of nationalist economic rights. The very structure of the labour market produces these tensions and contributes to the regulatory tug-of-war where some are perceived as winners of regulatory liberalisation and others as losers. For instance, later in May 2020,

---

[28] Zainab Mansoor, 'Oman to Not Renew Work Visas for Expats in Certain Professions', *Gulf Business*, 6 February 2020, sec. Oman, https://gulfbusiness.com/oman-to-not-renew-work-visas-for-expats-in-certain-professions/; 'Finance Ministry Issues Circular No. 14 On Omanisation Policy in Government Firms', *Oman News Agency*, accessed 15 June 2020, http://omannews.gov.om/description_bkp/ArtMID/867/ArticleID/12330/Finance-Ministry-Issues-Circular-No-14-On-Omanisation-Policy-in-Government-Firms.

[29] Castles, 'Migration, Crisis, and the Global Labour Market', 317.

[30] Sharma, *Home Rule*, 12–13.

expatriates received word that they would be able to change jobs more easily by 2021. They would no longer require a no-objection certificate from their employer to move to a new position and could avoid the two-year visa ban.[31] Moves like removing the NOC facilitates the mobility of foreign labour within the country and are welcomed by expatriates. Differing reactions to such moves indicate the embedded tensions of liberalising and regulating the labour market. Regulations that ease the labour market mobility of foreign workers are often viewed as damaging the prospects of citizens. This is a key aspect of relationality in Oman's labour market.[32]

After the re-emergence of protests in May 2021, the government issued another directive to create 32,000 new jobs. With austerity tightening even more, these jobs, it was stated, would include both full and part-time positions. Only 12,000 of these would be in the civil and security sectors; 2,000 of which would be temporary contracts. The government would, however, subsidise the wages of up to 15,000 fresh private sector employees with 200 OMR (520 USD) toward their monthly wage for up to two years. At the same time, the media reported on the declining numbers of foreigners in the public and private sector.[33] It was obvious from these stories and their placement

---

[31] Times News Service, 'Oman Removes NOC, Expats Can Switch Jobs', *Times of Oman*, 7 June 2020, sec. Oman, https://timesofoman.com/article/3015675/oman/government/oman-removes-noc-expats-can-switch-jobs.

[32] Karim Radhi, a trade union activist with the General Federation of Bahrain Trade Unions, recognises these relational patterns in Gulf labour markets and advocates against these attitudes and modes of differentiation. 'The term "foreigner" must be removed from the vocabulary of activists working with workers, as well as the term "servants," it must be replaced with "domestic workers." Trade union activists must shake off the condescending attitude that has become a part of the Khaleeji culture. We should consider that the right to transfer oneself from one job to another is the same as the right to transfer one's capital. This is not a shameful thing to do, nor an invasion, or an occupation, but rather each person's natural search for a living. Gulf citizens should remember that they too were migrants in the recent past.' Karim Radhi, 'Migrant Workers and Labor Unions in the Gulf: An Interview with Karim Radhi', *Jadaliyya*, 23 June 2014, www.jadaliyya.com/Details/30862.

[33] '32,000 Jobs for Omanis This Year', *Oman Daily Observer*, 26 May 2021, vol. 40, no. 193 edition; 'His Majesty Issues Directives to Offer 32,000 Jobs', *Times of Oman*, 25 May 2021, https://timesofoman.com/article/101705-his-majesty-issues-directives-to-offer-32000-jobs; Kabeer Yousuf, '12,000 More Jobs in the Pipeline for Nationals', *Oman Daily Observer*, 26 May 2021; '1,000 Jobs Every Month in Civil, Military Services', *Oman Daily Observer*, 27 May 2021, vol. 40, no. 194 edition.

in papers and news lineups that the underlying message was more jobs for Omanis equalled fewer jobs for expats. Thus, in attempting to ameliorate rising pressure for jobs, public messaging reproduced the implication of a zero-sum game even though much of the job contraction was due to the economic impact of the pandemic and border closures.

In this context, the public debate on what is regularly called the *lawbiyyāt* – an Arabised plural of lobby used to describe the dominance of certain communities of expatriates in various sectors of the economy – increased.[34] The discourse of *al-lawbiyyāt* usually applies to two contexts. The first, and arguably most predominant use, refers to the perception that particular (migrant) ethnicities are not only holding the majority of jobs in particular fields but also that managers and business leaders favour compatriots during recruitment and business deals. The second use refers to wealthy communities of businesspeople perceived as holding the reigns of economic power in the country. Both uses implicitly contain racialised or sectarianised undertones. The racialisation of discourse around the labour market and economy corresponds with the way minorities and migrants are framed and perceived as 'a threat to the conditions of local people' across multiple global contexts.[35] I discuss the first context in this section, while the second is included in the next.

Young Omanis explained the causes of youth unemployment in different ways in conversations, interviews, and surveys. Several themes emerged including government mismanagement, nepotism, corruption, and expatriates holding the available jobs. The latter reason was given frequently, often accompanied by their impression that employers blatantly favour foreigners over citizens. There is a strong perception that the private sector is a South Asian economic space. In it, Malayalis (Indian citizens from Kerala) only want to hire Malayalis, while Bengali managers only want to hire Bengalis. Within the business world, deals are understood to be enabled by which Malayali buyer knows which seller. Omanis, then, become necessary to business dealings only when the state has mandated it, such as the requirement for an Omani public relations officer (PRO) to file bureaucratic paperwork.

---

[34] Al-Mashīkhī, 'Ilā ayn dhahibūn fī idārat malaf al-tawẓīf?!'
[35] Castles, 'Migration, Crisis, and the Global Labour Market', 317.

Perceptions of exclusion from the private sector are common, especially among jobseekers, with several expressing their feeling that they
were explicitly excluded from jobs because managers and supervisors
are foreign. 'Because Indian people don't want us', explained one.[36]
There are 'more foreign managers and supervisors in the private
sector', explained another.[37] Numerous young people conveyed their
understanding that unemployment among Omanis existed because of
the private sector's 'dependence on expatriates' and habit of 'hiring'[38]
and 'favouring expats over Omanis'.[39] Others combined a second
reason alongside the 'existence of a large number of expatriates',[40]
pointing at government planning and describing it as lacking, 'bad', or
of 'poor level'.[41] Another added to the list, 'government policies, bad
investments, bad big projects, deterioration in tendering and no
Omanisation in companies'.[42] Alongside various perceptions of exclusion from the private sector, young Omanis also indicate a concern
with the attractiveness of working conditions. The long hours, low
salary, and weak job security associated with private sector work are
not especially appealing.

Even while blame for unemployment is often directed at the presence
of South Asian communities, some young people explain the cause in
economic terms rather than cultural ones. A young female jobseeker in
Muscat explains that 'there is unemployment because companies don't
want to pay Omanis because their salary is higher than other nationalities such as Indians. Omanis' basic salary for a bachelor's degree
holder is 600 OMR [$1,558 USD] compared to Indians which is way
less than that. And they give one employee tasks of maybe three or four
people so that they pay less people'.[43] Here she explicitly acknowledges the cost incentive for employers as well as an assumed implicit

---

[36] Female jobseeker, Muscat, 21 June 2018.
[37] Female jobseeker, Muscat, 20 June 2018.
[38] Young male jobseeker, Muscat, 25 June 2018.
[39] Young male recent geology graduate who secured a job within a year of
graduation, Muscat, 25 July 2018.
[40] Female entrepreneur who reported it took around five years to secure her first
job after graduating with a degree in accounting, Muscat, 17 April 2018.
[41] Male civil service employee, Sohar, 5 May 2018.
[42] Young male government employee, Sohar, 7 May 2018.
[43] Female jobseeker and recent geoscience graduate, Muscat, 25 June 2018. As of
2020, a system of wage levels based on academic qualifications was dropped
leaving the existing minimum wage for citizens as the common price floor.
Shaddad Al Musalmy, 'Wage Level Delinked from Academic Qualifications',

exploitability of a foreign employee. There is a sense that the ability of companies to subject foreign employees to additional exploitation, even when they are educated, promotes the attractiveness of international staff. The self-described tacit understanding is that Omanis will not accept exploitative conditions and overwork, reducing their competitiveness.

This sense of foreign domination of certain spaces of work is not only an outcome of the structural segmentations of the labour market, it is also an outcome of ways of constructing belonging – economic belonging in lieu of political belonging. Mehta and Onley's description of the Indian community in Oman demonstrates this fashioning of home and belonging in the diaspora:

> Despite their non-permanent legal status in Oman, Indians dominate the spaces they occupy, owning them in cultural and social terms, making them more Indian than Omani – a home away from home, even an extension of India itself. They employ a range of practices to accomplish this. Indian society permeates every aspect of life in Muscat – from the migrant labourers about whom so much has been written, to the professional classes about whom far less is known, to the millionaire owners of multinational firms who appear regularly in the pages of Arabian Business and national newspapers. Muscat's Indian society asserts its presence both socially – through the wearing of Indian clothing, the use of Indian house décor, and large public gatherings (for worship, cricket matches, concerts, and classical dances) – and physically, through establishments like Hindu temples and Indian restaurants and shops.[44]

This portrayal highlights the way that different communities find ways to belong even in spaces where citizenship is unavailable after a lifetime of living and working in the country. It also illuminates the multiple classes represented in the Indian diaspora in Oman.

Constructing belonging and contesting economic spaces thus goes hand in hand, especially within deeply segmented labour markets. On the one hand, the overlapping relations between Indians and Omanis in the workplace occur regularly in professional spaces of work. On the other hand, Oman jobseekers and young people on the

---

Muscat Daily, 22 September 2020, www.muscatdaily.com/2020/09/22/wage-level-delinked-from-academic-qualifications/.
[44] Sandhya Rao Mehta and James Onley, 'The Hindu Community in Muscat: Creating Homes in the Diaspora', *Journal of Arabian Studies* 5, no. 2 (2015): 157.

margins find the managerial and business-owning classes exclusionary, rich, and uncaring, leading to these perceptions of Indian or South Asian lobbies blocking the recruitment or promotion of citizens. Exclusions intensify perceptions of not belonging.

Omani business owners likewise complain of this so-called lobby, describing it as interrupting their ability to hire Omanis or even be successful without recruiting members of the community. 'I told you, I named the nationality, but now that we're recording I won't name it. There is a community that is controlling the market. They give business to each other because they are from the same country. So ... if you have salesmen from that community, you might be able to do stuff.'[45] If a company wants to be successful in selling products and getting customers, businesses owners report feeling a need to hire someone from the 'right' expatriate community. Another Omani businessperson said more bluntly,

One of the problems is job security. Listen I will tell you this and don't take it wrong. I hope you will understand ... hmm ... how do I say.... Listen I'm sorry I keep saying Indians. I just say this because, you know, they are the majority group here – so it's not about them, it's in general. But listen ... the companies with Omani CEO and management will hire more Omanis – not just owner Omani, but also operations management people Omani. The Indian – Keralite usually here – will only hire from his home state. They want to protect jobs and help their community. They will be the ones telling these stories – Omanis don't want to work, are lazy, go home early, etc. etc.[46]

The perception is that a lobby of a particular nationality – usually articulated as Indians although sometimes specified by state or linguistic group within India and other times used generically to refer to any South Asian nationality – controls the private sector and actively excludes Omani nationals.

A female jobseeker, an engineering graduate who had been on the job search for nearly two years, said she had not received any 'interviews or even assessment tests. I'm always rejected. I have registered with the Public Authority of Manpower Registry, I have participated in

[45] Interview with a young Omani business person from a major business family, Muscat, 26 October 2011.
[46] Interview with Omani owner of large shipping and transportation company, Muscat, 26 January 2019.

a government training program for jobseekers. I have used all possible ways'.[47] She felt there was a difference between how Omanis and expatriates were treated and remunerated 'because in Oman, an Omani receives less than the foreigner. Additionally, Omanis must pass through a recruitment process while foreigners are accepted directly'. Her sense of unfairness around recruitment process differences is not isolated. One can find social media calls for direct recruitment of fresh graduates trending annually at the end of the academic year. For most but the highest levels of jobs, recruitment of expatriates is carried out by agencies, and companies receive employees outside usual internal recruitment processes. This lends to an impression that Omani fresh graduates are held to a higher, more scrutinised standard.

Such impressions suggest that tensions are mounting and that populism has the potential to rise further even within this domestic context with a positive reputation for cross-national interaction. Notably, many interlocutors find Omani-expatriate social and workplace relations smooth, positive, and productive. There is often a great deal of social overlap and friendships amongst educated middle and upper classes, especially in urban centres. In fact, many young people who had some work experience initially described relations between foreigners and Omanis in the workplace quite positively. One described them as '*mumtī'a* [gratifying or enjoyable], because we can share experiences between us',[48] while another suggested they were 'friendly, welcoming', with good communication and exchange of information where there was interest 'to learn more about cultures'.[49] Others described relations as 'very friendly', 'collegial', 'pretty good and cooperative', 'excellent', 'healthy', 'normal and respectful', and 'cooperative and respectful'.[50] A young male from Al-Buraimi who graduated from GUTech and quickly secured a job in Muscat went as far as describing workplace relations between expatriates and Omanis as 'very lovely, we are like family'.[51]

[47] Female jobseeker, Muscat, 21 June 2018.
[48] Young unemployed female in Al-Buraimi, 4 July 2018.
[49] Male petroleum engineering graduate in a traineeship after nearly two years of job seeking, Muscat, 25 June 2018.
[50] Numerous impressions from recently employed graduates, Muscat, April to June 2018.
[51] Muscat, 19 June 2018.

The sense of a negative zero-sum game between foreigners and Omanis seems stronger among jobseekers, who specifically feel excluded and marginalised, than those working in a diverse workplace. These positive experiences do not negate the very real contentions around belonging and experiences of exclusion. It is important to develop understanding of multiple forms of relations including the experiences of the 'left-out' – those who sit on the margins of inclusion. The articulation of experiences in the workplace also vary once you dig beneath the surface. Some described relations as 'negative and competitive',[52] and I regularly heard young Omanis express the feeling that private sector employers are not only reluctant to hire them, when they do, they are unwilling to train them. There was likewise a sense that prevailing stereotypes of Omani unproductivity or unreadiness (see discussion in Chapter 3) coloured their encounters with the private sector. Section 5.2 further unpacks various forms and perceptions of not belonging on the job.

5.2 Perceptions of Not Belonging

The following composite characters offer glimpses into the perceptions of belonging and exclusion across various participants in the labour market. As described above, there is the young Omani college or university graduate who has already spent several years on the job market without success. There is also the aging expatriate who, after spending a forty-year career in the country, has to leave upon retirement and wonders where home is. A third includes the young Omani in a newly nationalised job who feels excluded from learning and knowledge transfer. Next to them, there is the expatriate who worries that by training a fresh Omani graduate they will render themself redundant. A fifth character is the Omani feeling excluded from a team discussion or decision-making process whilst their colleagues and manager conduct work conversations in their native tongue. Each of these composite characters represent common stories recounted to me again and again. They will ring familiar to many calling the Gulf home. It is a curious state to possess a coveted passport and yet feel trapped on the margins of belonging. These categories on the margins illustrate how policy measures that target finding jobs for

---

[52] Young female college lecturer, Muscat, 5 May 2018.

Omanis have adverse consequences for migrant workers. Here, louder public discourse about Omanisation is associated with job loss and potentially repatriation. These experiences of sitting on the margins of inclusion reveal how the precarity of one hinges on the precariousness of the other.

Feelings of not belonging within the workplace emerge from informal barriers to career mobility and on-the-job learning. Nurses share their frustration with me about foreign doctors and nurses consulting with each other in their shared language, which excludes them from participating in treatment planning and patient care. They feel their requests that these discussions be carried out in English or Arabic often fall on deaf ears. Likewise, new engineering and technician recruits complain they are often brushed aside as they try to learn new technical and operational processes while a team of expatriates do the work. One business owner offered a similar story. 'If you have, like normally, an all-Indian staff and not just all Indian – all Kerala or one place – they will only hire their own or they will keep the knowledge to themselves and exclude the other. This will happen with any [one nationality]. So the best is to have a mixed staff.'[53] This pattern is also criticised by Omani economists because of how it blocks the transfer of knowledge, skills, and innovation and perpetuates the structural dependence of Omanis on expatriates all the way down to the level of the individual.[54] While these forms of exclusion may often be unintentional, some exclusionary behaviour can also be interpreted as strategies to remain essential to work processes in order to secure jobs and by association livelihoods and the right to residency.

I regularly heard stories of frustration at being excluded from learning opportunities in the private sector.[55] 'One job was the most boring thing. They sat me alone in a room and told me to file some documents. I was done so quickly, and they wouldn't give me anything else to do. Just sit there in case they need me for something. They only wanted to

---

[53] Interview with Omani owner of large shipping and transportation company, Muscat, 26 January 2019.

[54] 'Murāqibūn wa muḥalilūn iqtiṣādī lil-waṭan al-iqtiṣādī: Duwal al-Majlis fī khaṭar wa lā bud min sīyāsat sarīʿa li- tanwiʿa maṣādar al-dakhl', *Al-Watan*, 4 November 2014, http://alwatan.com/details/37154;.

[55] While the discourse from the private sector is overwhelmingly a story of unproductivity of Omanis or an unwillingness to work, an alternative account emerges from new labour market entrants.

say, oh look we hired an Omani.'[56] This experience was common among college- and university-educated Omani millennials, especially fresh graduates. The practice of Omanisation being an accounting activity or CSR effort was not lost on them.

After university I had a few traineeships – an internship and a traineeship – I was bored. They didn't give me anything to do or learn. Both of them were at consultancies. One of them offered me a job when I finished, but it was going to be more of the same. There was no knowledge transfer, no actual training. It's like they just want you there so they can say, look, we have this many Omanis. I left to my current job [with the Special Economic Zone Authority Duqm], and here I have learned so much, and people ask my ideas, and I have input on processes and plans. My ideas are taken seriously and used. I can see an impact. You see that project there, I helped build it. You see that one, it was my idea. This would have never happened if I stayed in these private sector consultancies.[57]

In contrast to the experience of working for a private sector company, some had the experience that working for state-owned enterprises (SOEs) or the government side of a joint venture was a more attractive space to work and grow. There was a sense that one could belong as an Omani in this space, and be valued, rather than in the private sector where both their ideas and potential were dismissed.

Of course, working in the wide and varied public sector is not a clear-cut experience of belonging and growth. Many feel excluded from promotion and development opportunities, which has been made worse by recent pandemic austerity measures cutting bonuses and deferring annual increases.[58] Young people frequently point to the importance of *wāsṭa* as vital to achieving success and its absence instrumental in hampering career mobility.[59] Rahma elaborates,

---

[56] Female jobseeker, Muscat, July 2015.
[57] Young SEZAD employee, Duqm, 26 January 2020.
[58] Haider Abdulredha Al-Lawati, 'Private Sector Dilemma over 3% Annual Increment', *Oman Daily Observer*, 24 March 2021, www.omanobserver.om/article/1710/Opinion/private-sector-dilemma-over-3-annual-increment.
[59] The term *wāsṭa* best captures part of the informal mechanisms utilised to both navigate bureaucracy and access items, individuals, and action. It is somewhat comparable to the notion of having a 'connection' or an 'in.' As Barnett et al. note, 'One is said to 'have *wāsṭa*' when those from whom one can request assistance are in positions of power that make it possible for them to grant the requested assistance.' Andy Barnett, Bruce Yandle, and George Naufal, 'Regulation, Trust, and Cronyism in Middle Eastern Societies: The Simple

What happens when you feel that way? That there is no opportunity, that your skills and experience and ideas are not respected? You will feel demotivated. You will not be inspired, your productivity will go down. What else can you expect? How long can you feel that everything around is unjust? Where is the justice? We are the generation who are educated. We are the ones who are working. We are the ones building the country now. We are the ones who want to contribute to the country. If we don't feel respected, if we feel misused watching those get good positions because he is the son of a sheikh but he has no ideas and is scared to take a wrong decision – what will we do? I'll tell you. We will come together. We won't just stay alone all of us feeling this way. We will come together and things will have to change or we will leave. We will look outside to other countries for opportunities.[60]

Those with *wāsṭa* are viewed as having access to jobs, promotions, resources, government contracts, and business opportunities, while those without feel crushed under poorly defined bureaucratic processes, long wait times, and uninspiring work where they feel their skills are underutilised. What is also notable about Rahma's comments is how deeply citizens have internalised state narratives about individual contributions and responsibility to national development. Rahma's exasperation is not isolated. Others also muse in our conversations about seeking employment elsewhere in the Gulf or further afield.[61] Valeri already noted a 'revival of emigration by young Omanis to other GCC countries' in the 2000s, pointing to Kuwaiti recruiters who would come to recruit Omanis directly.[62] In fact, Oman still maintains an employment office in Doha, first opened in 2003, to facilitate employment in Qatar.

Although *wāsṭa* is often described as a social feature of the region, some suggest that it was the colonial powers that reinforced it as a socially constructed norm through economic incentives and access to economic and political power.[63] Steffen Hertog calls some individuals who have *wāsṭa* brokers. 'Brokers', he suggests, are 'intermediaries

---

Economics of "Wasta"', *The Journal of Socio-Economics* 44 (June 2013): 41, https://doi.org/10.1016/j.socec.2013.02.004

[60] Muscat, December 2021.

[61] One jobseeker suggested she will 'try to find a job outside the country' after two years of searching for a position as an engineering graduate, Muscat, 21 June 2018.

[62] Valeri, *Oman: Politics and Society in the Qaboos State*, 212.

[63] Andy Barnett, Bruce Yandle, and George Naufal, 'Regulation, Trust, and Cronyism in Middle Eastern Societies: The Simple Economics of "Wasta"', *The*

who hold privileged positions and can make such resources available to nationals and foreigners who are not as well connected. Such brokers are a defining feature of state-society relations in rentier states'.[64] Some brokers are people who have *wāsṭa*, while others are those who have been prescribed particular roles as intermediaries. In Oman, the public relations officer (PRO) is an example of the state 'deliberately' constructing regulations 'that encourage the emergence of brokers, and in many cases have made mere citizenship an important base for brokerage of state resources to non-nationals'.[65] All companies with employees require a PRO, and this person must be Omani. Their role includes handling the bureaucratic paperwork and intermediation between expatriate employees and the various authorities and processes necessary for work. Not only is this a way of generating employment, such roles facilitate and formalise patron-client networks throughout society. Brokerage is therefore both an employment role and a form of class. It is a way of mediating access and inclusion.

Many young Omanis still express the expectation that the state should be both welfare and job provider but recognise that the opportunities are much more limited in comparison to their parents' generation. Already 49.4 per cent of employed eighteen- to twenty-nine-year-olds work in the private sector.[66] Surveying the dwindling prospects in the public sector, some young people choose to pursue further education or simply postpone their graduation in order to continue collecting a small education subsidy and delay their entry into the job-wait period. These strategies are also manifestations of unemployment and underemployment that are not accounted for in national statistics. What is more, delay spreads into other aspects of everyday life – the later one starts to earn a living through work, the later one begins to support families, purchase a home, get married, or have children. Delay then contributes to a sense of being excluded from participation in expected social norms and processes.

Such alienation also affects perceptions of belonging derived from narratives of collective nation building. Over the decades, young

---

Journal of Socio-Economics 44 (June 2013): 44, https://doi.org/10.1016/j.socec.2013.02.004.

[64] Hertog, 'The Sociology of the Gulf Rentier Systems', 283.
[65] Hertog, 'The Sociology of the Gulf Rentier Systems', 283.
[66] 'al-Shabāb wa sūq al-'amal', 2.

people have been regularly called upon to contribute to national development through work. These calls are not only found in development plans but also in royal speeches and ministerial statements. Work is cast as part of a shared developmental responsibility and part of the citizen's patriotic duty. The experiences of many job market entrants then clash with this discourse, as they find few available government jobs and inhospitable private sector establishments. Pessimistic perceptions of the private sector are so widespread they are addressed in policy spaces. A speech delivered by the late Sultan Qaboos to the Council of Oman in 2012 chided both the private sector and citizens to reorient such views.

It is not acceptable that some citizens adopt the impression that the private sector relies on what the state offers to it, and that this sector does not contribute efficiently to the service of society and support of its social institutions and programmes or that the private sector only seeks to achieve profit and does not try to work more seriously in serving its society, environment, and its country . . .. Therefore, the private sector is required to work harder to eliminate this impression . . .. Such a positive attitude is capable of enhancing the confidence of citizens and their appreciation of the private sector's role. It will encourage Omani youth to work in this sector and to continue to keep their jobs and instil a spirit of belonging in this sector's institutions. This will in turn reflect positively on the performance of youth, their commitment to the ethics of work and will contribute to productivity. Therefore, the private sector will be an authentic partner in employment.[67]

It is noteworthy that even in the highest echelons of power there are references to the lack of a 'spirit of belonging' in the private sector.

Constructions and contestations of belonging in the labour market to a certain extent reflect larger socio-cultural and political navigation of belonging. Omani national discourse 'embraces the country's history of overseas empire and connections to the Indian Ocean rim and thus reinforces the Omani identity' of diverse tribes and non-tribal communities.[68] Valeri has shown how Oman under Qaboos worked to forge a feeling of belonging 'above other allegiances people were used to referring to, such as tribes and local communities' by presenting a less political and more unified history.[69] Even as Valeri notably

---

[67] Speech of His Majesty before the Council of Oman (13 November 2012) Al-Said, 'The Royal Speeches of His Majesty Sultan Qaboos Bin Said', 550.
[68] Peterson, 'Oman's Diverse Society', 33.   [69] Valeri, Oman, 119.

criticises this narration of Omani history as 'promoting political oblivion', he also demonstrates how successful it has been at constructing a 'timeless Omani national identity' co-existing with but superseding other ones.[70] As much as the workplace reproduces narratives of belonging as citizens, workplace practices also trail historical patterns of employment and migration in modern Oman. Thus, perceptions of tribal, sectarian, and ethnic difference intersect with those of heritage, class, race, and gender.

Oman is a historically diverse society. The linguistic diversity of Omanis alone is illustrative, where after Arabic at least eleven other languages are mother tongues.[71] Although Oman is associated with Ibadhism, it has been home to numerous religious and ethnic groups that share neither tribal nor *'Ibāḍī* roots since at least the seventeenth century. Thus, religious difference – whether an Omani citizen is *'Ibāḍī*, *Sunna*, or *Shī'a*, or part of other smaller religious minorities like the Hindu Banyan – sometimes intermixes with claims of belonging and authenticity.[72] Further, whether home is associated with life in Muscat or in *al-balad*, as many Omanis working in Muscat affectionately refer to their hometowns and villages outside the capital, interacts with place making and social capital building practices.

Coastal/interior distinctions came up regularly in musings about workforce development in the early days of Qaboos' reign. Fawzya Al-Kindy's 1976 article on the workforce and national development in *Al-Markazi*, the Central Bank of Oman's monthly publication, is telling.

At this stage of economic development in the Sultanate, it is not easy to say what an average Omani incentive is. This is complicated by the fact that life in the interior of Oman is different from life along the coast or the main towns namely Muscat and greater Muttrah. Briefly, in the interior life is strictly communal and until now tribal, and family affairs are the main

---

[70] Valeri, *Oman*, 132; 119.

[71] First languages in Oman include Arabic, Baluchi, Lawati, Zadjali, Gujarati, Swahili, Qarawi (Jibbali), Mahri, Habyoti, Bathari, Hikmani, and Harsusi, among others. Peterson, 'Oman's Diverse Society', 34.

[72] As John Wilkinson noted some time ago, 'Ibadi Oman and what people call Oman are not the same thing.' *The Imamate Tradition of Oman*, 72; See also Mehta and Onley, 'The Hindu Community in Muscat'; and Samuel Kutty and Sandhya Rao Mehta, *Oman-India Ties: Across Sea and Space* (Ruwi: Oman Daily Observer and Embassy of India Oman, 2021), 40–128, https://issuu.com/oeppa/docs/03-oman_india_book_printed_pages.

concern; whilst along the coast and in towns life is framed within a commercial atmosphere of businessmen's families of various races, cultures and traditions.[73]

This comment presents an interior/coastal divide from the perspective of an educated, urban citizen. Not only does the article follow a linear, liberal development ideology that prioritises growth within development, Al-Kindy suggests that the national workforce problem can 'only be solved by changing the typical Omani pattern of life'.[74] This view, we have seen, has persisted, fanning earlier notions of Omani labour as neither sufficiently industrious nor consumed by work. These characterisations are in turn used to necessitate a dependence on foreign labour. Such thinking, while rooted in the limited educational dissemination in Oman at the time, has continued and both generates and justifies the exclusion of Omanis from certain forms of employment. We can see, therefore, how elements of diversity and difference both take shape within and reproduce labour market dynamics in the country over time.[75]

Cultural and political experiences of negotiating belonging in the Omani nation have been explored by other scholars.[76] These include attempts to fortify ties to being Omani through an Arab identity where some prioritise 'Arabness' and tribal lineages from the interior as more authentically Omani than the diverse communities in coastal Oman. While the state's forging of a national Omani identity celebrates its historical diversity, it also absorbs the 'specific histories and lifeways of ethnic groups' into the 'singular historicism' of its unified narrative.[77] This contributes to a tacit atmosphere toward validating Omani-ness and tribal-ness within the microhistories of Omani minorities. Research shows that the ethno-cultural importance of 'Arabness' has

[73] Fawziya Al-Kindy, 'Manpower and Progress Go Hand in Hand', *Al-Markazi*, December 1976, 5, Central Bank of Oman Archive.

[74] Al-Kindy, 'Manpower and Progress Go Hand in Hand', 4.

[75] Social regulation is a powerful, intervening force of labour market governance.

[76] E.g., Al-Azri, *Social and Gender Inequality in Oman*; Mandana Limbert, *In the Time of Oil: Piety, Memory, and Social Life in an Omani Town* (Stanford: Stanford University Press, 2010); Sachedina, *Cultivating the Past, Living the Modern*; Valeri, *Oman*; Bhacker, *Trade and Empire in Muscat and Zanzibar*.

[77] Amal Sachedina, 'Assimilating the Heterogeneity of Migrant Populations through a National Past: Transforming a Shiʿa Minority Community in Post-Nationalist Oman', *Anthropological Quarterly* 95, no. 4 (2022): 848, https://doi.org/10.1353/anq.2022.0047.

generated struggles to lay claim to 'being Arab' by Ajami, Baluchi, and Khoja communities.[78] The contention for an Arab-Omani identity is perhaps most pronounced in the Lawati community, a religiously *Shī'a* minority often identified as Khoja and their competing origin stories. One links them to the Khoja community of the Kutch / Sindh regions of India and Pakistan whereas another distinguishes the Lawati of Oman from the wider Khoja by tracing an Arab genealogy based in the Arabian peninsula prior to their migration to the Indian subcontinent where they settled for centuries.[79] The Lawati are often associated with financial wealth and power based on their history of successful trade and commerce, but this association contributes to their racialisation as an 'other' especially during times of heightened economic malaise. Even as communities 'Arabise' and feel implicit pressure to embrace tribal associations, their incorporation into Omani national narrations of history can reinforce the effects of differentiation and transform communities' relationships with their communal past.[80]

Moreover, scholars are beginning to interrogate the impact of race and legacies of slavery more thoroughly. Despite a system of legal rights and obligations that treats all citizens equally and was designed to strengthen a homogenous national identity under a unified Oman, blood and lineage still seem to play a sizable role for some when it comes to things like marriage.[81] Some continue to find that patrilineal descent from enslaved peoples or members of historically subjected tribes still impact their social relations and mobility. Rahma, who is

---

[78] The Ajam, Baluch, and Khoja communities of Omani citizens are well known minorities, among others, long embedded in the social fabric of the country. Records indicate their ties to the modern Iranian, Pakistani, and Indian littoral. Peterson, 'Oman's Diverse Society', 33; Irtefa Binte-Farid, '"True" Sons of Oman: National Narratives, Genealogical Purity and Transnational Connections in Modern Oman', in *Gulfization of the Arab World*, ed. Marc Owen Jones, Ross Porter, and Marc Valeri (Berlin: Gerlach Press, 2018), 41–56.

[79] Zahir Bhalloo, 'Construction et Gestion Identitaire Chez Les Lawatiya Du Sultanat d'Oman, de Multân à Masqaṭ', *Journal Asiatique* 304, no. 2 (2016): 217–30.

[80] Sachedina, 'Assimilating the Heterogeneity of Migrant Populations through a National Past'; Chhaya Goswami, *The Call of the Sea: Kachchhi Traders in Muscat and Zanzibar, c. 1800–1880* (New Delhi: Orient Blackswan, 2011), 93–95.

[81] Binte-Farid, '"True" Sons of Oman'; Khalid Al-Azri, 'Change and Conflict in Contemporary Omani Society: The Case of Kafa'a in Marriage', *British Journal of Middle Eastern Studies* 37, no. 2 (2010): 121–37, https://doi.org/10.1080/13530191003794707; Sachedina, *Cultivating the Past, Living the Modern*, 179.

from Al-Sharqiyyah but lives in the capital, suggested that despite how 'bad' it sounded today, her community retained practices that impacted who she could marry. She recalled a time a young man from her region approached her family to propose marriage. He had a job and was educated, but her family went and looked into the suitor's family background to confirm his 'aṣl' (lineage/descent) and 'make sure he was pure Arab'. She intimated that despite that some of her family had gone to Zanzibar, they intentionally avoided marrying there to stay fully Arab and considered this an important point of differentiation. Her family did not readily share that they had ties to Zanzibar to avoid any stigma or assumptions this history could generate. They were also extra careful that their daughters should marry at their 'social level', alluding to the principle of kafā'a or equivalence in marriage.[82] Determinations of social level are necessarily subjective and intersect with race, class, and tribe. Kafā'a has created an identity and legal paradox because its enshrinement in family law clashes with both the idea of Omani equality and with the basic law by creating an avenue for tribal, caste, and racial discrimination.[83]

While those of khadam, bayāsir, or mawāla ancestry continue to be considered 'at the margins of respectability' in marriage and social interactions,[84] the younger generation have marshalled education and embraced the national identity narrative to find social mobility through the labour market. The generational gap is growing. I met an older woman, for example, who maintained rather traditional relationships with the families of a community where she behaved in a subordinate social position given her khadam class background. She interacted with the women as friends but was always there to help rather than socialise for the sake of it. She assisted with preparations for weddings and big social occasions, wore simpler clothes, and

---

[82] Kafā'a is an Arabic term that means equality. Within Islamic legal terminology and customs in Oman, kafā'a in marriage is a conception that dictates that a husband's family should be of equal or superior socio-economic and cultural status. Khalid Al-Azri argues that the legal recognition of kafā'a as a condition of marriage in the Omani Personal Status Law serves to reinforce and promote inequality as well as tribal cultural practices in Oman. Al-Azri, 'Change and Conflict in Contemporary Omani Society'.

[83] Al-Azri, 'Change and Conflict in Contemporary Omani Society'.

[84] Sachedina, Cultivating the Past, Living the Modern, 180; Limbert, 'Caste, Ethnicity, and the Politics of Arabness in Southern Arabia' See also n. 48 in Chapter 2 for a translation and explanation of these terms.

during the celebrations would be the one to initiate the various melodies, chants, and songs. Her daughter, in the millennial generation, would never attend such weddings or socialise with her mother's circle, keeping as much social distance from lingering stigma. She busied herself with education and work, creating different social circles. Likewise, Sachedina noted younger generations rejecting the 'historical implications of hierarchical domination' by seeking better professions and distancing themselves from the tribe and occupational roles of their parents' or grandparents' generation. Through these acts and work, young people 'were transforming the meaning of status and reputation'.[85]

As discussed in Chapter 2, economic development across the country, and especially the activity within population centres, meant that social networks and identities increasingly overlap. Shared spaces of work, education, and residence, intermarriage, and effective nation-building mean these differences are often secondary to the overarching identity of being Omani. Young Omanis of diverse backgrounds internalise national unity narratives to embrace their Omani-ness. Despite this, young people at the margins struggling in the labour market reach to various narratives of inclusion and exclusion to explain their economic struggle. Differences are not irrelevant to perceptions of belonging and access when discussing employment. Proximity to power and wealth, and perceptions of power and wealth, matter greatly to the conversation.

Three identities emerged regularly in conversations about job seeking and the workplace that held meaning for constructions and contestations of belonging in the economy – being *Zinjibārī*, being *tujjār*, and/or being perceived as close to political power. To some extent, these reproduce earlier historical identities and especially the post-1970 patterns of national development and return migration. Using the first example, many Zanzibari Omanis immigrated to Oman after Sultan Qaboos' call when he assumed the throne for Omanis abroad to return to their homeland and help build the 'modern' nation. Within Oman, those referred to as *Zinjibārī* – Zanzibari – include a wide range of people across racial, linguistic, sect, caste, and class boundaries. The term is used somewhat generically to include anyone with ties to East Africa. Some Omanis had long-

---

[85] Sachedina, *Cultivating the Past, Living the Modern*, 182.

standing connections to Zanzibar or elsewhere in East Africa from Oman's historical, colonial presence there, while others were emigrants over later decades in search of better economic fortunes. Some Zanzibari Omanis claim to have retained 'pure' Arab Omani blood, while others intermarried with indigenous communities and thereby 'mixed' their assumed racial and tribal 'purity'.[86] Some were from wealthy merchant and land-holding families and those with close proximity to the centre of Omani political power in Zanzibar, while others were from less-affluent communities with limited access to education.[87] Some maintained Arabic as a living, spoken language, while others abandoned Arabic and integrated into the linguistic Swahili-speaking world. These experiences, and their differences marked by class, race, and language, shape how Zanzibaris who 'returned' to Oman experienced the country and navigated the economy.

Meanwhile *tujjār*, meaning merchants or traders, is used to refer to a wide range of business families often perceived as either monopolising various markets or having an outsized influence on politics.[88] The *tujjār* or business class in Oman hail from diverse backgrounds, including Hindu, *'Ibāḍī*, *Shī'a*, and *Sunnī* ones, who earned economic and political power at diverse points in Oman's modern history. Allen and Rigsbee, Mehta, Onley, and Valeri offer detailed accounts of families and individuals with economic and political power that interested readers should turn to.[89] Among them, Valeri has done the most to

---

[86] See Binte-Farid, '"True" Sons of Oman'.

[87] For a discussion of caste, ethnicity, and race and the construction of 'Arabness' in Oman, see Limbert, 'Caste, Ethnicity, and the Politics of Arabness in Southern Arabia'; See also discussion of class in Chapter 2. Limbert, *In the Time of Oil*, 134–63.

[88] The second use of the term lobby discussed in the last section is applied to the *tujār*.

[89] See, for example, Calvin H. Allen and W. Lynn Rigsbee, *Oman under Qaboos: From Coup to Constitution, 1970–1996* (Routledge, 2000), 99–121; Mehta and Onley, 'The Hindu Community in Muscat'; Kutty and Mehta, *Oman-India Ties*, 61–85; James Onley, 'Indian Communities in the Persian Gulf, c. 1500–1947', in *The Persian Gulf in Modern Times: People, Ports, and History*, ed. Lawrence G. Potter (New York: Palgrave Macmillan, 2014), 231–66, https://doi.org/10.1057/9781137485779_10; Valeri, *Oman*, 103–16; Marc Valeri, 'Oligarchy vs. Oligarchy: Business and Politics of Reform in Bahrain and Oman', in *Business Politics in the Middle East*, ed. Steffen Hertog, Giacomo Luciani, and Marc Valeri (London: Hurst & Company, 2013), 17–42; Marc Valeri, 'High Visibility, Low Profile: The Shi'a in Oman under Sultan Qaboos', *International*

theorise this overlap and especially the political economy patterns in the Qaboos era. To illustrate for the purpose of this chapter, I will note a selection of families that constitute a diverse business and political class in the country. Large business families include those known as the Banyan merchant class, Gujarati and Kutchi Hindu families like Khimji Ramdas and Ratansi Purushottam, who have had a continuous presence in Oman since the 1800s.[90] Some Sunni business families are associated with extraordinary economic and political strength. For example, the Zubair and Al-Zawawi families run some of the largest economic groups in the country and each have a family member who, respectively, formerly served as economic advisor to the Sultan and deputy prime minister for finance and economy. Others include the Bahwan trading family of the al-Mukhaini tribe from Sur and leading Baluchi trading families like al-Raissi and Nasib Khan. Among note-worthy *Ibāḍī* families with overlapping business and political roles is the family of Saud Al-Khalili, decedents to the line of Imams from the interior of the country. Saud joined Qaboos' first cabinet and soon after founded the Al Taher business group. Other family members served as ministers and chairmen of banking groups and pension funds. Similarly, the Macki, Al-Jamali, and Abbas families of the *Bahārna* (an Arab *Shīʿa* community) have held powerful positions in the post-1970s government as ambassadors, ministers, and within the Diwan of the Royal Court. The Mohsen Haider Darwish company is perhaps one of the most well-known *Bahrani* (singular) family busi-nesses. The Sultan family, of the Khoja *Shīʿa* Al-Lawatiyya commu-nity, may be best known for one of the oldest merchant dynasties in Oman, the WJ Towell Group, and for Maqbool Sultan who was minister of Commerce and Industry from 1991–2011. Other large Al-Lawati companies include the Ali Redha and Al-Yusuf groups, the latter of which was chaired by Muhammad Musa Al-Yusef who held positions like undersecretary of financial affairs and minister of state

Journal of Middle East Studies 42, no. 02 (2010): 251–68, https://doi.org/10.1017/S0020743810000048.

[90] Bhacker, for example, writes about the pre-eminence of the Banyan in Omani trade and Indian Ocean commerce in the nineteenth century. Bhacker, *Trade and Empire in Muscat and Zanzibar*, 12–14, 68–74, 132–40. The label 'Banyan' specifically refers to Indians who belong to the Vanya caste and are Hindu, but British colonial records often inaccurately refer to all Gujrati merchants, regardless of their religious identity, as Banyan. Bhacker, *Trade and Empire in Muscat and Zanzibar*, 69.

for development before his imprisonment for fraud and embezzlement.[91] Such cases amplify perceptions of conflicts of interest between government and business that generate negative views of business families headquartered in the capital area.

For those on the margins, such patterns have resulted in *tujjār* sometimes being used pejoratively in reference to corruption or various feelings of insider-outsider treatment in political and economic spaces. Sometimes accusations are lodged against business families from minority groups, as observed during moments of high agitation around unemployment. For example, when the 2011 protestors in Sohar complained about corruption, they specifically named the ministers holding important economic portfolios – Maqbool Sultan, minister of Commerce and Industry, and Ahmed Macki, minister of National Economy. Since both ministers were from different *Shī'a ithnā 'asharī* communities, some felt as though these individuals were unfairly targeted from among much more ubiquitous conflicts of interests because of their minority status. Sachedina reported that her interlocutors in the Lawatiyya community suggested that Maqbool was named out of 'resentment' because he was from their community, which is 'perceived as rich, with a monopoly on Oman's business, banking, and trade resources, and ultimately as outsiders and exploiters'.[92] There are a multitude of ways through which the economy and the workplace is a site of contestation and one wherein crisis moments have a tendency to heighten malaise.

Professional positions that became available with the modern development of Oman's economy in the 1970s were staffed in large part by Omanis who had been in the diaspora, as well as British, Indians, and Arabs, among others. Many of the Omani diaspora in East Africa were already outside of Tanzania and Zanzibar after the 1964 revolution, particularly the well-educated and English-speaking class, having scattered to different parts of the world. When this community 'returned', they quickly found roles staffing the new bureaucracy, financial sector, and in oil and gas.[93] Along with Zanzibaris, this period of return

---

[91] Valeri, 'High Visibility, Low Profile', 255–57.

[92] Sachedina, *Cultivating the Past, Living the Modern*, 216.

[93] Swahili Omani language and culture continues to be quite prevalent in a range of work places. Even recently, new migrants from East Africa with no Omani ties tell me how quickly they felt at home in Muscat because of how widespread Swahili seemed in their official encounters.

migration also meant that thousands who had migrated for education or work to other Gulf, South Asian, and Middle Eastern countries (among others) in the 1950s and 1960s returned to assume positions as an educated class of professionals, civil servants, and oil workers. They also found quick opportunities to start businesses in the many gaps in the market.

These categories of experienced, educated Omanis populated professions in such a way that certain types of work or places of work became colloquially known as the domain of a particular community. As Shamsa, cited earlier, explained when I asked about possibilities in PDO for her: 'It's all Zanzibaris in oil and gas – not for people like me from Sharqiyyah.' Likewise Sara, another interlocutor, suggested she 'learned a lot about Swahili culture' when she briefly worked at Oman Oil. Al-Azri also notes a similar phenomenon of workplace associations in his research.[94] Security services and the Ministry of Interior, for example, are associated with Omanis of *'Ibāḍī* or tribal Arabic backgrounds, while Zanzibaris are viewed as dominating the petroleum sector. Similarly, certain banks became colloquially referred to as the domain of certain groups. For example, the Oman National Bank is widely perceived as Lawati. Such recent historical and cultural associations persist even when hiring stretches across the breadth of educated classes. More mundane than planned, and hardly surprising, since class by its nature reproduces itself.

Intersecting with ethnic and religious difference, gender too creates experiences of inclusion and exclusion in the labour market. This takes two main forms, the securitisation of male employment and gendered expectations of suitable jobs for women. Given the greater propensity of young men, rather than young women, to take to the streets with their employment demands, the issue of jobseekers has been effectively securitised. Not only is the very term 'unemployment' frowned upon, 'jobseekers' being favoured, but also the government has grown increasingly concerned and sensitive to any hint of public unrest. Along with more typical security reactions are quieter inactions. There are, for example, no visible attempts to prevent or discourage job ads from publicly including 'male' as a candidate requirement despite the existence of anti-discrimination laws. Some female jobseekers have intimated to me that they felt that even when there is no

---

[94] Al-Azri, *Social and Gender Inequality in Oman*, 49–51.

gender specified in an ad, they are not considered explicitly because they are female.

This phenomenon has not gone unnoticed by the very many female jobseekers and has entered the social domain. In an interview on an Al-Wisal programme focused on women in different fields of the private sector, Sihām al-Ḥārthiyya, an engineer, shares a story about how she decided to pursue a job that was advertised exclusively for males. She went to the interview day without an invitation because she wanted to know why this position was only advertised for men. She observed that several of the men waiting for the interview were her male classmates from university. She asked, 'Why only males? Where is the job – on Mars? Even if it is on Mars, I am ready to go. Just ask me if I am capable of doing the job or not capable! … there is nothing that's only specific for men – who put that?'[95] She later asked the job search committee why they even educate women in these fields if they won't employ them? The implicit and explicit prioritising of jobs for men has stimulated debate on social media, involving a range of voices including feminist as well as patriarchal ones who argue that men should have precedence on the labour market because of their social and religious role as the breadwinner who is expected to be responsible for the nuclear and extended family.[96]

Another dynamic of this phenomenon, as Sihām's story also goes on to indicate, is how certain social ideas about where women are willing to work and what jobs are female 'appropriate' continue to pervade the private sector imagination. Sihām was told that women would not want to go into the field, or be in the hot sun, and so the available engineering job was for men. Many of my interlocutors had similar experiences. Some women I encountered, especially from outside of urban areas, were initially reticent to work as the only female in a male-dominated workspace but often overcame such hesitation or

---

[95] 'al-Muhandisa Sihām al-Ḥārithiyya', *Ḥalū al-Wiṣāl* (Muscat: Al-Wiṣāl, 7 January 2022), www.youtube.com/watch?v=KKZamOc3uBI [Author translations].

[96] For another example of feminist and partriarchal debates on Omani Twitter, see Shaimaa Al-Essai, 'The Dualities of Traditions and Feminist Movements on the Omani Twitter Platform: An Extension of the Patriarchal Actuality or an Attempt to Create a Safer Space for Women?' (Konrad Adenauer Stiftung, December 2021), www.kas.de/documents/286298/8668222/Policy+Report+No +44+-+Dualities+of+Traditions+and+Feminist+Movements+on+the+Omani +Twitter+Platform.pdf/.

found ways to convince reluctant family members. Such concerns were less marked in the capital region, where patterns of access show not only the role of *wāsṭa* but also an urban-rural divide.[97] Some others, especially those with Zanzibari ties, were concerned that working with men would label them as '*maftūḥīn*' and give them away as Zanzibari with the alleged cultural assumptions about their foreign or liberal social habits.[98] Yet many women, like Sihām, were exasperated by such gendered or cultural assumptions. To these women, it should only be education and capabilities that mattered. They wanted to compete for the jobs and prove they could do them and found it extraordinarily frustrating that employers, whether Omani or foreign, would decide on their behalf that because of their gender they wouldn't or shouldn't perform certain types of work. The lack of positions in fields like engineering for women is especially notable given the so-called feminisation of engineering education in Oman like elsewhere in the Gulf.[99] The education of Omani women in a wide range of professional fields is celebrated in the country as representative of equality characterised by the post-*nahḍa* era. It is viewed as part of the embodiment of national development visions and plans, and women's education, work, and entrepreneurship are encouraged through training and mentorship programmes. Yet, simultaneously, the private sector informally regulates the feminisation of various fields by designating certain types of work as masculine or, at least, unsuitable for women. The private sector rationalises the gendered job ads by reproducing stereotypes of women being unwilling to work in certain fields or do certain types of work. These practices both frustrated and enhanced

---

[97] According to this study by Rahma Abdulkadir and Henriette Muller, most Omani female leaders were raised in urban areas. 'Between Leadership and Kinship: Women Empowerment in the GCC Countries', in *Corruption and Informal Practices in the Middle East and North Africa*, ed. Ina Kubbe and Aiysha Varraich (London: Routledge, 2019), 188–206.

[98] *Maftūḥīn* is often used to refer to those with a perceived more liberal cultural affinity or social upbringing in contrast to more conservative and traditional socio-cultural norms. Zanzibaris, by virtue of being from families raised and/or educated abroad, are often considered (sometimes labelled accusingly) as 'open'. This can carry unwanted insinuations for women especially.

[99] For interesting parallels in Qatar, see Danya Al-Saleh, '"Who Will Man the Rigs When We Go?" Transnational Demographic Fever Dreams between Qatar and Texas', *Environment and Planning C: Politics and Space*, 11 January 2022, https://doi.org/10.1177/23996544211063205.

the feelings of exclusion from the private sector. One more reason to work for the government, many suggested.

This section suggests that if the Omani labour market, and especially the private sector one, can be characterised in one way, it might be that economic activities and social relations are undergirded by an impression of *not* belonging. This 'not belonging' dances across inclusions and exclusions, and perceptions of foreigners or other constructed outsiders, actively excluding the job-seeking or early-career masses. As Alshehabi elucidated, 'foreigner' is not a pre-defined category but rather a site of contestation.[100] It is both a legal and jurisdictional struggle over who makes the cut of political belonging and also a struggle of social impressions about who has a right to belong and where. A commentary by Ali al-Kuwari in 2010 reflects some of the anxieties about the so-called demographic imbalance in Gulf countries. In it, he describes society in the Gulf as transforming into '*mujtama' mu'sakar 'amal'* – a work camp society. In his view, certain modes of rapid development and incentivised investment that begin offering residency to non-citizens facilitates a social structure that does not reflect indigenous culture and risks diminishing the role of Gulf nationals. He worries that the new social structure would be characterised by a multicultural, multi-religious, and multi-ethnic society that communicates in English where citizens are a weak minority whose power and role are at risk should administrative and legal protections be removed.[101] This is a potent reflection on the tensions and fears underlining the imaginations of the future of the workplace in everyday social life. It becomes even more vivid when considered together with rising xenophobia about the 'population imbalance' in some discourses and anxieties about economic citizenship and the right to jobs in others.

5.3 Conclusions on Belonging, Class, and Resistance

This chapter unravels the layers of inclusion and exclusions embedded within the Omani economy. It has shown how millennials

---

[100] AlShehabi, *Contested Modernity*, 145.
[101] ʿAlī al-Kūwārī, 'Makhāṭir al-Siyāsa al-Āmrīkiyya wa Taḥadiyāt Muwājahatihā - Ḥālat Duwal Majlis al-Taʿāwun', 16 March 2010, http://dr-alkuwari.net/node/125.html.

have internalised both neoliberal and nationalist narratives on economic belonging in Oman. They feel an urgency to work not only out of personal necessity but to be productive and to contribute to building the national economy. At the same time, they encounter a labour market space that is shaped by inclusions and exclusions, a space where they are confronted with the necessity to struggle and lay claims to their right to earn a living and be economically active.

Through this chapter, I am able to unpack arguments about belonging, about class, and about resistance. The empirics show two things: first, contestations around belonging and labour market experiences more generally emerge within the local structures of segmentation and the global nature of Oman's labour market. Second, in order to understand economic belonging and citizenship in the Gulf, class has to take a central role. The production of difference and competing identities of local regionalism, tribal and community affiliation, religion, interior and coastal cultures, race, heritage, and gender all matter but cannot be well understood without the intervening variable of class. This became apparent in the sections above. Even though identifications with class may rarely be expressed vocally by individuals, one can see its materialisation through the various struggles for belonging articulated above. Moving beyond the citizenship segmentation, there are levels and layers of class and belonging that influence labour market experiences. The subjectivity of experiences and perceptions of inclusion and exclusion exposes how the politics and practice of difference in global capitalism produces tensions, value, and forms of power that manifest in labour and class relations. These dynamics also generate resistance and contestation around the boundaries of inclusion and exclusion.

By focusing on labour and interrogating class *within* citizen populations and between economic actors, this work contributes to the nascent scholarship on class formation in the Gulf. Part of the analytical problem it confronts is pushing beyond the view that labour equals the working classes – that is, labour as limited to those who are engaged in productive sectors and/or work for a wage. Expansions of the classical Marxist definition of working class to encompass all wage-earners including those in service and reproductive work has furthered our understanding of labour in contemporary economies. Further scholarship considers and integrates forms of free and unfree labour and the cultural and social experience of particular classes.[102] Next to these forms, economies also feature communities of unemployed and under-employed people – those who desire work. The condition of unemployment should also be understood as a labour relation. The commonality that people as workers in the modern world have is not that they work entirely for wages but that they experience the 'coerced commodification of their labour power'.[103] Following this, I argue that we should understand labour in the Gulf to include all social relations between workers and capital, including the unemployed, not only between but also across foreigner and citizen divisions.

Understanding these nuances, and viewing the labour market as a whole, helps to de-exceptionalise narratives around Gulf economies and labour markets. Capitalist patterns of economic growth and of exploitation are not unique to the region and neither are struggles for belonging and contestations for economic space. Furthermore, this approach allows us to conceptualise and understand migrant workers, citizen workers, and unemployed workers, as part of a class relation of labour. We have seen how communities of Omani citizens and residents have rather different forms of class identity that intersect with race, ethnicity, gender, citizenship among others. The form of labour performed, and who has access to performing that labour, all shapes whether and how social relations occur within the workplace.

Within this context, young Omanis assert their agency in a variety of ways. One is through complaint, with virtual and sometimes physical protests, demanding jobs or pushing for economic reforms in their favour. This is a more vibrant form of youth mobilising than usually depicted, which utilises hashtags and memes on social media (especially WhatsApp and Twitter) as innovative ways to express dissent.[104]

---

[102] E.g., Ricardo Antunes, 'The Working Class Today: The New Form of Being of the Class Who Lives from Its Labour', *Workers of the World* 1, no. 2 (January 2013): 7–18; Marcel van der Linden, 'Who Are the Workers of the World? Marx and Beyond', *Workers of the World* 1, no. 2 (January 2013): 55–76; Judy Fudge, '(Re)Conceptualising Unfree Labour: Local Labour Control Regimes and Constraints on Workers' Freedoms', *Global Labour Journal* 10, no. 2 (May 2019): 108–22; Marcel van der Linden, 'The Promise and Challenges of Global Labor History', in *Global Histories of Work*, ed. Andreas Eckert, 1st ed. (Berlin: De Gruyter, 2016), 25–48.

[103] Marcel van der Linden, *Workers of the World: Essays Toward a Global Labor History* (Leiden: Brill, 2008), 34.

[104] Najma Al-Zadjali's scholarship has pioneered discourse analysis of Omani dissent on social media. 'Memes as Reasonably Hostile Laments: A Discourse

It demonstrates a capacity to contest and disrupt firms and the government in their efforts to deregulate and liberalise the mode of capitalist and rentier social relations. Another way of contestation is through the act of not doing something. For example, not joining the labour market at particular wage levels, deemed insufficient for living, is a form of resistance where the disenfranchised jobseekers muse why they should work to live in poverty.

This chapter also shared several examples of jobseeker protests that quickly received a government response. This is a broader pattern in the economy. Other spaces that have seen Omani agitation and protest include concerns about inflation, which, in 2011, prompted the government to establish the Public Authority for Consumer Protection, where the public can lodge their complaints about price fluctuations for a committee to investigate. Another space of economic contestation has been to fuel subsidy reductions, which, in 2017, resulted in a rapid government response to ameliorate the impact of subsidy cuts.[105] The state then serves as reformer but also provider and regulator. These examples illustrate how liberalisation and pro-competitive reforms are socially resisted. They also show that the socio-political space in Oman is neither quiet nor stagnant. Although it does not always take the 'traditional *form* of civil society', it certainly fulfils some of the '*function* of civil society'.[106] Through looking at the relationship between resistance and (re)regulation, we can better understand periods of plenty and stagnation and the tense, difficult efforts to reform the labour market

Viewing class through the nuances of belonging helps explain how labour regulation and reform is experienced, circumvented, and resisted. What is remarkable about the stories of labour resistance, whether they result in concessions for improved labour conditions or job creation or whether they result in new ways of disciplining labour, is 'how unremarkable' and 'unexceptional not only in a historical sense

Analysis of Political Dissent in Oman', *Discourse & Society* 28, no. 6 (1 November 2017): 573–94, https://doi.org/10.1177/0957926517721083; 'Repair as Activism on Arabic Twitter', in *Approaches to Discourse Analysis*, ed. Cynthia Gordon (Washington, DC: Georgetown University Press, 2021), 136–58.

[105] Ennis and Al-Saqri, 'Oil Price Collapse and the Political Economy of the Post-2014 Economic Adjustment in the Sultanate of Oman', 93–95.

[106] Moritz, 'Re-Conceptualizing Civil Society in Rentier States', 150.

but also in a geographical one' these activities are.[107] Studying labour in Oman as part of a comparative and global political economy opens these news directions that are not possible within a methodologically nationalist study of the country and region.

[107] Kanna, 'Class Struggle and De-Exceptionalizing the Gulf', 118.

6 *Pursuing Entrepreneurship for Employment*

SMEs for Women and Youth

Jobs are the number one issue for the country – well a big issue. Jobs are the number one issue for youth. Forget about youth activities – planning cultural activities, art installations – youth only want to know about their jobs.[1]

—Diwan employee

Youth, Millennials and Generation Z if you prefer such labels, and especially young women, are disproportionately represented among the numbers of jobseekers in Oman. Partly for this reason, they are specifically targeted by national initiatives promoting entrepreneurship in the country. Like in neighbouring Gulf states, entrepreneurship and small- and medium-sized enterprise (SME) promotion has been a key strategy throughout the 2010s, and continues. It is, on the one hand, viewed as integral to innovation policy and economic diversification and, on the other hand, as an alternative career path for Omani citizens. It thus tackles two major economic challenges that confront the country – dealing with a future where oil plays a less significant role and dealing with rising joblessness.

This dual economic rationale motivating entrepreneurship promotion is often framed in policy spaces by the first, the desire for entrepreneurial forms that stimulate the innovation necessary to grow and diversify the Omani economy. Yet it is the second – private sector jobs for citizens – that consumes most SME promotion initiatives and hype around entrepreneurship. That is, a great deal of entrepreneurship promotion, from education to funding to incubation, focuses on micro-enterprises and self-employment programmes encouraging citizens to create their own jobs. If the market is unwilling to hire citizens, perhaps the citizen can be encouraged to make their own market.

---

[1] Interview with individual working on youth issues at the Diwan of Royal Court, Muscat, 6 January 2020.

The promotion of entrepreneurship therefore allows the state to encourage a form of employment in the private sector, without necessarily addressing underlying structures that make the private sector so unattractive to citizens and, particularly, youth and women.

The valorisation of entrepreneurship and individual enterprise is a manifestation of neoliberal growth discourse that is ubiquitous across global economies. The focus on women and youth is also ideologically underpinned by neoliberal ideologies where the market is viewed as the power that can resolve exclusions and marginalisation. In a region typecast by weak gender development outcomes, female entrepreneurship is framed as a positive goal intended to liberate and empower women through the market. It is one more channel through which Western-rooted ideologies and institutions can 'save' women in the Middle East.[2] Thus, when a recent UNDP report suggests that the protracted unemployment crisis, especially among women and youth, is being worsened by the global pandemic, it also claims that 'increasing youth entrepreneurship will have a positive impact on the employment opportunities and economic growth of the Arab region'.[3] The report identifies individual behavioural barriers to youth and women's entrepreneurship and, as a solution, suggests behavioural interventions in the form of entrepreneurial training programmes to improve self-efficacy, growth mindsets, and personal initiative.[4] The individual – their behaviour and their choices – are viewed as instrumental both to personal livelihood and national economic success.

By some accounts, the effort of promoting entrepreneurship – from entrepreneurial education in school through to the public discourse, training courses, and funding and incubation opportunities – is starting to pay off. The NSCI's 2020 publication on youth in the labour market

---

[2] Lila Abu-Lughod, 'Do Muslim Women Really Need Saving? Anthropological Reflections on Cultural Relativism and Its Others', *American Anthropologist*, New Series, 104, no. 3 (1 September 2002): 783–90; Adrienne Roberts, 'The Political Economy of "Transnational Business Feminism"', *International Feminist Journal of Politics* 17, no. 2 (3 April 2015): 209–31, https://doi.org/10 .1080/14616742.2013.849968.

[3] 'Paving the Path to Successful Youth Entrepreneurship in the Arab States with Behavioural Science' (New York: United Nations Development Programme, 2021), 5, www.undp.org/publications/paving-path-successful-youth-entrepreneurship-arab-states-behavioural-science.

[4] 'Paving the Path to Successful Youth Entrepreneurship in the Arab States with Behavioural Science', 9.

reports that 17.7 per cent of Omani businesses are owned by eighteen-to twenty-nine-year-olds. Most of these youth-owned businesses are located in Muscat, Dhofar, and North Al Batinah and 77.7 per cent of them are owned by men, reflecting broader inequalities in the economy.[5] It is worth keeping in mind that this growth of entrepreneurship unfolds within the existing labour market and economic structure and is therefore subject to the same segmentations, challenges, and contradictions we have been exploring.

Oman's embrace of an entrepreneurial market discourse may seem to sit awkwardly next to the preponderance of the state in economic spaces. Yet it is perhaps this policy discourse that most clearly exhibits the marriage of rentierism with neoliberalism. It offers us an example of why autocratic, resource-dependent political economies actively promote entrepreneurship and how local youth and women respond to this agenda. By exploring the policy space and reception, this chapter contributes to a broader debate concerning the complementarity between neoliberalism and authoritarianism globally.[6] Through the space of entrepreneurship and private enterprise advocacy in the labour market, I demonstrate how rentier neoliberalism is a form of what Bruff and Tansel call authoritarian neoliberalism through its 'intertwinement of authoritarian statisms and neoliberal reforms'.[7]

This chapter focuses on the experiences of young people in internalising entrepreneurship promotion discourses and in starting personal businesses. It illustrates two key tensions – first, the tension between rentierism embedded within authoritarian governing structures, on the one hand, and the logic of neoliberal capitalism, on the other, and second, the tensions between rhetoric and realities of youth and female empowerment narratives.[8] Entrepreneurship is expressed and

---

[5] 'al-Shabāb wa sūq al-'amal', 7–8.

[6] Bruff, 'The Rise of Authoritarian Neoliberalism'; Hanieh, *Lineages of Revolt*; Samer N. Abboud, 'Economic Transformation and Diffusion of Authoritarian Power in Syria', in *Democratic Transition in the Middle East: Unmaking Power*, ed. Larbi Sadiki, Heiko Wimmen, and Layla Al-Zubaidi (London; New York: Routledge, 2013), 159–77.

[7] Bruff and Tansel, 'Authoritarian Neoliberalism', 239.

[8] As discussed in Chapter 1 in relation to Polanyian analysis, authoritarianism is a feature of neoliberalism. That is, the state wields its power on behalf of capital and profit maximisation through the way it regulates and deregulates economic activities. Rent-seeking is not a unique behaviour but is also a key feature of capitalism and its neoliberal variety. Actors pursue wealth through the extraction of rent from owning or pursuing surpluses from land ownership, government or

promoted as an empowering activity, and at times is experienced as such, but can also be used to legitimise or reconstitute patriarchal and authoritarian structures to accommodate the market. The space of entrepreneurship promotion is both a key tactic of labour market bandaging and a distinct illustration of rentier neoliberalism.[9] The remainder of this chapter unpacks this story; first, understanding entrepreneurship in rentier economies; second, interpreting how Omani female entrepreneurs confront competing tensions within three intersecting gendered political economy logics; and third, reflecting on capital, generational discourses, and entrepreneurial dreams of the young generations.

6.1 Contextualising Entrepreneurship in Neoliberal Rentier Spaces

The promotion of entrepreneurship in Oman reflects a global pulse where entrepreneurship has been high on the global development agenda. Three of the seventeen UN Sustainable Development Goals (SDGs) – goals four, eight, and nine – specifically reference entrepreneurship.[10] EU policy papers similarly view 'youth entrepreneurship as a way out of unemployment, inactivity, or social exclusion'.[11] Likewise, leading international financial institutions (IFIs), including the IMF, World Bank, WEF, among others have advocated entrepreneurship among their policy measures since the turn of the millennium. Such entrepreneurship advocacy in the region intensified after the global financial crisis and the Arab uprisings because of the assumption that entrepreneurial activities have a market stimulation effect and were therefore viewed as key to responding to the regional job crisis. 'Promoting women's entrepreneurship' in the region, a World Bank

---

commercial contracts, labour permits (where foreign labour is especially commodified under the *kafāla* system), as well as things like patents and copyrights.

[9] See Section 1.5.

[10] UN, 'Transforming Our World: The 2030 Agenda for Sustainable Development (United Nations Resolution 70/1)' (United Nations, 2015), www.un.org/ga/search/view_doc.asp?symbol=A/RES/70/1&Lang=E.

[11] Rossella Soldi and Simona Cavallini, 'Youth Initiative: A Framework for Youth Entrepreneurship' (European Union Committee of Regions, 2017), 1, https://cor.europa.eu/en/engage/studies/Documents/Youth_initiative/youth-initiative.pdf.

report claims, is important to 'create more and better jobs'.[12] The 2016 Arab Human Development Report (AHDR) further underscores youth entrepreneurship as a means to target the regional need to create more than sixty million new jobs within the decade for new labour force entrants.[13] This effect is being viewed as increasingly more essential in Oman after years of low oil prices and the pandemic-induced economic contraction.

States across the region embrace the policy advice from IFIs and consultancies to encourage entrepreneurship. In Oman, entrepreneurship features prominently in public life – praised and promoted in newspapers and government press releases, across universities, colleges, schools, and government ministries. State bodies, organisations, and commercial agencies have schemes and programmes geared to support entrepreneurs, foster their ideas, and launch them on the market, including training centres, incubators, accelerators, and funding instruments.[14] Entrepreneurship education and training initiatives start early, in primary school, and extend through secondary and tertiary education and include research funding around innovation and entrepreneurship.

Two interesting features characterise the entrepreneurship promotion landscape. First, the entrepreneurship ecosystem is grounded, like many activities in the country, in the government. It is primarily a top-down, deliberate government policy, and everything from education and training to funding and incubating is interweaved in government

---

[12] World Bank, 'The Environment For Women's Entrepreneurship in the Middle East and North Africa Region' (Washington, DC: The World Bank, 2007), foreword, http://web.worldbank.org/WBSITE/EXTERNAL/COUNTRIES/MENAEXT/0,,contentMDK:21517656~pagePK:146736~piPK:146830~theSitePK:256299,00.html.

[13] UNDP, 'Arab Human Development Report 2016: Youth and the Prospects for Human Development in Changing Reality' (New York: United Nations Development Programme, Regional Bureau for Arab States, 29 November 2016), 32, www.arab-hdr.org/reports/2016/english/AHDR2016En.pdf?download.

[14] E.g., Abishek Bhaya, 'Entrepreneurship Is the Way Forward in Oman, Says National Youth Commission', *Muscat Daily*, 22 April 2013; For more detail, see Crystal A. Ennis, 'Between Trend and Necessity: Top-Down Entrepreneurship Promotion in Oman and Qatar', *The Muslim World* 105, no. 1 (2015): 116–38, https://doi.org/10.1111/muwo.12083.

planning and often threaded to state or oil and gas sector financing. By the late 1990s, some initiatives had already gotten off the ground like Shell Intilaaqah (tied to Shell LiveWire International). This was launched in Oman in 1995 and offered training programmes for young Omani entrepreneurs. Another was Sharakah, a government fund for the establishment of youth projects, which started in 1998. It was designed to enter into partnerships with new SMEs. By 2007, the Ministry of Commerce and Industry set up an SME Development office, which liaised with the lending and training programmes sprouting up in the different government bodies but was geared to coordinate, centralise, and smooth the start-up process. Sheikh Salah Al-Mawali was tasked as the director general of this office, and, along with state-led entrepreneurship promotion, he and the centre received considerably more attention after 2011.

The top-down direction has caused a ripple effect with entrepreneurship support initiatives from private enterprises and public-private partnerships assembling around the government's vision – of their own accord or by direct encouragement. The substantial policy attention stimulated a space in which entrepreneurship support proliferated and through which a new interconnected and overlapping network of intermediaries and initiatives benefit from an extension of rentier distribution channels. The new policy space of the 2000s, aimed at fostering the private sector, extended the boundaries of rent circulation by allowing newer actors to become recipients – from the initiatives designed to promote and support entrepreneurial activities to the individual entrepreneurs benefitting from access to grants and loans and more favourable regulatory conditions to open their business.

Second, the entrepreneurship ecosystem is oriented toward, and rallies around, the idea that entrepreneurship produces jobs. The state wishes for the private sector to generate more jobs to meet the needs of the unemployed, so as to help reduce the size of Oman's bloated civil service. This was especially clear in new SME schemes the government introduced in 2016, which tried to incentivise civil servants to start an SME by offering the possibility to apply for a one-year leave, or up for four years of unpaid leave, to establish and run a business.[15] SME promotion was explicitly tied with job creation and Omanisation in the

---

[15] 'Ḍawābiṭ al-tafarrugh li-muwaẓẓafiyy al-Ḥukūma li-idārat Mū'assasātihim al-Khāṣṣa", *Atheer*, 22 February 2016, https://t.co/hOpxgkiJdO.

seventh FYP,[16] and there are multiple examples of how the government orients its entrepreneurship promotion as a job creation strategy. For example, the many educational initiatives in primary, secondary, and higher education try to encourage young people to consider being an entrepreneur as their career path. Also indicative is how the Ministry of Manpower refocused its Sanad programme on self-employment, established in 2001, within the entrepreneurship promotion landscape a decade later. By 2011 and 2012, the Sanad programme was freshly presented as 'an attractive option for the thousands of jobseekers currently enrolled with the MoM to receive unemployment payment' while lauding these jobseekers for 'taking advantage of the self-employment initiative'.[17] By 2013, Sanad merged into a collection of entrepreneurship support services under the SME Development Authority (known as Riyada).

Many ministries and government authorities became increasingly involved in the entrepreneurship promotion landscape after 2011, launching initiatives and holding symposiums, conferences, and workshops. In 2012, one such conference in which I participated, called 'Moving Mountains' convened by the Ministry of Higher Education, focused on promoting entrepreneurship among youth. Members of many of the leading training, funding, and SME advocacy organisations were present, as were senior government officials and a large number of college students. The best and the brightest from colleges around the country had been nominated to attend, engage in the workshops, and present nascent SME project ideas. During one of the days, I sat with a selection of the government officials present and we discussed the entrepreneurship landscape in the country and the promotion initiatives such as this conference. A senior official was very positive about the event, and the continuation of similar events in the future. He viewed such activities as politically and economically essential. He insisted the government '*must*' continue offering such experiences to students. 'Were you not here during February of [2011]? Did you see the events? There are significant numbers of youth

[16] 'The Seventh FYP 2006–2010', 427.
[17] Oxford Business Group, 'The Report: Oman 2012', 39.

who lack economic opportunities. We have to do something about this. Things have to change.'[18]

This was not an isolated perspective. Bureaucrats and policymakers never failed to mention the 2011 protests in my interviews during these years. They did so without my prompting. Frequently cited concerns included social agitation, rising levels of unemployment, and the growing numbers of graduates and school leavers. A senior official from the Ministry of Commerce and Industry (MOCI) specifically claimed that the motivation for entrepreneurship initiatives

is to create jobs for Omanis. We have a problem. Every year a big number graduates – around 50,000. The government cannot employ them. Big private companies cannot employ them, so they really have to start their own businesses. The contribution of SMEs to the GDP is only 23 per cent. We want to increase the contribution. We cannot just rely on the oil .... We have no choice! We have to encourage [entrepreneurs], to support them. Until now, we don't have a private sector in Oman that can really help the small businesses. So the government has to take a larger hand. If we don't help, I don't think we will be a success.[19]

Interviewees repeatedly referenced stability as a reason for support across different branches of government and non-governmental initiatives. Youth and potential unrest were viewed very much as a security issue, and hence jobs too become securitised. This contributes to a discourse of crisis in which it is perceived that there is no alternative to stimulating entrepreneurship for employment and strengthening privatisation and the private sector. It is both an economic and political necessity.

Clearly, entrepreneurship is offered as a way to save the national and the nation from the job-seeking epidemic. An Omani involved in promoting entrepreneurship described this connection explicitly:

The way I was brought up, you either become a police man, engineer, or doctor. This is why you're going to school. Get a degree and go work for a governmental organisation. If not, you go into the private sector and go work in PDO. This is the largest in Oman and they pay well. But now we need to change that mindset and we can't do it overnight. We need to create

---

[18] Conversation with senior government official, 18 March 2012, 'Moving Mountains: Entrepreneurship through Higher Education', Muscat, 17–19 March 2012.
[19] Interview, Muscat, 25 October 2011.

role models and let them know that entrepreneurship is an option when they start to think of their career. Tell them it is rewarding, when you give to it, it gives to you back. Start thinking like that.[20]

Entrepreneurship promotion targets individuals and what they can do to contribute to private sector growth and national development. It therefore has a 'labyrinthine relationship with neoliberal narratives and national developmentalist ones'.[21] Addressing youth, educators and policymakers emphasise the individual role in building the nation, stressing the importance not just of a getting good jobs but also the moral and loyal significance of creating good businesses. As I previously noted, it 'is a neoliberal paradigm equating entrepreneurship as citizenship; an imagined way to facilitate economic belonging in the private sector. If you cannot find a job in your field, surely you can make your own! Entrepreneurship then becomes a form of self-employment, and thereby a means of privatising and individualising the employment burden'.[22]

Entrepreneurship has political use as a mechanism of government, in the Foucauldian sense, which integrates the economic doctrine of free markets and private enterprise with individualism, obligation, and patriotism. This expression of neoliberalism urges individuals to 'give their lives a specific entrepreneurial form', while shifting the 'regulatory competence of the state onto "responsible" and "rational" individuals'.[23] Individuals then embody solutions to problems that would otherwise have been under the domain of the state. That the entrepreneurship agenda in the Gulf has centred on self-employment is also reflective of much wider global failures of political and economic systems. Like in Oman, colleges and universities around the world are expected to prepare students to create their own establishments with the logic that if graduates desire employment, they can make their own. The promotion of entrepreneurial behaviour becomes part of an

---

[20] Interview with Omani leading an entrepreneurship support initiative, 23 October 2011.

[21] Ennis, 'The Gendered Complexities of Promoting Female Entrepreneurship in the Gulf', 368.

[22] Crystal A. Ennis, 'Citizenship without Belonging? Contesting Economic Space in Oman', *International Journal of Middle East Studies* 52, no. 4 (November 2020): 763, https://doi.org/10.1017/S0020743820001063.

[23] Thomas Lemke, '"The Birth of Bio-Politics": Michel Foucault's Lecture at the Collège de France on Neo-Liberal Governmentality', *Economy and Society* 30, no. 2 (1 January 2001): 201–2, https://doi.org/10.1080/03085140120042271.

offshoring of collective or government responsibility onto the shoulders of individuals. The case of entrepreneurship promotion in Oman exemplifies how states with recent histories of rapid economic development 'seem to be converging on a style of governance that places an ethos of regulated self-reliance at its core'.[24] Starting your own business is not easy for new, young jobseekers; new businesses have high failure rates around the world. After failing, the individual bears the blame for not working sufficiently hard or being sufficiently successful. At a basic level, entrepreneurship becomes an attempt at correcting some of the systemic economic weaknesses by providing a means of self-employment. Yet it lacks the focus on structure and on innovation demanded by diversification imperatives.

These discourses focus on responsibilising either the private sector or citizens for national economic outcomes in order to offload the state's responsibility for failures. This blame shifting is at times placed on the individual and their productivity and ambition. At other times, it is placed on the private sector, which is accused of not pulling its weight or not being serious about national employment. Blame shifting is a useful technique of governance and one that is often wielded at moments when scapegoats are needed to excuse stagnating employment drives or weak economic outcomes.

Rapid economic development and modernisation in the Gulf are interweaved with a story of rentierism, where political loyalty is courted through the benevolence of the state in its redistributive role including the provision of jobs along with free education, health care, and other goods.[25] Today, the provision of new economic alternatives through forging an entrepreneurial ecosystem are important components to reframing and re-centring the state. Indeed, the connection between entrepreneurship, jobs, and the role of the state continues under the new Sultan. On 11 January 2022, his second anniversary since assuming the throne, Haitham bin Tariq said in his speech,

We look forward with hope, combined with determination, that all sectors of the State and the private sector will play the role expected of them in promoting employment, being the cornerstone of the economy and

---

[24] Catherine A. Honeyman, *The Orderly Entrepreneur: Youth, Education, and Governance in Rwanda* (Stanford: Stanford University Press, 2016), 5–6.

[25] Beblawi and Luciani, *The Rentier State*; Hvidt, 'Economic and Institutional Reforms in the Arab Gulf Countries'.

development. The aim is to provide jobs for our qualified sons and daughters and to qualify those who require to gain the necessary skills to join the labour market. As for our sons and daughters from among entrepreneurs who wish to establish their private projects, we are resolved to lend them our support and encourage their entrepreneurship programmes. We will offer necessary support and incentives to small and medium enterprises, given their vital role in stimulating economic activity and employment opportunities.[26]

Conveying these goals in terms of local growth and employment benefits while highlighting the state's support underscores its role as patron. At the same time, narrating the individual contribution connects personal action with national developmentalist and renaissance discourses.

Within the larger story of labour market reform, entrepreneurship promotion illustrates the dysfunctional relationship between rentierism and neoliberal capitalism well. The elite embrace of the prevailing neoliberal discourse, celebrating the virtues of the free market and private sector, is telling as it sits within a framework of a state that remains the most powerful economic actor. On the one hand, the state is dominant and, through its accumulation and recycling of oil receipts through contracts, jobs, and benefits, is intimately involved in the economic life of the country and the citizenry. On the other hand, there are continuous reform processes, as detailed in Chapter 5, aimed at reducing the financial burden of the state and privatising and liberalising the economy. In this context, entrepreneurship is framed as an elixir to labour market challenges while it simultaneously extends the arm of the state into new spaces. Such processes correspond with shifting regional landscapes from state developmentalism toward 'intrinsically authoritarian modalities of neoliberal government'[27] where authoritarianism and neoliberalism occur in conjunction.[28]

---

[26] Haitham bin Tariq Al-Said, 'The Royal Speech of HM Sultan Haitham Bin Tarik' (Ministry of Information, 11 January 2022), www.omaninfo.om/library/70/show/1227.

[27] Koenraad Bogaert, 'Contextualizing the Arab Revolts: The Politics behind Three Decades of Neoliberalism in the Arab World', *Middle East Critique* 22, no. 3 (2 September 2013): 215, https://doi.org/10.1080/19436149.2013.814945.

[28] Hanieh, *Capitalism and Class in the Gulf Arab States*; Bilge Yesil, *Media in New Turkey: The Origins of an Authoritarian Neoliberal State* (Urbana: University of Illinois Press, 2016); Buckley, 'Locating Neoliberalism in Dubai'; Ahmed Kanna,

6.2 Gendered Logics Shaping Entrepreneurial Praxis

Female and youth entrepreneurs and aspiring entrepreneurs confront competing tensions within three intersecting political economy logics in Oman: the logic of the economic structure, the logic of development narratives, and the logic of socio-economic organisation. This section examines how these interact with women's entrepreneurship in Oman.

6.2.1 Logic of the Economic Structure

Support for youth and women's entrepreneurship in Oman encounters entrenched economic structures – specifically hydrocarbon dependence and labour market segmentation. As articulated earlier, Oman and other Gulf states use public sector employment as an avenue to manage unemployment and redistribute hydrocarbon wealth. With this capacity under stress, entrepreneurship offers one way to shift some of the state's employment burden onto the private sector and individual, as discussed above. The entrepreneurship advocacy agenda therefore privatises and individualises the issue of national employment. At the same time, the logic of the economic structure remains and reproduces the economic and labour market realities visible throughout this book.

First, SMEs generally reproduce existing employment patterns and hiring practices, with small businesses especially keen to minimise costs and hire the cheapest available labour. SMEs are supposed to generate both GDP and employment growth. Globally, SME activity is said to account for 16, 39, and 51 per cent of GDP growth in low-income, middle-income, and high-income countries respectively. Yet in the Gulf, it only constitutes roughly 15 per cent of GDP.[29] The example of SMEs in Europe is further used to validate claims about job growth given that European SMEs contributed to approximately 85 per cent of employment growth in the 2000s.[30] Consistent with economic structures, job growth in GCC countries adds expatriates to the labour

---

Dubai: The City As Corporation (Minneapolis: University of Minnesota Press, 2011); Guazzone and Pioppi, *The Arab State and Neo-Liberal Globalization.*

[29] Oxford Business Group, 'The Report: Oman 2016', 21.

[30] Steffen Hertog, 'Benchmarking SME Policies in the GCC: A Survey of Challenges and Opportunities', The EU-GCC Chamber Forum (Brussels: Eurochambres, 2010), 23, www.europolitique.info/pdf/gratuit_fr/270047-fr .pdf.

market, contributing little to the employment of citizens. The low cost and high flexibility of foreign labour in the region perpetuates a segmented labour market between nationals and non-nationals that extends to fresh start-ups. Statistics show the largest companies in Oman's private sector hire the most nationals, while smaller companies primarily hire expatriates.[31] The dependence on expatriate workers in skilled and unskilled fields creates certain rigidities in the labour market that are difficult to alter. Despite the aim of entrepreneurship promotion to create national employment opportunities, new SMEs successfully lobby the government for exemptions from Omanisation quotas arguing that hiring locals, who require higher salaries, better benefits, and shorter working hours, is detrimental to their profit margins and competitiveness. For example, the government responded to pressure from the private sector in 2015 by granting new SMEs a two-year Omanisation exemption, allowing all labour needs to be met with foreign recruitment.[32]

Second, reflecting the larger labour market, entrepreneurs, and especially women entrepreneurs, confront dynamics that are gendered, raced, and classed. The segmentations detailed in Chapters 2 and 5 that characterise the Omani labour market – sectoral, skill, nationality, race, class, and gender – are naturally also part of the start-up landscape. The weak representation of Omani women in the private sector, for example, features among the considerations for aspiring entrepreneurs to navigate. This intersects with how gender continues to influence discourses around acceptable and desirable work, which in turn varies by class, education, and geography. Class is of substantial importance within this discussion, and as shown, holding an Omani or Gulf nationality can take on particular class formations that extend to the entrepreneurial ecosystem.[33]

Certainly there are successful female entrepreneurs. Those tied to elite circles, connected to large business dynasties or political power, more readily experience success by capitalising on their *wāsṭa*. Other highly educated women have launched successful enterprises within the entrepreneurial support ecosystems, creating training initiatives,

---

[31] Ennis and Al-Jamali, 'Elusive Employment', 10.
[32] 'Government to Ease Omanisation Norms for SME Sector: H E Sunaidy', *Muscat Daily*, 28 January 2015, www.muscatdaily.com/Archive/Oman/ Government-to-ease-Omanisation-norms-for-SME-sector-H-E-Sunaidy-3scp.
[33] See the discussion on wages and class in Chapter 2.

incubators, or funding instruments. In fact, the achievements of these ecosystems can most readily be seen through the successful entrepreneurship support initiatives incubated within them. Such entrepreneurs balance in the shifting boundary between being entrepreneurial and benefitting from rent recycling.[34]

To women in vulnerable financial circumstances, entrepreneurship is peddled as a form of economic self-help and mostly centres on micro-enterprises and the creation of small-scale, consumer-driven products. These are often business forms that can be started from home. Such 'women's businesses' showcased at exhibitions frequently include jewellery design, uniform design, *'abāya* embroidery, and baking. Again, rather than a focus on technological innovation required of entrepreneurship to respond to structural economic problems, these are self-employment alternatives.

6.2.2 Logic of Development Narratives

The second gendered political economy logic are the multiple development narratives wielded within entrepreneurship promotion. I consider two narratives especially relevant to this context. The first frames women as subjects who need to be liberated by the market. This narrative is concerned with locating women's freedom in the private sector and reframing them as market citizens. The second narrative frames women as empowered in the economy by the state. It is concerned with legitimising state feminist discourses by lauding women's patriotic roles within national development. This section unpacks these narratives by examining the overlapping domains of governance and politics that propel women forward as subjects of market liberalisation and change and concurrently as agents of stability.

Women in the Middle East are considered an 'untapped resource' by the World Bank, due to their lower labour market participation rates.[35] In this logic, they are viewed as market actors key to increasing national productivity. Along this vein, Oman's fifth FYP (1996–2000)

---

[34] For more on rent recycling and rentier class formation, see Hertog, 'The Sociology of the Gulf Rentier Systems'.

[35] World Bank, 'Gender and Development in the Middle East and North Africa: Women in the Public Sphere', MENA Development Report (Washington, DC: World Bank, 2004), 2, https://openknowledge.worldbank.org/handle/10986/15036.

noted that the goal of increasing Omani labour market participation rates 'applied particularly to women'[36] and therefore prioritised them in its human resource development strategy. By the seventh FYP (2006–2010), the attention began shifting to forms of self-employment as a means of encouraging women into the labour market. The plan focused on 'self-hiring projects' for Omani youth and conducted studies on 'proposals related to household and small scale projects which could be performed by Omani women'.[37] Increasingly women's entrepreneurship was viewed as a solution to increasing the number of women in Middle Eastern labour markets, because the gender gap in entrepreneurship was less marked than in employment.[38]

Such logics are heavily critiqued by feminist political economy due to the way economic production is measured in economies.[39] Social reproduction and work in the home are neither counted nor valued in measurements of economic development. Women 'count' by becoming market citizens, their value enumerated in market terms.[40] This form of promoting gender empowerment, through multinational corporations, development agencies, or the state, is what Kantola and Squires have called 'market feminism'.[41] It is a specific form of feminism critiqued for its 'neoliberalisation' and for abandoning its radical roots.[42] Moreover, casting women as market citizens has resulted in what Roberts characterises as 'a partial shift away from promoting women's social and economic dependence on men toward promoting

---

[36] 'The Fifth FYP 1996–2000', 470.   [37] 'The Seventh FYP 2006–2010', 126.

[38] OECD, 'Women in Business 2014: Accelerating Entrepreneurship in the Middle East and North Africa Region' (Paris: OECD, 2014), 55, http://dx.doi.org/10 .1787/9789264213944-en.

[39] Bakker, 'Social Reproduction and the Constitution of a Gendered Political Economy'; Silvia Federici, *Wages against Housework* (London; Bristol: Power of Women Collective and Falling Wall Press, 1975); Peterson, *A Critical Rewriting of Global Political Economy*; Laura Parisi, '"Disciplining" and "Engendering" the World Bank: A Comment', in *Feminist Economics and the World Bank: History, Theory, and Policy*, ed. Edith Kuiper and Drucilla K. Barker (London; New York: Routledge, 2006).

[40] Hoskyns and Rai, 'Recasting the Global Political Economy'.

[41] Johanna Kantola and Judith Squires, 'From State Feminism to Market Feminism?', *International Political Science Review* 33, no. 4 (2012): 382–400, https://doi.org/10.1177/0192512111432513.

[42] Elisabeth Prügl, 'Neoliberalising Feminism', *New Political Economy* 20, no. 4 (4 July 2015): 614–15, https://doi.org/10.1080/13563467.2014.951614.

their dependence on capitalist markets'.[43] Women's importance and freedom are hence tied to the market.

In Oman, market feminism takes on particular orientalised forms premised on the assumption that women in the region are awaiting exogenous economic liberation. Entrepreneurial narratives written *for* the Gulf point to its liberating potential within a space deemed restrictive for women.[44] The purchase of this narrative speaks to the prevalence of sensationalised Western stereotypes that have constructed contradictory images of Gulf women as either oppressed and silenced or as rich elites benefitting from vast oil wealth and abundant opportunities.[45] In both accounts, Western capitalism and private enterprise feature as saviours and champions of womenkind. Singularly framing entrepreneurship as a net positive for women because it facilitates their contribution to economic growth and empowers them as individuals ignores the inequalities, feminisation of labour and poverty, and wider economic structures that systematically marginalise women in global capitalism.[46] Inserting Omani women into entrepreneurship roots their productivity and value in the market while bolstering state narratives

---

[43] Adrienne Roberts, 'Financing Social Reproduction: The Gendered Relations of Debt and Mortgage Finance in Twenty-First-Century America', *New Political Economy* 18, no. 1 (1 February 2013): 26, https://doi.org/10.1080/13563467 .2012.662951.

[44] Christopher M. Schroeder, *Startup Rising: The Entrepreneurial Revolution Remaking the Middle East* (New York: Palgrave Macmillan, 2013), 149.

[45] Anita M. Weiss, 'Challenges for Muslim Women in a Postmodern World', in *Islam, Globalization, and Postmodernity*, ed. Akhbar S. Ahmed (New York: Routledge, 1994), 127–40; Meshal Al-Sabah, *Gender and Politics in Kuwait: Women and Political Participation in the Gulf* (London: I. B.Tauris, 2013); Madawi Al-Rasheed, *A Most Masculine State: Gender, Politics and Religion in Saudi Arabia* (Cambridge: Cambridge University Press, 2013); Schroeder, *Startup Rising*.

[46] Roberts, 'The Political Economy of "Transnational Business Feminism"'; Özlem Altan-Olcay, 'Entrepreneurial Subjectivities and Gendered Complexities: Neoliberal Citizenship in Turkey', *Feminist Economics* 20, no. 4 (2 October 2014): 235–59, https://doi.org/10.1080/13545701.2014.950978; Marianne H. Marchand and Anne Sisson Runyan, eds., *Gender and Global Restructuring: Sightings, Sites and Resistances*, Second (New York: Routledge, 2010); Spike V. Peterson, 'How (the Meaning of) Gender Matters in Political Economy', *New Political Economy* 10, no. 4 (1 December 2005): 499–521, https://doi.org/10 .1080/13563460500344468; Rai, *Gender and the Political Economy of Development*.

of supporting women in the economy and public life. It is therefore also part of state feminism.[47]

Entrepreneurship promotion narratives are politically expedient at the international and domestic levels. Oman can reach for some degree of legitimacy by speaking to international female empowerment agendas, on the one hand, while simultaneously speaking to economic diversification and employment generation locally, on the other. Neoliberal policy goals and female empowerment contribute to a country's status building and female-friendly branding.[48] Female entrepreneurship promotion thus becomes part of a wider state feminist discourse while also being integrated into government strategy aimed at legitimising liberal credentials. In authoritarian contexts, women's liberation can be used to paint autocratic governments as reformers. The paradox is government sponsorship of women's activities transpires alongside tight state controls, on the one hand, and governmental withdrawal from economic arenas, on the other.[49]

It is not only in development plans that the Omani state highlights women in employment and entrepreneurship strategies. Royal speeches also address women as neoliberal citizens and tie their economic productivity to their national developmental contribution.[50]

---

[47] State feminism is commonly top-down championing of women's liberation from the state. It usually refers to the effectiveness of alliances between policy agencies and women's movement activists in securing state responses to their demands. Kantola and Squires, 'From State Feminism to Market Feminism?', 382.

[48] Andrew F Cooper and Bessma Momani, 'The Challenge of Re-Branding Progressive Countries in the Gulf and Middle East: Opportunities through New Networked Engagements versus Constraints of Embedded Negative Images', *Place Branding and Public Diplomacy* 5, no. 2 (May 2009): 103–17, https://doi .org/10.1057/pb.2009.3.

[49] Emma C. Murphy, 'Women in Tunisia: Between State Feminism and Economic Reform', in *Women and Globalization in the Arab Middle East: Gender, Economy, and Society*, ed. Eleanor Abdella Doumato and Marsha Pripstein Posusney (Boulder: Lynne Rienner, 2003), 187; Wang Zheng, '"State Feminism"? Gender and Socialist State Formation in Maoist China', *Feminist Studies* 31, no. 3 (2005): 519–51, https://doi.org/10.2307/20459044.

[50] Al-Muftah unpacks similar dynamics around a women and development discourse in Qatar. 'al-Mara'a fī ẓill siyāsāt al-tanmiya: ḥālat Qaṭar'. al-Thābit wa al-Mutaḥawil 2016: al-Khalīj ba'd khams sanawāt min al-intifāḍāt al-'arabiyya (Gulf Centre for Development Policies, 2016), https://gulfpolicies.org/ 2019-10-30-17-42-40; and Jones speaks about the Emirati state trying to fashion 'entrepreneurial citizens' who are ready to contribute to market-driven economies. Calvert W. Jones, *Bedouins into Bourgeois: Remaking Citizens for Globalization* (Cambridge: Cambridge University Press, 2017).

In a 2009 speech to the council of Oman, Qaboos called 'upon Omani women everywhere, in villages and in cities, and both urban and Bedu communities ... to roll up their sleeves and contribute to the process of economic and social development .... The country needs every pair of hands for the progress of its development, stability, and prosperity'.[51] In the same speech, women were implored to 'prove their worth' by taking advantage of the opportunities the state granted to them.[52] The state is very much viewed as the enabler of Omani women's progress and success.[53] Likewise, by advocating local women in the economy, private sector actors in Oman are able to brand themselves as pro-national, patriotic, and contributing to national development.

Reflecting Kanna's work on Dubai, the Omani state's discourse around productive citizenship similarly focuses on 'national ethics and modes of proper and authentic citizenship'.[54] 'Readiness for hard work' and playing 'a part' in development 'for the sake of the nation' is cast as an obligation and responsibility of citizenship for both men and women.[55] Qaboos regularly spoke to an Omani pride, or nationalist sense of self, in his speeches on national day and to the Council of Oman. He declared that 'productive work – no matter how small – is a key element in the structure of the nation .... With productive work, there will be no place in our society for idle hands'.[56] Throughout speeches, being in tune with cultural values is stressed alongside the individual obligation to contribute to the nation.

Productive citizens contribute to both economic growth and to the reputation of the state. Omani women are frequently highlighted in media as part of state branding campaigns, the modernity associated with powerful women in business demonstrating national success.[57]

---

[51] Speech at the opening of the annual session of the Council of Oman (16 November 2009), Al-Said, 'The Royal Speeches of His Majesty Sultan Qaboos Bin Said', 522.

[52] Al-Said, The Royal Speeches of His Majesty Sultan Qaboos Bin Said', 523.

[53] See also, speech on the occasion of the opening of the Council of Oman (27 December 1997), Al-Said, 386.

[54] Kanna, 'Flexible Citizenship in Dubai', 104.

[55] Speech before the third session of the Council of Oman (21 November 2003), Al-Said, 'The Royal Speeches of His Majesty Sultan Qaboos Bin Said', 462–63.

[56] 26th National Day Speech (18 November 1996), Al-Said, 'The Royal Speeches of His Majesty Sultan Qaboos Bin Said', 369–70.

[57] 'Meet the Most Powerful Business Women in Oman', *Oman Economic Review*, 11 October 2015, http://oeronline.com/editor-pick/meet-the-most-powerful-business-women-in-oman.html; 'Three Omani Women Entrepreneurs to Share

Women are often provided platforms through media and conferences to praise the support of the state, demonstrating the 'gender equality machineries in nation states becoming ever more embedded in neoliberal market reform'.[58] Even in my interviews, participants regularly point to a perceived benevolence of the state in making way for women to have more powerful roles in business, politics, and society. The Omani entrepreneurship ecosystem is entangled with state propaganda.

6.2.3 Logic of Socio-economic Organisation

Just as neoliberalism places competing pressures on economic and political spaces, women experience complex pressures from the advocacy of individual responsibility for economic well-being alongside pressures from patriarchal structures and familial obligation. Female entrepreneurs try to adjust neoliberal individualism and responsibility with conservative social expectations. In this way, the 'adaptation of neoliberal conceptions of the self entail not a rejection of traditional patriarchal structures but a reinterpretation of them'.[59] Obligations placed on female entrepreneurs stretch to the market, the state, and the family. How these entrepreneurs perceive themselves, how they navigate economic life, and how they interpret their role within market, state, and society are important and reveal patterns where neoliberal economic deepening has especially complex interactions with gender.

Entrepreneurship promotion initiatives aim to encourage women into the private sector labour market to earn their own income. Most initiatives in the country are geared to promoting entrepreneurship in general, not specifically targeted toward women. Yet most initiative leaders I spoke with noted that a majority of their clients are women, whom they view as better prepared and more thorough in business and financial planning. 'Women are well-committed, hardworking, and do not cheat' noted a senior executive to explain his interpretation of women's high performance in work and business.[60] This is unsurprising when you consider that young women comprise the highest-

Experiences', *Times of Oman*, 13 September 2015, http://timesofoman.com/article/67499.
[58] Kantola and Squires, 'From State Feminism to Market Feminism?', 383.
[59] Kanna, 'Flexible Citizenship in Dubai', 104.
[60] Interview, Special Economic Zone Authority Duqm, Muscat, 8 January 2020.

educated demographic. Yet despite outperforming men in educational attainment, female graduates struggle to find jobs that match their training.[61] This partly explains both the focus on fashioning women entrepreneurs and the draw of the entrepreneurial option to women.

At the same time, discourses on female entrepreneurship in the region are imbued with appeals to women to prioritise work-family balance. Omani women are told that the opportunities they receive go 'alongside their greater role of building a family and implanting a sense of belonging and allegiance in the hearts and minds of the rising generations'.[62] Women's role in social reproduction is regularly highlighted. In the neighbouring UAE, state minister, Dr. Maitha Al-Shamsi, captured this succinctly when she said, 'only [a woman] who successfully runs a family can also be successful as an entrepreneur'.[63] In its encouragement of entrepreneurship, the state is careful to reinforce the importance of women's role in their families and societies. Some scholarship suggests that the oil state is viewed as liberating women from the financial necessity to work. That is, at the same time the Gulf state fostered literacy, education, and regulatory frameworks amenable to women's progress, there were counteracting cultural and religious forces encouraging their return to their homes to focus on their roles as mothers and wives.[64] As women are encouraged to enter the labour market and business initiatives, there are simultaneous signals pointing to the family. Conservative views on women's primary

---

[61] The is what the World Bank calls the 'gender paradox' of the Middle East (sometimes referred to as the 'MENA paradox'. World Bank, 'Capabilities, Opportunities, and Participation: Gender Equality and Development in the Middle East and North Africa Region' [Washington, DC: World Bank, 2011], http://siteresources.worldbank.org/INTMENA/Resources/World_Development_Report_2012_Gender_Equality_Development_Overview_MENA.pdf; World Bank, 'The Environment for Women's Entrepreneurship in the Middle East and North Africa Region'; UNCTAD, 'Science, Technology & Innovation Policy Review' [Geneva: United Nations Conference on Trade and Development (UNCTAD), 2014], 41, http://unctad.org/en/PublicationsLibrary/dtlstict2014d1_en.pdf.

[62] Speech on the occasion of the opening of the Council of Oman (27 December 1997), Al-Said, 'The Royal Speeches of His Majesty Sultan Qaboos Bin Said', 386.

[63] Sara-Ida Kaiser, Larissa Alles, and Franz J. H. Polenz, 'Female Entrepreneurs Needed', *Veranstalungsbeitrag*, October 2011, www.kas.de/wf/doc/kas_29078-1522-2-30.pdf?111127103848.

[64] Sean Foley, *The Arab Gulf States: Beyond Oil and Islam* (Boulder: Lynne Rienner, 2010), 180–84.

role in society are not exclusive to older generations, and one survey suggested that over half of young men in the Gulf feel that the primary role of women in society is to be a wife and mother whereas fewer than a quarter of women agree.[65] For the targets of women's entrepreneurship promotion, rhetoric around desirable economic behaviour produces tensions between collective cultural and national loyalty and the individual duty to be successful and productive in professional and personal life.

Not all Omani female entrepreneurs experience such gendered pressures in the same way. Women neither experience business and labour relations alike, nor do they experience discrimination, domination, or privilege or access, uniformly. As noted, gender intersects with class, ethnicity, education level and more, and these interactions shape entrepreneurial forms and the reasons an entrepreneurial path may be pursued. Many young Omani women I interviewed over the years seemed keen to respond to the state promotion of entrepreneurship and exploit the training, mentoring, and financial support available. Some viewed it in patriotic terms as part of their contribution to the economy, others as an important way to exercise freedom and independence, others as a nice part-time business hobby for extra income,[66] while others see it as a last option to earn after years of unemployment. Among the latter, there are those for whom entrepreneurship is experienced as a necessary possible path out of relative poverty. Other women also identify rural poverty alleviation and employment programmes as important opportunities for social entrepreneurship – thus both creating their own job and helping insert other women into wage earning.[67] As the last decade went on, with its high attention to entrepreneurship, women increasingly seemed to view

---

[65] Mona Almunajjed and Karim Sabbagh, 'Youth in GCC Countries: Meeting the Challenge' (Booz & Company, 2011), 39, www.booz.com/media/uploads/BoozCo-GCC-Youth-Challenge.pdf.

[66] Some women, and their male counterparts, dabble in entrepreneurship as a hobby. That is, they open a small side business to focus on after the working day. Moonlighting as an entrepreneur is facilitated by short public sector working hours and allows some activity within the private sector, without complete commitment and reliance upon it.

[67] See, for example, the story of Badriya Al Siyabi's creation of a sewing collective in the village is Sidab. Golam Mostafa Khan, 'Sidab Women's Sewing Group: An Example of Social Entrepreneurship in the Arabian Gulf', *International Journal of Entrepreneurship and Small Business* 18, no. 1 (2013): 47–56, https://doi.org/10.1504/IJESB.2013.050751.

entrepreneurship as aspirational and even noble. Even those in employment had ideas about early retirement to pursue small businesses.

Legal frameworks around the economy are not always reflected as part of the lived experience of entrepreneurship until specific issues arise which reveal them. Still these frameworks are relevant to the business environment in which women engage and should be mentioned here. Legal and financial barriers to entrepreneurship are said to impact female- and male-owned businesses equally in Oman and the Gulf, and gender discrimination is technically prohibited in commercial and labour law. However, there are a combination of laws on the status and mobility of women that, if exercised, have the potential to reduce their economic power. Many of these are framed as having been instituted in the interest of protecting women – for example, women cannot work at night or in dangerous jobs as easily as men. While laws penalise sexual harassment in employment, no laws fine pay discrimination. Maternity leave and benefits remained limited and weak, and there was no paternity leave at all until the introduction of the 2023 labour law.[68] Yet, in business, women can sign a contract, access credit, register a business, open a bank account, and have their ownership rights protected the same as men.[69] Certainly, intuitional and legal protections are important for women's engagement in the formal, calculated economy.

It is important that Oman's labour law stipulates that all workers should be treated equally.[70] Yet next to this, unwritten cultural codes may impact the feeling and experience of work and of running businesses in spaces perceived as heavily male-dominated. Women regularly exercise agency through their understanding of cultural norms,

---

[68] The 2023 labour law affords 98 days of combined pre- and postnatal maternity leave, up from 50 days previous. It also introduced 7 days of paternity leave (see Article 84). Royal Decree 53/2023, 'Issuing the Labour Law (Issued 25 July 2023, Published 30 July 2023)', Official Gazette 1504, [author translations from Arabic], 2023.

[69] World Bank, 'The Environment for Women's Entrepreneurship in the Middle East and North Africa Region'; Royal Decree 35/2003, 'Promulgating the Labour Law (Issued 26 April 2003, Published 3 May 2003)'; Royal Decree 74/2006, 'Amending Some Provisions of the Labour Law (Issued 8 July 2006, Published 15 July 2006)'; 'Women, Business and the Law 2021: Oman' (Washington, DC: World Bank, 2021), https://wbl.worldbank.org/content/dam/documents/wbl/2021/snapshots/Oman.pdf.

[70] See Article 24, Royal Decree 53/2023, 'Issuing the Labour Law (Issued 25 July 2023, Published 30 July 2023)'.

ways of 'negotiating practice',[71] and determining where or how such norms may be challenged. Aldossari and Calvard call this 'patternings of resistance and conformity' exercised by women in workplaces as they determine whether and how to resist or conform to diverse cultural norms and codes.[72] Such 'patternings' also capture when and how some women experience 'appropriate' professions and spaces as liberating in their own right. That is, some women pushed against discourses that frowned upon 'gender mixing' – as my young inter-locutors often called co-ed spaces and events – whereas others felt freer and more comfortable in these spaces. In focus groups, meetings, and in volunteer organisations and events, gender norms and the boundar-ies of the acceptable for women and young people were regularly discussed and contested. Law, religion, historical norms, and ideas about development are regularly invoked and inevitably confronted competing feminist perspectives.

Neoliberal ideologies intersect with religious, cultural, and nationalist interpretations of work and women in business. Capitalism and neoliberalism occupy the foundations of economic and social life across cultural and religious spaces and therefore often ground discourses in moral and religious codes. One can see evidence of how 'moral economies' are 'over-determined by existing market conditions and rhetorics' while religion can also 'permeate capital-ism'.[73] Research suggests that Islam may at times be invoked to set boundaries or justify ethical engagements with neoliberal economy.[74] Likewise, stories from Islamic history are sometimes used to legitimise and popularise the acceptability or importance of women's

[71] Kelly Knez and Lisahunter, 'The Paradox of Physical Activity for Qatari Women: Researcher Hysteresis and Reflexivity', in *Pierre Bourdieu and Physical Culture*, ed. Lisahunter, Wayne Smith, and Elke Emerald (London; New York: Routledge, 2015), 114.

[72] Maryam Aldossari and Thomas Calvard, 'The Politics and Ethics of Resistance, Feminism and Gender Equality in Saudi Arabian Organizations', *Journal of Business Ethics*, 24 September 2021, https://doi.org/10.1007/s10551–021–04949-3.

[73] Filippo Osella and Caroline Osella, 'Muslim Entrepreneurs in Public Life between India and the Gulf: Making Good and Doing Good', *The Journal of the Royal Anthropological Institute* 15 (2009): S217.

[74] Osella and Osella, 'Muslim Entrepreneurs in Public Life between India and the Gulf'.

entrepreneurial engagement.[75] Lived experiences of economic life, including 'patternings' of conformity, resistance, and rationalisation, help us recognise how neoliberalism, authoritarianism, and religion, which may seem competitive, can in fact be co-constitutive.

Moreover, some women interlocutors did not specify gender as a significant barrier to their experiences in entrepreneurship. When asked about the greatest barriers to their entrepreneurial ambitions, some responded with complaints about tedious bureaucratic processes required to register businesses or recruit employees from abroad. Some others responded with specific technological or policy constraints related to their particular endeavour or field. Gender often seemed secondary to their concerns. When probed, women sometimes discussed gendered concerns connected to household obligations, and the 'double work burden' that women often shoulder globally.[76] But even this often varied, depending on class, education, and access to hired help in the home. As discussed in Chapter 2, a great deal of care work in the country is delivered by live-in domestic workers from abroad. This has important implications for class formation and social reproduction in the country while also contributing to the availability of women for the labour market and business in the absence of robust socialised childcare and parental benefits. It is important for researchers to keep differential experiences in mind when examining issues of gender in the region and be cautious not to impose external perceptions of behaviours, patterns, and constraints onto their analyses.[77]

A story relayed to me in an interview is telling. An Omani director of a government fund aimed at financing start-ups shared the story of a

[75] 'How Women Entrepreneurs Are Driving Business in the Middle East', *Wamda*, 2 February 2012, www.wamda.com/2012/02/how-women-entrepreneurs-are-driving-business-in-the-middle-east-; Md. Maruf Ullah, Taskina Binta Mahmud, and Fatema Yousuf, 'Women Entrepreneurship: Islamic Perspective', *Islamic Management and Business 5*, no. 11 (2013): 44–52; 'Take Prophet's Wife as Model for Female Entrepreneurship, TOBB President Says', *Hürriyet Daily News*, 25 December 2012, www.hurriyetdailynews.com/take-prophets-wife-as-model-for-female-entrepreneurship-tobb-president-says-37604.

[76] Naila Kabeer, 'The Rise of the Female Breadwinner: Reconfigurations of Marriage, Motherhood, and Masculinity in the Global Economy', in *New Frontiers in Feminist Political Economy*, ed. Shirin M. Rai and Georgina Waylen (New York: Routledge, 2014), 67.

[77] Maya Mikdashi, 'How Not to Study Gender in the Middle East', Jadaliyya, 21 March 2012, www.jadaliyya.com/pages/index/4775/how-not-to-study-gender-in-the-middle-east.

female entrepreneur, I'll call her Khawla, who established an independent Omani chemical manufacturing company in the construction sector. She launched it in the early 2010s and toward the end of the decade it was thriving. The director's account of Khawla's story portrayed it as interesting in one major way – how she had to struggle against vested business interests that would see her fail. In his account, he characterised Khawla as coming from outside elite family circles and having a traditional, conservative background. As evidence of this, he suggested he had to expend quite some energy to convince Khawla to be in a photo at her manufacturing plant for his reporting. That she launched a successful business in a male-dominated sector and not in a field that was about consumption 'like making cupcakes at home or whatnot. This is a real economic activity that has real employment capabilities' was particularly meaningful. The crux of the story, however, was not that Khawla overcame a lot of conservative and patriarchal structures to be in this field and to launch this business. It was that Omani start-ups in general face a difficult environment because, in his view, established business families monopolise the market and government contracts. Accessing government contracts is the only way to really succeed in the private sector. He relayed receiving a private call from one such family about Khawla's business where they pressured him, as an investor, to force her business to close. She previously worked for one of their businesses, and although there were no laws preventing her from continuing to work in the field after leaving her position, they were unhappy she established a business that was becoming strong competition.

I tried to frame this as positive. I said – you should be so proud! Someone you trained, who worked with you, is now a successful entrepreneur running a business and contributing to the economy of the country! But they still tried to pressure me, and said, if you don't close it, we will force it to close – and they tried to make it very difficult for her business to thrive.[78]

At the time of our conversation, the pressure had not worked and the director had diffused the pressure by writing a detailed report of the call and emailing it to the individual asking for confirmation that this is what had transpired. Within seconds of receiving the email, the

---

[78] Interview with director of a public fund for new SMEs, Muscat, 27 February 2018.

individual called pleading for its deletion so that no record of the meeting could survive. The director had already sent a copy to the chairman of the fund and discussed his concerns. In his telling, such pressures would not work.

This story is an interesting case for our purposes for two reasons. First, it illustrates how gender-related struggles are not always the central obstacle to women's economic engagement even as it intersects with other variables, identities, structures, and oppressions. Second, the story demonstrates both the continuity of economic structures as well as the informal ways through which some established businesses attempt to maintain their access and dominance in government contracts and the market.

Women entrepreneurs confront logics related to the economic structure, related to narratives around development, and to socio-economic pressures. These three logics often overlap with each other and intersect with gender in revealing ways as detailed above. The emergence and management of micro- and SMEs by Omani women occurs within a combination of multiple interacting forces that may, in various cases, include neoliberal frameworks that champion private enterprise, desires for economic independence, financial need, and patriarchal constructs that render workplaces and economic behaviours appropriate or inappropriate for women.[79] Given this, women experience entrepreneurship differently. Some find entrepreneurship empowering because of the financial independence autonomous income offers. Yet some experience it more as a burden because they are driven by economic need and therefore must work in the formal economy whether they would prefer to or not. Still others experience entrepreneurship as liberating insofar as they can use it to participate in the economy on their own terms and away from male-dominated spaces if they so desire.[80] Such mixed interpretations speak to Prügl's assertion that the 'outcomes of the neoliberalisation of feminism are not

---

[79] See also Julia Elyachar, *Markets of Dispossession: NGOs, Economic Development, and the State in Cairo* (Durham: Duke University Press, 2005); Katharine N. Rankin, 'Governing Development: Neoliberalism, Microcredit, and Rational Economic Woman', *Economy and Society* 30, no. 1 (1 January 2001): 18–37, https://doi.org/10.1080/03085140020019070.

[80] Interviews and focus groups (2011–2014). Some of the ways women simultaneously negotiate patriarchal social and economic structures have already been addressed in Chapter 5 with the discussion of jobs advertised for men.

univocal ... [but] have contradictory effects in terms of the way in which they redirect power, strengthening some social forces and weakening others'.[81]

6.3 Capital and Entrepreneurial Dreams of the New Generations

The promotion of small businesses and entrepreneurship for employment emerges within a context of a history of an economic life surrounded by business and trade. As the economic structure transformed with the accumulation of oil wealth, business opportunities, activities, and employment took on particular shapes. By the early days of the country's oil era and Qaboos' reign, Oman was full of small shops and various forms of family businesses from those of earlier trading and merchant families to newer return migrants capitalising on new government contracts to build the development or security infrastructure of the *nahḍa* state. Forms of business activity and labour outcomes transformed during the expansion of the oil economy and the emergence of rentier neoliberalism in three distinct ways: first, by mandating partnership for foreign business owners with an Omani citizen; second, the growth of capital in the region and creation of large regional retailers; and third, changes in employment and overall downward pressure on wages and working conditions.

One way of channelling foreign investment to benefit Omanis was requiring investors opening business to go into partnership with a citizen. Until January 2020, Omanis needed to have a majority share (51 per cent) of any business except those under special regulatory frameworks like the Oman-USA FTA or those in special economic areas and free zones.[82] This requirement created a shadow space of income earning, in which some foreign investors would find a silent Omani partner and pay them an income connected with the business for the use of their name. Thus, a peculiar form of rent-seeking emerged around the business space that produced an opportunity for

---

[81] 'Neoliberalising Feminism', 627.
[82] Royal Decree 4/1974, 'Promulgating the Foreign Crafts and Foreign Capital Investment Law (Issued 21 January 1974, Published 16 February 1974)', Official Gazette 49, [author translations from Arabic], 1974; Royal Decree 102/ 1994, 'Promulgating the Foreign Capital Investment Law (Issued 16 October 1994, Published 1 November 1994)', Official Gazette 538, 1994.

citizen income generation. At the start of 2020, a new Foreign Capital Investment law came into force, which allowed full foreign ownership.[83] It is still too early to determine how many existing foreign investors bought out their Omani partners and whether this led to a meaningful change to these arrangements or not. As 2020 went on, regulatory frameworks around the new law continued to be adjusted by the Ministry of Commerce and Industry.[84] There are regulations, for example, preventing foreign investment in a specific set of business activities that are aimed at protecting common areas of small-scale Omani entrepreneurship and traditional handicrafts.[85] Overall, the regulations are aimed at encouraging further foreign investment in Oman, with specific incentives to invest in certain sectors (like IT and logistics) and certain areas (especially the least-developed regions of the country). One of the particularly interesting incentives for our purposes is the exemption from Omanisation rates for the first two years of operation for investment projects in less-developed regions.[86] We can see here how changes in laws around foreign capital investment impact not just the investment climate but also labour market outcomes.

The next two transformations are not especially unique outcomes in the global market. Internationally, as early as 1987, scholars like Harrod were already observing an international pattern of declining returns and working conditions in trading and shopkeeper forms of employment. Part of this decline was the difficulty competing with the growth of larger retailers and another was the decline of artisanal work and the concentration of suppliers into fewer hands.[87] This trend intensified in more recent decades with the expansion of transnational

---

[83] Royal Decree 50/2019, 'Promulgating the Foreign Capital Investment Law (Issued 1 July 2019, Published 7 July 2019)'.

[84] Ministry of Commerce and Industry, Ministerial Decision 72/2020, 'Issuing the Executive Regulations of the Foreign Capital Investment Law (Issued 14 June 2020, Published 21 June 2020)', Official Gazette 1346, [author translations from Arabic], 2020; Ministry of Commerce and Industry, Ministerial Decision 209/2020, 'Defining the List of Activities in Which Foreign Investment in Prohibited (Issued 9 December 2020, Published 13 December 2020)', Official Gazette 1370, [author translations from Arabic], 2020.

[85] Such clauses also demonstrate the same deregulation-protection tensions we see repeated throughout this book.

[86] See Article 17, Ministerial Decision 72/2020.

[87] Jeffrey Harrod, *Power, Production, and the Unprotected Worker* (New York: Columbia University Press, 1987), 271–73.

superstores – multinational companies and franchises functioning as super intermediaries between suppliers and consumers with such economies of scale they push out small businesses. In the same way, the growth of capital flows across the region has also encouraged the concentration of domestic and regional 'khaleeji capital', as Hanieh calls it.[88] Emirati capital like Majid al Futtaim's malls and hypermarkets, Indian capital like Yusuf Ali's Lulu hypermarket chain and malls or J. P. Kalwani's Al-Safeer Group of Companies, and Kuwaiti capital like the Sultan centres have led the way transforming the form and practices of retail-based consumption.

These forms of mega shopping centres had repercussions not only on small businesses and forms of shopping but also on the forms and availability of employment. Mega shops require staff as cashiers, shelf stockers, sales representatives, drivers, cooks, bakers, butchers, and department supervisors, among others. Many of these positions do not require sizeable levels of education and do not pay large salaries. South Asians staff many of the positions given their cost advantage and absence of a universally applied minimum wage. However, over the years these organisations have recognised the importance of demonstrating attention to Omanisation and have been subject to increased attention to do so. Lulu hypermarket, for example, has faced considerable pressure no less so than when it was thrust forward as a subject of angst as its Sohar branch was set on fire and looted by some of the protestors in 2011.[89] A few years later, in June 2014, Omani employees of Lulu hypermarkets around the country held a large-scale strike under the Lulu Workers Union. The workers had sixteen demands among which they were demanding a pay raise, a cost-of-living allowance, a bonus, and more Omanisation in accordance with a previous agreement signed by the company. The GFOW mediated between the union and Lulu and publicly blamed Lulu's 'intransigence' for the escalation. There was widespread support expressed on social media. The strike lasted for three days before work resumed.[90] This form of

[88] Hanieh, 'Khaleeji-Capital'.
[89] Saleh Al-Shaibany, 'Lulu Supermarket Set Ablaze by Oman Protesters', *The National*, 1 March 2011, www.thenational.ae/world/mena/lulu-supermarket-set-ablaze-by-oman-protesters-1.566581.
[90] 'Major LuLu Hypermarket Strike Ends in Oman', *Gulf News*, 29 June 2014, https://gulfnews.com/world/gulf/oman/major-lulu-hypermarket-strike-ends-in-oman-1.1353571.

pressure places such stores in the labour limelight, and the visibility of the staffing situation and demands gives jobseekers fodder to complain about the number of positions going to foreign employees. Indeed, some of the rhetoric included accusations against South Asians for sitting in jobs needed by Omanis. Lulu has since afforded significant attention to its image recovery. It now regularly highlights its support of Omanisation, including its offered training, commitment to Omani recruitment whenever a new hypermarket opens in another city, and its overall focus on 'empowering Omani youth'.[91]

These malls and mega-shopping complexes impact the viability of small shop ownership in various ways as well. Obviously, it is difficult to remain competitive given the scale of these centres. Yet the segmentation of the labour market has also allowed some to survive. The availability of a cheap supply of labour has an additional downward pressure on cost and working conditions. This has meant that some small shops can afford to employ low-skilled staff from abroad who are willing to work long shifts for low wages. Families are, however, then less likely to staff stores themselves than in earlier decades breaking the entrepreneurship–self-employment link. Some family businesses have grown to create chains of their small shops and can afford to do so and make a profit due to the small, basic nature of the shop set up and the employment of very low-cost foreign workers. With monthly salaries in the range of 80 to 90 rials (208 to 234 USD), even adding accommodation and flights home once every two years is significantly cheaper than hiring an Omani citizen. Indeed, many varieties of micro and small enterprises rarely contribute to national employment as they require so few staff to begin with and the available foreign workers are eminently more cost effective. So while these labour market distortions mean more families can continue to be small business owners, they too become party to systems that depress wages and working conditions for others.

Today, like in the rest of the world, it is cloud kitchens and dark stores that are beginning to transform the retail and food delivery

---

[91] 'Lulu Hypermarket Gearing up to Meet Residents' Needs in Ibri', *Times of Oman*, 24 July 2013, The Free Library, www.thefreelibrary.com/Lulu +Hypermarket+gearing+up+to+meet+residents%27+needs+in+Ibri.- a0337794853; 'Lulu Group Focuses on Empowering Omani Youth', *Black and White Oman*, 21 February 2022, sec. Newsworthy, https://blackandwhiteoman .com/lulu-group-focuses-on-empowering-omani-youth/.

space within urban areas of Oman and the Gulf region. For example, cloud or ghost kitchens are commercial spaces designed for speed and scale that operate as a hub for multiple brands at once. Using a cloud kitchen makes it easier for small start-ups to launch or test a new restaurant idea with low risk and capital. These contributions to the so-called platform economy also produce larger entrepreneurial opportunities for capital flush investors that open such kitchens and dark stores but struggle with the same trade-offs and tensions in the job creation landscape.[92] That is, the work of stocking, preparing, and delivering food is carried out by precariously employed migrant workers except for moments when the state steps in to mandate a percentage of Omani employment. Ideas like cloud kitchens took off in the wake of the global pandemic as a way to respond to changing consumption patterns. This is part of what van Doorn has called 'platform fixes', which seek to overcome limits of capital accumulation by responding to market needs while rearticulating the relationship between the market, state, and society.[93] For small restaurant owners, offloading their preparation and delivery to a ghost kitchen removes the burden of dealing with foreign recruitment and national hiring regulations and therefore offloads the responsibility for wages and working conditions onto these modern grocery and prepared food delivery services. For the larger investors too, the overall drive is to reduce costs and maximise profit, capitalising on a new entrepreneurial space.

It is understood as nearly impossible for a new start-up to only hire citizens, even if that is the public intention. As one young aspiring entrepreneur noted sheepishly, 'I will hire both expats and Omanis.

---

[92] To read more about gig work, the platform economy, and the creation of a so-called platform society, read José van Dijck, Thomas Poell, and Martijn de Waal, *The Platform Society* (New York: Oxford University Press, 2018), https://doi.org/10.1093/oso/9780190889760.001.0001; Niels van Doorn and Darsana Vijay, 'Gig Work as Migrant Work: The Platformization of Migration Infrastructure', *Environment and Planning A: Economy and Space*, 20 December 2021, https://doi.org/10.1177/0308518X211065049; Saori Shibata, 'Gig Work and the Discourse of Autonomy: Fictitious Freedom in Japan's Digital Economy', *New Political Economy* 25, no. 4 (6 June 2020): 535–51, https://doi.org/10.1080/13563467.2019.1613351.

[93] Niels van Doorn, 'Platform Capitalism's Social Contract', *Internet Policy Review* 11, no. 1 (22 March 2022), https://policyreview.info/articles/analysis/platform-capitalisms-social-contract.

The problem is the higher salary for an Omani.'[94] In private, many of those working in the entrepreneurship support and promotion space noted that they ultimately cannot impose Omanisation on the new businesses they fund or incubate. This is, one commented,

something difficult to do. We want to [require it] but we would not. Someone in our organisation would say you have to have 80 or 90 per cent Omanisation level. This is difficult. Firstly, even if you have Omanis working for you in your business if you're an entrepreneur, maintaining those staff is not something easy. Particularly given expatriates. In some types of industries like manufacturing, finding Omanis and pay them the minimum wage is costly and they will not stay a long time. And, except for rare cases, they are not as committed to that type of job. In many cases, some owners of SMEs have suffered from not having staff committed for a long time. Every now and then they have to recruit. That is not good for system abilities in the business. The short answer for the question is, no, we don't have specific Omanisation. But we try as much as we can to encourage the business owners to hire as many Omanis as possible. And that is a plus for us in the evaluation.[95]

Another said quite pointedly:

We are not so strict about Omani employees like the other initiatives like Sanad for example. Omanisation is killing the SME sector in Oman. SMEs cannot afford to pay the higher Omani wages for small jobs in the company. How can they pay 250 for an Omani when they can pay 90 for an expat? But we do ensure that the managers are Omani. That is why we do the entry interviews and the application procedures – we make sure – we check to determine how entrepreneurial the individual really is. We won't deal with non-Omanis and we have to be sure he or she has the skills to really be an entrepreneur.[96]

Eventually, this sentiment even received official acknowledgement when, in 2015, the government responded to lobbying by the start-up space and broader private-sector by granting new SMEs an exemption from conforming to Omanisation quotas for their first two years of operation.[97]

---

[94] Interview with aspiring entrepreneur, Nizwa, 21 January 2012.
[95] Interview with entrepreneurship funding and support initiative director, Muscat, 23 October 2011.
[96] Interview, staff member at GroFin, an SME financier, Muscat, 15 October 2011.
[97] 'Government to Ease Omanisation Norms for SME Sector: H E Sunaidy'.

New generations are no longer satisfied with the organisation of the economy, the dominance of large capital, and the weak labour market outcomes. The weakening of the rent-funded welfare provisions in recent years has underscored how the economic structures are not working out for them in the same way as earlier decades. Moreover, the push into entrepreneurship to secure an income has highlighted how difficult both the employment environment and the business environment is. The story of Khalfan, an entrepreneur from Izki who runs a small computer services and stationary shop in Nizwa, is telling of the types of challenge. He recounted the following experiences.[98]

I started my business two or three years ago, but my first attempt failed. Now it has been in operation for five months. The reasons for failure was that I had less money and experience, I had some problems with my partners, and really this is a far location. I work in the army, but the army provides a low salary. So if this business works well, I will quit. While I'm working, my brother runs the shop. I am back just after 2 p.m. .... In ten years I'd like to develop this to an Oman-wide business. I will start with a second branch in Izki and then expand around Oman. Maybe using E-bay and Amazon to expand globally. Now I'm just using E-Oman. Nowadays it's a bit easier because the government is helping. I had a one-week training at Sharakah. It was a visitor program. It was in Arabic and was run well. I finished university at a private college, and now am upgrading in another private college. All are in English.

Like many small entrepreneurs distant from elite circles, he suggested both bureaucracy and the dominance of large business houses made entering the market as an entrepreneur especially difficult.

In my opinion, the big business monopoly should end. You have to work hard, but they [the big family businesses] should be made to assist the smaller start-ups. They *yaḥtakirūn* [monopolise]. It's all about money and you can't challenge the big business with a little money and poor communication, poor connections with the ministries. Now there are plans in the Ministry to help small businesses. Now it's a little faster to get permission. There are difficulties. The major difficulty is money. Then time. Now I self-finance. I am trying Sharakah to help me expand / open new branch .... Registration process was between difficult and easy. There are rules about the look of the board, rules about safety, etc. It takes about three weeks to wait. The *baladiyya*

---

[98] Khalfan is a pseudonym.

[municipality] is difficult. I had to go six times. Every time they would tell you that you need something else, some other paper.[99]

Many young Omanis like Khalfan were keen to respond to the promotion of entrepreneurship, relishing the idea of financial independence. Encountering monopolisation and bureaucratisation of the business space often felt like one more example of their alienation from the private sector, as explored in Chapter 5.

At the same time, large businesses, both as employers and as those looking at struggling start-ups, place the blame on the individual young person for their failures to secure employment or succeed at business, as do government officials. As one suggested, 'The new generation they are lazy and do not want to work hard. They want to get a profit fast. They don't work for profit, they want it now and they blame the previous people.'[100] They often reach to generational stereotyping and reproduce both the narratives about entitled citizens that shapes rentier literature on the sociological effects of oil wealth and general narratives on lazy millennials.[101] A conversation with a retired minister was especially telling. He recalled his past, when in the early 1950s he had left Oman clandestinely to pursue an education in Bahrain, when Said bin Taymur had, with few exceptions, prevented education beyond primary school and banned those who studied abroad from returning.[102] He recollected how hard he worked during those days, working in the summer on a ship in the Gulf and studying in the winter. 'We got 10 rupees – Indian rupees – *rātib mālī* [salary] per day – Ha! 10 rupees! They gave us food of course . . .. But we had been working, why had we been working? Because if I don't work, I wouldn't be able to study. I wouldn't be able to eat. So, I mean, if I get something free, why should I work? This is what happens here now.' The solution to the laziness of recent generations, in his view, was to be

---

[99] Interview with aspiring entrepreneur, Nizwa, 21 January 2012.

[100] Interview with senior official, Ministry of Commerce and Industry, 25 October 2011.

[101] See sections 1.3 and 3.4 for further discussion on the so-called rentier mentality and narratives on millennials.

[102] Al-Saqri, 'Private Education in the Omani City of Maṭraḥ during the Reign of Sultan Saʿīd b. Taymūr (1932–1970)'; Juliette Honvault and Talal Al-Rashoud, 'Modern Education in the Arabian Peninsula: Social Dynamics and Political Issues', *Arabian Humanities*, no. 12 (6 November 2019), https://doi.org/10.4000/cy.4884.

far more austere – 'hire and fire!' This, he thought was the only solution to encourage more industriousness in the labour market. 'There is no discipline today. If you kick him out from his job, he will go to the court and complain that I have been kicked out. And then the court will not only send him back, and then you have to keep him – also as a company you have to pay something for him – compensation or whatever.'[103] This interpretation is common. The labour market protections in place are viewed as business and productivity obstacles rather than necessary social safety nets.

The desire of young people and young entrepreneurs for structural change was often greeted by dismay from an older generation, still reminiscent of days past and grateful for the development changes witnessed in their lifetime. Young people did not realise how fast things were moving and how great the development leaps there were, explained one interviewee.

From 1970 until now there is a huge difference … from '70 to '80 it was like the airplane takes off. And now it is like it is in the air. And in the air the airplane is moving fast, but you don't feel it. And they said in Oman they are moving fast, but to me as an Omani I feel they are moving very slow. There is nothing, but there is much improvement. Maybe you know because you were here years ago right? You saw Sohar ….[104]

What felt like a new environment of labour unrest and political protest sat uneasy next to a memory of dramatic change in the lifetime of anyone with memories before 1970. While discussing the 2011 protests, one business owner lamented,

The new generation are forgetting their fathers. They do not want to learn from the earlier generations and think themselves better because of their education or their modern thinking. The new generation, yes, they are more serious with work but they have no experience and want to make projects with their study only. Book learning is different from life …. They are asking heavy questions and making heavy requirements on the budget which is not healthy. They want increased salaries, then what of the roads? Health care? They should support the government to support their future and their families' future. They cannot eat everything and have everything.[105]

---

[103] Interview, retired minister, Muscat, 31 March 2018.
[104] Interview with senior official, Ministry of Commerce and Industry, 25 October 2011.
[105] Interview with business owner, Muscat, 8 January 2012.

In the intervening years since 2011, it has become clear that the millennial generation, and youth more broadly, expect more or resent that they cannot secure the same perceived level of opportunity as the prior generations. The convergence of expectations around the welfare offerings and government support, the promise of globalisation and economic growth, and an interest in freedom clashes with the reality of a difficult labour market situation and tightening economic reality.[106] As Marc Valeri presciently noted in 2009, the young generations no longer agree 'to abdicate, like their parents, their right to take part in the national debates in the name of socio-economic welfare'.[107] Memories of an impoverished past are now mere historical tale, and the gratitude for basic socio-economic welfare earlier generations felt is no longer relevant to youth.

In contrast to these stereotypes, Millennials and Gen Z view themselves as especially hard-working, creative, and innovative. They are 'the google generation, but aware of cultural roots'.[108] In entrepreneurship, young people characterise the 'new generations' as having 'more creative ideas than the old generation'.[109] 'The past generations are not innovative. The new generation innovates. The old are static and don't know how to innovate.'[110] Several interviewees pointed to a difference in enterprise and individual independence between the generations. They spoke of the 'closed minds' of earlier generations where 'everyone worked for the government and came home early' juxtaposed against the more convoluted reality of today. The present, including the difficult labour market that forced struggle, was representative of change. These senses suggest, as Al-Azri observed, 'both an awareness of tensions between traditional culture and social and economic development and an appetite for cultural renewal and genuine reform'.[111]

---

[106] Even the 2021 Annual Report from the Public Authority for Social Insurance acknowledges this generational gap by aiming for 'justice between generations' in their social security schemes, 11.

[107] Valeri, *Oman: Politics and Society in the Qaboos State*, 259.

[108] Interview with consultant at the Industrial Innovation Centre, Muscat, 11 October 2011.

[109] Interview with entrepreneurship support organisation, Muscat, 15 October 2011.

[110] Interview with entrepreneur, Muscat, 17 October 2017.

[111] Al-Azri, 'Change and Conflict in Contemporary Omani Society', 137.

The promotion of entrepreneurship has meant that some young people too are now looking to the market for their liberation but then become especially disenchanted and alienated when it does not deliver. They desire not just economic benefits but also articulate a dream for freedom. Freedom does not carry the same meaning for everyone. Various interlocutors seemed to attach different meanings to freedom including actions like being 'your own boss' or conditions such as being 'independent' or not having 'to rely on parents' to contribute to family well-being. Some interlocutors described freedom as something that would allow them to make a difference and help 'change the world' around them or pursue creative goals. Taken together, freedom evoked a whimsical anticipation of an imagined future that successful entrepreneurship could enable. At the same time, many indicated the struggle of navigating the bureaucratic processes associated with the start-up and operation of their businesses as hampering their potential and possibilities. Despite this, many described business ownership as liberating and empowering. In interviews and focus groups during 2011 and 2012, millennials who were aspiring entrepreneurs expressed a strong desire to be a part of the regional change narrative, but this motivation seemed to dissipate with distance and disillusionment about 2011 in the region. There was a sense implied in conversations that social and political freedom may be connected to their liberation through the market – and by contributing to the economy in this way they were not just achieving their own financial independence but also contributing to national development and change.

A young law graduate, Mohammad's story is telling.[112] After graduation and job training experiences in the courts, he received offers to continue and represent the government. He expressly did not wish to do this. He told me how much he valued freedom and felt that working for the state in that way would not do. He wanted the freedom to represent cases of interest to him and to have money independent of the state. His dream was to open his own law firm and also have the space to pursue his creative side and produce social commentary through literature. He succeeded at achieving these goals. Likewise, Yousef conceptualised freedom similarly. He was a young entrepreneur who when we first met had recently graduated and also finished a flagship training and entrepreneurship idea competition weekend at Knowledge

---

[112] Names have been changed.

Oasis Muscat. He was in the early period of his start-up endeavour and had already made the rounds seeking state-sponsored entrepreneurship support through training and financing. 'Being an entrepreneur', he said, 'was part of my vision that I was developing in the beginning of my university studies'.[113] When I asked him if he hoped to work for the government like so many of his contemporaries, he replied emphatically,

No. I never wanted to work in the government. The economy is growing and I want to be part of the growing economy. Myself, and people like me want to participate in the development of our country. As well, and this is very important, we want to make our own private income. The main reason however, is to get freedom and be free in thinking and free in movement. This freedom is what you will hear everyone tell you that is like me and wants to work independently and operate our own business. We want to develop our skills and provide new things for society.

Entrepreneurial dreams emerge in the crossroads of labour market conditions, the widespread promotion of entrepreneurship, and expectations of what the state should provide combined with the promises of future potentialities. They merge with discourses noted above on economic liberation, the state's protective eye, and the patriotic importance of contributing to national development. They also sometimes intersect with discourses and forms of contestation that seek to push against the norm, against the dominance of large capital, and against negatively perceived economic conditions and outcomes.

6.4 Conclusions on Entrepreneurship and the Political Economy of Labour

Through exploring the landscape of entrepreneurship promotion and pursuit with its special focus on young people and on women, this chapter further illustrates the dynamics of Oman's global labour market and concomitant neoliberalisation of the rentier state. Importantly, the study of entrepreneurship here offers the opportunity to reflect further on the global political economy of labour in Oman. We see how two trends, first, the impetus to increase foreign investor attractiveness and business friendliness by liberalising and deregulating

---

[113] Yousef, an aspiring entrepreneur, Muscat, 31 October 2011.

the private sector and, second, being able to draw from a global supply of inexpensive labour, both serve to depress wages and working conditions in the country. Whilst these trends stimulate SME creation and private sector growth, they continue to reproduce the same employment patterns present elsewhere in the labour market. Meanwhile, the state promotion of entrepreneurship has also retooled and re-embedded the state into yet another facet of economic life. This reveals the 'symbiotic configuration' of rentier neoliberalism 'whereby reforms are enacted and protected through existing mechanisms of authoritarian statecraft'.[114] One the one hand, the state engages a selection of austerity measures reducing the cost of certain benefits to citizens. On the other hand, it engages in the economy as a facilitator of the market and produces a micro-economy of rent-seeking where young people look for the benefit of training, funding, and contracts from the state to start and continue their entrepreneurial journeys.

At the same time, the responsibility for success and generating your own income becomes effectively placed upon the shoulders of the individual entrepreneur who is now supposed to perform as a productive businessperson. Failure then is not attributed to structural features but is individualised and explained in terms of attitude, training, productiveness, and experience. The purchase of the entrepreneurial narrative has resulted in a category of business hopefuls who embrace the idea of their freedom being realised through the market and through attaining independence. Among these are those who desire deeper social and political freedom, but a majority are looking for the economic freedom that success could bring. The precarity and insecurity that frequently coincides with small-scale entrepreneurship is at times unexpected and jarring. Blaming individuals for dominating and monopolising the market as the cause of entrepreneurial failures and the market's distortions displaces attention from the very structures of global capitalism and imperialism that have facilitated the injection of Oman into the global economy and fostered decades of segmentation disrupting labour's collective power and placing downward pressures on income.

Furthermore, the drive for the lowest priced labour eventually works against the twin goals of entrepreneurship promotion – the building of innovation to help diversify the economy and generating jobs for

---

[114] Bruff and Tansel, 'Authoritarian Neoliberalism', 239.

citizens. Notably, only 10.9 per cent of those employed in the country hold a university degree or higher.[115] As long as the price of labour stays low enough, it counters the incentive to invest in innovative technologies and upscale jobs in a way that may be more attractive to Omani workers. While labour markets in a global capitalist order may exhibit a certain cost 'efficiency', this carries an enormous destructive capacity for both communities and for economic life.[116] We see this clearly in the Omani labour space, with growing unemployment, rising youth disenfranchisement, continued weak social protections for migrant labour, and limited business innovation. This is because, in its current form, neoliberal capitalism promotes not only cost cutting and regulatory stripping, but it also 'breeds short-termism in social reproduction as well as in capitalist production'.[117] Omanisation discourses then, which partly prompted the entrepreneurial one, are subsequently rebuffed by entrepreneurs on the basis of cost and regulatory ineffectiveness. Rather, 'inequality, flexibility, and mobility are promoted as virtues', where the entrepreneurial salvation of the individual and the nation also become globally linked to the competitive and flexible global workforce.[118] The entrepreneurial pursuit occurs within the Omani labour market, partly in response to its maladies and yet is structured and takes shape within the same context and therefore reproduces the same disparities and marginalisations.

---

[115] NCSI, '2019 Statistical Year Book', 111.
[116] Karl Polanyi has shown this long ago. *The Great Transformation*, 77–80, 95–99.
[117] Peck, *Work-Place*, 238.
[118] See Jamie Peck's discussion on the geopolitics of labour regulation to consider how this process has worked in advanced capitalist and welfare states. Peck, *Work-Place*, 232–39.

Conclusion

Studying the Global Political Economy of Labour

Following labour of various sorts – from business executives to taxi drivers, from administrators to entrepreneur hopefuls and job hunters – reveals another side of the development story in Oman and the region. The geography of work and its reconfiguration based on local and global transformations embeds the pursuit of work in the Omani story within regional and global ruptures and transformations. From Omanis who left Oman in pursuit of education and work in the early twentieth century and encountered ideas and ideologies that wrapped them up in the antiimperialist and liberation movements of the age, to Omanis who benefitted from the rapid expansion of economic opportunities after the first oil boom, to jobseekers today in pursuit of meaningful, comparable, and sustainable work and economic life: the story of Oman's development is 'the story of living and working'.

Putting people first thereby recontextualises an appreciation of change and continuity. Young Omanis' engagements with the labour market in Oman take shape within a world of dreams and expectations for the future, within a context of rapid growth and ongoing spatial and economic transformation, and within a space where wealth and success are visible to all but achievable to few. Including the lived experiences, perceptions, and resistance of job seekers and workers engages 'global political economies of the everyday' and asks 'who acts' alongside 'who governs' to reveal new sites of agency and contestation.[1] This enables an understanding of how labour

---

[1] John M. Hobson and Leonard Seabrooke, 'Everyday International Political Economy', in *Routledge Handbook of International Political Economy (IPE)*, ed. Mark Blyth (London: Routledge, 2009), 290–306; Juanita Elias and Adrienne Roberts, 'Feminist Global Political Economies of the Everyday: From Bananas to Bingo', *Globalizations* 13, no. 6 (1 November 2016): 787–800, https://doi.org/10.1080/14747731.2016.1155797.

governance and reform unfolds from the bottom-up and the top-down.[2]

Part of the goal of this book has been to centre labour in development analysis and to de-exceptionalise narratives of Gulf political economy and citizens. Empirically, it set out to (1) understand Omani millennials' experiences in the labour market and the persistence of conditions leading to their alienation from the economy in general and the private sector in particular and (2) to explain why the state's economic development plans continue to fail to resolve these conditions despite appearing to respond so clearly to labour market problems. To fulfil this, the book has taken readers on a journey through the world of work in Oman, centring labour in its account and explanation of development and labour market outcomes in the region. Taken together, the chapters here offer a picture of the global embedded within Oman's labour market and develop this by unpacking the structure of the labour market and spaces of radical economic transformation alongside labour's struggles of belonging and pursuits of entrepreneurial salvation or independent financial life. This examination demonstrates how 'global market relations' and 'the everyday' interact in labour governance.[3]

A central argument of this book has been that Oman's labour market is global and for us to answer questions about the labour market today we must understand labour globally and relationally. This heterodox vision accounts for empirical and ideological competitions and contradictions, developing nuanced understanding of (a) the competing neoliberalising and nationalising pressures domestically, (b) structural segmentation in relation to global histories and contemporary transformations, (c) the multi-scalar nature of governance and

---

[2] As Morton argues, 'due recognition has to be granted to the intertwined histories of hegemonic and resistance practices'. Adam David Morton, 'Peasants as Subaltern Agents in Latin America: Neoliberalism, Resistance and the Power of the Powerless', in *Everyday Politics of the World Economy*, ed. John M. Hobson and Leonard Seabrooke (Cambridge: Cambridge University Press, 2007), 136, https://doi.org/10.1017/CBO9780511491375.007.

[3] Chisholm and Stachowitsch view 'global market relations and everyday practices as equally consitutive' of the processes of labour governance and security in global labour chains. 'Everyday Matters in Global Private Security Supply Chains: A Feminist Global Political Economy Perspective on Gurkhas in Private Security', *Globalizations* 13, no. 6 (1 November 2016): 815–29, https://doi.org/10.1080/14747731.2016.1155796.

governance reform pressures, (d) the ways through which perceptions and expectations take shape and in turn forge social regulation and generate claims on economic belonging, (e) the rentier state's neoliberal orientation, and (f) the ways that policies are constructed to advance capital interests while crafting a discourse of nationalist development achievements. Through the Omani case, the book demonstrates that the global political economy of labour and job seeking are intricately tied to the wider deterritorialisation, privatisation, and global governance of labour.

Three intersecting vectors run through this book, elucidating this argument and vision. Together they highlight how Gulf labour and Gulf classes must be understood within a wider global political economy of labour. The first establishes how the segmented labour markets of the region are embedded within global structures and processes, which in turn shape domestic and regional structures and the frames through which social relations and regulations unfold. The second vector suggests three historical junctures as especially important in shaping labour trajectories in the region. Finally, the third vector explains the liberalising and nationalising dialectic in labour governance.

The first vector directly speaks to the overarching argument and establishes the importance of the global and relational in traversing Oman's labour market. A global, relational perspective takes seriously the multiple segmentations that structure the domestic labour markets of the Gulf but understands their functions and outcomes through the region's embedding in the global political economy. Discourses grounded in the particularities of Gulf rentierism, tribal or cultural traditions, and rooted in isolated analysis of contained national spaces give the impression that labour and social relations in Omani and Gulf economies are a regional particularity. These explanations marginalise how entangled the region is in the development of global capitalism and elide how neoliberal ideologies and policies shape economic and labour governance in the region.[4]

The findings of this book therefore contest the conventional wisdom that Oman's, and by extension the Gulf's, labour markets are best

---

[4] This has particular relevance to both the wider study of global capitalism and to the study of regions across the "Global South" in development studies and comparative politics, offering an approach that can locate the political economy of diverse cases within a broader GPE of labour.

defined as segmented spaces under the exclusive governance of the state. Oman's labour market is segmented, but these segmentations are neither neat and tidy divisions that isolate labour nor unique spaces detached from the reconfiguration of the global labour market. Rather, these segmentations assume their structure in association with the spatial structuring of class across the global labour market and the state and capital's impetus to discipline and control labour.[5] The analysis of the Omani labour market shows the contours of a global labour regime that is a crucial accompaniment to the transformation of global capitalism in the very process of restructuring the social divisions of labour, its geographies, stratifications, and lineages of resistance. The trajectories and struggles of Omani labour today and over time speak to broader patterns of how capital seeks to control labour by promoting fragmentation and putting workers in competition with each other for the available jobs.[6] The particular means and ways through which regional labour markets are segmented and governed are not isolated from capitalism's larger fragmentations, but instead the ways labour is 'gendered, racialised, ethnicised, tribalised ... emerge as fundamental to the workings of the labour market'.[7] This conceptualisation of Oman's global labour market thus also speaks to Sassen's 'novel borderings', which demonstrates that global processes and governance regimes take place at subnational scales, entering national institutional space and geographic territory.[8]

Essentially, Oman's injection in a global market for labour is not only part of its global character but also part of the system of organising and governing the economic life of the country. Understanding Omani millennials in the labour market as part of labour requires understanding the broader forces, mechanisms, and discourses that structure and govern them. This means understanding the broader labour relations and mechanisms of inclusion and exclusion, of privilege and access, and of marginalisation, exploitation, and suppression. These inform how people as labour behave, interact, and assign value

---

[5] Indeed, this is a global story.

[6] David Harvey, *The Enigma of Capital and the Crises of Capitalism* (Oxford: Oxford University Press, 2010), 61; 104.

[7] Harvey, *The Enigma of Capital and the Crises of Capitalism*, 61.

[8] Saskia Sassen, 'When National Territory Is Home to the Global: Old Borders to Novel Borderings', *New Political Economy* 10, no. 4 (1 December 2005): 523–41, https://doi.org/10.1080/13563460500344476.

ascriptions to forms of labour. These also shape business actors and employers and how they discipline, pay, recruit, 'differentiate and differentially control', and govern labour.[9] And it connects to a wider global labour governance arena in which governmental and civil society actors operate transnationally and translocally.

Young people's experiences in the labour market are also shaped by that which came before. The second vector delineates three historical conjunctures that play particularly important roles in shaping labour outcomes and trajectories in Oman and the region: first, the partial incorporation of Omani labour and the transnational Asian labouring classes into global capitalism through colonial development; second, the wider integration of Gulf economies and labour markets into global capitalism through the expansion of the oil industry, which increased the regional and global circulation of capital and labour; and third, the increasing embeddedness of the region in neoliberal capitalism, entangling the present and future of Gulf classes within the broader process of integrating the Asian 'continent of labour' into global capitalism.[10] In examining the historical and contemporary experiences and records of labour, it is apparent that the structures of segmentation; racialised, gendered, and classed labour hierarchies; and labour regulation and governance have been directly informed by colonial capitalism, the legacies of oil industry recruitment and employment practices, neoliberal policies and discourses, and the integration of Oman in the GPE. While labour struggles and conditions occur in spatially specific ways, they are not unique. They exist globally.

This brings us to the third vector. The tensions around how to regulate the labour market – whether to liberalise or nationalise – and the competing global and local pressures that inform this tension show us something about labour's power and potential in Oman. I have used the term 'Oman's global labour market' to conceptualise both the empirical realities of diverse Gulf labour markets and the related developments throughout the world that have facilitated the emergence of a global labour market. Capital can access this market in two ways – through locating economic activities in lower-cost

---

[9] Jill Crystal, *Oil and Politics in the Gulf: Rulers and Merchants in Kuwait and Qatar* (Cambridge: Cambridge University Press, 1995), 80.

[10] Chang, 'From Global Factory to Continent of Labour'.

locations, on the one hand, or through recruiting from pools of international migrant workers, on the other. Gulf labour markets are competitive because they offer a space embedded within the economic transformation of Asia and because the Gulf economic model and migration regime is based on its access to abundant, flexible labour flows. The global labour market has inspired competing regimes for disciplining labour, on the one hand, and facilitating its mobility, on the other, and these regimes are caught in tensions between deregulating and liberalising in the interests of capital or protecting in the interests of social or environmental realities. The radical transformations of Sohar and Duqm provided vivid examples. This dialectic occurs at national and international scales of governance.

The story of Omani labour is thus also a story of pushback and how Omanis as social actors pressure the state to regulate in their interest. Omani labour – employees and job seekers – push for outcomes that generate employment or force capital to offer work, better pay, and career progression. Omani capitalists, on the other hand, push for open access to global labour pools and more flexible conditions domestically to allow them to hire and fire and pay workers less. International financial institutions and consultancies recommend the same. Yet rounds of economic reform are regularly confronted with social pressure to ameliorate the negative effects. The labour market reveals most clearly this social double movement. Contestation from Omani workers or job-hunters, or even the threat of agitation among these groups, prompts policy reaction. Notwithstanding a pattern of labour becoming more organised through the development of unions, most of labour's power at the present rests in its ability to inspire policy change. Labour's power is evident in the prospect of its discontent. The anticipation of social action and the manifestation of various forms of protest (from discontent on social networks like WhatsApp and Twitter to in-person demonstrations and combinations of the two) have led to policy change.

What then for the future? Within the current global structure, it is difficult to imagine the dramatic change necessary to unseat the historical and structural lineages and incentives underpinning labour market outcomes in Oman and the region. Short of a radical global restructuring, wages and benefits would need to be equalised and the rules of the game applied equally to all. This is not a call for deregulating the labour market for citizens and thereby weakening their protections but for applying protective regulation equally. The same wages, benefits, and protections should be put in place for both expatriates and citizens. It is only through fighting precarity for all that change is achievable. The internal structures, segmentations, and problems of the labour market cannot be resolved without equalising the rules of the game.

This then is also a lesson for labour organising – uniting labour across national and migrant divisions is key. Labour must prioritise extending solidarity. Diversity and solidarity do not have to be incompatible, and labour can look for ways to surmount colonial divisions and racial categories.[11] This book has shown examples where this happens but all too often segmentations push the interests of different labour parties in opposition. As Nielson says, 'If misunderstandings and performances of difference entrench the niche structure of the global economy and reaffirm the profitability of supply chains, we need new models of solidarity that can negotiate difference in ways that displace logistical power.'[12] Sustainable change would require global solidarity and wider empowerment of global labour.

The heterodox approach of this book offers a direction for future scholarship on the GPE of labour. It not only demonstrates how empirically grounded national and regional case studies can highlight and explain global patterns, but also reveals how the present and future of work in local spaces are entangled within the trajectories of global capitalist development. Understanding labour globally and relationally escapes methodologically nationalist treatments of development and offers a path for examining GPE where labour takes centre stage. Workplaces, labour policy-making spaces, and studies of economic life render the *global* evident and further untangle the protection–liberalisation dialectic. Future case studies can build from

[11] E. A. Wolff argues against viewing diversity and solidarity in opposition, pointing to how state and non-state actors construct racial categories and fix notions of 'in-groups'. 'Diversity, Solidarity and the Construction of the Ingroup among (Post)Colonial Migrants in The Netherlands, 1945–1968', *New Political Economy* (23 June 2023): 1–14, https://doi.org/10.1080/13563467.2023.2227120; See also, Gurminder K. Bhambra, 'Colonial Global Economy: Towards a Theoretical Reorientation of Political Economy', *Review of International Political Economy* 28, no. 2 (4 March 2021): 307–22, https://doi.org/10.1080/09692290.2020.1830831..

[12] Brett Neilson, 'Five Theses on Understanding Logistics as Power', *Distinktion: Scandinavian Journal of Social Theory* 13, no. 3 (2012): 337–38.

here, demonstrating how local capitalist, labouring, and job-seeking classes are immersed within the global labour market and global capitalism.

Throughout these vectors, this book has sketched various ways Omani young people dream of successful economic lives both to achieve their aspirations and to follow social mores and processes around work, marriage, and home. Some also want to contribute somehow, to do their part, in the development or change story of the country. This also is not a locally isolated story. Omani young people compare their experiences not just with those of their parents but also with their regional neighbours and international peers. In sharp contradiction to prevailing stereotypes, labour market assessments, and much academic and policy discourse, young people consistently articulate an interest, motivation, and desire to work, to be economically active, or economically valued.

Both economic structures and social policies around the world of work play a critical role in everyday life. The multi-scalar analysis that unfolded in the chapters of this book followed labour and labour regulation from the bottom up and the top town. It examined the intersections of global, regional, and local processes illustrating how the reconfiguration and structures of Oman's global labour market impact young people's dreams as well as their everyday experiences of the economy, institutional structures, and arrangements. At the same time, their experiences and perceptions shape their relations with others and their interpretations of economic outcomes. Across the different sites and spaces of investigation in this book, whether empirical sites like Sohar and Duqm, or themes like economic belonging, both the impact and power of different forms and levels of regulation as well as the presence of Omani labour become visible. Writing citizens into scholarly investigations of Gulf labour markets reveals how development occurs and affects different populations and classes unevenly and how class formation and social relations take shape in the labour market. It is only through understanding labour globally and relationally that we can attain a more rounded picture of what development means and how labour governance functions on the ground.

Bibliography

Abboud, Samer N. 'Economic Transformation and Diffusion of Authoritarian Power in Syria'. In *Democratic Transition in the Middle East: Unmaking Power*, edited by Larbi Sadiki, Heiko Wimmen, and Layla Al-Zubaidi, 159–77. London; New York: Routledge, 2013.

Abdulkadir, Rahma, and Henriette Muller. 'Between Leadership and Kinship: Women Empowerment in the GCC Countries'. In *Corruption and Informal Practices in the Middle East and North Africa*, edited by Ina Kubbe and Aiysha Varraich, 188–206. London: Routledge, 2019.

Abulibdeh, Ammar, Talal Al-Awadhi, Noura Al Nasiri, Ali Al-Buloshi, and Montasser Abdelghani. 'Spatiotemporal Mapping of Groundwater Salinity in Al-Batinah, Oman'. *Groundwater for Sustainable Development* 12 (1 February 2021): 100551. https://doi.org/10.1016/j.gsd.2021.100551.

Abu-Lughod, Lila. 'Do Muslim Women Really Need Saving? Anthropological Reflections on Cultural Relativism and Its Others'. *American Anthropologist*, New Series, 104, no. 3 (1 September 2002): 783–90.

'Administration Reports of the Persian Gulf, 1939 to 1944'. British Library: India Office Records and Private Papers, 1939–1944. IOR/R/15/1/719. Qatar Digital Library. www.qdl.qa/en/archive/81055/vdc_100000000193.0x0002b5.

Afonso, Alexandre, Samir Negash, and Emily Wolff. 'Closure, Equality or Organisation: Trade Union Responses to EU Labour Migration'. *Journal of European Social Policy* 30, no. 5 (1 November 2020): 528–42. https://doi.org/10.1177/0958928720950607.

Ahram Online. 'Oil Workers Strike for Wage Increases'. 15 March 2011. https://english.ahram.org.eg/NewsContentP/3/7769/Business/Oman-oil-workers-strike-for-wage-increases.aspx.

Al Alawi, Saleh, Yaqoub Al Mufargi, and Ikhlas Al Waili. *Oil and Gas Dictionary*. Muscat: Petroleum Development Oman, 2014.

Al Musalmy, Shaddad. 'Wage Level Delinked from Academic Qualifications'. *Muscat Daily*, 22 September 2020. www.muscatdaily.com/2020/09/22/wage-level-delinked-from-academic-qualifications/.

Al Zadjali, Mohamed Issa. 'Duqm: A Plug and Play City for Everyone'. *Times of Oman*, 14 July 2019. https://timesofoman.com/article/1607880/Oman/Duqm-A-Plug-and-Play-City-for-everyone.

Tahir Salim Al-ʿAmri, 'Ḥiwār ʿamal', *Majalat Sawaʿid Niqābīyya*, 2019, 12–14, www.gfow.om/?p=4333.

Alatas, Syed Hussein. *The Myth of the Lazy Native: A Study of the Image of the Malays, Filipinos and Javanese from the 16th to the 20th Century and Its Function in the Ideology of Colonial Capitalism*. London: Routledge, 2013.

Al-Aufi, Kathiya, Malik Al-Wardy, B. S. Choudri, and Mushtaque Ahmed. 'Analysis of Crops Cultivation Trend: A Shifting Scenario in a Coastal Wilayat, Oman'. *Environment, Development and Sustainability* 22, no. 3 (1 March 2020): 2685–98. https://doi.org/10.1007/s10668-019-00309-4.

Al-Azri, Khalid. 'Change and Conflict in Contemporary Omani Society: The Case of Kafaʾa in Marriage'. *British Journal of Middle Eastern Studies* 37, no. 2 (2010): 121–37. https://doi.org/10.1080/13530191003794707.

Social and Gender Inequality in Oman: The Power of Religious and Political Tradition. New York: Routledge, 2013.

Al-Badwawi, Khalfan. 'Human Rights: My Personal Experience'. The Omani Centre for Human Rights, 18 December 2018. https://ochroman.org/eng/2018/10/event1/.

'Laḥaẓat fī masīrat inhāʾ al-istiʿmār: ʿashar sanawāt ʿalā intafāḍat Ṣuḥār'. Al-Hamish, 2 March 2021. https://al-hamish.net/11522/.

Aldossari, Maryam, and Thomas Calvard. 'The Politics and Ethics of Resistance, Feminism and Gender Equality in Saudi Arabian Organizations'. *Journal of Business Ethics* 24 (September 2021). https://doi.org/10.1007/s10551-021-04949-3.

Al-Essai, Shaimaa. 'The Dualities of Traditions and Feminist Movements on the Omani Twitter Platform: An Extension of the Patriarchal Actuality or an Attempt to Create a Safer Space for Women?' Konrad Adenauer Stiftung, December 2021. www.kas.de/documents/286298/8668222/Policy+Report+No+44+-+Dualities+of+Traditions+and+Feminist+Movements+on+the+Omani+Twitter+Platform.pdf.

Al-Farsi, Sulaiman H. *Democracy and Youth in the Middle East: Islam, Tribalism and the Rentier State in Oman*. London; New York: I. B.Tauris, 2013.

al-Ghazālī, ʿAbdulmunʿim. *al-ʿUdwān al-briṭāniyy ʿalā ʿUmān wa-l-Yaman*. Cairo: Dār Al-Fikr, 1957.

Al-Hashimi, Said Sultan, ed. al-Rabīʿ al-ʿUmānī: qirāʾa fi al-siyāqāt w-al-dalālāt. *Beirut: Dār al-Farabī 2013*.

'The Omani Spring: Towards the Break of a New Dawn?' Arab Reform Brief. Arab Reform Initiative, November 2011. www.arab-reform.net/ publication/the-omani-spring-towards-the-break-of-a-new-dawn/.

''Umān: 'an Masālat al-ṭabaqa, wa-fī musā'lat al-wusṭā'. al-Mustaqbal al-'Arabī, no. 495 (May 2020): 65–81.

al-Hinai, Habiba. 'Silsilat Anīn al-Jidrān: Ghaḍafān ta'in'. Omani Association for Human Rights. Anīn al-Jidrān (blog), 8 April 2010. https://omanhr.org/.

al-Hutiyya, Anissa. 'Limādhā Ṣuḥār?' Al-Roya, 24 May 2021. https://alroya .om/p/282725.

Ali, Ali Hassan. 'Manpower Development in Oman'. Al-Markazi, January 1978. Central Bank of Oman Archive.

al-Itihād al-'ām l-'umāl salṭanat 'Umān. 2021. www.gfow.om/.

Al-Jamali, Ra'id Zuhair. 'Oman, Kind of Not Quiet?' Foreign Policy, 7 November 2011. http://mideast.foreignpolicy.com/posts/2011/11/07/ kind_of_not_quiet.

Al-Kindi, Ann. 'Muqāwamat al-'Aqaliyya al-rī'iyya', 5 November 2017. https://annalkindi.net/archives/2030.

Al-Kindy, Fawziya. 'Manpower and Progress Go Hand in Hand'. Al-Markazi, December 1976. Central Bank of Oman Archive.

Al-Kūwārī, 'Alī. 'Makhāṭir al-siyāsa al-Amrīkiyya wa taḥadiyāt muwājahatihā - Ḥālat Duwal Majlis al-Ta'āwun', 16 March 2010. http://dr-alkuwari.net/node/125.html.

Allam, Abeer. 'Kuwaitisation: Youth Demands Action to Meet Expectations'. Financial Times, 23 April 2013. www.ft.com/content/ 9fda70fc-a81d-11e2-b031-00144feabdc0.

Al-Lamki, Salma. 'Barriers to Omanization in the Private Sector: The Perceptions of Omani Graduates'. The International Journal of Human Resource Management 9, no. 2 (1998): 377–400.

Al-Lawati, Haider Abdulredha. 'Private Sector Dilemma over 3% Annual Increment'. Oman Daily Observer, 24 March 2021. www .omanobserver.om/article/1710/Opinion/private-sector-dilemma-over-3-annual-increment.

Al-Lawati, Hasan Shaban. 'Minister of Manpower Backs 2-Year Visa Ban in Oman'. Times of Oman, 16 January 2017. https://timesofoman.com/ article/25809-minister-of-manpower-backs-2-year-visa-ban-in-oman.

Allen, Calvin H. Oman: The Modernization of the Sultanate. London; New York: Routledge, 1987.

Allen, Calvin H., and W. Lynn Rigsbee. Oman under Qaboos: From Coup to Constitution, 1970–1996. London: Routledge, 2000.

Al-Markazi. 'Development of Skilled Labour in Oman'. November 1978. Central Bank of Oman Archive.

'Industry in the Economy of Oman'. November 1979. Central Bank of Oman Archive.

'PD(O) Becomes PDO'. May 1980. Central Bank of Oman Archive.

Al- Mashīkhī, Muhammad ʿAwaḍ. 'Ḥuriyyat al-taʿbīr fī zaman al-samāwāt al-maftūḥa'. *Al-Roya*, 27 December 2021. https://alroya.om/post/293656.

'Ilā ayn dhahibūn fī idārat malaf al-tawẓīf?!' *Al-Roya*, 31 May 2021. https://alroya.om/post/283134.

Al-Muftāḥ, Esraaʾ. 'al-Maraʾa fī ẓill siyāsāt al-tanmiya: ḥālat Qaṭar'. al-Thābit wa al-Mutaḥawil 2016: al-Khalīj baʿd khams sanawāt min al-intifāḍāt al-ʿarabiyya. Gulf Centre for Development Policies, 2016. https://gulfpolicies.org/2019-10-30-17-42-40.

'al-Muhandisa Sihām al-Ḥārithiyya'. *Ḥalū al-Wiṣāl*. Muscat: al-Wiṣāl, 7 January 2022. www.youtube.com/watch?v=KKZamOc3uBI.

Al-Mukrashi, Fahad. 'Liwa Residents Protest against Pollution, Want Relocation'. *Times of Oman*, 7 October 2012. www.pressreader.com/oman/times-of-oman/20121007/page/1.

'Omani Oil and Gas Unions Threaten Strike amid Oil Slump'. *Gulf News*, 29 October 2015. https://gulfnews.com/world/gulf/oman/omani-oil-and-gas-unions-threaten-strike-amid-oil-slump-1.1609750.

'Port Pollution Irks Liwa Residents'. *Times of Oman*, 7 October 2012. www.pressreader.com/oman/times-of-oman/20121007/281522223312253.

Almunajjed, Mona, and Karim Sabbagh. 'Youth in GCC Countries: Meeting the Challenge'. Booze & Company, 2011. www.booz.com/media/uploads/BoozCo-GCC-Youth-Challenge.pdf.

'al-Mūʾashirāt al-raʾīsiyya li-natāiʾj al-taʿdād al-iliktrūnī li-lsukān wa-l-masākin wa-l-munshāʾat 2020'. Muscat: E-Census Government of Oman, December 2020. www.ncsi.gov.om/Elibrary/.

Alpers, Edward A. 'On Becoming a British Lake: Piracy, Slaving, and British Imperialism in the Indian Ocean during the First Half of the Nineteenth Century'. In *Indian Ocean Slavery in the Age of Abolition*, edited by Robert W. Harms, Bernard K. Freamon, and David W. Blight, 45–58. New Haven: Yale University Press, 2013.

Al-Qasimi, Sultan Muhammad. *Omani-French Relations 1715–1900*. Translated by B. R. Pridham. London: Forest Row, 1996.

Al-Rasheed, Madawi. *A Most Masculine State: Gender, Politics and Religion in Saudi Arabia*. Cambridge: Cambridge University Press, 2013.

Al-Rashoud, Talal. 'From Muscat to the Maghreb: Pan-Arab Networks, Anti-Colonial Groups, and Kuwait's Arab Scholarships (1953–1961)'. *Arabian Humanities*, no. 12 (November 2019). https://doi.org/10.4000/cy.5004.

'The Omani Union (1952–1965): Would-Be Vanguard of the Imamate's Uprising'. Princeton University, 2019.

Alsaafin, Linah. 'Omani Parliamentarian Remains Imprisoned amidst Crackdown on Dissent'. *Middle East Eye*, 13 February 2015. www .middleeasteye.net/news/omani-parliamentarian-remains-imprisoned-amidst-crackdown-dissent.

Al-Sabah, Meshal. *Gender and Politics in Kuwait: Women and Political Participation in the Gulf*. London: I. B.Tauris, 2013.

Al-Said, Haitham bin Tariq. 'The Royal Speech of HM Sultan Haitham Bin Tarik'. Ministry of Information, 11 January 2022. www.omaninfo.om/ library/70/show/1227.

Al-Said, Sultan Qaboos bin Said. 'The Royal Speeches of His Majesty Sultan Qaboos Bin Said'. Muscat: Ministry of Information, 2015. www .omaninfo.om/english/files/Book/royal-speech.pdf.

Al-Saleh, Danya. '"Who Will Man the Rigs When We Go?" Transnational Demographic Fever Dreams between Qatar and Texas'. *Environment and Planning C: Politics and Space*, 11 January 2022. https://doi.org/10 .1177/23996544211063205.

Al-Saqri, Nasser Abdullah Salim. 'Private Education in the Omani City of Maṭraḥ during the Reign of Sultan Saʿīd b. Taymūr (1932–1970)'. *Arabian Humanities*, no. 12 (November 2019). https://doi.org/10 .4000/cy.5429.

Al-Saqri, Said. 'Al-Khazīna al-ʿAddad 18 November 2013'. *Cosmologymass* (blog), 13 December 2013. http://cosmologymass.blogspot.com/2013/ 12/18.html.

'al-Shabāb: silsilat al-iḥṣāʾāt al-mujtamʿiyya'. Muscat: National Centre for Statistics and Information, 2018.

'al-Shabāb wa-l-ʿamal'. Muscat: National Centre for Statistics and Information, 2017.

'al-Shabāb wa-sūq al-ʿamal'. Muscat: National Centre for Statistics and Information, 2020. www.ncsi.gov.om/Elibrary/.

Al-Shaibany, Saleh. 'Lulu Supermarket Set Ablaze by Oman Protesters'. *The National*, 1 March 2011. www.thenational.ae/world/mena/lulu-super market-set-ablaze-by-oman-protesters-1.566581.

'Oman Sultan to Cede Some Powers after Protests'. Reuters, 13 March 2011. www.reuters.com/article/us-oman-idUKTRE72C1WH20110313.

AlShehabi, Omar. *Contested Modernity: Sectarianism, Nationalism, and Colonialism in Bahrain*. London: OneWorld, 2019.

'Divide and Rule in Bahrain and the Elusive Pursuit for a United Front: The Experience of the Constitutive Committee and the 1972 Uprising'. *Historical Materialism* 21, no. 1 (1 January 2013): 94–127. https://doi .org/10.1163/1569206X-12341267.

'Policing Labour in Empire: The Modern Origins of the Kafala Sponsorship System in the Gulf Arab States'. *British Journal of Middle*

Eastern Studies 48, no. 2 (2021): 291–310. https://doi.org/10.1080/13530194.2019.1580183.

'Radical Transformations and Radical Contestations: Bahrain's Spatial-Demographic Revolution'. *Middle East Critique* 23, no. 1 (2 January 2014): 29–51. https://doi.org/10.1080/19436149.2014.896596.

AlShehabi, Omar Hesham, and Saleh Suroor. 'Unpacking "Accumulation By Dispossession", "Fictitious Commodification", and "Fictitious Capital Formation": Tracing the Dynamics of Bahrain's Land Reclamation'. *Antipode* 48, no. 4 (2016): 835–56. https://doi.org/10.1111/anti.12222.

Al-Shidi, Fatima. 'al-Mara'a al-ʿumāniyya w-al-Rabīʿ: bayn al- ḥuḍūr al-rāfil w-al-taghyīb al-muʾaṭar'. In *al-Rabīʿ al-ʿumānī: qirāʾa fi al-siyāqāt w-al-dalālāt*, edited by Said Sultan Al-Hashimi, 55–61. Beirut: Dar Al-Farabi, 2013.

Alston, Robert John, and Stuart Laing. *Unshook Till the End of Time: A History of Relations between Britain & Oman 1650–1970*. Fulham: Gilgamesh, 2012.

Altan-Olcay, Özlem. 'Entrepreneurial Subjectivities and Gendered Complexities: Neoliberal Citizenship in Turkey'. *Feminist Economics* 20, no. 4 (2 October 2014): 235–59. https://doi.org/10.1080/13545701.2014.950978.

'al-Taʿdād al-iliktrūniyy l-lsukān wa-l-masākin wa-l-munshaʾāt 2020'. Muscat: NCSI, January 2021. www.ncsi.gov.om/Elibrary/.

Alvi, Riazuddin. 'The Need for an Effective Training Programme in the Sultanate of Oman'. *Al-Markazi*, July 1976. Central Bank of Oman Archive.

Al-Wahaibi, Adil, and Ariana Zeka. 'Health Impacts from Living near a Major Industrial Park in Oman'. *BMC Public Health* 15, no. 524 (2015). https://doi.org/10.1186/s12889-015-1866-3.

Al-Watan. 'Murāqibūn wa-muḥalilūn iqtiṣādī lil-waṭan al-iqtiṣādī: Duwal al-Majlis fī khaṭar wa lā bud min sīyāsāt sarīʿa li-tanwiʿ maṣādar al-dakhl'. 4 November 2014. http://alwatan.com/details/37154.

Al-Yousef, Mohamed Bin Musa. *Oil and the Transformation of Oman: The Socio-Economic Impact*. London: Stacey International, 1996.

Al-Zidjaly, Najma. 'Memes as Reasonably Hostile Laments: A Discourse Analysis of Political Dissent in Oman'. *Discourse & Society* 28, no. 6 (1 November 2017): 573–94. https://doi.org/10.1177/0957926517721083.

'Repair as Activism on Arabic Twitter'. In *Approaches to Discourse Analysis*, edited by Cynthia Gordon, 136–58. Washington, DC: Georgetown University Press, 2021.

Al-ʿAmri, Tahir Salim. 'Ḥiwār ʿamal'. *Majalat Sawāʿid Niqābīyya*, 2019. www.gfow.om/?p=4333.

'Annual Report 2012'. Muscat: Petroleum Development Oman, 2012.

Antunes, Ricardo. 'The Working Class Today: The New Form of Being of the Class Who Lives from Its Labour'. *Workers of the World* 1, no. 2 (January 2013): 7–18.

Arabian Business. 'Gulf States Struggle to Shift Jobs to Choosy Locals'. 3 November 2011. www.arabianbusiness.com/gulf-states-struggle-shift-jobs-choosy-locals-428611.html.

Arshad, Syed Ali Naveed, and Maria Mariam Rabeaa Petrou. 'Major Projects: Environmental Risks in Oman: Overview'. Thomson Reuters Practical Law, 1 May 2017. https://uk.practicallaw.thomsonreuters.com/w-008-2712?transitionType=Default&contextData=(sc.Default)&firstPage=true#co_anchor_a118297.

Ashiagbor, Diamond. 'Race and Colonialism in the Construction of Labour Markets and Precarity'. *Industrial Law Journal* 50, no. 4 (2021): 506–31. https://doi.org/10.1093/indlaw/dwab020.

Aslop, Ron. 'The "Trophy Kids" Go to Work'. *Wall Street Journal*, 21 October 2008. http://online.wsj.com/article/SB122455219391652725.html.

Atabaki, Touraj, Elisabetta Bini, and Kaveh Ehsani, eds. *Working for Oil: Comparative Social Histories of Labor in the Global Oil Industry*. Cham: Springer, 2018.

Atheer. 'Ḍawābiṭ al-tafarrugh li-muwaẓẓafiyy al-Ḥukūma li-idārat Mū'assasātihim al-Khāṣṣa'. 22 February 2016. https://t.co/hOpxgkiJdO.

Babar, Zahra R. 'The Vagaries of the In-Between: Labor Citizenship in the Persian Gulf'. *International Journal of Middle East Studies* 52, no. 4 (November 2020): 765–70. https://doi.org/10.1017/S0020743820001075.

Bair, Jennifer. 'On Difference and Capital: Gender and the Globalization of Production'. *Signs* 36, no. 1 (2010): 203–26. https://doi.org/10.1086/652912.

Bakker, Isabella. 'Social Reproduction and the Constitution of a Gendered Political Economy'. *New Political Economy* 12, no. 4 (1 December 2007): 541–56. https://doi.org/10.1080/13563460701661561.

'Barnāmaj nuqṭat niẓām ḥawl qaḍiyat talawuth'. idhāʿat al-wiṣāl, May 2010. www.youtube.com/watch?v=0B16jA0xrA0.

Barnett, Andy, Bruce Yandle, and George Naufal. 'Regulation, Trust, and Cronyism in Middle Eastern Societies: The Simple Economics of "Wasta"'. *The Journal of Socio-Economics* 44 (June 2013): 41–46. https://doi.org/10.1016/j.socec.2013.02.004.

Barth, Fredrik. *Sohar: Culture and Society in an Omani Town*. Baltimore: John Hopkins University Press, 1983.

Batutu, Hanna. *The Old Social Classes and the Revolutionary Movements of Iraq: A Study of Iraq's Old Landed and Commercial Classes and of Its Communists, Ba'thists and Free Officers*. Princeton: Princeton University Press, 1978.

Baumann, Hannes. 'Avatars of Eurocentrism in International Political Economy Textbooks: The Case of the Middle East and North Africa'. *Politics*, 28 October 2021. https://doi.org/10.1177/02633957211054739.

Baumann, Hannes, and Roberto Roccu. 'International Political Economy and the State in the Middle East'. *Globalizations* (2023): 1–13. https://doi.org/10.1080/14747731.2023.2223951.

BBC News Arabic. 'Ṣuḥār: Limādhā tuthīr al-iḥtijājāt wa al-mūājahāt fī ʿUmān al-makhāwif min tikrār aḥdāth 2011? 24 May 2021. www.bbc.com/arabic/trending-57231803.

Beblawi, Hazem. 'The Rentier State in the Arab World'. In *The Rentier State*, edited by Hazem Beblawi and Giacomo Luciani, 49–62. New York: Routledge, 1987.

Beblawi, Hazem, and Giacomo Luciani. *The Rentier State*. New York: Routledge, 1987.

Beck, Martin, and Thomas Richter, eds. *Oil and the Political Economy in the Middle East: Post-2014 Adjustment Policies of the Arab Gulf and Beyond*. Manchester: Manchester University Press, 2021.

Bello, Walden. 'States and Markets, States versus Markets: The Developmental State Debate as the Distinctive East Asian Contribution to International Political Economy'. In *Routledge Handbook of International Political Economy (IPE): IPE as a Global Conversation*, edited by Mark Blyth, 180–200. London: Routledge, 2010.

Bennett, Andrew, and Colin Elman. 'Complex Causal Relations and Case Study Methods: The Example of Path Dependence'. *Political Analysis* 14, no. 3 (20 June 2006): 250–67. https://doi.org/10.1093/pan/mpj020.

Benny, Joseph. 'Oman: Over 3,000 Workers of Construction Firm on Strike Demanding Unpaid Wages'. *Muscat Daily / Business Human Rights*, 20 December 2015. www.business-humanrights.org/en/latest-news/oman-over-3000-workers-of-construction-firm-on-strike-demanding-unpaid-wages/.

Bhacker, M. Reda. *Trade and Empire in Muscat and Zanzibar: The Roots of British Domination*. London; New York: Routledge, 1994.

Bhalloo, Zahir. 'Construction et Gestion Identitaire Chez Les Lawatiya Du Sultanat d'Oman, de Multân à Masqaṭ'. *Journal Asiatique* 304, no. 2 (2016): 217–30.

Bhambra, Gurminder K. 'Colonial Global Economy: Towards a Theoretical Reorientation of Political Economy'. *Review of International Political Economy* 28, no. 2 (4 March 2021): 307–22. https://doi.org/10.1080/09692290.2020.1830831.

Bhambra, Gurminder K., and John Holmwood. 'Colonialism, Postcolonialism and the Liberal Welfare State'. *New Political Economy* 23, no. 5 (2018): 574–87. https://doi.org/10.1080/13563467.2017.1417369.

Bhattacharyya, Gargi. *Rethinking Racial Capitalism: Questions of Reproduction and Survival*. Lanham: Rowman & Littlefield, 2018.

Bhaya, Abishek. 'Entrepreneurship Is the Way Forward in Oman, Says National Youth Commission'. *Muscat Daily*, 22 April 2013.

Bilgin, Pinar. '"Contrapuntal Reading" as a Method, an Ethos, and a Metaphor for Global IR'. *International Studies Review* 18, no. 1 (2016): 134–46. https://doi.org/10.1093/isr/viv018.

'How to Remedy Eurocentrism in IR? A Complement and a Challenge for the Global Transformation'. *International Theory* 8, no. 3 (2016): 492–501. https://doi.org/10.1017/S1752971916000178.

Binte-Farid, Irtefa. '"True" Sons of Oman: National Narratives, Genealogical Purity and Transnational Connections in Modern Oman'. In *Gulfization of the Arab World*, edited by Marc Owen Jones, Ross Porter, and Marc Valeri, 41–56. Berlin: Gerlach Press, 2018.

Bishara, Fahad Ahmad. *A Sea of Debt: Law And Economic Life In The Western Indian Ocean, 1780–1950*. Cambridge: Cambridge University Press, 2017.

'The Many Voyages of Fateh Al-Khayr: Unfurling the Gulf in the Age of Oceanic History'. *International Journal of Middle East Studies* 52, no. 3 (August 2020): 397–412. https://doi.org/10.1017/S0020743820000 367.

Bitwize. 'Omani Students Undergo Training at Chinese Centre'. *Times of Oman*, 14 July 2018 edition. Accessed 13 December 2021. https://timesofoman.com/article/138105/Oman/Omani-students-undergo-training-at-Chinese-centre.

Black and White Oman. 'Lulu Group Focuses on Empowering Omani Youth'. 21 February 2022, sec. Newsworthy. https://blackandwhiteoman.com/lulu-group-focuses-on-empowering-omani-youth/.

Blarel, Nicolas, and Crystal A. Ennis. 'Contested Governance and Sovereignty in the Kerala-Dubai Migration Corridor'. In *The South Asia to Gulf Migration Governance Complex*, edited by Crystal A. Ennis and Nicolas Blarel, 147–72. Bristol: Bristol University Press, 2022. https://bristoluniversitypressdigital.com/view/book/9781529221510/ch007.xml.

Bogaert, Koenraad. 'Contextualizing the Arab Revolts: The Politics behind Three Decades of Neoliberalism in the Arab World'. *Middle East Critique* 22, no. 3 (2 September 2013): 213–34. https://doi.org/10 .1080/19436149.2013.814945.

Borrowman, Mary, and Stephan Klasen. 'Drivers of Gendered Sectoral and Occupational Segregation in Developing Countries'. *Feminist Economics* 26, no. 2 (2 April 2020): 62–94. https://doi.org/10.1080/13545701.2019.1649708.

Bose, Sugata. *A Hundred Horizons: The Indian Ocean in the Age of Global Empire*. Cambridge, MA: Harvard University Press, 2006.

'Briefings from Oman: Agriculture & Fisheries'. Muscat; Ithraa: The Public Authority for Investment Promotion and Export Development, December 2016. https://issuu.com/ithraaoman/docs/ithraa_briefing_agriculture_eng_aw.

'Briefings from Oman Waste Management'. Ithraa: The Public Authority for Investment Promotion and Export Development, December 2016. https://ithraa.om/portals/0/IthraaPDF/Brochures/PDF/ithraa_briefings_waste_engAW.pdf.

Bruff, Ian. 'The Rise of Authoritarian Neoliberalism'. *Rethinking Marxism* 26, no. 1 (2 January 2014): 113–29. https://doi.org/10.1080/08935696.2013.843250.

Bruff, Ian, and Cemal Burak Tansel. 'Authoritarian Neoliberalism: Trajectories of Knowledge Production and Praxis'. *Globalizations* 16, no. 3 (2019): 233–44. https://doi.org/10.1080/14747731.2018.1502497.

Buckley, Michelle. 'Locating Neoliberalism in Dubai: Migrant Workers and Class Struggle in the Autocratic City'. *Antipode* 45, no. 2 (2013): 256–74. https://doi.org/10.1111/j.1467-8330.2012.01002.x.

'BW 91/757: TETOC: Oman – General Correspondence'. British Council Archives. London: The National Archives, Kew, 1978 1974. A/OMA/2. Kew.

Cairo Institute for Human Rights Studies. 'Oman: Drop Cases against Online Activists "Defaming the Sultan" Sentences Part of Wider Repression Campaign', 21 July 2012. https://cihrs.org/oman-drop-cases-against-online-activists-'defaming-the-sultan'-sentences-part-of-wider-repression-campaign/?lang=en.

'The Sultanate of Silence . . . Full Scale Crackdown on Omani Democracy Activists', 18 December 2012. https://cihrs.org/the-sultanate-of-silence-full-scale-crackdown-on-omani-democracy-activists/?lang=en.

Castelier, Sebastian, and Quentin Mueller. 'Oman's Duqm, a New Port City for the Middle East?' *Middle East Eye*, 10 February 2019. www.middleeasteye.net/news/omans-duqm-new-port-city-middle-east.

'Omani Fishermen Swept up in Belt and Road Wave'. *Asia Times*, 11 January 2019. https://asiatimes.com/2019/01/omani-fishermen-swept-up-in-belt-and-road-wave/.

Castles, Stephen. *The Age of Migration: International Population Movements in the Modern World*. 2nd ed. Hampshire: Macmillan International Higher Education, 1998.

'Migration, Crisis, and the Global Labour Market'. *Globalizations* 8, no. 3 (1 June 2011): 311–24. https://doi.org/10.1080/14747731.2011.576847.

Cawthorne, Pamela. 'Identity, Values and Method: Taking Interview Research Seriously in Political Economy'. *Qualitative Research* 1, no. 1 (1 April 2001): 65–90. https://doi.org/10.1177/146879410100100104.

Chalcraft, John. 'Migration and Popular Protest in the Arabian Peninsula and the Gulf in the 1950s and 1960s'. *International Labor and Working-Class History*, no. 79 (2011): 28–47.

Chalil, Gemsheer Mon. 'The New Investment Wave into Aquaculture in Middle East Countries: Opportunities and Challenges'. GLOBEFISH – Information and Analysis on World Fish Trade. Food and Agriculture Organization of the United Nations. Accessed 11 December 2021. www.fao.org/in-action/globefish/fishery-information/resource-detail/en/c/338614/.

Chang, Daeoup. 'From Global Factory to Continent of Labour: Labour and Development in Asia'. *Asian Labour Review* 1, no. 1 (1 January 2015): 5–48.

Chang, Dae-oup. 'Informalising Labour in Asia's Global Factory'. *Journal of Contemporary Asia* 39, no. 2 (May 2009): 161–79. https://doi.org/10.1080/00472330902723766.

Chatty, Dawn. 'Bedouin Economics and the Modern Wage Market: The Case of the Harasiis of Oman'. *Nomadic Peoples* 4, no. 2 (December 2000): 68–83. https://doi.org/doi/10.3167/082279400782310593.

'Boarding Schools for Mobile Peoples: The Harasiis in the Sultanate of Oman'. In *The Education of Nomadic Peoples: Issues, Provision and Prospects*, edited by Caroline Dyer, 213–31. Oxford; New York: Berghahn Press, 2006.

Mobile Pastoralists: Development Planning and Social Change in Oman. New York: Columbia University Press, 1996.

'Petroleum Exploitation and the Displacement of Pastoral Nomadic Households in Oman'. *Center for Migration Studies Special Issues* 11, no. 4 (1994): 87–106. https://doi.org/10.1111/j.2050-411X.1994.tb00799.x.

'The Bedu and Al-Badiyah in Oman'. *PDO News*, 1991.

Chaudhry, Kiren Aziz. 'Economic Liberalization and the Lineages of the Rentier State'. *Comparative Politics* 27, no. 1 (1994): 1–25. https://doi.org/10.2307/422215.

Chisholm, Amanda, and Saskia Stachowitsch. 'Everyday Matters in Global Private Security Supply Chains: A Feminist Global Political Economy Perspective on Gurkhas in Private Security'. *Globalizations* 13, no. 6 (1 November 2016): 815–29. https://doi.org/10.1080/14747731.2016.1155796.

Choudri, B. S., Mahad Baawain, Mushtaque Ahmed, A. Al-Sidairi, and H. Al-Nadabi. 'Relative Vulnerability of Coastal Wilayats to Development: A Study of Al-Batinah North, Oman'. *Journal of Coastal Conservation* 19, no. 1 (2015): 51–57.

Chowdhry, Geeta. 'Edward Said and Contrapuntal Reading: Implications for Critical Interventions in International Relations': *Millennium: Journal of International Studies* 36, no. 1 (2007): 101–16. https://doi .org/10.1177/03058298070360010701.

Christophers, Brett. 'Class, Assets and Work in Rentier Capitalism'. *Historical Materialism* 29, no. 2 (19 March 2021): 3–28. https://doi .org/10.1163/1569206X-29021234.

Clark, Terence. *Underground to Overseas: The Story of Petroleum Development Oman*. London: Stacey International, 2007.

'Coll 27/9(2) "Passports. British-Protected Persons. Travel Documents for Persons Proceeding to, and for Natives of, Certain British Protectorates and Arab States"'. British Library: India Office Records and Private Papers, Februry 1939–March 1948. IOR/L/PS/12/3370. Qatar Digital Library. www.qdl.qa/en/archive/81055/vdc_100000000602.0x00039a.

'Coll 30/9(2) "Admin. Reports of the Persian Gulf – 1945–"'. British Library: India Office Records and Private Papers, 1945. IOR/L/PS/12/ 3720A. Qatar Digital Library. www.qdl.qa/en/archive/81055/vdc_ 100000000648.0x00011b.

'Coll 30/232 "Arab Sheikdoms of the Persian Gulf"'. British Library: India Office Records and Private Papers, 1949. IOR/L/PS/12/3974. Qatar Digital Library. www.qdl.qa/archive/81055/vdc_100000000648 .0x000224.

Collier, David. 'Understanding Process Tracing'. *PS: Political Science & Politics* 44, no. 4 (October 2011): 823–30. https://doi.org/10.1017/ S1049096511001429.

'Commercial Export of Oil'. Foreign and Commonwealth Office. London: The National Archives, 1967–1968. FCO 8/600. Arabian Gulf Digital Archives. www.agda.ae/en/catalogue/tna/fco/8/600.

Construction Week. 'Workers Strike in Oman over Pay and Conditions'. 8 September 2013. www.constructionweekonline.com/appointments/ article-24155-workers-strike-in-oman-over-pay-and-conditions.

Cooper, Andrew F, and Bessma Momani. 'The Challenge of Re-branding Progressive Countries in the Gulf and Middle East: Opportunities through New Networked Engagements versus Constraints of Embedded Negative Images'. *Place Branding and Public Diplomacy* 5, no. 2 (May 2009): 103–17. https://doi.org/10.1057/pb.2009.3.

Crystal, Jill. *Oil and Politics in the Gulf: Rulers and Merchants in Kuwait and Qatar*. Cambridge: Cambridge University Press, 1995.

Dauvergne, Catherine, and Sarah Marsden. 'The Ideology of Temporary Labour Migration in the Post-Global Era'. *Citizenship Studies* 18, no. 2 (17 February 2014): 224–42. https://doi.org/10.1080/13621025.2014 .886441.

De Bel-Air, Françoise. 'Demography, Migration, and the Labour Market in Bahrain'. Gulf Labour Market and Migration (GLMM) Programme, 2015. https://cadmus.eui.eu/handle/1814/35882.

Delacroix, Jacques. 'The Distributive State in the World System'. *Studies In Comparative International Development* 15, no. 3 (1980): 3–21. https://doi.org/10.1007/BF02686463.

Dept, International Monetary Fund Middle East and Central Asia. 'Oman: 2021 Article IV Consultation-Press Release; Staff Report; and Statement by the Executive Director for Oman'. *IMF Staff Country Reports* 2021, no. 206 (12 September 2021). www.elibrary.imf.org/view/journals/002/2021/206/article-A001-en.xml.

Development Council. 'Resolution on Aims and Objectives of Economic Development Policy in the Sultanate (Issued at Its Meeting of Sunday, 9 February 1975)'. In *The Five-Year Development Plan 1976–1980*, 106–9. Muscat: Sultanate of Oman Development Council, 1976.

'Development Projects in Oman'. Foreign and Commonwealth Office. London: The National Archives, 1971. FCO 8/1683. Arabian Gulf Digital Archives. www.agda.ae/en/catalogue/tna/fco/8/1683.

Dietrich, Christopher R. W. *Oil Revolution: Anticolonial Elites, Sovereign Rights, and the Economic Culture of Decolonization*. Cambridge: Cambridge University Press, 2017.

Dijck, José van, Thomas Poell, and Martijn de Waal. *The Platform Society*. New York: Oxford University Press, 2018. https://doi.org/10.1093/oso/9780190889760.001.0001.

Diplomatic Staff. 'Curfew Quells Disorders in Omani Towns'. *The Times*, 2 September 1971.

Dito, Mohammed. 'Kafala: Foundations of Migrant Exclusion in GCC Labour Markets'. In *Transit States: Labour, Migration & Citizenship in the Gulf*, edited by Abdulhadi Khalaf, Omar AlShehabi, and Adam Hanieh, 79–100. London: Pluto Press, 2015. www.press.uchicago.edu/ucp/books/book/distributed/T/bo21636617.html.

'Documents of the National Struggle in Oman and the Arabian Gulf [Trans. from the Arabic and Ed. by the Gulf Committee]'. Arabic Original, Dar at-Talia, Beirut. 9th June Studies. London: Gulf Committee, 1974. International Institute of Social History (Az15 – Bro E 760 – Bro E 4898).

Doorn, Niels van. 'Platform Capitalism's Social Contract'. *Internet Policy Review* 11, no. 1 (22 March 2022). https://policyreview.info/articles/analysis/platform-capitalisms-social-contract.

Doorn, Niels van, and Darsana Vijay. 'Gig Work as Migrant Work: The Platformization of Migration Infrastructure'. *Environment and Planning A: Economy and Space*, 20 December 2021. https://doi.org/10.1177/0308518X211065049.

Draves, William August, and Julie Coates. *Nine Shift: Work, Life and Education in the 21st Century*. River Falls: LERN Books, 2004.

Dutton, Roderic W. *Changing Rural Systems in Oman: The Khabura Project*. London: Kegan Paul International, 1999.

'Economic Situation in Oman, Part C'. Foreign and Commonwealth Office. London: The National Archives, 1975. FCO 8/2465. Arabian Gulf Digital Archives. www.agda.ae/en/catalogue/tna/fco/8/2465.

The Economist. 'From Oil to Toil'. 10 September 2016. www.economist .com/middle-east-and-africa/2016/09/10/from-oil-to-toil.

Ehsani, Kaveh. 'Disappearing the Workers: How Labor in the Oil Complex Has Been Made Invisible'. In *Working for Oil: Comparative Social Histories of Labor in the Global Oil Industry*, edited by Touraj Atabaki, Elisabetta Bini, and Kaveh Ehsani, 11–34. Cham: Springer, 2018.

Eickelman, Dale F. 'Oman's Next Generation: Challenges and Prospects'. In *Crosscurrents in the Gulf: Arab, Regional and Global Interests*, edited by H. Richard Sindelar III and J. E. Peterson, 157–80. London; New York: Routledge, 1988.

Eickelman, Dale F., and M. G. Dennison. 'Arabizing the Omani Intelligence Services: Clash of Cultures?' *International Journal of Intelligence and CounterIntelligence* 7, no. 1 (1 March 1994): 1–28. https://doi.org/10 .1080/08850609408435235.

Elias, Juanita, and Adrienne Roberts. 'Feminist Global Political Economies of the Everyday: From Bananas to Bingo'. *Globalizations* 13, no. 6 (1 November 2016): 787–800. https://doi.org/10.1080/14747731 .2016.1155797.

El-Khatib, M. Fathalla, and Issam Kabbani. 'British Aggression against the Imamate of Oman'. In *British Imperialism in Southern Arabia*, 43–57. Information Papers 6. New York: Arab Information Center, 1958.

Elyachar, Julia. *Markets of Dispossession: NGOs, Economic Development, and the State in Cairo*. Durham: Duke University Press, 2005.

Emerson, Robert, Rachel Fretz, and Linda Shaw. 'Participant Observation and Fieldnotes'. In *Handbook of Ethnography*, edited by Paul Atkinson, 352–68. Thousand Oaks: SAGE, 2001.

Ennis, Crystal A. 'Between Trend and Necessity: Top-Down Entrepreneurship Promotion in Oman and Qatar'. *The Muslim World* 105, no. 1 (2015): 116–38. https://doi.org/10.1111/muwo.12083.

'Citizenship without Belonging? Contesting Economic Space in Oman'. *International Journal of Middle East Studies* 52, no. 4 (November 2020): 759–64. https://doi.org/10.1017/S0020743820001063.

'The Gendered Complexities of Promoting Female Entrepreneurship in the Gulf'. *New Political Economy* 24, no. 3 (2019): 365–84. https://doi.org/ 10.1080/13563467.2018.1457019

'Networking through Kafala: Skilled Workers and Transnational Networks in the Governance of Health Care Migration in the Gulf'. In *Global Migration, Gender and Professional Credentials*, edited by Margaret Walton-Roberts, 145–66. Toronto: University of Toronto Press, 2022.

Ennis, Crystal A., and Ra'id Z. Al-Jamali. 'Elusive Employment: Development Planning and Labour Market Trends in Oman'. Research Paper. London: Chatham House, September 2014. www .chathamhouse.org/sites/files/chathamhouse/field/field_document/ 20140916ElusiveEmploymentOmanEnnisJamali.pdf.

Ennis, Crystal A., and Said Al-Saqri. 'Oil Price Collapse and the Political Economy of the Post-2014 Economic Adjustment in the Sultanate of Oman'. In *Oil and the Political Economy in the Middle East: Post-2014 Adjustment Policies of the Arab Gulf and Beyond*, edited by Martin Beck and Thomas Richter, 79–101. Manchester: Manchester University Press, 2021.

Ennis, Crystal A., and Nicolas Blarel, eds. *The South Asia to Gulf Migration Governance Complex*. Bristol: Bristol University Press, 2022.

eds. *The South Asia to Gulf Migration Governance Complex*. Bristol: Bristol University Press, 2022.

Ennis, Crystal A., and Margaret Walton-Roberts. 'Labour Market Regulation as Global Social Policy: The Case of Nursing Labour Markets in Oman'. *Global Social Policy* 18, no. 2 (2018): 169–88. https://doi.org/10.1177/1468018117737990.

Ernst & Young. 'Oman: Private Sector Training Needs Assessment'. Bureau for Private Enterprise, US Agency for International Development, December 1990. http://pdf.usaid.gov/pdf_docs/pnabh460.pdf.

'Facts & Figures 2010'. Muscat: Ministry of National Economy, June 2011.

Fargues, Philippe, and Nasra M. Shah, eds. *Skilful Survival: Irregular Migration to the Gulf*. Nicosia: European University Institute and Gulf Research Center, 2017. https://gulfmigration.org/publications/book/.

Fayṣal, Fayṣal ʿAlī. *al-Qaḍiyya al-ʿUmāniyya*. Solo: Dār al-Hanāʾ, ca 1960.

'FCO 8/1848 Annual Review of Oman for 1971'. Foreign and Commonwealth Office. London: The National Archives, Kew, 1972. File NB/M14. Kew.

'FCO 8/2224: Economic Situation in Oman'. Foreign and Commonwealth Office. London: The National Archives, 1974. NBL 5/2. Kew.

Federici, Silvia. *Wages against Housework*. London; Bristol: Power of Women Collective and Falling Wall Press, 1975.

'File 2/21 R.A.F. Landing Ground at Beit al Falaj (Petrol Store at Muscat)'. British Library: India Office Records and Private Papers, 17 February 1938. IOR/R/15/6/99. Qatar Digital Library. www.qdl.qa/en/archive/ 81055/vdc_100000000831.0x0002eb.

'File 8/72 Muscat State Affairs: Muscat Levies Strike; Muscat Customs Strike'. British Library: India Office Records and Private Papers, September 1942–September 1944. IOR/R/15/6/266. Qatar Digital Library. www .qdl.qa/en/archive/81055/vdc_100000000831.0x000166.

'File 13/5 "Foreign Consular Representation in Kuwait (and Persian Gulf)"'. British Library: India Office Records and Private Papers, 1 November 1933. IOR/R/15/5/315. Qatar Digital Library. www.qdl.qa/en/archive/ 81055/vdc_100000000831.0x000166.

'File 18/54 (A 89) Muscat Order in Council, 1867: New Regulations'. British Library: India Office Records and Private Papers, 4 April 1911. IOR/R/ 15/1/297. Qatar Digital Library. www.qdl.qa/en/archive/81055/vdc_ 100023834010.0x000012.

'File 29/7 I Consular: Passport and Visa Regulations (Governing Bahrain, Muscat, Kuwait and Other Shaikhdoms)'. British Library: India Office Records and Private Papers, December 1929–October 1934. IOR/R/15/ 2/1748. Qatar Digital Library. www.qdl.qa/en/archive/81055/vdc_ 100000000282.0x0001e3.

'File 15331: Oil Exploration'. Foreign Office. London: The National Archives, 1954. FO 1016/330. Arabian Gulf Digital Archives. www .agda.ae/en/catalogue/tna/fo/1016/330.

Finnie, David. 'Recruitment and Training of Labor: The Middle East Oil Industry'. *Middle East Journal* 12, no. 2 (1958): 127–43.

Foley, Sean. *The Arab Gulf States: Beyond Oil and Islam*. Boulder: Lynne Rienner, 2010.

Freitag, Ulrike, and Achim Von Oppen. 'Translocality: The Study of Globalising Processes from a Southern Perspective'. In *Introduction. 'Translocality': An Approach to Connection and Transfer in Area Studies*, edited by Ulrike Freitag and Achim Von Oppen, 1–21. Leiden: Brill, 2010.

Fudge, Judy. '(Re)Conceptualising Unfree Labour: Local Labour Control Regimes and Constraints on Workers' Freedoms'. *Global Labour Journal* 10, no. 2 (May 2019): 108–22.

Gardner, Andrew M. *City of Strangers: Gulf Migration and the Indian Community in Bahrain*. Ithaca: Cornell University Press, 2010.

'General Census of Population, Housing, and Establishments 2010'. Muscat: Census Administration, National Centre for Statistics and Information, 2010.

George, Alexander L., and Andrew Bennett. *Case Studies and Theory Development in the Social Sciences*. Cambridge, MA: The MIT Press, 2005.

Ghosh, Basu. 'Health Workforce Development Planning in the Sultanate of Oman – a Profile (1991–2009)'. Muscat: Directorate General of Planning, Ministry of Health, 28 October 2009. MOH Library.

Glubb, Faris. 'The Role of the Workers in the Struggle of British-Occupied Arabia'. Translation of a lecture delivered to the Arab Students Union by Faris Glubb, Secretary of the Committee for the Rights of Oman on the occasion of Occupied South Yemen Day. London: Omani News, 1966. Collection Documentation and Leaflets Great Britain, ARCH01732. International Institute of Social History.

Gonzalez, Gabriella, Lynn A. Karoly, Louay Constant, Hanine Salem, and Charles A. Goldman. *Facing Human Capital Challenges of the 21st Century: Education and Labor Market Initiatives in Lebanon, Oman, Qatar, and the United Arab Emirates.* Santa Monica: Rand Corporation, 2008.

Gordon, David M. 'Reading the Archives as Sources'. In *The Oxford Encyclopedia of African Historiography: Methods and Sources.* Oxford: Oxford University Press, 2019.

Goswami, Chhaya. *The Call of the Sea: Kachchhi Traders in Muscat and Zanzibar, c. 1800–1880.* New Delhi: Orient Blackswan, 2011.

Gray, Matthew. 'A Theory of "Late Rentierism" in the Arab States of the Gulf'. Center for International and Regional Studies Georgetown University School of Foreign Service in Qatar, Occasional Paper, no. 7 (2011).

GreenPort. 'Rotterdam/Oman Environmental Protection Service', 12 May 2008. www.greenport.com/news101/europe/rotterdamoman-environ mental-protection-service.

Guazzone, Laura, and Daniela Pioppi, eds. *The Arab State and Neo-Liberal Globalization: The Restructuring of State Power in the Middle East.* Cairo: American University in Cairo Press, 2009.

Gulf News. 'Major LuLu Hypermarket Strike Ends in Oman'. 29 June 2014. https://gulfnews.com/world/gulf/oman/major-lulu-hypermarket-strike-ends-in-oman-1.1353571.

'Octal Employees Continue to Strike in Oman'. 6 March 2014. https://gulfnews.com/world/gulf/oman/octal-employees-continue-to-strike-in-oman-1.1300525.

'Oman Bans Strikes in Essential Services'. 11 November 2013. https://gulfnews.com/world/gulf/oman/oman-bans-strikes-in-essential-services-1.1253912.

'Rights Activists Held over Oil Field Strike in Oman'. 1 June 2012. https://gulfnews.com/world/gulf/oman/rights-activists-held-over-oil-field-strike-in-oman-1.1030409.

'Tear Gas Used on Protesters in Oman'. 23 August 2013. https://gulfnews.com/world/gulf/oman/tear-gas-used-on-protesters-in-oman-1.1223268.

Gulf Solidarity: Bulletin on Oman and the Gulf. 'Omani Regime: Dependency and Reform'. 1977. International Institute of Social History (IISG ZK 35376).

Hall, Stuart. *The Fateful Triangle: Race, Ethnicity, Nation*. Cambridge, MA: Harvard University Press, 2017.

Halliday, Fred. *Arabia without Sultans*. London: Saqi Books, 1974.

Hamadah, Faisal. 'Kafala and Social Reproduction: Migration Governance Regimes and Labour Relations in the Gulf'. In *The South Asia to Gulf Migration Governance Complex*, edited by Crystal A. Ennis and Nicolas Blarel, 173–89. Bristol: Bristol University Press, 2022. https://bristoluniversitypressdigital.com/view/book/9781529221510/ch008.xml.

Hanieh, Adam. *Capitalism and Class in the Gulf Arab States*. New York: Palgrave Macmillan, 2011.

'Khaleeji-Capital: Class-Formation and Regional Integration in the Middle-East Gulf'. *Historical Materialism* 18, no. 2 (2010): 35–76. https://doi.org/10.1163/156920610X512435.

Lineages of Revolt: Issues of Contemporary Capitalism in the Middle East. Chicago: Haymarket Books, 2013.

Money, Markets, and Monarchies: The Gulf Cooperation Council and the Political Economy of the Contemporary Middle East. Cambridge: Cambridge University Press, 2018.

'Overcoming Methodological Nationalism: Spatial Perspectives on Migration to the Gulf Arab States'. In *Transit States: Labour, Migration & Citizenship in the Gulf*, edited by Abdulhadi Khalaf, Omar AlShehabi, and Adam Hanieh, 57–76. London: Pluto Press, 2015.

Hardy, Cynthia, Nelson Phillips, and Bill Harley. 'Discourse Analysis and Content Analysis: Two Solitudes?' *Qualitative & Multi-Method Research* 2, no. 1 (31 March 2004): 19–22.

Harms, Robert W., Bernard K. Freamon, and David W. Blight, eds. *Indian Ocean Slavery in the Age of Abolition*. New Haven: Yale University Press, 2013.

Harrod, Jeffrey. *Power, Production, and the Unprotected Worker*. New York: Columbia University Press, 1987.

'Towards an International Political Economy of Labour'. In *Global Unions? Theory and Strategies of Organized Labour in the Global Political Economy*, edited by Jeffrey Harrod and Robert O'Brien, 49–63. London; New York: Routledge, 2002.

Harvey, David. *The Enigma of Capital and the Crises of Capitalism*. Oxford: Oxford University Press, 2010.

Henderson, Christian. 'Gulf Capital and Egypt's Corporate Food System: A Region in the Third Food Regime'. *Review of African Political Economy* 46, no. 162 (2 October 2019): 599–614. https://doi.org/10.1080/03056244.2018.1552583.

'Land Grabs Reexamined: Gulf Arab Agro-Commodity Chains and Spaces of Extraction'. *Environment and Planning A: Economy and Space* 53, no. 2 (1 March 2021): 261–79. https://doi.org/10.1177/0308518X20956657.

Herb, Michael. 'No Representation without Taxation? Rents, Development, and Democracy'. *Comparative Politics* 37, no. 3 (1 April 2005): 297–316. https://doi.org/10.2307/20072891.

The Wages of Oil: Parliaments and Economic Development in Kuwait and the UAE. Ithaca: Cornell University Press, 2014.

Hertog, Steffen. 'A Comparative Assessment of Labor Market Nationalization Policies in the GCC'. In *National Employment, Migration and Education in the GCC*, edited by Steffen Hertog. Berlin: Gerlach Press, 2012.

'Arab Gulf States: An Assessment of Nationalisation Policies'. GLMM – Research Paper. Gulf Labour Markets and Migration (GLMM), 2014. https://cadmus.eui.eu/bitstream/handle/1814/32156/GLMM%20ResearchPaper_01–2014.pdf?sequence=1&isAllowed=y.

'Benchmarking SME Policies in the GCC: A Survey of Challenges and Opportunities'. The EU-GCC Chamber Forum. Brussels: Eurochambres, 2010. www.europolitique.info/pdf/gratuit_fr/270047-fr.pdf.

'Defying the Resource Curse: Explaining Successful State-Owned Enterprises in Rentier States'. *World Politics* 62, no. 2 (2010): 261–301. https://doi.org/10.1017/S0043887110000055.

Princes, Brokers, and Bureaucrats: Oil and the State in Saudi Arabia. Ithaca: Cornell University Press, 2010.

'The Sociology of the Gulf Rentier Systems: Societies of Intermediaries'. *Comparative Studies in Society and History* 52, no. 2 (2010): 282–318. https://doi.org/10.1017/S0010417510000058.

'State and Private Sector in the GCC after the Arab Uprisings'. *Journal of Arabian Studies* 3, no. 2 (2013): 174–95. https://doi.org/10.1080/21534764.2013.863678.

Hirschman, Charles. 'The Making of Race in Colonial Malaya: Political Economy and Racial Ideology'. *Sociological Forum* 1, no. 2 (1 March 1986): 330–61. https://doi.org/10.1007/BF01115742.

'Historical Summary of Events in the Persian Gulf Shaikhdoms and the Sultanate of Muscat and Oman, 1928–1953'. British Library: India Office Records and Private Papers, 1953. IOR/R/15/1/731(1). Qatar Digital Library. www.qdl.qa/archive/81055/vdc_100000000193.0x0002c1.

Hobson, John M., and Leonard Seabrooke. 'Everyday International Political Economy'. In *Routledge Handbook of International Political Economy (IPE)*, edited by Mark Blyth, 290–306. Routledge, 2009.

Hofmann, Erin Trouth, and Cynthia J. Buckley. 'Global Changes and Gendered Responses: The Feminization of Migration From Georgia'.

International Migration Review 47, no. 3 (2013): 508–38. https://doi
.org/10.1111/imre.12035.

Hofstede, Geert. *Culture's Consequences: Comparing Values, Behaviors,
Institutions and Organizations Across Nations*. 2nd ed. Thousand
Oaks: SAGE, 2001.

*Culture's Consequences: International Differences in Work-Related
Values*. Thousand Oaks: SAGE, 1984.

Honeyman, Catherine A. *The Orderly Entrepreneur: Youth, Education, and
Governance in Rwanda*. Stanford: Stanford University Press, 2016.

Honvault, Juliette, and Talal Al-Rashoud. 'Modern Education in the
Arabian Peninsula: Social Dynamics and Political Issues'. *Arabian
Humanities*, no. 12 (6 November 2019). https://doi.org/10.4000/cy
.4884.

Hopper, Matthew. 'Slaves of One Master: Globalization and the African
Diaspora in Arabia in the Age of Empire'. In *Indian Ocean Slavery in
the Age of Abolition*, edited by Robert W. Harms, Bernard K. Freamon,
and David W. Blight, 223–40. New Haven: Yale University Press, 2013.

Hoskyns, Catherine, and Shirin M. Rai. 'Recasting the Global Political
Economy: Counting Women's Unpaid Work'. *New Political Economy*
12, no. 3 (1 September 2007): 297–317. https://doi.org/10.1080/
13563460701485268.

Howarth, Stephen, and Joost Jonker. *Powering the Hydrocarbon
Revolution, 1939–1973, A History of Royal Dutch Shell*. Vol. 2.
Oxford: Oxford University Press, 2007.

Howe, Neil, and William Strauss. *Millennials Rising: The Next Great
Generation*. Random House, 2000.

'Human Development Report 2010: The Real Wealth of Nations: Pathways
to Human Development'. New York: United Nations Development
Programme, November 2010. www.hdr.undp.org/sites/default/files/
reports/270/hdr_2010_en_complete_reprint.pdf.

Hürriyet Daily News. 'Take Prophet's Wife as Model for Female
Entrepreneurship, TOBB President Says'. 25 December 2012. www
.hurriyetdailynews.com/take-prophets-wife-as-model-for-female-entre
preneurship-tobb-president-says-37604.

Hvidt, Martin. 'Economic and Institutional Reforms in the Arab Gulf
Countries'. *The Middle East Journal* 65, no. 1 (2011): 85–102.

'The State and the Knowledge Economy in the Gulf: Structural and
Motivational Challenges'. *The Muslim World* 105, no. 1 (2015):
24–45. https://doi.org/10.1111/muwo.12078.

International Institute for Strategic Studies. 'Armed Forces Personnel (% of
Total Labor Force)'. World Bank Data, 2017. https://data.worldbank
.org/indicator/MS.MIL.TOTL.TF.ZS.

International Labour Organisation. 'ISCO: International Standard Classification of Occupations', 18 September 2004. www.ilo.org/public/english/bureau/stat/isco/isco88/major.htm.

Jones, Calvert W. *Bedouins into Bourgeois: Remaking Citizens for Globalization*. Cambridge: Cambridge University Press, 2017.

'Seeing Like an Autocrat: Liberal Social Engineering in an Illiberal State'. *Perspectives on Politics* 13, no. 1 (March 2015): 24–41. https://doi.org/10.1017/S1537592714003119.

Jones, Jeremy, and Nicholas Ridout. *A History of Modern Oman*. New York: Cambridge University Press, 2015.

Kabeer, Naila. 'The Rise of the Female Breadwinner: Reconfigurations of Marriage, Motherhood, and Masculinity in the Global Economy'. In *New Frontiers in Feminist Political Economy*, edited by Shirin M. Rai and Georgina Waylen, 62–84. New York: Routledge, 2014.

Kaiser, Sara-Ida, Larissa Alles, and Franz J. H. Polenz. 'Female Entrepreneurs Needed'. *Veranstalungsbeitrag*, October 2011. www.kas.de/wf/doc/kas_29078-1522-2-30.pdf?111127103848.

Kamrava, Mehran, ed. *Political Economy of the Persian Gulf*. 1st ed. Oxford: Oxford University Press, 2012.

Kamrava, Mehran, and Zahra Babar, eds. *Migrant Labor in the Persian Gulf*. New York: Columbia University Press, 2012.

Kang, Charles, Frank Germann, and Rajdeep Grewal. 'Washing Away Your Sins? Corporate Social Responsibility, Corporate Social Irresponsibility, and Firm Performance'. *Journal of Marketing* 80, no. 2 (1 March 2016): 59–79. https://doi.org/10.1509/jm.15.0324.

Kang, Gye-Man, and Hyo-jin Kim. 'DSME, Hyundai Heavy Win String of Crude Carrier Orders'. *Maeil Business Newspaper*, 18 January 2019, sec. english. www.mk.co.kr/news/english/view/2019/01/38110/.

Kanna, Ahmed. 'The Arab World's Forgotten Rebellions: Foreign Workers and Biopolitics in the Gulf'. *South Asian Magazine for Action and Reflection (SAMAR)*, 31 May 2011. http://samarmagazine.org/archive/articles/357.

'Class Struggle and De-Exceptionalizing the Gulf'. In *Beyond Exception: New Interpretations of the Arabian Peninsula*, by Ahmed Kanna, Amélie Le Renard, and Neha Vora, 100–122, Illustrated ed. Ithaca: Cornell University Press, 2020.

Dubai: The City as Corporation. Minneapolis: University of Minnesota Press, 2011.

'Flexible Citizenship in Dubai: Neoliberal Subjectivity in the Emerging "City-Corporation"'. *Cultural Anthropology* 25, no. 1 (February 2010): 100–29.

'A Politics of Non-Recognition? Biopolitics of Arab Gulf Worker Protests in the Year of Uprisings'. *Interface* 4, no. 1 (May 2012): 146–64.

Kanna, Ahmed, Amélie Le Renard, and Neha Vora. *Beyond Exception: New Interpretations of the Arabian Peninsula*. Ithaca: Cornell University Press, 2020.

Kantola, Johanna, and Judith Squires. 'From State Feminism to Market Feminism?' *International Political Science Review* 33, no. 4 (2012): 382–400. https://doi.org/10.1177/0192512111432513.

Kerr, Simeon. 'Oman Gets Tough with Striking Teachers in Revival of Unrest'. *Financial Times*, 24 October 2013. www.ft.com/content/5bc595a5-5491-3874-a93f-1a8cade2fe8b.

Khalaf, Abdulhadi, Omar AlShehabi, and Adam Hanieh, eds. *Transit States: Labour, Migration & Citizenship in the Gulf*. London: Pluto Press, 2015.

Khalili, Laleh. *Sinews of War and Trade: Shipping and Capitalism in the Arabian Peninsula*. London: Verso Books, 2020.

Khan, Golam Mostafa. 'Sidab Women's Sewing Group: An Example of Social Entrepreneurship in the Arabian Gulf'. *International Journal of Entrepreneurship and Small Business* 18, no. 1 (2013): 47–56. https://doi.org/10.1504/IJESB.2013.050751.

Kinninmont, Jane. 'To What Extent Is Twitter Changing Gulf Societies?' London: Chatham House, February 2013. www.chathamhouse.org/sites/default/files/public/Research/Middle%20East/0213kinninmont.pdf.

Knez, Kelly, and Lisahunter. 'The Paradox of Physical Activity for Qatari Women: Researcher Hysteresis and Reflexivity'. In *Pierre Bourdieu and Physical Culture*, edited by Lisahunter, Wayne Smith, and Elke Emerald, 108–16. London and New York: Routledge, 2015.

Kubursi, Atif A. 'Prospects for Arab Economic Integration After Oslo'. In *The Middle East Dilemma: The Politics and Economics of Arab Integration*, edited by Michael C. Hudson, 299–319. New York: Columbia University Press, 1999.

Kunz, Sarah. 'A Business Empire and Its Migrants: Royal Dutch Shell and the Management of Racial Capitalism'. *Transactions of the Institute of British Geographers* 45 (2020): 377–91. https://doi.org/10.1111/tran.12366.

Kuttapan, Rejimon. 'Thumbs up for NOC Compromise in Oman'. *Times of Oman*, 30 November 2016. https://timesofoman.com/article/97693/Oman/Thumbs-up-for-NOC-compromise-by–bosses-workers-and-government-bodies-in-Oman.

Kutty, Samuel, and Sandhya Rao Mehta. *Oman-India Ties: Across Sea and Space*. Ruwi: Oman Daily Observer and Embassy of India Oman, 2021. https://issuu.com/oeppa/docs/03-oman_india_book_printed_pages.

'LAB 13/2740 Gulf States Labour Reports'. British Council Archives. London: The National Archives, Kew, 1973. 4/OS192/1973. Kew.

'Labour Force Participate Rate by Sex and Age'. Labour Force Survey, Labour Force Statistics. ILOSTAT. Geneva: International Labour Organization. Accessed 12 December 2022. https://ilostat.ilo.org/data/.

'Labour Relations'. Foreign and Commonwealth Office. London: The National Archives, 1967–1968. FCO 8/588. Arabian Gulf Digital Archives. www.agda.ae/en/catalogue/tna/fco/8/588.

'Labour Relations'. Foreign and Commonwealth Office. London: The National Archives, 1968. FCO 8/70. Arabian Gulf Digital Archives. www.agda.ae/en/catalogue/tna/fco/8/70.

Lalji, Nadira. 'Labor Law Matters'. *Harvard International Review* 28, no. 3 (Fall 2006): 12–13.

'Labor Law Matters: Trade Liberalization in Oman'. *Harvard International Review* 28, no. 3 (22 September 2006): 12–14.

Las Heras, Jon. 'International Political Economy of Labour and Collective Bargaining in the Automotive Industry'. *Competition & Change* 22, no. 3 (2018): 313–31. https://doi.org/10.1177/1024529418764350.

'International Political Economy of Labour and Gramsci's Methodology of the Subaltern'. *The British Journal of Politics and International Relations* 21, no. 2 (2019): 462–80. https://doi.org/10.1177/1369148118815403.

Lawson, Fred H. 'Geo-Political Complications of US Free Trade Agreements with Gulf Arab Countries'. In *Shifting Geo-Economic Power of the Gulf: Oil, Finance and Institutions*, edited by Matteo Legrenzi and Bessma Momani, 199–210. Farnham: Ashgate, 2011.

Le Renard, Amélie. *A Society of Young Women: Opportunities of Place, Power, and Reform in Saudi Arabia.* Stanford: Stanford University Press, 2014.

Lemke, Thomas. '"The Birth of Bio-Politics": Michel Foucault's Lecture at the Collège de France on Neo-Liberal Governmentality'. *Economy and Society* 30, no. 2 (1 January 2001): 190–207. https://doi.org/10.1080/03085140120042271.

Limbert, Mandana. '"If You Catch Me Again at It, Put Me to Death": Slave Trading, Paper Trails, and British Bureaucracy in the Indian Ocean'. In *Indian Ocean Slavery in the Age of Abolition*, edited by Robert W. Harms, Bernard K. Freamon, and David W. Blight, 120–40. New Haven: Yale University Press, 2013.

In the Time of Oil: Piety, Memory, and Social Life in an Omani Town. Stanford: Stanford University Press, 2010.

Limbert, Mandana E. 'Caste, Ethnicity, and the Politics of Arabness in Southern Arabia'. *Comparative Studies of South Asia, Africa and the Middle East* 34, no. 3 (2014): 590–98.

Linden, Marcel van der. 'The Promise and Challenges of Global Labor History'. In *Global Histories of Work*, edited by Andreas Eckert, 1st ed., 25–48. Berlin: De Gruyter, 2016.

'Who Are the Workers of the World? Marx and Beyond'. *Workers of the World* 1, no. 2 (January 2013): 55–76.

Workers of the World: Essays toward a Global Labor History. Leiden: Brill, 2008.

Lori, Noora. *Offshore Citizens: Permanent Temporary Status in the Gulf*. Cambridge: Cambridge University Press, 2019.

Losman, Donald L. 'The Rentier State and National Oil Companies: An Economic And Political Perspective'. *The Middle East Journal* 64 (Summer 2010): 427–45. https://doi.org/10.3751/64.3.15.

Louër, Laurence. 'The Arab Spring Effect on Labor Politics in Bahrain and Oman'. *Arabian Humanities. Revue Internationale d'archéologie et de Sciences Sociales Sur La Péninsule Arabique/International Journal of Archaeology and Social Sciences in the Arabian Peninsula*, no. 4 (12 January 2015). http://cy.revues.org/2865.

Lynch, Marc, and Michael Herb, eds. *The Politics of Rentier States in the Gulf*. Washington, DC: POMEPS, 2019. https://pomeps.org/pomeps-studies-33-the-politics-of-rentier-states-in-the-gulf.

Macartney, Huw, and Stuart Shields. 'Space, the Latest Frontier? A Scalar-Relational Approach to Critical IPE'. In *Critical International Political Economy: Dialogue, Debate and Dissensus*, edited by Stuart Shields, Ian Bruff, and Huw Macartney, 27–42. London: Palgrave Macmillan, 2011. https://doi.org/10.1057/9780230299405_3.

Machado, Pedro. *Ocean of Trade: South Asian Merchants, Africa and the Indian Ocean, c. 1750–1850*. Cambridge: Cambridge University Press, 2014.

Mahmood, S.M.I. 'Training and Its Benefits to the Employees'. *Al-Markazi*, September 1976. Central Bank of Oman Archive.

Mansoor, Zainab. 'Oman to Not Renew Work Visas for Expats in Certain Professions'. *Gulf Business*, 6 February 2020, sec. Oman. https://gulfbusiness.com/oman-to-not-renew-work-visas-for-expats-in-certain-professions/.

Marawid. 'Marawid Press Releases', 2010–2013. www.mawaridmining.com/press.html.

Marchand, Marianne H., and Anne Sisson Runyan, eds. *Gender and Global Restructuring: Sightings, Sites and Resistances*. 2nd ed. New York: Routledge, 2010.

Marcus, George E. *Ethnography through Thick and Thin*. Princeton: Princeton University Press, 1998.

Mathew, Johan. *Margins of the Market: Trafficking and Capitalism Across the Arabian Sea*. Oakland: University of California Press, 2016.

Matthiesen, Toby. *The Other Saudis: Shiism, Dissent And Sectarianism*. Cambridge: Cambridge University Press, 2014.

Mehta, Sandhya Rao. 'Contesting Victim Narratives: Indian Women Domestic Workers in Oman'. *Migration and Development* 6, no. 3 (2 September 2017): 395–411. https://doi.org/10.1080/21632324.2017.1303065.

Mehta, Sandhya Rao, and James Onley. 'The Hindu Community in Muscat: Creating Homes in the Diaspora'. *Journal of Arabian Studies* 5, no. 2 (2015): 156–83.

Menoret, Pascal. *Joyriding in Riyadh: Oil, Urbanism, and Road Revolt.* Cambridge: Cambridge University Press, 2014.

Middle East Eye. 'Omani Government Promises to Address Unemployment after Nationwide Protests'. 3 January 2019. www.middleeasteye.net/news/omani-government-promises-address-unemployment-after-nation wide-protests.

Mikdashi, Maya. 'How Not to Study Gender in the Middle East'. Jadaliyya, 21 March 2012. www.jadaliyya.com/pages/index/4775/how-not-to-study-gender-in-the-middle-east.

Ministry of Commerce and Industry. Ministerial Decision 72/2020. 'Issuing the Executive Regulations of the Foreign Capital Investment Law (Issued 14 June 2020, Published 21 June 2020)'. Official Gazette 1346, [author translations from Arabic], 2020.

Ministerial Decision 209/2020. 'Defining the List of Activities in Which Foreign Investment in Prohibited (Issued 9 December 2020, Published 13 December 2020)'. Official Gazette 1370, [author translations from Arabic], 2020.

Ministry of Foreign Affairs. '25,000 Jobs for Omanis in Public, Private Sectors'. 5 October 2017. www.mofa.gov.om?p=10333&lang=en.

Ministry of Manpower. 'Open Data', 2019. www.manpower.gov.om/OpenData/home/home.

Ministry of Manpower. Ministerial Decision 47/2020. 'Regulating the Practice of Some Professions (Issued 29 January 2020, Published 2 February 2020)'. Official Gazette 1328, [author translations from Arabic], 2020.

Ministerial Decision 294/2006. 'Regulating Collective Bargaining, Peaceful Strikes, and Closures (Issued 29 October 2006, Published 2 December 2006)'. Official Gazette 828, [author translations from Arabic], 2006.

Ministry of Regional Municipalities, Environment, and Water Resources. Ministerial Decision 159/2005. 'Promulgating Regulation for the Discharge of Liquid Effluents into the Marine Environment (Issued 19 June 2005, Published 2 July 2005)'. Official Gazette 794, [author translations from Arabic], 2005.

Mitchell, Timothy. *Carbon Democracy: Political Power in the Age of Oil.* London; New York: Verso Books, 2011.

Mogielnicki, Robert. *A Political Economy of Free Zones in Gulf Arab States*. Berlin: Springer Nature, 2021.

Mongia, Radhika. *Indian Migration and Empire: A Colonial Genealogy of the Modern State*. Durham; London: Duke University Press, 2018.

'Monthly Statistical Bulletin'. Muscat: National Centre for Statistics and Information, January 2019.

Moore, Phoebe. 'Where Is the Study of Work in Critical IPE?' *International Politics* 49, no. 2 (1 March 2012): 215–37. https://doi.org/10.1057/ip.2011.40.

Moritz, Jessie. 'Re-Conceptualizing Civil Society in Rentier States'. *British Journal of Middle Eastern Studies* 47, no. 1 (2020): 136–51. https://doi.org/10.1080/13530194.2020.1714268.

'Reformers and the Rentier State: Re-Evaluating the Co-Optation Mechanism in Rentier State Theory'. *Journal of Arabian Studies* 8, no. 1 (2018): 46–64. https://doi.org/10.1080/21534764.2018.1546933.

Morton, Adam David. 'Peasants as Subaltern Agents in Latin America: Neoliberalism, Resistance and the Power of the Powerless'. In *Everyday Politics of the World Economy*, edited by John M. Hobson and Leonard Seabrooke, 120–38. Cambridge: Cambridge University Press, 2007. https://doi.org/10.1017/CBO9780511491375.007.

Morton, Michael Quentin. *Buraimi: The Struggle for Power, Influence and Oil in Arabia*. London; New York: I. B. Tauris, 2013.

Murphy, Emma C. 'Women in Tunisia: Between State Feminism and Economic Reform'. In *Women and Globalization in the Arab Middle East: Gender, Economy, and Society*, edited by Eleanor Abdella Doumato and Marsha Pripstein Posusney, 169–94. Boulder: Lynne Rienner, 2003.

Muscat Daily. 'Construction of Oman's Largest Fishing Port Completed in Duqm'. 20 October 2021. www.muscatdaily.com/2021/10/20/construction-of-omans-largest-fishing-port-completed-in-duqm/.

'Government to Ease Omanisation Norms for SME Sector: H E Sunaidy'. 28 January 2015. www.muscatdaily.com/Archive/Oman/Government-to-ease-Omanisation-norms-for-SME-sector-H-E-Sunaidy-3scp.

'Visa Ban on 87 Jobs in Private Sector Extended: MOM'. 4 February 2019. https://muscatdaily.com/Archive/Oman/Visa-ban-on-87-jobs-in-private-sector-extended-MoM-5cyh.

Muscat Economic Affairs. Foreign and Commonwealth Office. London: The National Archives, 1968 1967. FCO 8/589. Arabian Gulf Digital Archives. www.agda.ae/en/catalogue/tna/fco/8/589.

Nagraj, Aarti. 'Thousands Of South Asian Workers Strike At Oman Airport'. *Gulf Business*, 12 March 2013. https://gulfbusiness.com/thousands-of-south-asian-workers-strike-at-oman-airport/.

National Centre for Statistics and Information (NCSI), 2021. www.ncsi.gov.om/Pages/NCSI.aspx.

'218,000 Expatriate Workers Left Oman in the Past 12 Months'. 23 May 2021. www.ncsi.gov.om/News/Pages/NewsCT_20210523131776647 .aspx.

'2019 Statistical Year Book'. Muscat: National Centre for Statistics and Information, August 2019. www.ncsi.gov.om/Elibrary/.

'Khaṣāʾiṣ al- Bāḥthīn ʿan ʿamal'. Muscat: National Centre for Statistics and Information, 2015. www.ncsi.gov.om/Elibrary/.

'Monthly Statistical Bulletin'. Muscat: National Centre for Statistics and Information, February 2020. www.ncsi.gov.om/Elibrary/.

'Statistical Year Book 2021'. Muscat: National Centre for Statistics and Information, August 2021. www.ncsi.gov.om/Elibrary/.

'National Democratic Working Plan: Peoples Front for Liberation of Oman and Arabian Gulf'. Constituent Conference at Ahleesh (Dhofar), December 1972. Collection Documentation and Leaflets Great Britain, ARCH01732/468. International Institute of Social History.

Neilson, Brett. 'Five Theses on Understanding Logistics as Power'. *Distinktion: Scandinavian Journal of Social Theory* 13, no. 3 (2012): 323–40.

O'Brien, Robert. 'Labour and IPE: Rediscovering Human Agency'. In *Global Political Economy: Contemporary Theories*, edited by Ronen Palan, 89–99. London: Routledge, 2000. https://doi.org/10.4324/9780203978740.

'The Varied Paths to Minimum Labour Standards'. In *Global Unions? Theory and Strategies of Organized Labour in the Global Political Economy*, edited by Jeffrey Harrod and Robert O'Brien, 221–34. London; New York: Routledge, 2002.

OECD. 'Women in Business 2014: Accelerating Entrepreneurship in the Middle East and North Africa Region'. Paris: OECD, 2014. http://dx .doi.org/10.1787/9789264213944-en.

Office of the United States Trade Representative. 'Free Trade Agreements'. Accessed 13 July 2021. https://ustr.gov/trade-agreements/free-trade-agreements.

'Oil'. Foreign Office. London: The National Archives, 1965. FO 371/ 179828. Arabian Gulf Digital Archives. www.agda.ae/en/catalogue/ tna/fo/371/179828.

'Oil in Muscat and Oman'. Foreign Office. London: The National Archives, 1963. FO 371/168719. Arabian Gulf Digital Archives. www.agda.ae/ en/catalogue/tna/fo/371/168719.

'Oil Prospecting'. Foreign Office. London: The National Archives, 1964. FO 371/174573. Arabian Gulf Digital Archives. www.agda.ae/en/cata logue/tna/fo/371/174573.

Okruhlik, Gwenn. 'Rentier Wealth, Unruly Law, and the Rise of Opposition: The Political Economy of Oil States'. *Comparative Politics* 31, no. 3 (1999): 295–315. https://doi.org/10.2307/422341.

Oman: A Class Analysis. Translated from Arabic, Originally published by 9th June Studies, Beirut, 1973. London: The Gulf Committee, 1974.

Oman Daily Observer. '1,000 Jobs Every Month in Civil, Military Services'. 27 May 2021, Vol. 40, No. 194 edition.

'32,000 Jobs for Omanis This Year'. 26 May 2021, Vol. 40, No. 193 edition.

'All Port of Duqm Employees Relocated from Muscat'. 29 May 2021, sec. Oman. www.omanobserver.om/article/1101497/oman/labour/all-port-of-duqm-employees-relocated-from-muscat.

'MoHUP Reissues Tenders for Demolition Works in Al Batinah Coastal Road Project'. 26 January 2021. www.omanobserver.om/article/4478/Front%20Stories/mohup-reissues-tenders-for-demolition-works-in-al-batinah-coastal-road-project.

'Role of Labour Unions, Members in Focus'. 23 January 2012. http://main.omanobserver.om/node/80476.

Oman Drydock Company. 'About Oman Drydock Company', 2021. www.omandrydock.com/about_us.html.

Oman Economic Review. 'At a Crossroads'. September 2003.

'Meet the Most Powerful Business Women in Oman'. 11 October 2015. http://oeronline.com/editor-pick/meet-the-most-powerful-business-women-in-oman.html.

Oman News Agency. 'Council of Ministers / Statement'. 2 February 2013. www.omannews.gov.om/ona/english/newsDetailsPrint.jsp?newsID=160144.

'Finance Ministry Issues Circular No. 14 On Omanisation Policy in Government Firms'. Accessed 15 June 2020. http://omannews.gov.om/description_bkp/ArtMID/867/ArticleID/12330/Finance-Ministry-Issues-Circular-No-14-On-Omanisation-Policy-in-Government-Firms.

Oman Observer. 'Scraping of NOC in Oman: Balancing Act for Employees and Employers'. 26 December 2020. www.omanobserver.om/noc-scrapping-balancing-act-for-employees-and-employers/.

'OMN/01 - Talib Al Mamari: Decision Adopted Unanimously by the IPU Governing Council at Its 195th Session'. In *Results of the 131st Assembly and Related Meetings of the Inter-Parliamentary Union*, 105–8. Geneva: Inter-Parliamentary Union, 2014. http://archive.ipu.org/conf-e/131/results.pdf.

Ong, Aihwa. *Spirits of Resistance and Capitalist Discipline: Factory Women in Malaysia*. 2nd ed. New York: State University of New York Press, 2010. http://muse.jhu.edu/book/1369.

Onley, James. 'Indian Communities in the Persian Gulf, c. 1500–1947'. In *The Persian Gulf in Modern Times: People, Ports, and History*, edited by Lawrence G. Potter, 231–66. New York: Palgrave Macmillan, 2014. https://doi.org/10.1057/9781137485779_10.

Osella, Filippo, and Caroline Osella. 'Muslim Entrepreneurs in Public Life between India and the Gulf: Making Good and Doing Good'. *The Journal of the Royal Anthropological Institute* 15 (2009): S202–21.

Overbeek, Henk. 'Neoliberalism and the Regulation of Global Labor Mobility'. *The Annals of the American Academy of Political and Social Science* 581, no. 1 (1 May 2002): 74–90. https://doi.org/10.1177/0002716202581001108.

Oxford Business Group. 'The Report: Oman 2012'.

'The Report: Oman 2016'.

Palan, Ronen. 'New Trends in Global Political Economy'. In *Global Political Economy*, 2nd ed. Routledge, 2012.

Parisi, Laura. '"Disciplining" and "Engendering" the World Bank: A Comment'. In *Feminist Economics and the World Bank: History, Theory, and Policy*, edited by Edith Kuiper and Drucilla K. Barker 199–206. London; New York: Routledge, 2006.

'PASI Annual Report 2021'. Muscat: Public Authority for Social Insurance, 23 February 2023. www.pasi.gov.om/?page_id=15396&lang=en.

'Paving the Path to Successful Youth Entrepreneurship in the Arab States with Behavioural Science'. New York: United Nations Development Programme, 2021. www.undp.org/publications/paving-path-successful-youth-entrepreneurship-arab-states-behavioural-science.

PDO Public Relations. 'PDO's Training Efforts'. Al-Markazi, December 1978. Central Bank of Oman Archive.

Peck, Jamie. *Work-Place: The Social Regulation of Labor Markets*. New York: The Guilford Press, 1996.

Peck, Jamie, and Nik Theodore. 'Labour Markets from the Bottom Up'. In *Handbook of Employment and Society: Working Space*, 87–105. Cheltenham: Edward Elgar, 2010.

People's Daily Online. 'Spotlight: Belt and Road Generates Growing Passion for China among Middle East Youths'. 12 September 2018. http://en.people.cn/n3/2018/0912/c90000–9499750.html.

Percot, Marie. '"We Sent Our Sons across the Seven Rivers": Tracing the Migratory Network and the Risky Migration of Bangladeshi Fishermen to Oman'. In *The South Asia to Gulf Migration Governance Complex*, edited by Crystal A. Ennis and Nicolas Blarel, 125–43. Bristol: Bristol University Press, 2022.

Peterson, J. E. *Oman in the Twentieth Century: Political Foundations of an Emerging State*. London: Routledge, 2016.

'Oman's Diverse Society: Northern Oman'. *The Middle East Journal* 58, no. 1 (January 2004): 32–51. https://doi.org/info:doi/10.3751/58.1.12.

Oman's Insurgencies: The Sultanate's Struggle for Supremacy. London: Saqi Books, 2007.

Peterson, Spike V. 'How (the Meaning of) Gender Matters in Political Economy'. *New Political Economy* 10, no. 4 (1 December 2005): 499–521. https://doi.org/10.1080/13563460500344468.

Peterson, V. Spike. *A Critical Rewriting of Global Political Economy: Integrating Reproductive, Productive and Virtual Economies.* London; New York: Routledge, 2003.

Philpott, Simon. 'The Natural Order of Things? From "Lazy Natives" to Political Science'. *Inter-Asia Cultural Studies* 4, no. 2 (1 January 2003): 249–63. https://doi.org/10.1080/1464937032000112980.

Piketty, Thomas. *Capital in the Twenty-First Century.* Translated by Arthur Goldhammer. Cambridge, MA; London: Belknap Press of Harvard University Press, 2014.

Polanyi, Karl. *The Great Transformation: The Political and Economic Origins of Our Time.* Boston: Beacon Press, 1944.

'Political Situation in Oman'. Foreign and Commonwealth Office. London: The National Archives, 1972. FCO 8/1844. Arabian Gulf Digital Archives. www.agda.ae/en/catalogue/tna/fco/8/1844.

'Political Situation in Oman'. Foreign and Commonwealth Office. London: The National Archives, 1972. FCO 8/1845. Arabian Gulf Digital Archives. www.agda.ae/en/catalogue/tna/fco/8/1845.

'Political Situation in Oman'. Foreign and Commonwealth Office. London: The National Archives, 1974. FCO 8/2215. Arabian Gulf Digital Archives. www.agda.ae/en/catalogue/tna/fco/8/2215.

Power Engineering International. 'Oman Leads Gulf States in Reform and Privatization of Electricity and Water Sectors'. 30 June 2011. www .powerengineeringint.com/news/oman-leads-gulf-states-in-reform-and-privatization/.

Prabhu, Conrad. 'Construction Work to Resume on Batinah Coastal Road Project'. *Oman Daily Observer*, 29 September 2019. www .omanobserver.om/article/23818/Business/construction-work-to-resume-on-batinah-coastal-road-project.

'Major Industrial Hazardous Waste Treatment Project Planned in Liwa in Oman'. *Zawya*, 10 May 2015. www.zawya.com/mena/en/business/ story/Major_industrial_hazardous_waste_treatment_project_planned_ in_Liwa_in_Oman-ZAWYA20150510051307/.

Pradeep, Angitha. 'New 3,500 Home Residential Community for Project Announced for Liwa in Oman'. *ME Construction News*, 11 October 2020. https://meconstructionnews.com/43791/new-3500-home-residen tial-community-project-announced-for-liwa-in-oman.

Prügl, Elisabeth. 'Neoliberalising Feminism'. *New Political Economy* 20, no. 4 (4 July 2015): 614–31. https://doi.org/10.1080/13563467.2014 .951614.

Radhi, Karim. 'Migrant Workers and Labor Unions in the Gulf: An Interview with Karim Radhi'. *Jadaliyya*, 23 June 2014. www .jadaliyya.com/Details/30862.

Rai, Shirin M. *Gender and the Political Economy of Development: From Nationalism to Globalization*. Cambridge: Polity Press, 2002.

Rankin, Katharine N. 'Governing Development: Neoliberalism, Microcredit, and Rational Economic Woman'. *Economy and Society* 30, no. 1 (1 January 2001): 18–37. https://doi.org/10.1080/03085140020019070.

Reilly, Benjamin J. 'A Well-Intentioned Failure: British Anti-Slavery Measures and the Arabian Peninsula, 1820–1940'. *Journal of Arabian Studies* 5, no. 2 (3 July 2015): 91–115. https://doi.org/10.1080/ 21534764.2015.1114735.

'Rethinking Arab Employment: A Systemic Approach for Resource-Endowed Economies'. Geneva: World Economic Forum, October 2014. http://wef.ch/1uAr60x.

Roberts, Adrienne. 'Financing Social Reproduction: The Gendered Relations of Debt and Mortgage Finance in Twenty-First-Century America'. *New Political Economy* 18, no. 1 (1 February 2013): 21–42. https://doi.org/ 10.1080/13563467.2012.662951.

'The Political Economy of "Transnational Business Feminism"'. *International Feminist Journal of Politics* 17, no. 2 (3 April 2015): 209–31. https://doi.org/10.1080/14616742.2013.849968.

Roediger, David. 'Raced Markets: Prefatory Note'. *New Political Economy* 23, no. 5 (3 September 2018): 531–33. https://doi.org/10.1080/ 13563467.2017.1417365.

Roediger, David R., and Elizabeth D. Esch. *The Production of Difference: Race and the Management of Labor in U.S. History*. New York: Oxford University Press, 2012.

Rosales, Antulio. 'Venezuela's Deepening Logic of Extraction'. *NACLA Report on the Americas* 49, no. 2 (3 April 2017): 132–35. https://doi .org/10.1080/10714839.2017.1331794.

Ross, Michael L. 'Does Oil Hinder Democracy?' *World Politics* 53, no. 03 (2001): 325–61. https://doi.org/10.1353/wp.2001.0011.

'Oil, Islam, and Women'. *American Political Science Review* 102, no. 1 (February 2008): 107–23. https://doi.org/10.1017/ S0003055408080040.

Royal Decree 34/1973. 'Promulgating the Labour Law (Issued 15 November 1973, Published 1 Dec 1973)'. Official Gazette 44, [author translations from Arabic], 1973.

Royal Decree 4/1974. 'Promulgating the Foreign Crafts and Foreign Capital Investment Law (Issued 21 January 1974, Published 16 February 1974)'. Official Gazette 49, [author translations from Arabic], 1974.

Royal Decree 64/1978. 'Promulgating the Law of Expropriation for the Public Interest (Issued 24 December 1978, Published 1 January 1979)'. Official Gazette 161, [author translations from Arabic], 1978.

Royal Decree 75/1987. 'Amending Some Provisions of the Law of Expropriation for the Public Interest (Issued 14 October 1987, Published 1 November 1987)'. Official Gazette 370, [author translations from Arabic], 1987.

Royal Decree 39/2011. 'Granting the Council of Oman Legislative and Oversight Powers (Issued 12 March 2011, Published 15 March 2011)'. Official Gazette 931, [author translations from Arabic], 1991.

Royal Decree 72/1991. 'Promulgating the Social Security Law (Issued 2 July 1991, Published 15 July 1991)'. Official Gazette 459, [author translations from Arabic], 1991.

Royal Decree 102/1994. 'Promulgating the Foreign Capital Investment Law (Issued 16 October 1994, Published 1 November 1994)'. Official Gazette 538, 1994.

Royal Decree 42/1996. 'Approving the Privatisation Policies and Controls (Issued 8 June 1996, Published 15 June 1996)'. Official Gazette 577, [author translations from Arabic], 1996.

Royal Decree 114/2001. 'Promulgating the Law on the Protection of the Environment and the Prevention of Pollution (Issued 14 November 2001, Published 17 November 2001)'. Official Gazette 707, [author translations from Arabic], 2001.

Royal Decree 35/2003. 'Promulgating the Labour Law (Issued 26 April 2003, Published 3 May 2003)'. Official Gazette 742, 2003.

Royal Decree 78/2004. 'Promulgating the Law for the Regulation and Privatisation of the Electricity and Related Water Sector (Issued 20 July 2004, Published 1 August 2004)'. Official Gazette 772, 2004.

Royal Decree 74/2006. 'Amending Some Provisions of the Labour Law (Issued 8 July 2006, Published 15 July 2006)'. Official Gazette 819, [author translations from Arabic], 2006.

Royal Decree 85/2006. 'Determining the Character of the Public Interest for the Duqm City Development Project in Al-Wusta (Issued 25 July 2006, Published 1 August 2006)'. Official Gazette 820, [author translations from Arabic], 2006.

Royal Decree 62/2007. 'Organising the Colleges of Applied Sciences (Issued 3 July 2007, Published 15 July 2007)'. Official Gazette 843, [author translations from Arabic], 2007.

Royal Decree 123/2010. 'Establishing the Free Zone in Sohar (Issued 20 December 2010, Published 1 January 2011)'. Official Gazette 926, [author translations from Arabic], 2011.

Royal Decree 119/2011. 'Establishing the Special Economic Zone Authority at Duqm and Issuing Its System (Issued 26 October 2011, Published 29 October 2011)'. Official Gazette 949, [author translations from Arabic], 2011.

Royal Decree 22/2019. 'Establishing the National Centre for Employment and Issuing Its System (Issued 28 February 2019, Published 3 March 2019)'. Official Gazette 1283, [author translations from Arabic], 2019.

Royal Decree 50/2019. 'Promulgating the Foreign Capital Investment Law (Issued 1 July 2019, Published 7 July 2019)'. Official Gazette 1300, [author translations from Arabic], 2019.

Royal Decree 82/2020. 'Promulgating the Employment Security System (Issued 17 August 2020, Published 19 August 2020)'. Official Gazette 1353, 2020.

Royal Decree 105/2020. 'Establishing the Public Authority for Special Economic Zones and Free Zones and Defining Its Terms of Reference (Issued 18 August 2020, Published 19 August 2020)'. Official Gazette 1353, [author translations from Arabic], 2020.

Royal Decree 121/2020. 'Promulgating the Value Added Tax Law (Issued 12 October 2020, Published 18 October 2020)'. Official Gazette 1362, 2020.

Royal Decree 6/2021. 'Promulgating the Basic Statute of the State (Issued 11 January 2021, Published 12 January 2021)'. Official Gazette 1374, 2021.

Royal Decree 33/2021. 'Regarding the Systems for Retirement and Social Security (Issued 7 April 2021, Published 11 April 2021)'. Official Gazette 1387, [author translations from Arabic], 2021.

Royal Decree 50/2021. 'Ratifying the Unified Agreement for Value Added Tax for the States of the Cooperation Council for the Arab States of the Gulf (Issued 7 July 2021, Published 11 July 2021)'. Official Gazette 1399, 2021.

Royal Decree 53/2023. 'Issuing the Labour Law (Issued 25 July 2023, Published 30 July 2023)'. Official Gazette 1504, [author translations from Arabic], 2023.

Sachedina, Amal. 'Assimilating the Heterogeneity of Migrant Populations through a National Past: Transforming a Shiʿa Minority Community in Post-Nationalist Oman'. *Anthropological Quarterly* 95, no. 4 (2022): 839–68. https://doi.org/10.1353/anq.2022.0047.

   Cultivating the Past, Living the Modern: The Politics of Time in the Sultanate of Oman. Ithaca: Cornell University Press, 2021.

Safar, Jihan, and Melissa Levaillant. 'Irregular Migration in Oman: Policies, Their Effects and Interaction with India'. In *Skilful Survival: Irregular*

Migration to the Gulf, edited by Philippe Fargues and Nasra M. Shah, 115–33. Nicosia: European University Institute and Gulf Research Center, 2017. https://gulfmigration.org/media/pubs/book/BookChapters/GLMM %20-%20IMVolume%20-%20Chapter%20VII%20-%20Extract%20-%202017-05-16.pdf.

Said, Edward W. *Culture and Imperialism*. New York: Vintage Books, 1993. *Reflections on Exile and Other Essays*. Cambridge, MA: Harvard University Press, 2000.

Said, Ibrahim bin. "Awdat al-i'itişāmāt: Wājib al-Kalima'. *Alfalq*, 25 May 2021. www.alfalq.com/?p=24654.

Salisbury, Peter. 'Insulting the Sultan in Oman'. *Foreign Policy*, 19 October 2012. https://foreignpolicy.com/2012/10/19/insulting-the-sultan-in-oman/.

Sardar, Ziauddin. 'Development and the Locations of Eurcentrism'. In *Critical Development Theory: Contributions to a New Paradigm*, edited by Denis O'Hearn, 44–62. London: Zed Books, 1999.

Sarkhel, Sushmita. 'Oman Tender Board Awards Contracts Worth Over 724 Million Rials in 2019'. *Oman Economic Review Live*, 18 August 2019. www.oerlive.com/economy/oman-tender-board-awards-contracts-worth-over-724-million-rials-in-2019/.

Sasikumar, S. K., and Seeta Sharma. 'Minimum Referral Wages for International Migrant Workers from India: An Assessment'. ILO Decent Work Team for South Asia and Country Office for India. New Delhi: International Labour Organization, 2016. www.ilo.org/wcmsp5/ groups/public/—asia/—ro-bangkok/—sro-new_delhi/documents/publi cation/wcms_538168.pdf.

Sassanpour, Cyrus, Ghazi Joharji, Alexei Kireyev, and Martin Petri. 'Labor Market Challenges and Policies in the Gulf Cooperation Council Countries'. In *Financial Systems and Labor Markets in the Gulf Cooperation Council Countries*, 26–50. Washington, DC: International Monetary Fund, 1997. www.imf.org/external/pubs/FT/gcc/.

Sassen, Saskia. 'When National Territory Is Home to the Global: Old Borders to Novel Borderings'. *New Political Economy* 10, no. 4 (1 December 2005): 523–41. https://doi.org/10.1080/13563460500344476.

Schaumberg, Heike. '"Disorganisation" as Social Movement Tactic: Reappropriating Politics during the Crisis of Neoliberal Capitalism'. In *Marxism and Social Movements*, edited by Colin Barker, Laurence Cox, John Krinsky, and Alf Gunvald Nilsen, 377–400. Leiden: Brill, 2013. https://doi.org/10.1163/9789004251434_019.

Schroeder, Christopher M. *Startup Rising: The Entrepreneurial Revolution Remaking the Middle East*. New York: Palgrave Macmillan, 2013.

'Seventh Five-Year Development Plan (2006–2010)'. Muscat: Ministry of National Economy, 2006.

SEZAD Decision 22/2020. 'Amending Some Provisions of the Regulation of Urban Planning and Building Licenses in the Special Economic Zone at Duqm (Issued 10 February 2020, Published 23 February 2020)'. Official Gazette 1330, [author translations from Arabic], 2020.

Shah, Nasra. 'Recent Labor Immigration Policies in the Oil-Rich Gulf: How Effective Are They Likely to Be?' *International Publications* 52, Working Paper no. 3 (1 January 2008). http://digitalcommons.ilr.cornell.edu/intl/52.

Sharma, Nandita. *Home Rule: National Sovereignty and the Separation of Natives and Migrants*. Durham: Duke University Press, 2020.

Shehabi, Ala'a, and Marc Owen Jones, eds. *Bahrain's Uprising: Resistance and Repression in the Gulf*. 1st ed. London: Zed Books, 2015.

Shepard, Wade. '"Five Years Ago There Was Nothing": Inside Duqm, the City Rising from the Sand'. *The Guardian*, 6 August 2018, sec. Cities. www .theguardian.com/cities/2018/aug/06/five-years-ago-there-was-nothing-inside-duqm-the-city-rising-from-the-sand-oman-city-sand-luxury-hotels-housing.

Sheriff, Abdul. *Slaves, Spices and Ivory in Zanzibar: Integration of an East African Commercial Empire into the World Economy, 1770–1873*. Rochester: Boydell and Brewer, 1987. www.cambridge.org/core/books/slaves-spices-and-ivory-in-zanzibar/8BBA2BA56875E3637C05D875E04280CD.

Shibata, Saori. 'Gig Work and the Discourse of Autonomy: Fictitious Freedom in Japan's Digital Economy'. *New Political Economy* 25, no. 4 (6 June 2020): 535–51. https://doi.org/10.1080/13563467.2019.1613351.

Sluyterman, Keetie. *Keeping Competitive in Turbulent Markets, 1973–2007: A History of Royal Dutch Shell*. Vol. 3. Oxford: Oxford University Press, 2007.

Smith, Benjamin. *Market Orientalism: Cultural Economy and the Arab Gulf States*. Syracuse: Syracuse University Press, 2015.

Smith, Benjamin, and David Waldner. *Rethinking the Resource Curse*. Cambridge: Cambridge University Press, 2021.

Snider, Erin A. 'International Political Economy and the New Middle East'. *PS: Political Science & Politics* 50, no. 3 (July 2017): 664–67. https://doi .org/10.1017/S104909651700035X.

Sohar Environmental Unit. 'Omani Environmental Regulations International References Documents SEU Guidance Notes'. Advanced Regulatory Wiki Application. Sohar: Ministry of Environment and Climate Affairs, July 2013. www.soharportandfreezone.com/PDF/Complete%20pack%20Omani%20Environmental%20Regulations,%20International%20References%20Documents%20and%20SEU%20Guidance%E2%80%A6.pdf.

'Sohar Freezone Investor Guide (Version 1)'. Sohar Port/Freezone, 2019.

'Sohar Freezone LLC Guidance Notes on Labour and Visas'. Sohar Port/Freezone, 2019.

'Sohar Port Information Guide'. Sohar Port/Freezone, 2021. https://soharportandfreezone.com/PDF/Sohar%20Port%20Information%20Guide%20V9_single_page.pdf.

Soldi, Rossella, and Simona Cavallini. 'Youth Initiative: A Framework for Youth Entrepreneurship'. European Union Committee of Regions, 2017. https://cor.europa.eu/en/engage/studies/Documents/Youth_initiative/youth-initiative.pdf.

Spradley, James P. *Participant Observation*. Long Grove: Waveland Press, 2016.

'Statistics on Youth'. International Labour Organization, 2022. https://ilostat.ilo.org/topics/youth/.

Stephenson, Lindsay. 'Rerouting the Persian Gulf: The Transnationalisation of Iranian Migrant Networks, c. 1900–1940'. Dissertation. Princeton University, June 2018. https://dataspace.princeton.edu/handle/88435/dsp016h440w16b.

Stoler, Ann. *Along the Archival Grain: Epistemic Anxieties and Colonial Common Sense*. Princeton: Princeton University Press, 2010.

Strange, Susan. *The Retreat of the State: The Diffusion of Power in the World Economy*. Cambridge University Press, 1996.

———. *States and Markets*. 2nd ed. London: A&C Black, 1994.

Sukarieh, Mayssoun, and Stuart Tannock. *Youth Rising? The Politics of Youth in the Global Economy*. London: Routledge, 2014.

'Sultanate of Muscat and Oman: Petroleum Concessions Ltd.: Agreement, Dated 24th June, 1937, Relating to Sultanate Exclusive of Dhofar'. Oil in Muscat and Oman. Foreign Office. London: The National Archives, 1963. FO 371/168719. Arabian Gulf Digital Archives. www.agda.ae/en/catalogue/tna/fo/371/168719.

'Sustainable Management of the Fisheries Sector in Oman: A Vision for Shared Prosperity'. World Bank Advisory Assignment. Washington, DC: World Bank Group and Ministry of Agriculture and Fisheries Wealth, December 2015. https://documents1.worldbank.org/curated/en/901371480601979449/pdf/110678-WP-Summary-Oman-Fisheries-PUBLIC.pdf.

Takriti, Abdel Razzaq. *Monsoon Revolution: Republicans, Sultans, and Empires in Oman, 1965–1976*. Oxford: Oxford University Press, 2013.

Tansel, Cemal Burak, ed. *States of Discipline: Authoritarian Neoliberalism and the Contested Reproduction of Capitalist Order*. Lanham: Rowman and Littlefield, 2017. www.rowmaninternational.com/buy-books/product-details/.

Tansey, Oisín. 'Process Tracing and Elite Interviewing: A Case for Non-Probability Sampling'. *PS: Political Science and Politics* 40, no. 4 (1 October 2007): 765–72.

Teacher Solidarity. 'Oman Teachers Strike', 14 October 2013. https://teachersolidarity.com/blog/oman-teachers-strike.

The Energy Year. 'Oman Strike Called Off'. 16 November 2015. https://theenergyyear.com/news/oman/.

'The Fifth Five-Year Development Plan 1996–2000'. Muscat: Ministry of Development, 1997.

'The Five-Year Development Plan 1976–1980'. Muscat: Sultanate of Oman Development Council, 1976.

'The Fourth Five-Year Development Plan 1991–1995'. Muscat: Development Council General Secretariat, November 1991.

The Free Library / Al Bawaba. 'Employees of ONEC Branches Continue Strike'. 30 April 2008.

'The General Framework of the Sixth Five-Year Development Plan 2001–2005, Volume I'. Muscat: Ministry of National Economy, February 2002.

The People's Front for the Liberation of Oman and the Arab Gulf. '"National Programme of the People's Front for the Liberation of Oman", in Documents of the National Struggle in Oman and the Arabian Gulf [Transl. From the Arabic and Ed. By the Gulf Committee]'. Arabic Original, Dar at-Talia, Beirut. 9th June Studies. London: Gulf Committee, 5 August 1974. International Institute of Social History (Az15 – Bro E 760 – Bro E 4898).

'The Second Five-Year Development Plan 1981–1985'. Muscat: Sultanate of Oman Development Council, 1981.

'The Third Five-Year Development Plan 1986–1990'. Muscat: Sultanate of Oman Development Council, 1987.

Therborn, Göran. 'Class in the 21st Century'. *New Left Review*, Issue 78, (November/December 2012): 5–29.

Thompson, Mark C. *Being Young, Male and Saudi: Identity and Politics in a Globalized Kingdom*. Cambridge: Cambridge University Press, 2019.

Tilley, Lisa, and Robbie Shilliam. 'Raced Markets: An Introduction'. *New Political Economy* 23, no. 5 (3 September 2018): 534–43. https://doi.org/10.1080/13563467.2017.1417366.

The Times. 'Oman Inquiry Ordered into Rioters' Grievances'. 4 September 1971.

Times News Service. '161 Companies Penalised for Violating Omanisation Law'. *Times of Oman*, 14 May 2018. http://timesofoman.com/article/134058.

'His Majesty Issues Directives to Offer 32,000 Jobs'. 25 May 2021. https://timesofoman.com/article/101705-his-majesty-issues-directives-to-offer-32000-jobs.

'Lulu Hypermarket Gearing up to Meet Residents' Needs in Ibri'. 24 July 2013. The Free Library. https://www.thefreelibrary.com/Lulu+Hypermarket+gearing+up+to+meet+residents%27+needs+in+Ibri.-a0337794853.

'More than 2,200 Omanis Laid off in 2019'. *Times of Oman*, 2 December 2019. https://timesofoman.com/article/2320658/oman/more-than-2200-omanis-laid-off-in-2019.

'Oman Removes NOC, Expats Can Switch Jobs'. *Times of Oman*, 7 June 2020, sec. Oman. https://timesofoman.com/article/3015675/oman/government/oman-removes-noc-expats-can-switch-jobs.

'Three Omani Women Entrepreneurs to Share Experiences'. 13 September 2015. http://timesofoman.com/article/67499.

Tinker, Hugh. *A New System of Slavery: The Export of Indian Labour Overseas, 1830–1920*. Oxford: Oxford University Press, 1974.

Twenge, Jean M. *Generation Me: Why Today's Young Americans Are More Confident, Assertive, Entitled – and More Miserable Than Ever Before*. New York: Free Press, 2006.

Ullah, Md. Maruf, Taskina Binta Mahmud, and Fatema Yousuf. 'Women Entrepreneurship: Islamic Perspective'. *Islamic Management and Business 5*, no. 11 (2013): 44–52.

Ulrichsen, Kristian Coates. *The Gulf States in International Political Economy*. New York: Palgrave Macmillan, 2016.

UN. 'Transforming Our World: The 2030 Agenda for Sustainable Development (United Nations Resolution 70/1)'. United Nations, 2015. www.un.org/ga/search/view_doc.asp?symbol=A/RES/70/1&Lang=E.

UNCTAD. 'Science, Technology & Innovation Policy Review'. Geneva: United Nations Conference on Trade and Development (UNCTAD), 2014. http://unctad.org/en/PublicationsLibrary/dtlstict2014d1_en.pdf.

UNDP. 'Arab Human Development Report 2016: Youth and the Prospects for Human Development in Changing Reality'. New York: United Nations Development Programme, Regional Bureau for Arab States, 29 November 2016. www.arab-hdr.org/reports/2016/english/AHDR2016En.pdf?download.

United States Trade Representative. 'Final Text of the U.S.-Oman FTA', 1 January 2009. http://ustr.gov/trade-agreements/free-trade-agreements/oman-fta/final-text.

Unnikrishnan, Deepak. 'The Hidden Cost of Migrant Labor'. *Foreign Affairs*, 11 February 2020. www.foreignaffairs.com/articles/india/2020-02-07/hidden-cost-migrant-labor.

Vaidya, Sunil K. 'Heavy Security Prevents Friday Protests in Sohar, Oman'. Gulf News, 8 April 2011. http://gulfnews.com/news/gulf/oman/heavy-security-prevents-friday-protests-in-sohar-oman-1.789074.

'Oman Private Companies Find Youth Reluctant to Take up Jobs'. *Gulf News*, 10 August 2012. https://gulfnews.com/world/gulf/oman/oman-private-companies-find-youth-reluctant-to-take-up-jobs-1.1060229.

Vale. 'Partnership Between Vale and the Ministry of Agriculture & Fisheries Generates Positive Results to the Fishing Community in Liwa'. Press

Release, 30 June 2014. www.vale.com/oman/EN/press/releases-local/ Pages/partnership.aspx.

Valenta, Marko, and Jo Jakobsen. 'Moving to the Gulf: An Empirical Analysis of the Patterns and Drivers of Migration to the GCC Countries, 1960–2013'. *Labor History* 57, no. 5 (19 October 2016): 627–48. https://doi.org/10.1080/0023656X.2016.1239885.

Valeri, Marc. 'High Visibility, Low Profile: The Shi'a in Oman under Sultan Qaboos'. *International Journal of Middle East Studies* 42, no. 02 (2010): 251–68. https://doi.org/10.1017/S0020743810000048.

'Oligarchy vs. Oligarchy: Business and Politics of Reform in Bahrain and Oman'. In *Business Politics in the Middle East*, edited by Steffen Hertog, Giacomo Luciani, and Marc Valeri, 17–42. London: Hurst, 2013.

Oman: Politics and Society in the Qaboos State. London: Hurst, 2009.

'So Close, So Far. National Identity and Political Legitimacy in UAE-Oman Border Cities'. *Geopolitics* 23, no. 3 (3 July 2018): 587–607. https://doi.org/10.1080/14650045.2017.1410794.

'The Ṣuḥār Paradox: Social and Political Mobilisations in the Sultanate of Oman since 2011'. *Arabian Humanities. Revue Internationale d'archéologie et de Sciences Sociales Sur La Péninsule Arabique/ International Journal of Archaeology and Social Sciences in the Arabian Peninsula*, no. 4 (12 January 2015). https://doi.org/10.4000/cy.2828.

Virdee, Satnam. 'Racialized Capitalism: An Account of Its Contested Origins and Consolidation'. *The Sociological Review* 67, no. 1 (1 January 2019): 3–27. https://doi.org/10.1177/0038026118820293.

'Vision for Oman's Economy – 2020: Long-Term Development Strategy (1996–2020), 2nd Edition'. Muscat: Ministry of National Economy, 2007.

Vitalis, Robert. *America's Kingdom: Mythmaking on the Saudi Oil Frontier*. Stanford: Stanford University Press, 2007.

Vora, Neha. 'From Golden Frontier to Global City: Shifting Forms of Belonging, "Freedom," and Governance among Indian Businessmen in Dubai'. *American Anthropologist* 113, no. 2 (2011): 306–18. https://doi.org/10.1111/j.1548-1433.2011.01332.x.

Impossible Citizens: Dubai's Indian Diaspora. Durham; London: Duke University Press, 2013.

Vora, Neha, and Natalie Koch. 'Everyday Inclusions: Rethinking Ethnocracy, Kafala, and Belonging in the Arabian Peninsula'. *Studies in Ethnicity and Nationalism* 15, no. 3 (2015): 540–52. https://doi.org/10.1111/sena.12158.

WAF. '3601 Retired from Oman's Civil Government Bodies in 9 Months'. 17 November 2020. https://wafoman.com/2020/11/17/3601-retired-from-omans-civil-government-bodies-in-9-months/?lang=en.

Waldner, David, and Benjamin Smith. 'Rentier States and State Transformations'. In *The Oxford Handbook of Transformations of the State*, edited by Stephan Leibfried, Evelyne Huber, Matthew Lange, Jonah D. Levy, and John D. Stephens. Oxford: Oxford University Press, 2015. https://doi.org/10.1093/oxfordhb/9780199691586.013.38.

Walters, Rosie. 'Varieties of Gender Wash: Towards a Framework for Critiquing Corporate Social Responsibility in Feminist IPE'. *Review of International Political Economy* 29, no. 5 (3 September 2022): 1577–1600. https://doi.org/10.1080/09692290.2021.1935295.

Wamda. 'How Women Entrepreneurs Are Driving Business in the Middle East'. 2 February 2012. www.wamda.com/2012/02/how-women-entre preneurs-are-driving-business-in-the-middle-east-.

Weiss, Anita M. 'Challenges for Muslim Women in a Postmodern World'. In *Islam, Globalization, and Postmodernity*, edited by Akhbar S. Ahmed, 127–40. New York: Routledge, 1994.

Wikan, Unni. *Behind the Veil in Arabia: Women in Oman*. Chicago: University of Chicago Press, 1982.

Wilkinson, J. C. 'Bayāsirah and Bayādīr'. *Arabian Studies* 1, no. 1 (1974): 75–85.

Wilkinson, John C. *The Arabs and the Scramble for Africa*. Sheffield; Bristol: Equinox, 2014.

The Imamate Tradition of Oman. Cambridge: Cambridge University Press, 1987.

Williamson, John. 'What Washington Means by Policy Reform'. Washington: Peterson Institute for International Economics, April 1990. www.iie.com/publications/papers/paper.cfm?researchid=486.

Winckler, Onn. *Arab Political Demography: Population Growth, Labor Migration and Natalist Policies*. Rev. and expanded 2nd ed. Sussex: Sussex Academic Press, 2009.

Wolff, Emily Anne. 'Diversity, Solidarity and the Construction of the Ingroup among (Post)Colonial Migrants in The Netherlands, 1945–1968'. *New Political Economy* (23 June 2023): 1–14. https://doi .org/10.1080/13563467.2023.2227120.

'Women, Business and the Law 2021: Oman'. Washington, DC: World Bank, 2021. https://wbl.worldbank.org/content/dam/documents/wbl/ 2021/snapshots/Oman.pdf.

World Bank. 'Capabilities, Opportunities, and Participation: Gender Equality and Development in the Middle East and North Africa Region'. Washington, DC: World Bank, 2011. http://siteresources .worldbank.org/INTMENA/Resources/World_Development_Report_ 2012_Gender_Equality_Development_Overview_MENA.pdf.

'The Environment For Women's Entrepreneurship in the Middle East and North Africa Region'. Washington, DC: The World Bank, 2007. http://

web.worldbank.org/WBSITE/EXTERNAL/COUNTRIES/MENAEXT/0,,
    contentMDK:21517656~pagePK:146736~piPK:146830~theSiteP
    K:256299,00.html.
'Gender and Development in the Middle East and North Africa: Women
    in the Public Sphere'. MENA Development Report. Washington, DC:
    World Bank, 2004. https://openknowledge.worldbank.org/handle/
    10986/15036.
'Oman Country Program', 4 December 2016. www.worldbank.org/en/
    country/gcc/brief/oman-country-program.
'Oman's Economic Outlook - April 2018'. Washington, DC: World Bank,
    16 April 2018. www.worldbank.org/en/country/gcc/publication/eco
    nomic-outlook-april-2018-oman.
'Sultanate of Oman: Sustainable Growth and Economic Diversification'.
    Washington, DC: World Bank, 31 May 1994.
'Unlocking the Employment Potential in the Middle East and North
    Africa: Toward a New Social Contract'. Washington, DC: World
    Bank, 2004.
'World Development Indicators'. World Bank Databank, 2019. https://
    databank.worldbank.org/reports.aspx?source=world-development-
    indicators#.
Wright, Andrea. *Between Dreams and Ghosts: Indian Migration and Middle
    Eastern Oil*. Stanford: Stanford University Press, 2021.
Wright, Erik Olin. 'Class Analysis, History and Emancipation'. *New Left
    Review*, Issue I/202, (Nov/December 1993): 15–35.
'Understanding Class: Towards an Integrated Analytical Approach'. *New
    Left Review*, no. 60 (1 December 2009): 101–16.
Yeates, N., ed. *Globalizing Care Economies and Migrant Workers: Explorations
    in Global Care Chains*. London: Palgrave Macmillan, 2008.
Yesil, Bilge. *Media in New Turkey: The Origins of an Authoritarian
    Neoliberal State*. Urbana: University of Illinois Press, 2016.
Yom, Sean L. 'Oil, Coalitions, and Regime Durability: The Origins and
    Persistence of Popular Rentierism in Kuwait'. *Studies in Comparative
    International Development* 46, no. 2 (1 June 2011): 217–41. https://doi
    .org/10.1007/s12116–011-9087-y.
Yousuf, Kabeer. '12,000 More Jobs in the Pipeline for Nationals'. *Oman
    Daily Observer*, 26 May 2021.
Zaibet, L., H. Boughanmi, T. Al-Hinai, and A. Al-Marshudi.
    'Internationalization of Oman Fisheries Firms After the European
    Union Ban'. *Agricultural and Marine Sciences* 9, no. 2 (2004): 1–6.
Zawya. 'Oman Developing Eight New Fishing Harbours and Ports'. 25 December
    2016. www.zawya.com/mena/en/business/story/Oman_developing_eight_
    new_fishing_harbours_and_ports-ZAWYA20161225041102.

Zheng, Wang. '"State Feminism"? Gender and Socialist State Formation in Maoist China'. *Feminist Studies* 31, no. 3 (2005): 519–51. https://doi .org/10.2307/20459044.

Ziadah, Rafeef. 'Constructing a Logistics Space: Perspectives from the Gulf Cooperation Council'. *Environment and Planning D: Society and Space* 36, no. 4 (2018): 666–82. https://doi.org/10.1177/0263775817742916.

Zidjaly, Najma Al. 'WhatsApp Omani Teachers: Social Media and the Question of Social Change'. *Multimodal Communication* 3, no. 1 (1 June 2014): 107–30. https://doi.org/10.1515/mc-2014-0007.

Zorob, Anja. 'Intraregional Economic Integration: The Cases of GAFTA and MAFTA'. In *Beyond Regionalism? Regional Cooperation, Regionalism and Regionalization in the Middle East*, edited by Cilja Harders and Matteo Legrenzi, 169–83. Farnham: Ashgate, 2008.

Index

For EU product safety concerns, contact us at Calle de José Abascal, 56–1°,
28003 Madrid, Spain or eugpsr@cambridge.org.

www.ingramcontent.com/pod-product-compliance
Ingram Content Group UK Ltd.
Pitfield, Milton Keynes, MK11 3LW, UK
UKHW021846150226
468058UK00008B/156